Formal Demography

The Plenum Series on Demographic Methods and Population Analysis

Series Editor: Kenneth C. Land, *Duke University, Durham, North Carolina*

ADVANCED TECHNIQUES OF POPULATION ANALYSIS
Shiva S. Halli and K. Vaninadha Rao

THE DEMOGRAPHY OF HEALTH AND HEALTH CARE
Louis G. Pol and Richard K. Thomas

FORMAL DEMOGRAPHY
David P. Smith

MODELING MULTIGROUP POPULATIONS
Robert Schoen

A Continuation Order Plan is available for this series. A continuation order will bring delivery of each new volume immediately upon publication. Volumes are billed only upon actual shipment. For further information please contact the publisher.

Formal Demography

David P. Smith

University of Texas
Houston, Texas

Plenum Press • *New York and London*

Library of Congress Cataloging-in-Publication Data

Smith, David P., 1944-
    Formal demography / David P. Smith.
        p.   cm. -- (The Plenum series on demographic methods and
    population analysis)
    Includes bibliographical references and indexes.
    ISBN 0-306-43869-0
    1. Demography--Methodology.   I. Title.   II. Series.
HB849.4.S63   1992
304.6'072--dc20   91-37248
                                                                    CIP

ISBN 0-306-43869-0

© 1992 Plenum Press, New York
A Division of Plenum Publishing Corporation
233 Spring Street, New York, N.Y. 10013

Printed in the United States of America

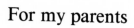
For my parents

Preface

This book is intended as a relatively nontechnical introduction to current demographic methods. It has been several years in preparation, beginning from occasional class handouts I wrote to elaborate on essential points of demographic methodology. Its growth from scattered notes to an integrated text was a natural process, if a gradual one.

The content of the book addresses three objectives. First, I have tried to avoid demographic methods that are now dated. In some chapters, that has meant concentrating on formulas most demographers recognize. In the chapters on life tables, it meant testing competing formulas on a variety of real and synthetic data sets, and dropping or relegating to footnotes those that were least accurate.

Second, I have attempted to give readers a sense of the limits of different formulas and methods. I am a terse writer, however, and for the reader that means most sentences carry weight. Chapters should be read attentively, with careful regard to commentary as well as to formulas and examples.

Finally, I have tried to make the principal methodologies of the book accessible, by offering explanations for formulas that are not obvious, by keeping examples to the forefront, and by placing relatively specialized topics in chapter appendices.

The book begins with an overview of demographic concepts and measures, including population pyramids and the Lexis diagram, to introduce readers to usual population configurations. Chapter 2 reviews data adjustment techniques that are widely used in demography, and includes elementary formulas for curve fitting, osculatory interpolation, and a selection of parametric distributions which find applications in fertility analysis. The chapter also introduces integral and derivative fittings for polynomial distributions, used in conjunction with the life table. Data adjustment by direct and indirect standardization is treated separately in Chapter 3.

Chapters 4–6 focus on life table methodology. The treatment is detailed, since the broad applicability and flexibility of the life table make it the centerpiece of demography. Topics that are covered include basic formulas, multiple decrement and cause elimination formulas, methods for mortality projection, and multistate analysis of tables with both increments and decrements to the survivor population.

The later chapters of the book discuss fertility analysis, population projections and migration, and stable population theory. In fertility analysis (Chapter 7), the principal fertility measures are introduced, with emphasis on their interrelationships and on the implications current fertility levels have for long-term population change. The chapter appendix introduces fertility exposure analysis, a partitioning of the time spent in various exposure states, which provides insights into the determinants of family sizes in different populations. Population projections are discussed in Chapter 8. The chapter reviews both elementary formulas for projection and the more detailed information required for component projections and projection matrices. The analysis introduces stable age distributions by forward projection, and the more limited applications of reverse and back projection. Section 8.11 generalizes projection matrices to other types of demographic problems.

Chapter 9 focuses on migration and small-area population estimation, both of which introduce problems in population analysis that require a more heuristic treatment than is usually taken in fertility and mortality analysis. Much of the chapter discussion focuses on methods to partly correct implausible results, a problem that can arise even where source data are of high quality.

In five areas of substantial demographic importance, my coverage of methods is thinner. The first is historical demography, which is touched upon only in the context of backward population projection. The second area is methodologies for extracting information from limited or defective data, principally of concern to analysts working with information from the poorer of the developing nations. The third is stable population theory, introduced in the text as an extension of population projection but not generalized to most of its current applications. The fourth area is mathematical modeling, especially of birth processes and population heterogeneity. The models contribute to our understanding of individual variability, but require strong assumptions, and have only limited applicability at the population level. Finally, the book does not address linear modeling in detail, although the rapid advance of computer technology has brought it into widespread use. These five areas are difficult to introduce competently in a short space, and are well handled in other works referenced in the text.

The book does not have chapter problems, with the exception of several short exercises on the life table in the summary to Chapter 4, placed there because they did not fit well in the main text. In place of formal exercises, problems and solutions permeate the text. They are introduced by phrases such as "the reader may confirm that . . . ." The problems are intended to be free of surprises, and readers should attempt them, and rework the text examples, to satisfy themselves that they understand the concepts and methods that are addressed.

The various examples and illustrations in the text are drawn from my interests. The writing has been done at the University of Texas School of Public Health, and the reader will recognize a public health emphasis in much of the book. My earlier training in sociology will also be evident. Except for standardization (Chapter 3), which has been supplanted by linear models in many of its early applications outside public health, the methods that are emphasized in the text are relevant to both the social sciences and health professions. In the presentation I have not tried to differentiate between the two areas.

The book is written for readers familiar with algebra and at least not intimidated by logarithms. Parts of the text also introduce matrix algebra for the conciseness of its notation, but the level is elementary and easily learned. The calculus is used to a limited extent where a point is more easily made with continuous than with discrete analysis. In each case the choice is determined by the nature of the information to be conveyed: algebra predominates because most of the applications in the text are to discrete data.

A number of people have helped to bring this book to fruition. Most important has been Barbara Fredieu, who put much of the manuscript on a word processor in the days when those were truly cumbersome. PCs and manageable software eventually lifted that burden, but not my indebtedness to her. I also need to thank Eun Sul Lee, to whom the book's emphasis on statistical testing is due. What merit the book has also owes much to my earlier training under Nathan Keyfitz, an outstanding teacher and friend. Two doctoral students, Yuan-Who Chen and Douglas Mains, helped correct typos and occasional content errors in the text. I am grateful to these and several other friends. I am responsible for the errors and oversights that may remain.

David P. Smith

Houston, Texas

Contents

CHAPTER 1

Introduction

1. Having been born, and bred in the City of London, *and having always observed, that most of them who constantly took in the weekly Bills of* Mortality, *made little other use of them, then to look at the foot, how the* Burials *increased, or decreased; And, among the* Casualties, *what had happened rare, and extraordinary in the week currant: so as they might take the same as a* Text *to talk upon, in the next Company; and withall, in the Plague-time, how the* Sickness *increased, or decreased, that so the* Rich *might judge of the necessity of their removall, and* Trades-men *might conjecture what doings they were like to have in their respective dealings:*

2. Now, I thought that the Wisdom of our City had certainly designed the laudable practice of takeing, and distributing these Accompts, for other, and greater uses then those above-mentioned, or at least, that some other uses might be made of them: And thereupon I casting mine Eye upon so many of the General Bills, *as next came to hand, I found encouragement from them, to look out all the* Bills *I could, and (to be short) to furnish my self with as much matter of that kind, even as the Hall of the* Parish-Clerks *could afford me; the which, when I had reduced into Tables (the Copies whereof are here inserted) so as to have a view of the whole together, in order to the more ready comparing of one* Year, Season, Parish, *or other* Division *of the City, with another, in respect of all the* Burials, *and* Christnings, *and of all the* Diseases, *and* Casualties *happening in each of them respectively; I did then begin, not onely to examine the Conceits, Opinions, and Conjectures, which upon view of a few scattered* Bills *I had taken up; but did also admit new ones, as I found reason, and occasion from my* Tables.

3. Moreover, finding some Truths, *and not commonly-believed Opinions, to arise from my Meditations upon these neglected* Papers, *I proceeded further, to consider what benefit the knowledge of the same would bring to the World . . .*

4. How far I have succeeded in the Premisses, I now offer to the World's censure. Who, I hope, will not expect from me, not posessing Letters, things demonstrated with the same certainty, wherewith Learned men determine in their Scholes; *but will take it well, that I should offer a new thing, and could forbear presuming to meddle where any of the Learned Pens have ever touched before, and that I have taken the pains, and been at the charge, of setting out those* Tables, *whereby all men may both correct my* Positions, *and raise others of their own . . .*

—JOHN GRAUNT (1662)

1.1. INTRODUCTION

Demography traces its modern origins to the second half of the 17th century, when John Graunt published his "Natural and political observations mentioned in a following index, and made upon on the Bills of Mortality" (1662). The bills, first compiled during the plague outbreak of 1592, recorded sex, approximate age, and cause of death for all decedents. His *Observations* are still a valuable introduction to the assessment of data quality and to the epidemiology of plague. Combining mortality statistics with limited information on christenings, Graunt was also able to draw a fairly comprehensive profile of the populations of London and England in his time. He erred at a few points where wrong methods gave reasonable results,* but otherwise handled his data with imaginativeness and care. Much of the later development of demography, better life tables in 1693, age-specific fertility rates in 1800, and component population projections in 1895, is anticipated in his work. His is also the earliest formal use of population estimation from a sample survey. Thomas Robert Malthus has received far more attention than Graunt, but in demography it is for contributions that were far smaller.†

1.2. SOURCES OF DEMOGRAPHIC DATA

Apart from the least developed countries, for whom censuses and vital registration systems are not a high priority, national population statistics are

---

* Among his errors, from his estimate that about 40% of infants survived to age 16, and about 6% survived to 56, he concluded that $40 - 6 = 34\%$ of the population would be aged 16–55. The formula is wrong, in the life table 34% of deaths are at these ages, but his answer was close enough to the correct estimate for his life table (41%) that he missed his mistake. His analysis of London's recovery after plagues (see the opening quotation in Chapter 9) would also not satisfy modern analysts, as he could have done more with his information on the age distribution of plague deaths.

† For a perspective on Malthus's mastery of formal demography, the reader should see Behar (1987). Other valuable comments will be found in the collections of articles edited by Dupâquier and Grebenik (1983) and Wood (1986). The reader should also see William Farr [New York Academy of Medicine, 1975 (1885), pp. 12–19], whose 19th century perspective conveys a sensitivity to poverty missing in Malthus and in much of the modern discussion of his work. We begin Chapter 3 with a quotation from Farr. Malthus's initial *Essay* (1798) and *Summary View* (1830) are reprinted in Malthus (1970). A fine introduction to Graunt will be found in Greenwood (1977).

generated regularly nearly everywhere in the world. Their quality is not uniformly high. Even in the United States, where reporting of births and deaths is virtually complete, about 10% of birth certificates omit information on the infant's father. In the U.S. census, information on family incomes is omitted even more often, despite substantial efforts to assure essentially complete reporting. In the developing countries, as in the United States until this century, problems of accuracy and completeness are substantial.

The nature of the census contributes to the difficulty of assuring its quality. By intent, a census is a complete count of the population either present (de facto) or residing (de jure) in a defined area on a specific date. Locating an entire population is an extraordinary undertaking. In the United States we largely succeed, despite severe problems enumerating two groups: persons in the country illegally and those who are poor, chronically unemployed, and outside the national welfare system. The former group is disproportionately Mexican in origin, the latter predominantly black and male. Because the black population is U.S. born, and because females are more completely counted, the omission of black males is largely statistically correctable both nationally and at the state level. Less can be said for the undocumented. Their numbers include both temporary and permanent immigrants. With cross-border traffic apparently much exceeding net inflows, there is little that can be done to fix the numbers in either group to more than the nearest million. We may not do that well.

Despite its errors and omissions, the census is the basis for many demographic measures. Most measures using total population as denominators are not seriously compromised by census errors; nor are estimates of U.S. life expectancy, since population is counted well at the ages where mortality is highest. For the black and Hispanic origin populations, particularly at the working ages, data adjustment is much more often needed.

The information collected in the U.S. census extends well beyond its constitutional mandate, for which age, sex, and limited information to track omissions would suffice. Since the 1960s, ethnicity has become an important component for determining compliance with civil rights legislation. More recently, residence and poverty information have come into use as elements in funding formulas for welfare and educational service programs.* The list

---

* The inclusion of census data in federal funding formulas has put the Bureau at odds with states and municipalities with substantial black and Hispanic populations, who want counts adjusted upward. The Supreme Court, in the role of arbiter, has thus far been loathe to override Bureau decisions in the absence of a congressional mandate to conduct census operations differently. At issue is the Bureau's role as the only honest player in a political poker game: the predominant state and local interest is in higher counts, not correct counts. On the prospect for improvement the reader should see Freedman and Navidi (1986) and Ericksen *et al.* (1989). Legal aspects of the census are discussed in Keyfitz (1981b).

can be extended, and is supplemented by indicators included in the census at the behest of corporations, universities, and a variety of other data users. On occasion, entries have been added that are almost wholly political, as the 1980 and 1990 questions asking respondents about Hispanic ancestry.*

In contrast to the census, birth and death registration in the United States has been virtually complete for several decades.† The documents are filed by service providers (that is, by professionals) in nearly all cases, which contributes to both completeness and accuracy. Even so, problems exist. Birth certificate information includes the parents' names, ages, occupations, and in some states education, normally provided by the mother. If she does not know, or does not give, the infant's father's attributes, they will not appear on the certificate. Other information that is indifferently reported includes the date the mother first received prenatal care and her number of prenatal visits. The infant's gestational age is more often a problem than it should be: fairly precise physical indicators can establish gestational age, but the remembered date of the mother's last menstrual period is also widely used, introducing recall error.

Death certificates are usually completed by funeral homes, with information provided by the physician attending the death or by a coroner's office. Besides the decedent's age, which may be misreported by surviving family members, particularly for the elderly, the certificates include occupation and place and cause of death information. Space is included on the forms for both immediate and contributing causes of death. These are reviewed by nosologists, who translate the descriptions into International Classification of Diseases (ICDA) cause of death codes.‡ The United States also maintains a National

---

* Similar questions on Caucasian ancestry would define nearly the whole of the black population as white. In contrast to the confusions of Hispanic origin and descent categories, black self-identification is highly consistent from census to census and has not required probing. A brief history of ethnic delimiters in the census will be found in Petersen and Petersen (1986, pp. 280–284). For a sympathetic view of the Bureau's effort to identify Hispanics in 1980, see Choldin (1986), who does not, however, attempt to build a case for the quality of the result.

† The completeness and detail of NCHS marriage and divorce tables are much lower, and their demographic applications limited.

‡ ICDA codes are revised about every 10 years, to keep abreast of changes in diagnoses. In revision years a sample of death certificates are coded using both the old and new codes to determine comparability. The user should consult the reviews of changes whenever mortality rates by cause of death are analyzed across revision years. References for changes in the seventh and eighth revisions and the eighth and ninth revisions are Klebba and Dolman (1975), Klebba and Scott (1980), and Duggar and Lewis (1987).

Two problems in the codes require specific warnings. First, causes of death for periods in which criteria were evolving should be analyzed with care, since apparent changes may reflect revisions in codes as well as in disease frequency. Sudden infant death syndrome and HIV-related deaths are current examples. Second, some revisions do not take hold. As examples, over the past few revisions the hypertensive heart disease category has increased sharply for the

Death Index, which computerizes names and attributes of decedents as well as cause-of-death information. Among its other uses, the NDI allows tracking of individuals lost to medical studies to confirm any deaths that have occurred. Some matching of birth with death certificates is done federally and at the state level for analysis of infant mortality.

The United States produces other censuses and surveys, of which the Current Population Survey is probably the best known. The CPS is completed monthly with a rotating sample of 55,000 and is used for current unemployment estimates and consumer outlook and spending intentions. Special topics are included from time to time, including marriage and divorce histories, for which vital statistics are not of much value. Fertility and family planning are surveyed about every 5 years in the National Surveys of Family Growth. Other federal surveys of interest to demographers include the National Natality Survey, National Fetal Mortality Survey, National Longitudinal Survey, and in public health the National Health Interview Survey and National Health and Nutrition Examination Survey. Information on methodology and findings for these surveys is presented in issues of Vital and Health Statistics. For the history of the census the reader may consult Alterman (1969). A compact introduction to the modern census, Current Population Survey, and vital statistics is Rives and Serow (1984).

1.3. DEMOGRAPHIC TERMS AND NOTATION

Demography begins with populations, either enumerated in censuses or followed from anniversaries, such as date of birth. The two bases are conceptually distinct. Censuses and intercensal population estimates enumerate persons in age intervals. The census population age 0, for example, comprises all infants not yet 1 year old. The count includes both newborns and infants near their first birthday. By contrast, an anniversary count enumerates persons at milestones: at age 0 the anniversary population is all those born during a specified period, only some of whom may be living or still under age 1 at a subsequent census. We will distinguish the two bases as

---

first few years of the new codes, and then dropped back to its previous level as coders have paid it less attention. Other revisions of cardiovascular disease codes have created more confusion than clarification with respect to trends. For a discussion of some of these problems the reader may see Slater and Smith (1985). A fine general introduction to cause-of-death coding will be found in Benjamin (1968, pp. 72–91).

A continuing difficulty is separation of immediate from underlying causes of death. The number of conditions listed on death certificates tends to increase with the age of the decedent, and the point at which control over events is lost in a particular case may not be apparent. For an appreciation of this problem the reader may see Wrigley and Nam (1987) and Manton and Myers (1987).

$N(x)$ = the number of persons surviving at xth anniversary

$_nN_x$ = the number in the age or duration interval x (1.1)

to $x + n$ at enumeration

In other texts the reader may see K or P used to denote populations. Subscript usage is also not uniform. In studies that use anniversary enumeration exclusively, the term N_x may replace $N(x)$ without confusion. Analogous to N_x, the term l_x (or ℓ_x) is used to denote the anniversary population in the life table, with $l(x)$ largely restricted to works requiring calculus. The life table also includes an interval population analogous to our $_nN_x$, the life table population $_nL_x$.*

Where subscripts are used, a right subscript (usually a or x) will denote the start of the age or duration interval of concern, and a left subscript (usually n) will denote the interval width, as in $_nN_x$. The reader will find texts in which left subscripts are omitted, usually when interval widths are 1 unit. Thus, in some works N_x substitutes for $_1N_x$ to denote the population in the interval x to $x + 1$. The context will normally make clear whether N_x or equivalent terms are intended as anniversary or interval estimators. However, even demographers occasionally misread each other's work.

In this volume, $N(x)$ will *always* represent persons surviving as of the xth anniversary and $_nN_x$ will always represent persons in the interval x to $x + n$, as indicated in expression (1.1). In applications to national populations, we also adopt the convention that $_nN_x$ represents the interval population at *midyear*. Other dates could be used, but the midyear population is usually a better estimate of the average number in the interval during the year than is the population at an earlier or later date.

Births may be denoted in two ways. As the population enumerated at exact age 0 they can be represented by $N(0)$, while as events occurring to males or females at ages x to $x + n$ they are denoted $_nB_x$. The two terms are related by the equality

$$N(0) = \sum_{x=0}^{\omega-n} {}_nB_x = \sum_x {}_nB_x$$

* Ages are always given in the Western (Gregorian) calendar days and years. Among other systems, lunar calendars, ceremonially important in China, Korea, and Japan, begin at age 1 (birth) and add 1 year at each lunar new year. In the lunar calendar the number of months varies between 12 and 13, and new year and holiday dates shift, but the calendar is precise and conversion to Western ages and dates is exact.

where Σ_x represents the sum of births across all parental ages x [that is, from $x = 0$ to $x = \omega - n$, where ω (omega) represents the oldest age to which anyone survives; $\omega - n$ denotes the start of the final interval], for parents of one or the other sex. In Chapters 7 and 8 we will distinguish the sex of children (m, f) and parents (M, F) by additional subscripts, as in $_nB_{x,f,M}$, which would denote births of daughters to males ages x to $x + n$.

Associated with births are age-specific fertility rates, which display the ratio of infants born to males or females ages x to $x + n$ during year t to the midyear population at one of their parents' ages, either:

$$_nf_{x,M} = {_nB_{x,M}^{(t,t+1)}}/{_nN_{x,M}^{(t+1/2)}}$$

$$_nf_{x,F} = {_nB_{x,F}^{(t,t+1)}}/{_nN_{x,F}^{(t+1/2)}} \qquad (1.2)$$

where the subscripts indicate that the denominators are either males or females and the superscripts indicate annual $(t, t + 1)$ and midyear $(t + \frac{1}{2})$ estimates. Births of both sexes are counted in the numerator. Age-specific fertility rates are found by age of mother far more often than by age of father, and the user may assume mothers are intended when parental subscripts are omitted from the numerator terms. The 1980 ASFR distribution for U.S. females is displayed as Fig. 2.1; rates for the period 1917–1985 are shown in Fig. 7.1.

The reader might note that age-specific fertility rates are not a count of the number of males or females parenting infants. About 1% of confinements and 2% of births each year are twins, and in populations of any size the number of fathers is nearly always smaller than the number of mothers, whether or not that is acknowledged. As aggregate measures, fertility rates are independent of the identities of the parents.

Deaths or events are denoted by $_nD_x$, where the interval x to $x + n$ is the age or exposure duration at occurrence. The time dimension over which events are measured is often implicit. In national life tables, both births and deaths are summed over single calendar years. For deaths, however, the number $_nD_x$ can represent annual deaths among persons ages x to $x + n$, or deaths over the next n years among persons surviving at x. Either interpretation identifies $_nD_x$ as the sum $_1D_x + {_1D_{x+1}} + {_1D_{x+2}} + {_1D_{x+3}} + \cdots + {_1D_{x+n-1}}$. Introducing right superscripts denoting time, for $n = 5$ years the two quantities will be the period count for year t

$$_1D_x^{(t,t+1)} + {_1D_{x+1}^{(t,t+1)}} + {_1D_{x+2}^{(t,t+1)}} + {_1D_{x+3}^{(t,t+1)}} + {_1D_{x+4}^{(t,t+1)}}$$

and the cohort count for years t through $t + 4$,

$$_1D_x^{(t,t+1)} + {_1D_{x+1}^{(t+1,t+2)}} + {_1D_{x+2}^{(t+2,t+3)}} + {_1D_{x+3}^{(t+3,t+4)}} + {_1D_{x+4}^{(t+4,t+5)}}$$

If cohort sizes and mortality rates are relatively constant, the event counts $_1D_{x+a}^{(t, t+1)}$ and $_1D_{x+a}^{(t+a, t+a+1)}$ will be similar, and we may be indifferent as to which measure is used. This point will be discussed further in connection with the Lexis diagram in Section 1.5.

Age-specific death rates are estimated from annual deaths and the midyear population, using

$$_nM_x = {_nD_x^{(t, t+1)}}/{_nN_x^{(t+1/2)}} \tag{1.3}$$

The population and event counts are usually for one sex, as U.S. male death rates are higher than female rates at all ages. That pattern holds in most other countries, and for most causes of death that occur to both sexes. 1980 ASDRs for the United States are graphed as Fig. 3.1.

Age-specific migration rates are estimated like death rates, using annual counts of immigrants ($_nI_x^{(t, t+1)}$) and emigrants ($_nE_x^{(t, t+1)}$) divided by the mid-year population for the same age interval ($_nN_x^{(t+1/2)}$).

Generalizing from age-specific rates, a number of summary measures exploiting population, birth, and death estimates are universally recognized. The most widely used measures are crude rates of birth, death, migration, and population growth or decrease:

$$\text{CBR} = {_\omega B_0^{(t, t+1)}}/{_\omega N_0^{(t+1/2)}}$$

$$= \text{(Annual births)/(Midyear population)}$$

$$\text{CDR} = {_\omega D_0^{(t, t+1)}}/{_\omega N_0^{(t+1/2)}}$$

$$= \text{(Annual deaths)/(Midyear population)}$$

$$\text{CMR} = ({_\omega I_0^{(t, t+1)}} - {_\omega E_0^{(t, t+1)}})/{_\omega N_0^{(t+1/2)}} \tag{1.4}$$

$$= \text{(Annual immigrants} - \text{Annual emigrants)/}$$

$$\text{(Midyear population)}$$

$$\text{CGR} = ({_\omega B_0^{(t, t+1)}} - {_\omega D_0^{(t, t+1)}} + {_\omega I_0^{(t, t+1)}} - {_\omega E_0^{(t, t+1)}})/{_\omega N_0^{(t+1/2)}}$$

$$= \text{(Annual births} - \text{Annual deaths} + \text{Annual immigrants}$$

$$- \text{Annual emigrants)/(Midyear population)}$$

The expressions use interval widths of $n = \omega$ to count births, population, and deaths across all ages. The infinity symbol (∞) conveys the same meaning as a measure of the length of life.* In most applications, the four rates are multiplied by 1000 to yield integer values. *In this volume, rates will usually be expressed per 1 person rather than per 1000 persons*, since in some contexts the scale factors invite math errors. Crude birth and death rates for several populations are presented in Tables 3.1 and 7.1. The U.S. rates are about $1\frac{1}{2}\%$ and 1% for the CBR and CDR, respectively; the U.S. crude migration rate is about $1/2\%$.

Leaving aside migration, which will be addressed in Chapter 9, the difference between the crude birth and death rates is an approximate measure of annual population growth or decrease. It is not an exact measure: the midyear population in year $t + 1$ will be the midyear population in year t, plus *midyear-to-midyear* births and minus *midyear-to-midyear* deaths. It is not the midyear population adjusted by *annual* events. Where migration occurs, the same consideration applies.

The exact measure of population change is given by the *balancing equation*

$$_{\omega}N_0^{(t+1)} = {_{\omega}N_0^{(t)}} + {_{\omega}B_0^{(t, t+1)}} - {_{\omega}D_0^{(t, t+1)}} + {_{\omega}I_0^{(t, t+1)}} - {_{\omega}E_0^{(t, t+1)}} \qquad (1.5)$$

where time is indexed at the exact points t, $t + 1$, and over the interval $(t, t + 1)$. For the rate of population increase or decrease, the terms in (1.5) would be divided by $_{\omega}N_0^{(t)}$.

Although (1.4) does not estimate annual population change, its terms, annual events over midyear populations, may be interpreted as measures of the average intensity* of fertility, mortality, and migration during year t. If the intensities are constant over time, the approximate population change, omitting migration, will be found by the exponential

$$_{\omega}N_{0, \text{exp}}^{(t+1\ 1/2)} = {_{\omega}N_0^{(t+1/2)}}\exp[({_{\omega}B_0^{(t, t+1)}} - {_{\omega}D_0^{(t, t+1)}})/{_{\omega}N_0^{(t+1/2)}}]$$

$$= {_{\omega}N_0^{(t+1/2)}}e^{\text{CGR}} \qquad (1.6)$$

The expression is applied to U.S. population projections in Section 8.2.

---

* The reader might note that of the crude rates, those for deaths and migration are age-specific rates for age intervals $(0, \omega)$ or $(0, \infty)$, and may be defined either for one or both sexes. The CBR is an age-specific rate only when computed for children to parents of one sex. Since parents may be of different ages, an age-specific fertility rate for males and females ages x to $x + n$ would need to fractionally allocate births depending on whether one or both parents were included in the denominator.

† We will use age-specific death rates $_nM_x$ as measures of the intensity of mortality, or mortality *hazard*, to estimate survival probabilities in Chapter 4. The estimating formula is presented as expression (4.10).

Two measures, the infant mortality rate and life expectancy, are widely used as indicators of health status and economic level. The IMR is found as the number of calendar year deaths at ages under 1 divided by calendar year births, or

$$\text{IMR} = {_1}D_0^{(t,\,t+1)}/N(0)^{(t,\,t+1)} \qquad (1.7)$$

The rate can also be estimated from all deaths at ages under 1 that occur to the birth cohort $N(0)$. The cohort IMR would include infant deaths occurring both in the cohort's year of birth and in the following year. In the developed countries the cohort rate typically differs only marginally from the calendar year rate, since most infant deaths occur near the time of birth. Those that come in the following year can be closely approximated by deaths in the base year among infants born the year before.

As of 1985 the U.S. IMR was about 10 per 1000. That is, about 1% of infants die in their first year of life. The rate is higher in the black population than in the white population, for reasons largely associated with lower birth weights, and is higher among boys than among girls at almost every birth weight. The rates are like those of other developed countries, and far below the 15% infant mortality that the United States suffered in 1900, and that is still suffered in 1990 in some of the world's poorest nations.

The life expectancy at age x, e_x or $\mathring{e}_x$, is the mean number of years of life remaining to individuals at the xth birthday.* It is usually found as a *synthetic* estimate, from the population and deaths occurring in a particular year. In human populations the median lifetime, or the age by which half of infants born will have died, is slightly older due to the high concentration of deaths near the end of life. The U.S. life expectancy was about 72 years at birth for males in 1985 and 79 for females. It is about 5 years lower for both sexes in the black population. In 1900, and some of the poorest nations in the 1980s, life expectance was about 45 years for both sexes.

A widely used variant of the age-specific death rate is the *Pearl Index* (Pearl, 1933), introduced historically as an estimate of fecundability, and more recently to measure contraceptive effectiveness. The index divides events (pregnancies in the risk population) over a fixed period by total exposure time during the same period. That is,

$$_tM_{0,\,\text{Pearl}} = {_t}D_0/{_t}N_0 \qquad (1.8)$$

---

* In some texts, both e_x and $\mathring{e}_x$ are used, with the former interpreted as a *curtate life expectancy*, or life expectancy omitting fractional years, and the latter taken to be the complete life expectancy. We will use e_x to represent the complete life expectancy.

where $_tD_0$ represents events and $_tN_0$ is exposure time in the interval $(0, t)$. The measure is analogous to the age-specific death rate at ages 0 to t, with the substitution of exposure time in the interval for the conventional midyear population. In the limiting case, as $t \rightarrow \infty$, the measure resembles a crude death rate.

As a measure of fecundability, and in many of its other applications, the Index is biased due to sample heterogeneity: if risk varies across individuals, events to those at highest risk will concentrate disproportionately in early intervals and events to those at lower risk in later intervals. In consequence, as the observation time lengthens, the rate at which new events accrue slows and the Index decreases. Formally, for $x > 0$, the Pearl Indexes for the intervals 0 to t, 0 to $t + x$, and x to $t + x$ become:

$$_tD_0/_tN_0 > {}_{t+x}D_0/_{t+x}N_0 > {}_tD_x/_tN_x$$

An example of the Index is given by Trussell and Menken (1980), who use it to measure pregnancy rates among IUD users in the 1973 National Survey of Family Growth, and find after 12 and 24 months of observation:

$$_{12}M_0 = {}_{12}D_0/_{12}N_0 = 18/7865 = 0.00229$$

$$_{12}M_{12} = {}_{12}D_{12}/_{12}N_{12} = 5/5695 = 0.00088$$

$$_{24}M_0 = {}_{24}D_0/_{24}N_0 = 23/13,560 = 0.00170$$

Erosion of value over time is not a desirable property for indexes, and limits the use of the Pearl Index to comparisons between samples with equal exposure durations. For the crude death rate we do not have the equivalent option of setting *age distributions* to be equal between populations, which makes it also a poor comparative measure. (In the case of the CDR, the critical problem is the heterogeneity of mortality by age, evident in the pronounced concentration of mortality very late in life. The age heterogeneity results in much lower death rates for younger than for older populations with similar life expectancies.)

1.4. THE POPULATION PYRAMID

Differences in population age distributions around the world are marked, and crude birth and death rates are not easily understood without an appreciation of the impact that age structure has on them. An easy way to display

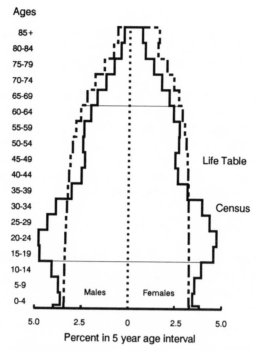

Figure 1.1. U.S. 1980 population pyramid and 1980 life table population.

age distributions is the population pyramid. The pyramid is a histogram, with age measured on the ordinate (vertical axis) and population size on the abscissa (horizontal axis), usually with males in the left quadrant and females in the right. Figure 1.1 displays the U.S. 1980 population pyramid, using percentages by age as the measure of size. The source data for the pyramid are displayed in Table 1.1.

Superimposed on the pyramid is the U.S. 1980 life table, which displays the population age and sex distribution (the life table term $_nL_x$, introduced in Chapter 4) as it would appear if the number of annual births had been constant over time, if mortality rates remained at 1980 levels, and if no migration occurred.*

---

* For the superposition we have scaled births in the male and female life tables to the ratio 1.05:1, about the same ratio as in U.S. births, and set the total life table population to equal the actual population. The life table estimates satisfy the equality $k(1.05T_{0,\,\mathrm{M}} + T_{0,\,\mathrm{F}}) = {}_\omega N_0$, where T_0 is the 1980 NCHS life table population, introduced in Chapter 4. These conventions were adopted to bring differences between the actual and life table populations into sharp focus.

Table 1.1. U.S. July 1 1980 Total Population by Age
and Sex. *Source:* Hollmann (1989)

Ages	Males	Females	Total
0–4	8,417,000	8,040,000	16,458,000
5–9	8,495,000	8,114,000	16,609,000
10–14	9,314,000	8,923,000	18,236,000
15–19	10,776,000	10,382,000	21,159,000
20–24	10,882,000	10,702,000	21,584,000
25–29	9,897,000	9,906,000	19,804,000
30–34	8,845,000	8,977,000	17,822,000
35–39	6,964,000	7,160,000	14,124,000
40–44	5,756,000	5,988,000	11,744,000
45–49	5,376,000	5,677,000	11,054,000
50–54	5,619,000	6,080,000	11,700,000
55–59	5,480,000	6,136,000	11,616,000
60–64	4,700,000	5,466,000	10,145,000
65–69	3,919,000	4,894,000	8,812,000
70–74	2,873,000	3,968,000	6,841,000
75–79	1,862,000	2,966,000	4,828,000
80–84	1,026,000	1,928,000	2,954,000
85+	688,000	1,582,000	2,269,000
0–14	26,226,000	25,077,000	51,303,000
15–44	53,120,000	53,115,000	106,237,000
15–64	74,295,000	76,454,000	150,750,000
65+	10,366,000	15,338,000	25,704,000
Total	110,888,000	116,869,000	227,757,000
Median age	28.8	31.3	30.0

Examining the population pyramid, the reader will recognize the bulge centered at age 20 as the postwar baby boom population. Births and fertility rates increased by nearly two-thirds from about 1940 to 1960 and declined as precipitously from 1960 to 1980 (from 2.6 million births in 1940 to 4.3 million in 1960 and 3.6 million in 1980; the corresponding total fertility rates were 2.3, 3.7, and 1.8 children). At older ages, some effect of World War II and Korean War mortality is apparent in the ratio of males to females, but U.S. losses were low in proportion to the total population and are spread across several age cohorts. At these and older ages, a more striking pattern is the difference between the actual and life table populations: the observed population represents survivors from a period of lower annual births and higher mortality than we currently experience. At the oldest ages, females greatly outnumber males in both the observed and life table distributions.

One of the most widely used summary measures developed from the population pyramid is the *dependency ratio*, defined as the ratio of the population under 15 and 65 and over to the population ages 15–64:

$$D = (_{15}N_0 + _{\omega-65}N_{65})/_{50}N_{15} \qquad (1.9)$$

For the United States, the ratio is $D = (51,303,000 + 25,704,000)/150,750,000 = 0.51$. In many developing countries, where family sizes are 2–3 times as large as in the United States, the ratio reaches about 1.0. If U.S. family sizes remain near their present level (about 2 children per family), the ratio will rise to 0.61 in 2025, when the peak baby boom cohorts reach age 65.*

A better measure of dependency is the size of the nonworking population relative to the working population. The U.S. 1980 labor force numbered 109 million out of a total population of 228 million, yielding a ratio of 0.48 ignoring unemployment. At 1980 labor force participation rates, the labor force would number about 139 million in 2025 out of a total population of 301 million, reducing the ratio to 0.46. The change is smaller than the change in the dependency ratio since part of the population over 65 is employed.

Besides dependency ratios, the pyramid draws attention to a remarkable pattern in U.S. historical mortality. The ratio of male to female births has been fairly constant over time at about 105 to 100, and we would expect deaths to be in the same ratio, but for most of the 20th century annual male deaths have outnumbered female deaths in the ratio 110–130 to 100. The result has been a gradual increase in the proportion of the total population that is female, from about 49% during 1900–1930 and about 50% at the end of World War II to $51\frac{1}{2}$% in 1980. Three factors contributed to the changes: increasing life expectancies, past population growth, and the concentration of mortality at the older ages. From 1900 to 1980, male life expectancy increased from about 46 years to 70 years, and female life expectancy from about 48 years to 77 years, with increasing concentration of mortality at the oldest ages. The widening female lead and mortality concentration have meant that annual female deaths have centered on cohorts older, and because of population growth, smaller than the cohorts contributing to male deaths. We may contrast 1940, when the median ages of males and females dying were 65 and 69 years, respectively, with 1980, when the median ages were 70 and 76 years. The medians correspond to 1875 and 1871 male and female birth cohorts in 1940, and to 1910 and 1904 birth cohorts in 1980. Birth cohort sizes became more uniform between 1910 and 1940, and with the narrowing of the male–female life expectancy differential that began about 1980, the death ratios will reverse for two or three decades after 1990.

---

* The projection is from the Bureau of the Census Middle Series (Spencer, 1984).

The changing U.S. age distributions and death ratios underscore the complexity of demographic processes, and may reinforce for the reader the hazards of comparing demographic measures across populations whose age structures differ. Anticipating part of the discussion of Chapters 3 and 8, in Fig. 1.2 we display the 1980 age distributions of the United States, Mexico, and the Soviet Union, the latter dramatically influenced by collapsing birth rates during both world wars and the brutal disruption accompanying collectivization in the 1930s. The mortality of the three periods, perhaps 50 million persons, affects the whole of the age structure at ages above 35. Mexico's pattern is one of increasing rates of population growth for most of the century, followed by decreasing fertility rates and stabilizing numbers of births during the 1970s. We display a 1960 pyramid for Mexico, scaled to the 1980 population size, to clarify the change now occurring. (The 1960 pyramid is nearer that of the United States in 1900 or 1910, when American birth rates were also high, than to either Mexico or the United States in 1980.) The reader may note that the 1980 population of Mexico at ages 20 and above comprises survivors of the 1960 population at ages 0 and above, and is therefore similar in shape and area to the 1960 pyramid. The actual population change over the 20-year period was from 40 million persons to 75 million. Disaggregating the change, about one-sixth of those alive in 1960 had died by 1980, but a number greater than the 1960 total population was added at ages under 20. Table 3.1 displays 1980 crude birth and death rates for the three countries.

Pyramids might also be constructed for subpopulations, such as urban or rural populations, ethnic groups, native and foreign-born populations, migrant populations, and students, the labor force, or retirees. These groups can also be differentiated on a single pyramid, as can different marital status categories. Life table populations ($_nL_x$) can be similarly disaggregated, to show the distribution patterns as they would appear with constant birth and mortality rates.

Construction of the pyramids is straightforward, since they are no more than graphic displays of population numbers ($_nN_{x,\,F}$, $_nN_{x,\,M}$) or proportions ($_nN_{x,\,F}/_\omega N_0$, $_nN_{x,\,M}/_\omega N_0$). The two points at which comments are appropriate are with respect to infancy, where the interval widths in Fig. 1.1 are 1 year and 4 years, and ages 85+, where we have collapsed ages 85–89, 90–94, 95–99, and 100+ into a 5-year block.

At the youngest ages the proportions in the age intervals are not indicated on the scale. To preserve the appearance of the 5-year interval distribution, the proportion at age 0 is multiplied by 5 and the proportion ages 1 through 4 by 5/4. Without the scale adjustment, the base would be about one-fourth as wide for infants age 0 as for children 1 through 4, and four-fifths as wide for children 1 through 4 as for older age groups. Visually, we would find the numbers of infants and small children difficult to relate to the numbers at

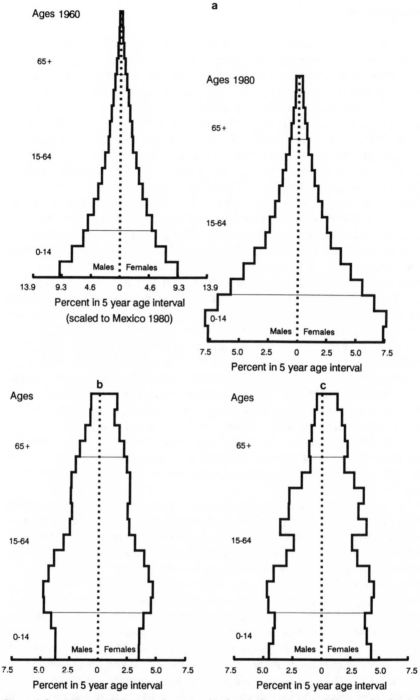

Figure 1.2. 1960 and 1980 population pyramids for Mexico (a), and 1980 pyramids for the United States (b) and the Soviet Union (c) *Source:* United Nations (1989).

older ages. Besides ages under 5, scales are also adjusted in pyramids that contain both 5-year and 10-year age intervals. By convention, usually only the principal scale used in the pyramid is indicated.

1.5. THE LEXIS DIAGRAM

The distinction between $N(x)$, the population surviving at xth birthday or anniversary, and $_nN_x$, the population in the interval x to $x + n$, is brought out in the Lexis diagram, Fig. 1.3, introduced in 1875. On the Lexis diagram, ages are followed along one axis (here, the vertical axis) and time on the other (horizontal). Lifelines are represented by diagonals, of which five are illustrated: individual α, dying in year t at age $x + 1$; individual β, dying in year $t + 1$ at age $x + 1$; γ, dying in year t at age x; δ, dying after year $t + n$ at an age beyond $x + n$; and ε, dying at age x in year $t + 1$. (As Fig. 1.3 is drawn, we would need to extend the lifelines downward and to the left to locate the dates of the individuals' births if x represents an age greater than about 2 years.)

On the Lexis diagram, $N(x)$ is the population surviving at xth birthday, and comprises all lifelines crossing **af**. $_1N_x$ is the population that would be enumerated in a midyear census, and comprises the lifelines crossing **gh**. (The n year population $_nN_x$ comprises lifelines crossing **gi**.) The two populations $N(x)$ and $_1N_x$ only partly overlap: in a midyear census only survivors in the subset **ag** of **af** would be age x at enumeration. The subset **gf** would still be age $x - 1$. At a point later in the year the overlap would be greater; earlier in the year it would be less.

Deaths, $_1D_x$ or $_nD_x$, are recorded differently for $N(x)$ and $_1N_x$ or $_nN_x$. For the cohort $N(x)$, deaths between ages x and $x + n$ occur in the parallelogram **ajkf**, bounded by age x (**af**) and $x + n$ (**jk**). Annual deaths at the same ages fall in the rectangle **acdf**. The reader should note that the areas and ages spanned by the rectangle (deaths at ages x to $x + n$ in year t) and parallelogram (deaths at ages x to $x + n$ in the cohort **af**) are the same. The equivalence should suggest that the two $_nD_x$ counts will be similar if rates of mortality and population sizes are relatively constant in the two periods. That is, counting deaths to one age cohort over several years is essentially equivalent to counting deaths to several age cohorts over one year, provided that cohort sizes and event rates are close to each other.

In the diagram we have forced period and cohort equivalence by displaying two deaths (β, γ) to the cohort, one in year t and one in year $t + 1$, and two (α, γ) in the year t count, one (γ) to the cohort $N(x)$ and the other to the older cohort $N(x + 1)$. If the figure were for a real population, the

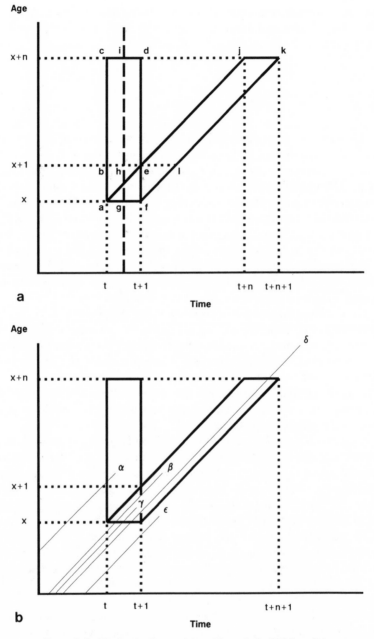

Figure 1.3. The Lexis diagram (a) and hypothetical lifelines (b).

density of lifelines (the amount of time that is lived) in **acdf** and **ajkf** would also be expected to be similar.

We may use the Lexis diagram to introduce an important substitution of period for cohort data in national vital statistics. If we set age $x = 0$, individuals β, γ, and δ, whose lifelines originate in **af**, represent the birth cohort for year t. The cohort infant mortality rate [expression (1.7)] will be found as deaths in **aelf** divided by births **af**: for the example, $_1D_0/N(0) = \gamma/(\beta, \gamma, \delta) = 0.33$. Since **aelf** extends into year $t + 1$, however, the rate is not determinable until the start of year $t + 2$, when all surviving infants will have reached their first birthday. To estimate the calendar year IMR, events in **abe**, representing year t deaths at ages under 1 to infants born in year $t - 1$, are substituted for events in **fel**.

Since about half of infant deaths in the United States occur in the first 7 days of life and 65% are within the first month, the impact of the substitution of **abe** for **fel** is small, affecting about $12\frac{1}{2}\%$ of infant deaths. This proportion is the *separation factor* for infant deaths. The reader may see Shryock and Siegel (1971, pp. 411–415) for its calculation. At older ages, where the distribution of deaths is more nearly linear, separation factors are close to $1/2$. They are closely related to the life table term $_na_x$ [expression (4.28)] which represents the mean age at death of persons dying in the interval x to $x + n$.

1.6. MEASUREMENT PRECISION

Most of the calculations that are presented in this book are to five significant digits. That would seem an easy convention to follow in every case, but it is not. American demographers are habituated to rates per 1000 population for crude birth and death measures and for age-specific birth rates; to rates per 10,000 for age-specific death rates; and to rates per 100,000 for life table measures and age-specific death rates for rare causes of death.

With at least these three sets of conventions, we easily lose track of the number of significant digits we can fairly claim and the number we need. Even in the U.S. National Center for Health Statistics (NCHS) life tables, mortality probabilities $(_nq_x)$ are printed to one less digit than the cumulative survival estimates (l_x) constructed from them. Nor can demographers use published NCHS age-specific death rates $(_nM_x)$, which have no better than two or three digit precision at most ages, to construct life tables. Unfortunately, students try.

In this volume we will continue with the conventions for numbers of significant digits that are most widely used, except where readers require additional digits to duplicate text examples. For formulas that are commonly written to use either source data (e.g., the age-specific death rate $_nD_x/_nN_x$) or an intermediate estimator $(_nM_x = {}_nD_x/{}_nN_x)$, we will usually display the expression in its source information form.

For readers who have not confronted measures of indifferent precision, it may be useful to indicate what is meant by the number of significant digits that are claimed. The rule to follow in all cases is to count as significant only digits coming *after* leading zeros. As examples, the numbers 1000, 10.00, and 0.01000 have four significant digits, while 1.0 and 0.010 have two. To see the distinction between these terms, the reader may establish the range each number is bounded by. The first number lies within the range 999.5–1000.5, the second within 9.995 and 10.005, and so forth. Precision is lost as we operate on the numbers: the quotient of 10.00/1000 lies between 9.995/1000.5 and 10.005/999.5, or between 0.009990 and 0.01001. It may be fixed at 0.0100 which has better than three significant digits but not four.

Unfortunately, demography does not strictly adhere to the limits of its data. In national life tables we estimate survivors to the nearest 1/100,000, even when denominators would permit estimation to the nearest 1 or 10 million. Because it is a familiar base, we claim the same precision when our data are from sample surveys that may have counted fewer than 100,000 persons at all ages combined and no more than a few thousand in any single interval. The convention is too well established to be easily overturned. It is not a problem where confidence intervals or significance tests are used, since they are estimates of the precision achievable at the given sample size. If such measures are not available, the reader will need to be cautious in the amount of precision he or she ascribes to life table estimates.

1.7. SUMMARY

Demography has its modern origins in the English Bills of Mortality and the systems of vital statistics that followed, and in the development of censuses of reasonable completeness and accuracy. These sources provide estimates of deaths for periods and cohorts $(_nD_x)$, and the base populations $[N(x), {}_nN_x]$ in which they occur.

Relationships between populations and events are brought out graphically in the Lexis diagram, which follows individuals from birth across age and time to death, and in the population pyramid, which displays the population age and sex structure at a single time point. The Lexis diagram is of greater technical interest, since it clarifies distinctions between cohort and period information. Both are widely used, period information in current NCHS life tables, which summarize survival experience during a single calendar year, and cohort information in many historical analyses and in medical studies.

In applications of demographic methods, the user needs to keep data sources, quality, and interpretation in mind. Besides data errors, confusion sometimes arises both by the use of nonstandard notation, and by nonstandard uses of standard notation. This is not a problem that will be resolved, since the variety of problems that are amenable to demographic analysis is wide and many have parallels in other fields, which lend their own notation to demographic analysis. The reader needs to be attentive to these differences.

A problem that is often more critical is the widespread use of measures, particularly the age-specific death rate ($_nM_x$), that are too aggressively rounded in published sources to be useful in further applications. Rounded to only one or two significant digits, death rates will not yield either standardized measures (Chapter 3) or life tables (Chapter 4) of usable quality, but that is how they are normally presented in NCHS tables. The reader will avoid many difficulties by using source data in place of derived estimates wherever the precision of the derived measures is low. For the same reasons, the reader should not round intermediate terms to fewer significant digits than are expected in his or her final result.

CHAPTER 2

General Data Adjustment

When a series ov quantitys proceed by a regular law, ther is no difficulty in interpolating between each ajacent two ov them any number ov terms with any desired degree ov accuracy. The methods to be adopted for this purpos hav been described in varios original and reprinted papers contain in the Jurnl *ov the* Institute *ov* Actuarys. . . . *We sometimes, however, hav to interpolate between quantitys which do not accuratly follo any law. For instance, we may hav calculated premiums for every quinquennial age, and wish to obtain the premiums for the intermediat ages by interpolation. In this case, it wil somtimes happen that the ordinary formulas ov interpolation do not giv satisfactory results, unles we take a very large number ov differences, and then the amount ov labor is offen more than the result is worth. In my paper* On the Value ov Anuitys payabl half-yearly, quarterly, *etc.,* I *indicated briefly a method ov interpolation which* I *tho't miht be employd with advantage in such cases (xiii, 322), and it is now my intention to work out the formulas resulting from that method, and giv a practical ilustration ov their use.*

—Thomas B. Sprague (1881)

2.1. INTRODUCTION

In many situations, researchers are confronted with data distributions that display substantial irregularity due to sample sizes being small or responses being concentrated at preferred values. Or a data set may be coded using groupings different from those the researcher would prefer. In such cases, data may need to be smoothed (graduated) or regrouped before they can be used. Regrouping is also needed when data sets with different interval categories are to be merged, and when categories need to be expanded, as from 5-year to 1-year intervals.

A number of methodologies exist for handling these situations. All have limitations of two types. First, they do not correct for *directional* biases in the source data. If persons round their ages to preferred numbers (ages ending in the digits 0, 2, and 5, for example), data smoothing can remove much of the resulting distortion. If they overstate their ages, or both round and overstate them, data smoothing will not set the data right.

A second limitation of the methods is that all necessarily work by parameterization, or curve fitting by mathematical formulas. A linear curve will give different results than a cubic or higher-order fitting to the same data set. Each samples a different range of the source data and uses its own set of weights for data adjustment. Cubic fittings, for example, use information from four intervals and fifth-order polynomials sample slightly differently from six. If the information provided by outlying intervals is irrelevant to the adjustment of the interval of interest, nothing may be gained by their inclusion in the fitting expression. Thus, in a fitting that graduates mortality in the age interval 0–4 to mortality at single year ages, little of value will be realized by formulas that sample from ages 10–14 or 15–19: even the interval 5–9 may be of limited help since mortality experience in the first year of life is unlike that at any later age. By contrast, after age 25 or 30 mortality patterns stabilize enough that sampling from several 5-year age intervals may improve the quality of interpolated or graduated estimates. That is also true for fittings to fertility distributions, whose curvature over 5-year age intervals is too sharp for satisfactory interpolation by two-point (linear) formulas.

2.2. DATA INTERPOLATION

Interpolation is the estimation of an intermediate value for a series of points $n_1, n_2, n_3, \ldots$, with ordinates $g(n_1), g(n_2), g(n_3), \ldots$. For the linear estimator the ordinate $g(n_1 + \alpha)$ is found as

$$g(n_1 + \alpha)_{\text{linear}} = [(n_2 - n_1 - \alpha)/(n_2 - n_1)]g(n_1)$$
$$+ [\alpha/(n_2 - n_1)]g(n_2) \tag{2.1}$$

If $n_1 + \alpha$ is the interval midpoint, (2.1) reduces to the simpler form

$$g(n_1 + \alpha) = g[\tfrac{1}{2}(n_1 + n_2)] = \tfrac{1}{2}[g(n_1) + g(n_2)] \qquad |\alpha = \tfrac{1}{2}(n_2 - n_1)$$

The general formula applies for all values α, including those for which $n_1 + \alpha$ falls outside the range (n_1, n_2).

For two-point fittings, an alternative to (2.1) is the exponential

$$g(n_1 + \alpha)_{\text{exp}} = g(n_1)^{(n_2 - n_1 - \alpha)/(n_2 - n_1)} g(n_2)^{\alpha/(n_2 - n_1)} \tag{2.2}$$

Again, if $n_1 + \alpha$ is the interval midpoint, the expression simplifies, becoming

$$g(n_1 + \alpha) = g[\tfrac{1}{2}(n_1 + n_2)] = [g(n_1)g(n_2)]^{1/2} \qquad |\alpha = \tfrac{1}{2}(n_2 - n_1)$$

To find intermediate points for a series of values $g(n_1)$, $g(n_2)$, $g(n_3)$, ..., we fit the distribution piecewise, using first n_1, $g(n_1)$ and n_2, $g(n_2)$ to find $g(n_1 + \alpha)$, then n_2, $g(n_2)$ and n_3, $g(n_3)$ to find $g(n_2 + \alpha)$, and so forth.

Most readers will find the expressions intuitive. Formally, (2.1) is found by solving the linear equations

$$g(n_1) = a_1 + a_2 n_1$$

$$g(n_2) = a_1 + a_2 n_2$$

Rearranging the equations, we have

$$a_1 = [n_2 g(n_1) - n_1 g(n_2)]/(n_2 - n_1)$$

$$a_2 = [g(n_2) - g(n_1)]/(n_2 - n_1)$$

Substituting these values into $g(n_1 + \alpha) = a_1 + a_2(n_1 + \alpha)$ yields (2.1). The reader can confirm the correctness of (2.2), by solving the expression $g(n) = a_1 a_2^n$ given the points n_1 and n_2 and the ordinates $g(n_1)$ and $g(n_2)$.

Besides interpolation of intermediate values, expressions (2.1) and (2.2) are widely used in population projections. For the simplest case, in which equidistant time points n_1 and $n_2 = n_1 + t$ are used to project the population at $n_1 + \alpha = n_1 + 2t$, the expressions reduce to:

$$g(n_1 + \alpha)_{\text{linear}} = [(n_2 - n_1 - \alpha)/(n_2 - n_1)]g(n_1) + [\alpha/(n_2 - n_1)]g(n_2)$$

$$= 2g(n_2) - g(n_1)$$

$$g(n_1 + \alpha)_{\text{exp}} = g(n_1)^{(n_2 - n_1 - \alpha)/(n_2 - n_1)} g(n_2)^{\alpha/(n_2 - n_1)}$$

$$= g(n_2)^2/g(n_1)$$

An example is given in Section 8.2.

The fitting of higher-order polynomials is more complex and is most easily approached through matrix algebra, introduced in Appendix 2A.1. The methodology will be less important to most readers than the fitting expressions. We present several below, beginning with polynomial expressions for midpoint estimates. We then introduce revised expressions when the value to be fitted is the integral or derivative of the polynomial. All of the expressions presented will assume equidistant source points n, $2n$, $3n$, ... Readers who follow the mechanics of the formulas will be able to use them to find coefficients for arbitrarily spaced points and to set boundary restrictions on the estimates.

For interpolation of midpoint values given equally spaced observations, we replace the generalized notation $g(n_0)$, $g(n_1)$, $g(n_2)$, $g(n_3)$, . . . by the simpler g_0, g_n, g_{2n}, g_{3n}, ... For the linear, cubic, and fifth-order polynomials, and the exponential, the fittings through points on either side of the midpoint $g_{(1/2)n}$ have the forms

$$g_{(1/2)n,\,\text{linear}} = (1/2)(g_0 + g_n) \tag{2.3a}$$

$$g_{(1/2)n,\,\text{cubic}} = (9/16)(g_0 + g_n) - (1/16)(g_{-n} + g_{2n}) \tag{2.3b}$$

$$g_{(1/2)n,\,\text{5th order}} = (150/256)(g_0 + g_n) - (25/256)(g_{-n} + g_{2n})$$
$$+ (3/256)(g_{-2n} + g_{3n}) \tag{2.3c}$$

$$g_{(1/2)n,\,\text{exp}} = (g_0 g_n)^{1/2} \tag{2.3d}$$

The reader should note that each function essentially finds $g_{(1/2)n}$ as the average of g_0 and g_n, with the cubic and fifth-order expressions incorporating some information on the distribution shape from outlying points.

The formula differences may be made clearer by an example. In Table 2.1 we display U.S. 1980 age-specific fertility rates for women in 5-year age intervals, together with fittings to midinterval values for the three polynomials given above.* At ages 15–19 and 40–44 we show both the calculated rates and, for the cubic and fifth-order distributions, revised rates that incorporate the residuals generated at younger and older ages by the expressions.

The original and interpolated rates are graphed in Fig. 2.1. It is not evident from the table and figure, but of the interpolated estimates those for the cubic and fifth-order polynomial are nearer the values found from 1-year rates than are the linear estimates. Substituted for the original age-specific fertility rates, both also yield very close approximations to the roots of the renewal equation, introduced in Chapters 7 and 8.

---

* The example will be used for population projection in Chapter 8.

Table 2.1. U.S. 1980 Female Age-Specific Fertility Rates and
Interpolated Estimates

| | | | | | Interpolated estimates [b] | | | | |
| | | | | | Cubic | | 5th order | | |
Ages	Female population $_5N_x$	Births[a] $_5B_x$	ASFR $_5f_x$	Linear est.	Est.	Adj.	Est.	Adj.	Ages
0–4									
							0.0006		2.5–7.4
5–9									
					−0.0034		−0.0039		7.5–12.4
10–14									
				0.0270	0.0232	0.0198	0.0217	0.0184	12.5–17.4
15–19	10,412,715	562,330	0.0540						
				0.0845	0.0881	0.0881	0.0888	0.0888	17.5–22.4
20–24	10,655,473	1,226,200	0.1151						
				0.1140	0.1210	0.1210	0.1225	0.1225	22.5–27.4
25–29	9,815,812	1,108,291	0.1129						
				0.0874	0.0899	0.0899	0.0900	0.0900	27.5–32.4
30–34	8,884,124	550,354	0.0619						
				0.0409	0.0386	0.0386	0.0378	0.0378	32.5–37.4
35–39	7,103,793	140,793	0.0198						
				0.0119	0.0096	0.0096	0.0093	0.0093	37.5–42.4
40–44	5,961,198	24,290	0.0041						
				0.0020	0.0011	0.0008	0.0012	0.0011	42.5–47.4
45–49									
					−0.0003		−0.0002		47.5–52.4
50–54									
							0.0001		52.5–57.4

[a] Births at ages 10–14 are included with births at 15–19, and births at 45–49 are included with births at 40–44.
[b] For the cubic and 5th-order fittings, the residuals at ages under 15 and over 45 may be included in the terms for $12\frac{1}{2}$–$17\frac{1}{2}$ and $42\frac{1}{2}$–$47\frac{1}{2}$, respectively. The adjustments correspond to the end-point estimators:

$g_{(1/2)n,\text{ cubic, lower bound}} = (1/2)g_n - (1/16)g_{2n}$
$g_{(1/2)n,\text{ cubic, upper bound}} = (1/2)g_0 - (1/16)g_{-n}$
$g_{(1/2)n,\text{ 5th order, lower bound}} = (128/256)g_n - (22/256)g_{2n} + (3/256)g_{3n}$
$g_{(1/2)n,\text{ 5th order, upper bound}} = (128/256)g_0 - (22/256)g_{-n} + (3/256)g_{-2n}$

2.3. OSCULATORY INTERPOLATION

Besides recentering distributions, researchers sometimes need to interpolate from 5- or 10-year age or rate distributions to single year estimates. That is commonly done using tables of Sprague (1881) and Beers (1945) multipliers,* which are the coefficients of fourth-order polynomial splines

---

* Beers coefficients were used by the National Center for Health Statistics to graduate U.S. 1980 age and 1979–1981 mortality distributions from 5-year to single year intervals for constructing decennial life tables (NCHS, 1985, 1987).

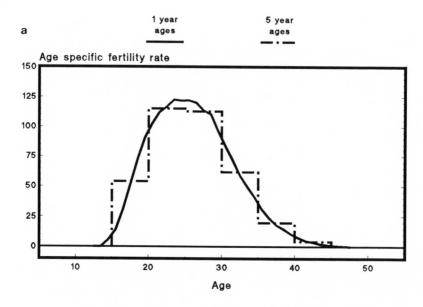

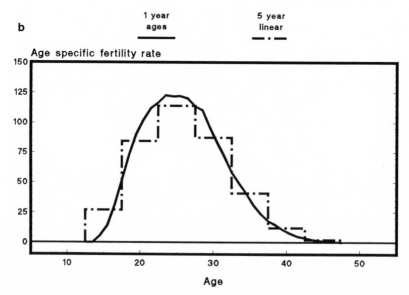

Figure 2.1. U.S. 1980 female age-specific fertility rates and interpolated estimates: (a) 1 and 5 year ages, (b) linear interpolation, (c) cubic interpolation, and (d) fifth-order interpolation. *Source:* National Center for Health Statistics (1984–1985).

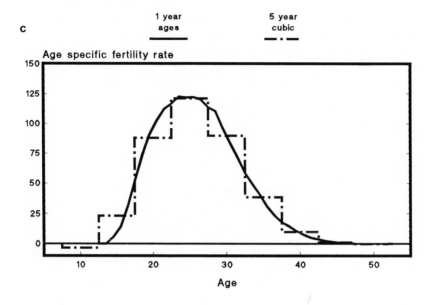

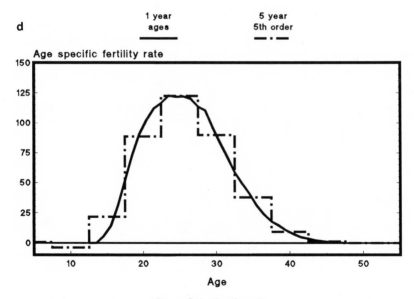

Figure 2.1 (Continued)

satisfying the condition that the first and second derivatives (the tangent and radius of curvature) at an interval endpoint x will be equal for fittings passing through $x - n$ and those passing through $x + n$. [The term osculatory ("kissing") is used for fittings meeting these conditions]. Sprague and Beers coefficients also have the property that the interpolated 1-year terms add to the interval total.*

Sprague coefficients are displayed in Table 2.2 for graduation from 5-year to single year ages.† Five age intervals are used for all except the endpoint fittings. At the end points the distribution is fitted to four intervals, since only some data sets (as in the example of Table 2.1) allow values to be imputed outside the distribution range for use with central panel multipliers. The reader should note that the column coefficients for the age interval to be fitted sum to 1.0, and that coefficients of other columns sum to 0, which establishes that the interpolated estimates will correctly sum to the 5-year estimate. Summing across, all row totals equal 0.2. (The coefficients should be multiplied by 5 when they are used to graduate rates since, unlike ages, 5-year rates average rather than sum 1-year rates.)

Beers coefficients are shown in Table 2.3. The Beers multipliers are like Sprague multipliers in that the interpolated estimates sum to the 5-year total. They produce a smoother fitting at distribution end points by minimizing residuals, but unlike the Sprague coefficients, they produce different and inconsistent estimates for fifths and for tenths of intervals. The coefficients fit distribution end points using five age intervals, as against four for Sprague coefficients, which increases their dependence on more distant information for those intervals. Except for these distinctions the two sets of multipliers are close.

The reader can use Table 2.2 or 2.3 to estimate single year age-specific fertility rates from the 5-year rates of Table 2.1. He or she will find that for Table 2.2 the peak of the fertility distribution will be

$$_1f_{24, \text{ Sprague 2nd panel}} = 5(-0.0176 \times 0.0540 + 0.1408 \times 0.1151$$

$$+ 0.0912 \times 0.1129 - 0.0144 \times 0.0619) = 0.1233$$

$$_1f_{24, \text{ Sprague central panel}} = 5(0.0016 \times 0.0 - 0.0240 \times 0.0540 + 0.1504$$

$$\times 0.1151 + 0.0848 \times 0.1129 - 0.0128 \times 0.0619) = 0.1240$$

---

* For a more complete discussion of interpolation the reader is referred to Greville (1944), Shryock and Seigel (1971, pp. 681–691), and Keyfitz (1977b, pp. 223–245). An accessible introduction to polynomial splines is given in McNiel *et al.* (1977).

† Other coefficients are used for interpolating between point values, such as the life table population l_x surviving at exact age x, or life expectancy e_x at x; and for subdividing intervals into halves or tenths. For these the reader should see Shryock and Siegel (1971, pp. 876–877).

Table 2.2. Sprague Multipliers for Graduating from 5-Year Ages to Single Years[a]

First panel (*Example: ages 0–4*)

	First age (0–4)	Next age (5–9)	Next age (10–14)	Next age (15–19)
First year (0)	0.3616	−0.2768	0.1488	−0.0336
Second year (1)	0.2640	−0.0960	0.0400	−0.0080
Third year (2)	0.1840	0.0400	−0.0320	0.0080
Fourth year (3)	0.1200	0.1360	−0.0720	0.0160
Fifth year (4)	0.0704	0.1968	−0.0848	0.0176

Second panel (*Example: ages 5–9*)

	First age (0–4)	Second age (5–9)	Next age (10–14)	Next age (15–19)
First year (5)	0.0336	0.2272	−0.0752	0.0144
Second year (6)	0.0080	0.2320	−0.0480	0.0080
Third year (7)	−0.0080	0.2160	−0.0080	0.0000
Fourth year (8)	−0.0160	0.1840	0.0400	−0.0080
Fifth year (9)	−0.0176	0.1408	0.0912	−0.0144

Central panels (*Example: ages 10–14*)

	First age (0–4)	Next age (5–9)	Cent. age (10–14)	Next age (15–19)	Next age (20–24)
First year (10)	−0.0128	0.0848	0.1504	−0.0240	0.0016
Second year (11)	−0.0016	0.0144	0.2224	−0.0416	0.0064
Third year (12)	0.0064	−0.0336	0.2544	−0.0336	0.0064
Fourth year (13)	0.0064	−0.0416	0.2224	0.0144	−0.0016
Fifth year (14)	0.0016	−0.0240	0.1504	0.0848	−0.0128

Second to last panel transposes second panel
Last panel transposes first panel

[a] Coefficients should be multiplied by 5 for graduating from 5-year to 1-year rates.

$$_1 f_{25, \text{ Sprague central panel}} = 5(-0.0128 \times 0.0540 + 0.0848 \times 0.1151 + 0.1504$$

$$\times\, 0.1129 - 0.0240 \times 0.0619 + 0.0016 \times 0.0198) = 0.1230$$

At these and most other ages the estimates are in close agreement with 1980 1-year fertility tables. We note that since the fertility distribution progresses smoothly from $_5 f_0 = {}_5 f_5 = {}_5 f_{10} = 0$ to $_5 f_{15} = 0.0540$ and $_5 f_{20} = 0.1151$, either first panel or central panel coefficients might be appropriate for graduation between ages 15 and 20, and either second or central panel coefficients might

Table 2.3. Beers Multipliers for Graduating from 5-Year Ages to Single Years[a]

First panel (*Example: ages 0–4*)

	First age (*0–4*)	Next age (*5–9*)	Next age (*10–14*)	Next age (*15–19*)	Next age (*20–24*)
First year (*0*)	0.3333	−0.1636	−0.0210	0.0796	−0.0283
Second year (*1*)	0.2595	−0.0780	0.0130	0.0100	−0.0045
Third year (*2*)	0.1924	0.0064	0.0184	−0.0256	0.0084
Fourth year (*3*)	0.1329	0.0844	0.0054	−0.0356	0.0129
Fifth year (*4*)	0.0819	0.1508	−0.0158	−0.0284	0.0115

Second panel (*Example: ages 5–9*)

	First age (*0–4*)	Second age (*5–9*)	Next age (*10–14*)	Next age (*15–19*)	Next age (*20–24*)
First year (*5*)	0.0404	0.2000	−0.0344	−0.0128	0.0168
Second year (*6*)	0.0093	0.2268	−0.0402	0.0028	0.0013
Third year (*7*)	−0.0108	0.2272	−0.0248	0.0112	−0.0028
Fourth year (*8*)	−0.0198	0.1992	0.0172	0.0072	−0.0038
Fifth year (*9*)	−0.0191	0.1468	0.0822	−0.0084	−0.0015

Central panels (*Example: ages 10–14*)

	First age (*0–4*)	Next age (*5–9*)	Cent. age (*10–14*)	Next age (*15–19*)	Next age (*20–24*)
First year (*10*)	−0.0117	0.0804	0.1570	−0.0284	0.0027
Second year (*11*)	−0.0020	0.0160	0.2200	−0.0400	0.0060
Third year (*12*)	0.0050	−0.0280	0.2460	−0.0280	0.0050
Fourth year (*13*)	0.0060	−0.0400	0.2200	0.0160	−0.0020
Fifth year (*14*)	0.0027	−0.0284	0.1570	0.0804	−0.0117

Second to last panel transposes second panel
Last panel transposes first panel

[a] Coefficients should be multiplied by 5 for graduating from 5-year to 1-year rates.

be appropriate between ages 20 and 25. The differences are brought out in Fig. 2.2, which displays both all panel and central panel fittings.

Sprague and Beers coefficients are most often used to estimate single year ages or single year deaths from the numbers in 5-year age intervals, where the single year data are unavailable or of poor quality due to heaping on preferred digits. The graduated estimates will typically be low at ages 0–2, where censuses also suffer serious omissions, but will usually be satisfactory at older ages. The researcher should also be aware that the graduated estimates will smooth real irregularities in the source data (Jaffe, 1960, pp. 94–96),

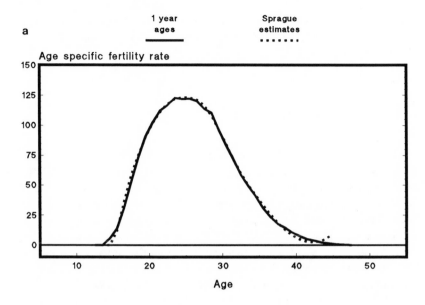

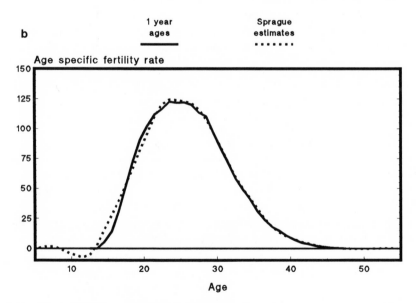

Figure 2.2. U.S. 1980 1-year female age-specific fertility rates and Sprague estimates from 5-year rates: (a) all panels and (b) central panel only.

and that for some types of distributions, including mortality probabilities $_nq_x$, interpolated or graduated estimates may be systematically biased (Pollard, 1979).

2.4. DATA SMOOTHING

Where single year values are available but of indifferent quality due to small sample sizes or data heaping, graduation can be used for adjusting the source estimates. The data are first grouped into 5-year intervals, chosen so that values displaying marked heaping are toward the middle of each interval rather than at its end points. (For example, if ages ending in 0 and 5 are favored, as is common where dates of birth are poorly remembered, grouping in intervals 3–7, 8–12, 13–17, . . . will produce smoother-fitted 1-year estimates than grouping in intervals 0–4, 5–9, 10–14, ... By centering at distribution peaks, depleted adjacent ages are brought within the interval.) The adjusted estimates should be graphed with the original data, with careful attention to points at which irregularities in the source distribution reflect real historical events and should not be smoothed. Judgment is an invaluable asset.

Smoothing is also widely accomplished by the use of moving averages. Given values g_{-n}, g_0, and g_n, a simple moving average estimator for g_0 will be

$$g_{0,\text{ linear}} = (g_{-n} + g_0 + g_n)/3 \qquad (2.4)$$

Using 5-year age intervals, the ratio $g_0/g_{0,\text{ linear}} = {_35}N_x/({_5}N_{x-5} + {_5}N_x + {_5}N_{x+5})$ is taken as an index of the smoothness of census age distributions. If numbers are constant or decline linearly by age, the indexes will equal 1.0; with population growth, the indexes will be slightly lower. For uneven age distributions, the indexes will fluctuate irregularly with age.*

In a different context, the formula is used to average deaths for the 3 years centered on each census year. The averages are divided by the census population to construct mortality rates for U.S. decennial life tables.

---

* The index is sometimes called an Age Accuracy Index [Shryock and Siegel (1971, pp. 218–219)] but the title is a misnomer. The index measures accuracy of age reporting only to the extent that the irregularities it identifies are not present in the true age distribution.

More aggressive data smoothing is achieved by Grabill's weighted moving average of Sprague coefficients (Shryock and Siegel, 1971, pp. 702, 878), given by*,†

$$g_{0, \text{ Grabill}} = 0.4390 g_0 + 0.2641(g_{-n} + g_n) + 0.0164(g_{-2n} + g_{2n}) \quad (2.5)$$

Where heaping is suspected, various measures can be used to gauge its extent both before and after adjustment. A particularly useful indicator because of its low bias is Myers' (1940) blended method, which tests preferences for all digits. Beginning with age 10, for each terminal digit i the method constructs the sum

$$M_i = (1 + i)(_1N_{10+i} + _1N_{20+i} + _1N_{30+i} + _1N_{40+i} + \cdots)$$

$$+ (9 - i)(_1N_{20+i} + _1N_{30+i} + _1N_{40+i} + \cdots)$$

$$= (1 + i)_1N_{10+i} + (10)(_1N_{20+i} + _1N_{30+i} + _1N_{40+i} + \cdots) \quad (2.6)$$

$$M = \sum_{i=0}^{9} M_i$$

In the absence of age heaping, the ratio M_i / M will be approximately 0.1 for each i. Any substantial divergence suggests that digit preference ($M_i > 0.1$) or digit avoidance ($M_i < 0.1$) is occurring.

The weightings on the terms $_1N_{10+i}$ are symmetric. At age 10 we have $M_0 = 1(_1N_{10}) + 10(_1N_{20} + _1N_{30} + _1N_{40} + \cdots)$. If we were to begin at age 9, weights would be $M_9 = M_{-1} = 0(_1N_9) + 10(_1N_{19} + _1N_{29} + _1N_{39} + \cdots)$.

---

* I have found the formula valuable for age smoothing where distributions are erratic due to small sample sizes, but caution that in smoothing age distributions it increases the proportions in the oldest age intervals and may be biasing with respect to mortality rates and related measures at those ages.

† For interval splitting, or for smoothing distributions so as to preserve the source total for two adjacent values g_x, g_{x+n} the researcher can also use the Carrier–Farrag (1959; Shryock and Siegel, 1971, pp. 223–224) ratio formula

$$\hat{g}_{x+n} = (g_x + g_{x+n}) / \{1 + [(g_{x-2n} + g_{x-n})/(g_{x+2n} + g_{x+3n})]^{1/4}\}$$

$$\hat{g}_x = (g_x + g_{x+n}) - \hat{g}_{x+n}$$

The formula assigns equal values to $\hat{g}_x$ and $\hat{g}_{x+n}$ when $(g_{x-2n} + g_{x-n}) = (g_{x+2n} + g_{x+3n})$.

These are the same weights as at age 19, where we have $M_9 = 10({}_1N_{19})$ $+ 10({}_1N_{29} + {}_1N_{39} + {}_1N_{49} + \cdots)$. Between its extreme values the formula achieves approximate balance by increasing the weighting on its first term ${}_1N_{10+i}$ to compensate for the successively smaller population sizes generated by its second term, $10({}_1N_{20+i} + {}_1N_{30+i} + {}_1N_{40+i} + \cdots)$, as the age indexes increase.

For human population distributions, where mortality concentrates at the oldest ages, the expression is marginally biased. An example is given in Table 2.4, using 1980 midyear U.S. population estimates and the U.S. 1980 life table population. For the life table, which should not display digit preferences, the coefficients increase systematically from M_0/M to M_9/M. The pattern is

Table 2.4. U.S. 1980 Population and 1979–1981 Life Table ${}_nL_x$ Distribution, and Myers' Blended Estimates of Digit Preference. *Sources:* Miller (1983), National Center for Health Statistics (1984, Vol. 2, Sect. 6)

Age	${}_1N_x$	${}_1L_x$	Age	${}_1N_x$	${}_1L_x$	Age	${}_1N_x$	${}_1L_x$	Age	${}_1N_x$	${}_1L_x$
10	3714	98,324	30	3742	96,350	50	2340	91,196	70	1532	66,927
11	3616	98,304	31	3670	96,221	51	2307	90,631	71	1448	64,772
12	3531	98,282	32	3645	96,089	52	2344	90,017	72	1377	62,515
13	3622	98,252	33	3886	95,954	53	2341	89,351	73	1278	60,159
14	3746	98,208	34	2884	95,814	54	2357	88,631	74	1210	57,709
15	3993	98,147	35	2922	95,666	55	2381	87,856	75	1128	55,170
16	4172	98,069	36	2906	95,509	56	2341	87,022	76	1043	52,546
17	4228	97,976	37	2064	95,341	57	2312	86,125	77	963	49,840
18	4257	97,871	38	2663	95,162	58	2321	85,159	78	886	47,058
19	4479	97,758	39	2573	94,968	59	2266	84,120	79	813	44,204

Myers' coefficients

| | | | | | | | | | Digit (i) | M_i/M | |
										${}_1N_x$	${}_1L_x$
20	4429	97,639	40	2493	94,757	60	2177	83,033	0	0.0995	0.0962
21	4367	97,513	41	2396	94,527	61	2089	81,805	1	0.0990	0.0972
22	4324	97,383	42	2349	94,277	62	2017	80,523	2	0.0997	0.0981
23	4306	97,250	43	2260	94,003	63	1943	79,154	3	0.1017	0.0990
24	4187	97,118	44	2255	93,703	64	1910	77,696	4	0.0971	0.0998
25	4155	96,987	45	2220	93,374	65	1807	76,146	5	0.0990	0.1006
26	4052	96,858	46	2166	93,014	66	1898	74,502	6	0.1009	0.1013
27	3967	96,730	47	2203	92,620	67	1827	72,762	7	0.0974	0.1020
28	3758	96,604	48	2179	92,188	68	1766	70,922	8	0.1013	0.1026
29	3834	96,477	49	2281	91,714	69	1690	68,977	9	0.1044	0.1031

characteristic of rectangular distributions, where mortality is concentrated in one or a few ages at the end of life. The 1980 U.S. age distribution has a similar but less marked pattern, and does not display heaping at ages where it has historically been present: ages ending in 0 and 5, and to a lesser extent, 2 and 8 (Shryock and Siegel, 1971, p. 208).

Because of residual bias in Myers' coefficients, where the method identifies modest age heaping the researcher should exercise caution in attributing the heaping to method bias or digit preference, or to true irregularities in the age distribution. The researcher can more confidently interpret large deviations as evidence of heaping.

2.5. INTEGRAL AND DERIVATIVE FITTINGS

Besides interpolation and graduation, polynomial fittings are used to estimate integrals and derivatives for the life table terms l_x (life table survivors at exact age or duration x) and $_nL_x$ (persons in the age interval x to $x + n$). The $_nL_x$ distribution, which is used to estimate life expectancies, is found as the integral of l_x between x and $x + n$.

Following our earlier formulas, we will restrict the integral and derivative estimators to fittings from equally spaced observations $g_0, g_n, g_{2n}, g_{3n}, \ldots$, which will be considered *point* observations. We define the integrals $\int_0^n g(a) \times da$, $\int_n^{2n} g(a)\, da$, $\int_{2n}^{3n} g(a)\, da$, $\ldots$, to be the corresponding interval observations $_nG_0, _nG_n, _nG_{2n}, \ldots$, representing the areas between the g values.

For the linear, cubic, and fifth-order polynomials and the exponential introduced earlier, the integral estimators will be:

$$_nG_{0,\text{ linear}} = (n/2)(g_0 + g_n) \tag{2.7a}$$

$$_nG_{0,\text{ cubic}} = n[(13/24)(g_0 + g_n) - (1/24)(g_{-n} + g_{2n})] \tag{2.7b}$$

$$_nG_{0,\text{ 5th order}} = n[(802/1440)(g_0 + g_n) - (93/1440)(g_{-n} + g_{2n})$$
$$+ (11/1440)(g_{-2n} + g_{3n})] \tag{2.7c}$$

$$_nG_{0,\text{ exp}} = n(g_n - g_0)/(\ln g_n - \ln g_0) \tag{2.7d}$$

The derivative estimators for the three polynomials and the exponential are:

$$g_{0,\text{ linear}} = (_nG_{-n} + _nG_0)/(2n) \tag{2.8a}$$

$$g_{0,\text{ cubic}} = [(7/12)(_nG_{-n} + _nG_0) - (1/12)(_nG_{-2n} + _nG_n)]/n \tag{2.8b}$$

$$g_{0,\ \text{5th order}} = [(37/60)(_nG_{-n} + {_nG_0}) - (8/60)(_nG_{-2n} + {_nG_n})$$
$$+ (1/60)(_nG_{-3n} + {_nG_{2n}})]/n \tag{2.8c}$$

$$g_{0,\ \text{exp}} = {_nG_{-n}}\ {_nG_0}(\ln{_nG_0} - \ln{_nG_{-n}})/[n({_nG_0} - {_nG_{-n}})] \tag{2.8d}$$

The reader will find applications of these formulas as expressions (4.15), (4.16), and (6.4).* Like the expressions for interpolation and graduation, the formulas may provide fair rather than ideal representations of source data. We also caution that the integral and derivative functions are not symmetric: if one first computes integrals and then derivatives, with rare exceptions the derivatives will be smoothed estimates of the initial data. In most applications the fifth-order polynomial best reconstructs its source data, followed by the cubic.

2.6. OTHER DATA ADJUSTMENT METHODS

Several techniques for data adjustment are presented in later chapters, in the contexts in which they are most often used. Standardization, used in many contexts, is the subject of Chapter 3. Two other techniques that are widely used are distribution smoothing by fittings to model tables (used for ages at marriage, fertility distributions, and life table $_np_x$ and l_x terms), and parametric approximations (for fertility distributions and life table $_np_x$ terms). In the former category are the Coale *et al.* (1983) model life tables, Coale and McNiel (1972) age at marriage tables, Lesthaeghe and Page (1980) model amenorrhea and breastfeeding tables, and Coale and Trussell (1974) model fertility schedules. Logit fitting of observed survival probabilities to life tables, due to Brass (Brass and Coale, 1968, pp. 127–135; Brass, 1975, pp. 85–105), is introduced in Section 6.3.

Among parametric functions, the normal, gamma, and beta distributions are used to approximate fertility distributions and distributions of susceptibility

---

* Expressions (2.8a) and (2.8b) are also used by Jordan (1975, pp. 18, 33) to estimate the force of mortality μ_x from life table survivors l_x at age x. The estimators are

$$\mu_{x,\ \text{linear}} = (1/l_x)d/dx\ l_x = ({_1d_{x-1}} + {_1d_x})/(2l_x) = (l_{x-1} - l_{x+1})/(2l_x)$$

$$\mu_{x,\ \text{cubic}} = [7({_1d_{x-1}} + {_1d_x}) - ({_1d_{x-2}} + {_1d_{x+1}})]/(12l_x)$$

$$= [8(l_{x-1} - l_{x+1}) - (l_{x-2} - l_{x+2})]/(12l_x)$$

to various types of risk, particularly in mathematical modeling. The normal distribution has the ordinates

$$r(x) = R \exp[-(x - \mu)^2/2\sigma^2]/(\sigma\sqrt{2\pi}) \tag{2.9}$$

where R is a scale factor (in Table 2.1 it would be the total fertility rate). The normal distribution is symmetric about its mean μ and is unbounded between $-\infty$ and ∞. An alternative distribution that can also be fitted using the distribution mean and variance is the Pearson Type III (gamma) distribution,

$$r(x) = Rc^k x^{k-1} e^{-cx}/\Gamma(k) \tag{2.10}$$

where as before R is a scale factor, and $\Gamma(k)$ is the gamma function. For integer values of k, $\Gamma(k) = (k - 1)! = (k - 1)(k - 2) \cdots (1)$. For nonintegers we may use Stirling's approximation*:

$$\Gamma(k) \simeq \sqrt{2\pi k}\, k^{k-1} e^{-k}[1 + 1/(12k) + 1/(288k^2)$$
$$- 139/(51{,}840k^3) - 571/(2{,}488{,}320k^4)]$$

The constants c and k are found from the distribution mean (μ) and variance (σ^2 or μ_2) as

$$c = \mu/\mu_2$$

$$k = \mu^2/\mu_2$$

The distribution is defined over the range $(0, \infty)$ and is skewed toward the right. We may shift the origin from 0 to a using three moments, for which we have:

$$r(x) = Rc^k(x - a)^{k-1} e^{-c(x-a)}/\Gamma(k)$$

$$a = \mu - 2\mu_2^2/\mu_3$$

$$c = (\mu - a)/\mu_2 \tag{2.11}$$

$$k = (\mu - a)^2/\mu_2$$

---

* For $k < 3$ the expression is accurate to five or fewer significant digits. To improve accuracy the reader may substitute the equivalent terms $\Gamma(k + 1)/k$ or $\Gamma(k + 2)/[k(k + 1)]$ for $\Gamma(k)$.

Applications of both functions to fertility distributions will be found in Keyfitz (1977b, pp. 140–149) and Wicksell (1931, pp. 149–157). The distribution is used to model susceptibility to mortality risks in Manton and Stallard (1984), in their analysis of survival probabilities in heterogeneous populations.

Among distributions with both lower and upper bounds, the Pearson Type I (beta), which takes values in the range (a_1, a_2), is used occasionally to approximate fertility distributions (Mitra and Romaniuk, 1973), and is used in Potter and Parker (1964) and Sheps and Menken (1973) to model the distribution of fecundability. The Type I distribution has ordinates

$$r(x) = R\Gamma(b_1 + b_2)(x - a_1)^{b_1-1}(a_2 - x)^{b_2-1}/$$

$$[\Gamma(b_1)\Gamma(b_2)(a_2 - a_1)^{b_1+b_2-1}] \tag{2.12}$$

For the moment fitting we set (Smith and Keyfitz, 1977, pp. 315–316)*

$$c_1 = -(\mu_2^3 + \mu_3^2 - \mu_2\mu_4)/(\mu_2^3 + \mu_3^2/2 - \mu_2\mu_4/3)$$

$$c_2 = \mu_3(c_1 + 2)/2\mu_2$$

$$c_3 = |[c_2^2 + 4\mu_2(c_1 + 1)]^{1/2}|$$

$$a_1 = \mu - \tfrac{1}{2}(c_3 - c_2)$$

$$a_2 = a_1 + c_3$$

$$b_1 = \tfrac{1}{2}c_1(1 - c_2/c_3)$$

$$b_2 = c_1 - b_1$$

Sheps and Menken (1973, pp. 97–101) introduce an iterative maximum likelihood fitting to the Type I distribution that has better theoretical properties than the moment fitting. The higher moments in particular are very sensitive to values the distribution takes at its extremes.

---

* If the constant terms in expressions (2.10)–(2.12) are large, the expressions may need to be expanded and multiplications balanced against divisions to prevent computer over- or underflows. For example, the expression $c^k/\Gamma(k)$ can be evaluated as $[c/(k - 1)][c/(k - 2)]c^{k-2}/\Gamma(k - 2)$.

Table 2.5. U.S. 1980 Fertility Rates and Moment Fittings to the Normal,
Pearson Type I, and Pearson Type III Distributions[a]

Ages	ASFR $_sf_x$	Fitted estimates			
		Normal	Type I	Type III	
a_1		13.026	0	−2.2572	
a_2		52.159			
b_1		3.1469			
b_2		6.3348			
c			0.80299	0.87266	
k			20.889	24.671	
0–4		0.0000		0.0000	0.0000
5–9		0.0009		0.0000	0.0001
10–14	0.0000	0.0088	0.0018	0.0047	0.0051
15–19	0.0540	0.0437	0.0541	0.0470	0.0468
20–24	0.1151	0.1044	0.1150	0.1164	0.1153
25–29	0.1129	0.1209	0.1081	0.1151	0.1156
30–34	0.0619	0.0679	0.0624	0.0598	0.0604
35–39	0.0198	0.0185	0.0222	0.0194	0.0194
40–44	0.0041	0.0024	0.0040	0.0044	0.0043
45–49	0.0000	0.0002	0.0002	0.0008	0.0007
50–54		0.0000		0.0001	0.0001

[a] Distribution moments:
$\mu = 26.014$
$\mu_2 = \sigma^2 = 32.397$
$\mu_3 = 74.248$
$\mu_4 = 2878.9$

Table 2.5 displays U.S. 1980 fertility rates estimated by moment fittings
to expressions (2.9)–(2.12). For the fittings we require the integrals $_nf_{x, \text{fitted}}$
$= \int_x^{x+n} r(a)\, da$, which can be approximated by computer or programmable
calculator. In place of the exact integrals, the user can also substitute the cubic
or fifth-order integral approximations of expression (2.7).

2.7. SUMMARY

Interpolation and graduation of intermediate values between data points
are valuable in many demographic applications. For small data sets, or when
digit preferences limit data quality, common graduation formulas may provide
enough smoothing to improve overall distribution quality. In cases where two
or more data sets are to be compared, the techniques may be needed to align
age or attribute distributions that are differently grouped in source documents.

For other distributions, and particularly in the construction of life tables (Chapters 4–6), we may need to fit an integral or derivative of a fitted curve to a data set to estimate quantities that cannot be found or approximated more directly.

None of the techniques we introduce are intended to remove directional biases in source data, and none can be assumed to improve on the quality of the source information with certainty. When irregularities in the source data are real and not artifacts of small sample sizes or reporting errors, adjustments may yield poorer estimates than those from which the researcher began. Errors may also be introduced when data are smoothed more aggressively than the problems in the source data will justify. The researcher's knowledge of the data set to which the techniques are to be applied, and his or her judgment as to the amount of adjustment that is warranted, are essential whenever corrections are attempted.

Judgment also enters in the use of ancillary information in data adjustment, and in adjustment by inspection. The reader should be aware that in competent hands both options are highly respected. Many problems arise with historical data and with contemporary data of uncertain quality for which formula adjustments are of no real help. As an example, comparisons of populations by age across several censuses may suggest systematic biases (one that is almost universal is the undernumeration of infants) that are not well addressed by general formulas. Or comparisons may suggest that one or more censuses in a series are of a different standard of quality than others. Family reconstruction and backward population projections, both important tools in historical demography, may require judgment at many points. The same is true for extraction of fertility and mortality estimation for recent periods from data on surviving family members in a single census.

For developing countries, where a variety of data problems arise, a number of techniques have been developed that have broad applicability. For these the reader may see Brass and Coale (1968), Brass (1971, 1975), Carrier and Hobcraft (1971), Arthur and Stoto (1983), and United Nations (1983, 1988a,b). We will comment on some of these in later chapters, and on other data adjustment techniques. Those we will emphasize include standardization (Chapter 3), data fitting to reference tables (Chapter 6), and parametric approximations (Chapter 4 and Appendix 7A.1).

APPENDIX 2A.1. MATRIX ALGEBRA OF DISTRIBUTION FITTING

The polynomials introduced in Section 2.2 were for fittings where data points are equally spaced, but the procedure is far more general. We will illustrate it using matrix algebra.* For simplicity, we define the point to be fitted to be $n_j = 0$. We seek the ordinate $g(n_j)$, given the series n_h, n_i, n_k, n_l, n_m, n_n, . . . , and ordinates $g(n_h)$, $g(n_i)$, $g(n_k)$, $g(n_l)$, $g(n_m)$, $g(n_n)$, ... For a cubic fitting to $g(n) = a_1 + a_2n + a_3n^2 + a_4n^3$, we will require any four of the data points: we will use n_h, n_i, n_k, and n_l, and will solve the simultaneous equations:

$$a_1 + a_2n_h + a_3n_h^2 + a_4n_h^3 = g(n_h)$$

$$a_1 + a_2n_i + a_3n_i^2 + a_4n_i^3 = g(n_i)$$

$$a_1 + a_2n_k + a_3n_k^2 + a_4n_k^3 = g(n_k) \quad (2A.1)$$

$$a_1 + a_2n_l + a_3n_l^2 + a_4n_l^3 = g(n_l)$$

In matrix format the equations become

$$
\begin{bmatrix}
1 & n_h & n_h^2 & n_h^3 \\
1 & n_i & n_i^2 & n_i^3 \\
1 & n_k & n_k^2 & n_k^3 \\
1 & n_l & n_l^2 & n_l^3
\end{bmatrix}
\begin{bmatrix}
a_1 \\ a_2 \\ a_3 \\ a_4
\end{bmatrix}
=
\begin{bmatrix}
g(n_h) \\ g(n_i) \\ g(n_k) \\ g(n_l)
\end{bmatrix}
\quad (2A.2)
$$
$$\mathbf{M} \qquad\quad \mathbf{a} \;=\; \mathbf{g(n)}$$

where each term of $\mathbf{g(n)}$ is the product sum of the corresponding row of $\mathbf{M}$ and the column vector $\mathbf{a}$, as displayed in the four equations.

The matrix expression is solved for the coefficients $\mathbf{a}$ by multiplying both sides by $\mathbf{M}^{-1}$, the inverse of $\mathbf{M}$, to yield $\mathbf{M}^{-1}\mathbf{g(n)} = \mathbf{a}$. Denoting the coefficients of the inverse by i_{ij}, we have

$$
\begin{bmatrix}
i_{11} & i_{12} & i_{13} & i_{14} \\
i_{21} & i_{22} & i_{23} & i_{24} \\
i_{31} & i_{32} & i_{33} & i_{34} \\
i_{41} & i_{42} & i_{43} & i_{44}
\end{bmatrix}
\begin{bmatrix}
g(n_h) \\ g(n_i) \\ g(n_k) \\ g(n_l)
\end{bmatrix}
=
\begin{bmatrix}
a_1 \\ a_2 \\ a_3 \\ a_4
\end{bmatrix}
\quad (2A.3)
$$
$$\mathbf{M}^{-1} \qquad\qquad \mathbf{g(n)} \;=\; \mathbf{a}$$

Hence, for a_1 we would have

$$a_1 = i_{11}g(n_h) + i_{12}g(n_i) + i_{13}g(n_k) + i_{14}g(n_l)$$

---

* For readers not familiar with matrices, good general introductions are Searle (1966), Namboodiri (1984), and Caswell (1989, pp. 280–295).

The inversion is tedious by hand calculation, as the algebra is that required for solving the simultaneous equations, but besides computers a number of programmable calculators include matrix inversion routines. We may also reduce the complexity of the solution by centering the unknown value $g(n_j)$ at $g(0)$ and scaling other points n_k to integer or half-integer values.

As an example, we will repeat the cubic fitting for the fertility estimates of Table 2.1, but revise the source points by replacing g_n with g_{3n} in (2.3b). We have:

$$g_{(1/2)n,\ \text{cubic}} = \alpha_1 g_{-n} + \alpha_2 g_0 + \alpha_3 g_{2n} + \alpha_4 g_{3n} \qquad (2A.4)$$

Setting $n = 1$ and relocating the origin from $\frac{1}{2}n$ to 0, (2A.4) takes the simpler form

$$g_{0,\ \text{cubic}} = \alpha_1 g_{-1.5} + \alpha_2 g_{-0.5} + \alpha_3 g_{1.5} + \alpha_4 g_{2.5} \qquad (2A.5)$$

For the cubic, we require the solution to

$$g_{(1/2)n,\ \text{cubic}} = a_1 + a_2(\tfrac{1}{2}n) + a_3(\tfrac{1}{2}n)^2 + a_4(\tfrac{1}{2}n)^3$$

At the point $x = 0$, the expression reduces to

$$g_{0,\ \text{cubic}} = a_1 + a_2(0) + a_3(0)^2 + a_4(0)^3 = a_1 \qquad (2A.6)$$

Equating (2A.5) and (2A.6), for $g_{0,\ \text{cubic}}$ we find

$$g_{0,\ \text{cubic}} = a_1 = \alpha_1 g_{-1.5} + \alpha_2 g_{-0.5} + \alpha_3 g_{1.5} + \alpha_4 g_{2.5} \qquad (2A.7)$$

The solution we seek is the estimate of a_1 found by inverting expression (2A.2). As we have formulated the problem, the coefficients α_j correspond to the terms i_{1j} of the matrix inverse (2A.3). Thus, for the example we find:

$$\mathbf{M} = \begin{bmatrix} 1 & -1\frac{1}{2} & (-1\frac{1}{2})^2 & (-1\frac{1}{2})^3 \\ 1 & -\frac{1}{2} & (-\frac{1}{2})^2 & (-\frac{1}{2})^3 \\ 1 & 1\frac{1}{2} & (1\frac{1}{2})^2 & (1\frac{1}{2})^3 \\ 1 & 2\frac{1}{2} & (2\frac{1}{2})^2 & (2\frac{1}{2})^3 \end{bmatrix}$$

$$\mathbf{M}^{-1} = \begin{bmatrix} -5/32 & 15/16 & 5/16 & -3/32 \\ -7/48 & -3/8 & 17/24 & -3/16 \\ 7/24 & -5/12 & 1/12 & 1/24 \\ -1/12 & 1/6 & -1/6 & 1/12 \end{bmatrix}$$

Applying (2A.3), the estimator for $g_{0,\,\text{cubic}}$ becomes

$$g_{0,\,\text{cubic}} = a_1 = i_{11}g_{-1.5} + i_{12}g_{-0.5} + i_{13}g_{1.5} + i_{14}g_{2.5}$$

$$= -(5/32)g_{-1.5} + (15/16)g_{-0.5} + (5/16)g_{1.5} - (3/32)g_{2.5} \quad (2A.8)$$

Rewriting the estimator in the generalized notation of age-specific fertility rates, it becomes

$$_nf_{x+(1/2)n,\,\text{cubic}} = (-5/32)_nf_{x-n} + (15/16)_nf_x$$
$$+ (5/16)_nf_{x+2n} - (3/32)_nf_{x+3n} \quad (2A.9)$$

The reader might note that the sum of the coefficients (the first row of $\mathbf{M}^{-1}$) is 1.0, and therefore that the complete set of interpolated fertility rates will sum to the TFR, like the source and interpolated rates in Table 2.1. He or she can also confirm that for the data of Table 2.1, the expression estimates $_5f_{22.5}$ from $_5f_{15}$, $_5f_{20}$, $_5f_{30}$, and $_5f_{35}$ as $_5f_{22.5} = 0.1170$. The estimate is of lower quality than the estimate in Table 2.1 (0.1233) found from $_5f_{15}$, $_5f_{20}$, $_5f_{25}$, and $_5f_{30}$, but illustrates the flexibility of polynomial interpolation.

The reader might also confirm that the coefficients of the cubic introduced in Section 2.2 can be found from the first row of the inverse of the matrix (or other matrices whose principal terms are multiples of $-3, -1, 1, 3$):

$$\mathbf{M} = \begin{bmatrix} 1 & -3 & (-3)^2 & (-3)^3 \\ 1 & -1 & (-1)^2 & (-1)^3 \\ 1 & 1 & 1^2 & 1^3 \\ 1 & 3 & 3^2 & 3^3 \end{bmatrix}$$

Suppose now that the problem is to estimate the integral of a polynomial expression, we will use the cubic, between two points. From calculus, the cubic $g(n) = a_1 + a_2n + a_3n^2 + a_4n^3$, has as its integral between k_1 and k_2

$$_{k_2-k_1}G_{k_1} = a_1(k_2 - k_1) + a_2(k_2^2 - k_1^2)/2$$
$$+ a_3(k_2^3 - k_1^3)/3 + a_4(k_2^4 - k_1^4)/4 \quad (2A.10)$$

As before, the coefficients $\mathbf{a}$ are found from (2A.1)–(2A.3), in matrix form $\mathbf{Ma} = \mathbf{g(n)}$. From the matrix inverse $\mathbf{M}^{-1}\mathbf{g(n)} = \mathbf{a}$ we will have

$$a_1 = i_{11}g(n_h) + i_{12}g(n_i) + i_{13}g(n_k) + i_{14}g(n_l)$$

$$a_2 = i_{21}g(n_h) + i_{22}g(n_i) + i_{23}g(n_k) + i_{24}g(n_l)$$

$$a_3 = i_{31}g(n_h) + i_{32}g(n_i) + i_{33}g(n_k) + i_{34}g(n_l)$$

$$a_4 = i_{41}g(n_h) + i_{42}g(n_i) + i_{43}g(n_k) + i_{44}g(n_l)$$

On substituting these values into (2A.10), the integral becomes

$$_{k_2-k_1}G_{k_1} = [i_{11}(k_2 - k_1) + i_{21}(k_2^2 - k_1^2)/2 + i_{31}(k_2^3 - k_1^3)/3$$

$$+ i_{41}(k_2^4 - k_1^4)/4]g(n_h) + [i_{12}(k_2 - k_1) + i_{22}(k_2^2 - k_1^2)/2$$

$$+ i_{32}(k_2^3 - k_1^3)/3 + i_{42}(k_2^4 - k_1^4)/4]g(n_i) + [i_{13}(k_2 - k_1)$$

$$+ i_{23}(k_2^2 - k_1^2)/2 + i_{33}(k_2^3 - k_1^3)/3 + i_{43}(k_2^4 - k_1^4)/4]g(n_k) \qquad (2A.11)$$

$$+ [i_{14}(k_2 - k_1) + i_{24}(k_2^2 - k_1^2)/2 + i_{34}(k_2^3 - k_1^3)/3$$

$$+ i_{44}(k_2^4 - k_1^4)/4]g(n_l) = \alpha_1 g(n_h) + \alpha_2 g(n_i)$$

$$+ \alpha_3 g(n_k) + \alpha_4 g(n_l)$$

The reader can confirm that for the simplest case, in which all intervals $k_j - k_i = n$ and we are fitting $_{k_2-k_1}G_{k_1} = {}_nG_0$ from g_{-n}, g_0, g_n, g_{2n}, the terms in k_1 vanish (since $k_1 = 0$) and the α coefficients become $\alpha_1 = \alpha_4 = -n/24$, and $\alpha_2 = \alpha_3 = 13n/24$. These coefficients are found from the inverse of the matrix $\mathbf{M}$, after solving (2A.11). The reader can show that for $n = 1$, the matrix $\mathbf{M}$ to be inverted will be

$$\mathbf{M} = \begin{bmatrix} 1 & -1 & (-1)^2 & (-1)^3 \\ 1 & 0 & 0^2 & 0^3 \\ 1 & 1 & 1^2 & 1^3 \\ 1 & 2 & 2^2 & 2^3 \end{bmatrix}$$

Estimation of polynomial derivatives is similar to estimation of integrals. We illustrate as before with the cubic $g(n) = a_1 + a_2 n + a_3 n^2 + a_4 n^3$, and its integral between k_1 and k_2 [expression (2A.10)],

$$_{k_2-k_1}G_{k_1} = a_1(k_2 - k_1) + a_2(k_2^2 - k_1^2)/2 + a_3(k_2^3 - k_1^3)/3 + a_4(k_2^4 - k_1^4)/4$$

Given the integrals $_{k_2-k_1}G_{k_1}$, $_{k_4-k_3}G_{k_3}$, $_{k_6-k_5}G_{k_5}$, $_{k_8-k_7}G_{k_7}$, the coefficients $\mathbf{a}$ are found from $\mathbf{M}^{-1}\mathbf{G}(\mathbf{k}) = \mathbf{a}$, where $\mathbf{M}$ has the entries

$$
\mathbf{M} = \begin{bmatrix} (k_2 - k_1) & (k_2^2 - k_1^2)/2 & (k_2^3 - k_1^3)/3 & (k_2^4 - k_1^4)/4 \\ (k_4 - k_3) & (k_4^2 - k_3^2)/2 & (k_4^3 - k_3^3)/3 & (k_4^4 - k_3^4)/4 \\ (k_6 - k_5) & (k_6^2 - k_5^2)/2 & (k_6^3 - k_5^3)/3 & (k_6^4 - k_5^4)/4 \\ (k_8 - k_7) & (k_8^2 - k_7^2)/2 & (k_8^3 - k_7^3)/3 & (k_8^4 - k_7^4)/4 \end{bmatrix}
$$

For the simplest case, in which all intervals $k_j - k_i = n$, and we are fitting g_0 from $_nG_{-2n}$, $_nG_{-n}$, $_nG_0$, $_nG_n$, the reader will find that $\alpha_1 = \alpha_4 = -1/(12n)$, and $\alpha_2 = \alpha_3 = 7/(12n)$. The solution is analogous to (2A.6)–(2A.8), in requiring only the first row of the matrix inverse $\mathbf{M}^{-1}$. For $n = 1$, and with $k_1 = -2$, $k_2 = k_3 = -1$, $k_4 = k_5 = 0$, $k_6 = k_7 = 1$, $k_8 = 2$, the matrix $\mathbf{M}$ becomes

$$
\mathbf{M} = \begin{bmatrix} 1 & -3/2 & 7/3 & -15/4 \\ 1 & -1/2 & 1/3 & -1/4 \\ 1 & 1/2 & 1/3 & 1/4 \\ 1 & 3/2 & 7/3 & 15/4 \end{bmatrix}
$$

CHAPTER 3

Standardized Rates

Method for comparing Local with Standard Death-rates.—*We have no means of ascertaining what the rate of mortality would be among men living in the most favourable sanitary conditions; otherwise observations for a term of years on a considerable number of such persons would supply a standard rate with which other rates could be compared.*

In the absence of such a standard, the districts of England in which the mortality rate did not exceed 17 annual deaths in 1,000 living, have been selected as the basis of a new life table which will shortly be published, as the nearest approximation we can obtain to a table representing the human race in the normal state.

The 5th column in the annexed table shows the rates of mortality at 12 different ages in the districts of England which we call, for the sake of distinction, healthy. The sanitary conditions are often defective, but the defects are counter-balanced; so that the districts being much less unhealthy than the average, may be so designated.

It will be observed that if the population (2,373,983) be multiplied by 17, and the product be divided by 1,000, the resulting number (40,358) will represent the annual deaths that would take place in London if mortality were at the rate of 17 in 1,000 annually. The actual rate of mortality in those districts was 17.72 in 1,000 males, and 17.33 in 1,000 females.

But the population experienced very different rates of mortality at different ages, and the proportional numbers living in London at the various periods of life is not the same as it is in the country districts, which send out emigrants. London is supported partly by immigrants and partly by births. It has hence an excessive number of people in the prime of life. Accordingly, it is found that with the population as it was distributed in 1851 the annual deaths in London would not exceed 36,179, or the annual mortality would be 15 in 1,000 if the rates of mortality at each of the 12 periods of life were the same as those prevailing in the healthy districts. . . .

It is shown in the table that, on an average, 57,582 persons died in London annually during the five years 1849-53, whereas the deaths should not, at rates of mortality then prevailing in certain districts of England, have exceeded

METHOD for comparing the RATES of MORTALITY in the HEALTHY DISTRICTS of ENGLAND, with the Rates prevailing in other Districts; LONDON given as an example

LONDON

AGES 1	Population estimated to the middle of 1851 2	Average Annual Deaths in the 5 Years 1849–53 3	Average Annual Rate of Mortality in the 5 Years 1849–53 4	Average Annual Mortality in Healthy Districts (1849–53) 5	Average Annual Deaths which would have occurred if the Mortality had been the same as in Healthy Districts 6
			MALES		
0-	147,390	12,156	0.08247	0.04348	6367
5-	121,977	1,274	0.01045	0.00674	817
10-	107,745	569	0.00528	0.00384	412
15-	208,028	1,669	0.00802	0.00691	1432
25-	195,983	2,178	0.01111	0.00818	1596
35-	145,165	2,504	0.01725	0.00928	1341
45-	96,559	2,542	0.02632	0.01273	1223
55-	54,479	2,396	0.04398	0.02294	1243
65-	26,514	2,299	0.08670	0.05486	1446
75-	7,387	1,294	0.17522	0.12817	942
85-	794	272	0.34247	0.28350	225
95 and upwards-	48	19	0.40047	0.40000	19
All Ages-	1,112,069	29,172	0.02623	*0.01534	17,063
			FEMALES		
0-	147,969	10,635	0.07187	0.03720	5473
5-	123,082	1,220	0.00991	0.00702	859
10-	109,701	540	0.00492	0.00480	524
15-	248,763	1,619	0.00651	0.00765	1896
25-	233,846	2,213	0.00947	0.00894	2082
35-	165,265	2,345	0.01419	0.00998	1642
45-	113,007	2,241	0.01983	0.01192	1338
55-	69,308	2,460	0.03549	0.02162	1487
65-	36,496	2,645	0.07247	0.04992	1809
75-	12,582	1,936	0.15384	0.11866	1483
85-	1,793	514	0.28685	0.26711	477
95 and upwards-	102	42	0.41611	0.45000	46
All ages-	1,261,914	28,410	0.02251	*0.01515	19,116
Persons	2,373,983	57,582	0.02425	*0.01524	36,179

* This is the rate of mortality that would prevail in the healthy districts at *all ages* if the distribution of the ages were the same as they were in London in 1851.

36,179; consequently 21,403 unnatural deaths took place every year in London. It will be the office of the Boards of Works to reduce this dreadful sacrifice of life to the lowest point, and thus to deserve well of their country.

In Liverpool, by the same method, it is found that 6,418 lives were lost in the year 1857, in excess of the deaths at the healthy rates. In Manchester the sickness and mortality are also excessive.

—WILLIAM FARR (1857)

3.1. INTRODUCTION

A problem common to many summary measures is that they confuse the effects of target variables with the effects of other variables they were not intended to express. Among demographic measures, confounding effects are especially strongly felt in crude death rates. Since most human deaths occur in old age, the CDR is typically higher in populations with relatively high proportions of elderly than in populations with younger age structures, even when life expectancy is substantially better in the older populations. In fertility analysis, crude birth rates are much less sensitive to age distributions, and consequently can be more safely used as summary measures. As an illustration, Table 3.1 shows the proportions in various age categories and selected summary measures for several national populations about 1980 (see also Table 7.1).

The closeness in proportions at the reproductive ages in the seven countries shown is striking and virtually assures that the ratios of births to total

Table 3.1. Population Characteristics for China, the USSR, the United States, Mexico, Italy, France, and Zaire, c. 1980. *Sources:* United Nations (1989), and United Nations Demographic Yearbooks and Population Reference Bureau World Population Data Sheets (Various Years)

Country	Population	Proportion					Crude birth rate	Crude death rate	Total fert. rate	Life exp.
		0–14	15–44		45–64	65+				
			Male	Female						
China	1,000,000,000	0.33	0.24	0.23	0.15	0.05	0.022	0.007	2.8	65
USSR	250,000,000	0.24	0.24	0.24	0.18	0.10	0.018	0.010	2.3	65
USA	225,000,000	0.22	0.23	0.24	0.19	0.12	0.016	0.009	1.9	75
Mexico	75,000,000	0.46	0.21	0.21	0.09	0.03	0.032	0.006	4.8	65
Italy	55,000,000	0.21	0.21	0.21	0.23	0.14	0.011	0.010	1.7	70
France	55,000,000	0.22	0.22	0.21	0.22	0.13	0.015	0.010	2.0	75
Zaire	25,000,000	0.46	0.20	0.21	0.10	0.03	0.046	0.019	6.1	45

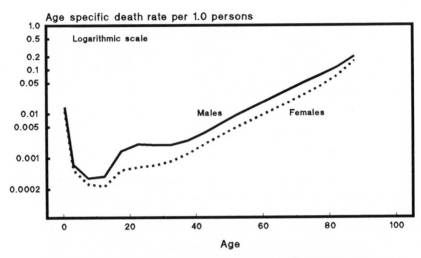

Figure 3.1. U.S. 1980 age-specific death rates. *Source:* NCHS (1984–1985).

population will correlate reasonably well with family sizes. At ages over 45 and over 65, where mortality is most heavily concentrated (Fig. 3.1), the populations differ much more sharply. As a result, the ratios of deaths to population correlate poorly with life expectancies.

One possibility for improving the comparability of mortality rates is to weight the underlying age distributions to be similar to each other. In *direct standardization* that is what is done: the proportion of the population in each age or attribute group is set equal to the proportion in a reference population, and deaths are rescaled to match. The resulting death rates will be comparable to death rates for other populations fitted to the same reference age distribution.

Besides deaths, two directly standardized rates, the total fertility rate and the gross reproduction rate, are used in fertility analysis. To construct the TFR, age-specific fertility rates for one sex, we will specify females, are summed over the fertile ages, a procedure that is equivalent to standardizing on a population of 1 (or 1000) persons at each single year of age. The sum is an estimate of the completed family size. The GRR is similar, except that at each age the ASFR is multiplied by the proportion of births that are female, about 0.49, to estimate the number of daughters born.

Direct standardization has other applications that go much beyond comparisons of birth and death rates. Many surveys are constructed using different sample weights for population subgroups, usually to increase the sample size for populations that are small. The sample is weighted—standardized—for tables that are intended to be representative of the whole population.

Index numbers, risk scores, and psychometric and sociometric scales are also standardized measures if they are created by applying weights to the values of component variables to produce a summary number. Like standardized death rates, but unlike survey weights or the TFR, the scores typically lack intuitive meaning and depend for their use on acceptance by the research community.

3.2. DIRECT STANDARDIZATION

For direct standardization we begin with two populations $_\omega N_{0,i}$ having $_n N_{x,i}$ persons and $_n D_{x,i}$ annual deaths in the age interval x to $x + n$, and $_\omega N_{0,j}$ having $_n N_{x,j}$ persons and $_n D_{x,j}$ deaths in $(x, x + n)$. The complete age distribution is represented by $(0, \omega)$, ω (omega) being the oldest age to which anyone survives. We will specify population j to be a reference population and will refer to i as a source population.

The two populations will have the *crude death rates* [expression (1.4)]:

$$\text{CDR}_i = {_\omega D_{0,i}}/{_\omega N_{0,i}} = \sum_x {_n D_{x,i}} \Big/ \sum_x {_n N_{x,i}} = \sum_x {_n M_{x,i}}({_n N_{x,i}}/{_\omega N_{0,i}})$$

$$\text{CDR}_j = {_\omega D_{0,j}}/{_\omega N_{0,j}}$$

where $_n M_x = {_n D_x}/{_n N_x}$ is the age-specific death rate at ages x to $x + n$ [expression (1.3)].

At the age-specific death rates of population i, deaths at ages x to $x + n$ in the reference population (j) would number:

$$_n D_{x,j,\text{ at pop } i \text{ ASDR}} = {_n N_{x,j}}({_n D_{x,i}}/{_n N_{x,i}})$$

Repeating the calculation for other age intervals and summing the expected deaths will give total deaths expected in population j at the population i rates. Dividing this total by the number in population j yields the *directly standardized death rate:*

$$\text{DSDR}_{\text{pop } i \text{ rates, } pop\, j\, ages} = \sum_x {_n D_{x,j,\text{ at pop } i \text{ ASDR}}} \Big/ {_\omega N_{0,j}}$$

$$= \sum_x ({_n D_{x,i}}/{_n N_{x,i}})({_n N_{x,j}}/{_\omega N_{0,j}}) \qquad (3.1)$$

$$= \sum_x {_n M_{x,i}}({_n N_{x,j}}/{_\omega N_{0,j}})$$

In the expression, $\sum_x$ represents the sum of the terms on the right over all age intervals. *Italics* are used to identify the population taken as the reference, which for the DSDR is *always* the population whose age or attribute distribution is used.*

Table 3.2 provides the data for standardizing deaths for Mexico on the age distribution of the United States as the reference population. (For purposes of illustration, only four age intervals are used. In real applications, 1-year, 5-year, or 10-year age categories would be used, giving a larger number of intervals and more accurate standardized rates.) The DSDR for Mexico found from the table, 0.0114, may be compared with other directly standardized rates that also use the United States as the reference population, and with the U.S. CDR since the latter also has the U.S. population as its base. The DSDR is not comparable to any of the other crude death rates in Table 3.1.

We interpret the DSDR to mean that if Mexico had an age distribution like that of the United States, its CDR would be 0.0114, as compared to the U.S. rate of 0.0088. Before making that conclusion, however, we should check the individual age-specific death rates for the two populations to determine whether the pattern is consistent. If we found that Mexico's age-specific death rates were higher than those of the United States at some ages but lower at others, we might decide that the standardized rate does not provide an adequate picture of the differences between the populations. Table 3.3 shows the age-specific death rates for the two populations. For this example they are consistent with the DSDR difference.

Table 3.3 also displays the U.S. DSDR standardized on Mexico's age distribution. The new DSDR can be compared with the Mexican CDR, which also has the Mexican age distribution as its base. The difference in the two sets of standardized rates, 0.0114 and 0.0088 using the United States as a reference, but 0.0062 and 0.0038 using Mexico as a reference, will suggest the importance of the choice of reference populations. The United States, with more than twice the proportion of elderly that Mexico has, gives standardized rates that are also about twice the level of rates standardized on Mexico's age distribution. Other choices of reference populations would give other values. Because standardized rates are simply index numbers used to represent mortality, there are no formal rules for selecting a "best" reference population from among the many possibilities the user might have. Some informal guidelines will be suggested later.

The range of standardized death rates is not limitless, whatever reference population may be selected. Like the CDR, the DSDR is a weighted average of the age-specific death rates of the source population. Hence, it is bounded:

---

* We note for the reader that unless $_nM_{x,i}$ terms are available to a high degree of precision, the DSDR should be estimated using $_nD_{x,i}/_nN_{x,i}$.

Table 3.2. Illustration of the Calculation of Directly Standardized Death Rates,
United States and Mexico c. 1980

	Source population (Mexico)		Reference population (United States)		
Ages	Persons $_nN_{x,\,source}$ (1)	Deaths $_nD_{x,\,source}$ (2)	Persons $_nN_{x,\,index}$ (3)	Deaths $_nD_{x,\,index}$ (4)	Expected deaths $_nD_{x,\,index,\,at\,source\,rates}$ (3) × (2)/(1)
0–14	34,640,000	151,900	51,300,000	64,400	225,000
15–44	30,900,000	87,800	105,200,000	157,700	298,900
45–64	7,020,000	78,550	44,500,000	425,300	497,900
65+	2,440,000	149,150	25,500,000	1,341,800	1,558,700
Total	75,000,000	467,400	226,500,000	1,989,200	2,580,500

$$CDR_{source\,(Mex)} = 467,400/75,000,000 = 0.0062$$
$$CDR_{ref\,(US)} = 1,989,200/226,500,000 = 0.0088$$
$$DSDR_{source\,rates,\,ref\,ages} = 2,580,500/226,500,000 = 0.0114$$

standardizing the Mexican data of Tables 3.2 and 3.3 on *any* age distribution
will give a DSDR between 0.0028 and 0.0611, while standardizing the U.S.
data on *any* age distribution will give a DSDR between 0.0013 and 0.0526.
(If we had used more age intervals in the examples, the range between the
lowest and highest age-specific death rates would be wider.) Within the limits
of the source population ASDRs, the level of the DSDR will depend in substantial measure on the age distribution of the reference population.

Table 3.3. U.S. and Mexican Age-Specific
Death Rates, c. 1980

Ages	Mexico $_nN_x/_nD_x$	United States $_nN_x/_nD_x$
0–14	0.0044	0.0013
15–44	0.0028	0.0015
45–64	0.0112	0.0096
65+	0.0611	0.0526
CDR	0.0062	0.0088
$DSDR_{Mex\,rates,\,US\,ages}$	0.0114	
$DSDR_{US\,rates,\,Mex\,ages}$		0.0038

3.3. INDIRECT STANDARDIZATION

When total deaths and the age distribution of a population are known but deaths are not available by age, or when the population size is small and age-specific death rates fluctuate sharply across ages, indirect standardization can be used for population comparisons. To standardize indirectly, with population j taken as the reference as before, we first calculate a DSDR using the rates of population j and the age distribution of i (recall that we used the rates of i and age distribution of j when we standardized directly). That is, we first find

$$\text{DSDR}_{\text{rates } j, \text{ ages } i} = \sum_x (_nD_{x,j}/_nN_{x,j})(_nN_{x,i}/_\omega N_{0,i}) \qquad (3.2)$$

We emphasize that the reference population for the DSDR used in indirect standardization is population i, as indicated by the subscripted italics, and not j. Population j will become the reference after two additional steps. For now, in (3.2) we have estimated a DSDR that displays the overall death rate population i would have at the age-specific rates of population j.

Dividing the CDR for population i by the DSDR in (3.2) yields a scale factor, the *standardized mortality ratio,* that is greater than 1 when the source population crude death rate CDR_i is higher than it would be at the age-specific death rates of population j, and is less than 1 when CDR_i is lower than it would be at population j rates. Formally:

$$\text{SMR}_i = \text{CDR}_i / \text{DSDR}_{\text{rates } j, \text{ ages } i} \qquad (3.3)$$

To complete the *indirectly standardized death rate,* the SMR is multiplied by the reference population CDR, here CDR_j, to scale it to the same approximate magnitude. We have:

$$\text{ISDR}_{\text{rates } j, \text{ ages } i, \, CDR_j} = (\text{CDR}_j)(\text{SMR}_i)$$
$$(3.4)$$
$$= \text{CDR}_j(\text{CDR}_i / \text{DSDR}_{\text{rates } j, \text{ ages } i})$$

By adjusting the reference CDR upward or downward in proportion to the change in the source population CDR after substitution of the reference age-specific rates, the ISDR operates as a substitute for the direct application of population i rates to population j ages in the directly standardized rate $\text{DSDR}_{\text{rates } i, \text{ ages } j}$. It does not use population i age-specific death rates, but exploits the SMR as a summary measure of their overall level relative to the death rates of the reference population. For two critical cases it agrees exactly with the DSDR: if the age distributions of populations i and j are the same, the ISDR equals CDR_i (because $DSDR_{rates\ j,\ ages\ i} = CDR_j$); while if the two populations have the same age-specific death rates it will equal CDR_j, the reference CDR (because $DSDR_{rates\ j,\ ages\ i} = CDR_i$). These are the same values the DSDR would take in the two cases.

More generally, the ISDR will substitute for the DSDR when either the two population age distributions are similar or their age-specific death rates follow the same pattern. It is a poorer measure when the patterns of the age-specific rates differ sharply, and when both the age distributions and mortality patterns differ. These are cases for which the DSDR may also be an inappropriate measure of population differences. (The quality of the measures can be checked by examining age-specific death rates for both populations if they are available.)

Having calculated DSDRs for the United States and Mexico, the ISDRs require little additional effort. The ISDR for Mexico using the United States as the reference population is

$$ISDR_{US\ rates,\ Mex\ ages,\ US\ CDR} = CDR_{US}(CDR_{Mex}/DSDR_{US\ rates,\ Mex\ ages})$$

$$= (0.0088)(0.0062)/(0.0038) = 0.0144$$

and for the United States using Mexico as the reference population we have

$$ISDR_{Mex\ rates,\ US\ ages,\ Mex\ CDR} = CDR_{Mex}(CDR_{US}/DSDR_{Mex\ rates,\ US\ ages})$$

$$= (0.0062)(0.0088)/(0.0114) = 0.0048$$

For this example the ISDRs are about 25% above the DSDRs for which they would substitute (0.0144 versus 0.0114 and 0.0048 versus 0.0038, respectively), but both convey the correct impression of higher Mexican than U.S. mortality rates. Looking again at Table 3.3, the two countries will be seen to share a common pattern of low death rates at young ages and much higher rates at older ages. That is a universal human pattern and allows us to use ISDRs for comparisons of mortality differences in national populations with some confidence.

3.4. REFERENCE DISTRIBUTIONS

The choice of reference populations for rate standardization is a matter of judgment. In occasional cases, as in the example of total fertility rates, which are interpretable as measures of family size, a particular reference distribution will find universal acceptance. Most often, however, the selection of a reference distribution is left to the researcher.

Some choices suggest themselves easily. If the researcher is extending a published data series or working with a related series, the reference population used for the published series may serve well. More generally, defining poor choices of reference populations is easier than defining ideal choices. Populations to be avoided include any with irregular age distributions, or that have relatively few persons at the ages at which rate differences are expected to be pronounced. In both cases the user risks understressing key differences or overstressing minor ones, without a clear awareness of what has occurred. It is also important that the reference population include about the same age range as the populations to be standardized: in direct standardization, unused ages are treated as ages of zero mortality.

A common convention when no reference population clearly suggests itself and when the age distributions of the populations to be compared are reasonably smooth is to construct a reference distribution by averaging their *proportions* at each age. Because the reference population is intermediate to the two populations in form, the standardized death rates will be nearer their crude rates than would be true for more arbitrary reference choices. That is an advantage for readers who are at least somewhat familiar with the crude rates. (For the example of Table 3.2, U.S. and Mexican DSDRs standardized on an intermediate population with 34.2% under age 15, 44.1% at ages 15–44, 14.3% at ages 45–64, and 7.4% at ages 65+ would be $DSDR_{US\ rates,\ immediate\ ages} = 0.0063$ and $DSDR_{Mex\ rates,\ intermediate\ ages} = 0.0089$. Since both DSDRs are standardized on the same age distribution, they may be compared with each other. Neither should be compared with the U.S. or Mexican CDR, since the age distributions of both countries differ from the reference age distribution.)

Notice that standardization on an intermediate distribution is equivalent to averaging each CDR with the DSDR standardized on the age distribution of the other population. For the example,

$$DSDR_{US\ rates,\ intermediate\ ages} = \tfrac{1}{2}(CDR_{US} + DSDR_{US\ rates,\ Mex\ ages})$$

$$DSDR_{Mex\ rates,\ intermediate\ ages} = \tfrac{1}{2}(CDR_{Mex} + DSDR_{Mex\ rates,\ US\ ages})$$

The relationship also allows the user to construct rates standardized on either population from rates standardized on the intermediate age distribution.

Our comments on the choice of reference populations apply to directly standardized rates more than to indirectly standardized rates. For the latter, the smoothness of the reference age-specific death rate distribution is also important, since it is used in constructing the denominator of the ISDR. It is also important that the pattern of the age-specific death rates be similar in the two populations insofar as they are both known. In standardizing indirectly we essentially impute the pattern of the reference rates to the source population. Finally, since the ISDR multiplies the standardized mortality ratio by the reference CDR, it is also critical that the two populations be enumerated over roughly the same age range. A reference CDR spanning a much broader or narrower age range than was required for the DSDR may produce ISDRs that are largely uninterpretable.

None of these restrictions should appear onerous to the reader. Essentially what we seek in a reference population are an age distribution and a rate distribution that enhance the comparability of the populations without imposing objectionable or nonrelevant features of their own.

3.5. DECOMPOSITION OF DIFFERENCES BETWEEN CRUDE RATES

A means of decomposing two crude rates to measure the relative importance of age differences versus rate differences that exploits DSDRs was introduced by Kitagawa in 1955 (Kitagawa, 1955, 1964). She suggested rewriting the difference of the two rates (for populations i and j) as:

$$\text{CDR}_i - \text{CDR}_j = \text{Age effect} + \text{Rate effect} - \text{Interaction effect}$$

Emphasizing population i, its *age effect* is the difference between its CDR and the DSDR with population j ages and population i age-specific death rates. That is:

$$\text{Age effect}_i = \text{CDR}_i - \text{DSDR}_{\text{rates } i, \text{ ages } j}$$

$$= \sum_x [(_nN_{x, i}/_\omega N_{0, i})_nM_{x, i} - (_nN_{x, j}/_\omega N_{0, j})_nM_{x, i}] \quad (3.5)$$

$$= \sum_x [(_nN_{x, i}/_\omega N_{0, i}) - (_nN_{x, j}/_\omega N_{0, j})]_nM_{x, i}$$

The expression measures the change in the death rate when the age distribution of population j is substituted for the age distribution of population i, keeping the age-specific death rates the same.

The *rate effect* for i is the difference between the CDR of population i and the DSDR with population i ages and population j age-specific death rates. That is:

Rate effect$_i$ = CDR$_i$ − DSDR$_{rates\ j,\ ages\ i}$

$$= \sum_x [(_nN_{x,\ i}/_\omega N_{0,\ i})_nM_{x,\ i} - (_nN_{x,\ i}/_\omega N_{0,\ i})_nM_{x,\ j}] \quad (3.6)$$

$$= \sum_x (_nN_{x,\ i}/_\omega N_{0,\ i})(_nM_{x,\ i} - {}_nM_{x,\ j})$$

The expression measures the change in the death rate when the rate distribution of population j is substituted for the rate distribution of population i, keeping the age distribution the same.

These two effects do not add to the difference of the crude death rates, but actually represent the crude death rate of population i counted twice (it is the first term of the age effect and of the rate effect), minus two standardized death rates. To correct the equality we need to *subtract out* an *interaction term* that contains both crude death rates (CDR$_i$ is present twice, in both the rate effect and age effect terms, CDR$_j$ is omitted) and the two standardized rates already present. The necessary expression is

Interaction = CDR$_i$ + CDR$_j$ − DSDR$_{rates\ i,\ ages\ j}$ − DSDR$_{rates\ j,\ ages\ i}$

$$= \sum_x (_nN_{x,\ i}/_\omega N_{0,\ i})_nM_{x,\ i} + \sum_x (_nN_{x,\ j}/_\omega N_{0,\ j})_nM_{x,\ j}$$

$$- \sum_x (_nN_{x,\ j}/_\omega N_{0,\ j})_nM_{x,\ i} - \sum_x (_nN_{x,\ i}/_\omega N_{0,\ i})_nM_{x,\ j} \quad (3.7)$$

$$= \sum_x [(_nN_{x,\ i}/_\omega N_{0,\ i}) - (_nN_{x,\ j}/_\omega N_{0,\ j})](_nM_{x,\ i} - {}_nM_{x,\ j})$$

The interaction effect is thus the difference between the crude and standardized rates, or the product of the difference in the population and difference in the death rate at each age.

An important limitation of decomposition is that the separation of age and rate effects is specific to the population of emphasis, whose CDR enters into both the age and rate formulas. If the two populations are switched, the age and rate effects change. For the United States and Mexico, the two sets of effects are:

For the United States as population of emphasis:

Age effect = CDR$_{US}$ − DSDR$_{US\ rates,\ Mex\ ages}$

= 0.0088 − 0.0038 = 0.0050

$$\text{Rate effect} = CDR_{US} - DSDR_{\text{Mex rates, } US \text{ ages}}$$

$$= 0.0088 - 0.0114 = -0.0026$$

$$\text{Interaction} = CDR_{US} + CDR_{Mex} - DSDR_{US \text{ rates, } Mex \text{ ages}}$$

$$- DSDR_{\text{Mex rates, } US \text{ ages}}$$

$$= 0.0088 + 0.0062 - 0.0038 - 0.0114 = -0.0002$$

$$CDR_{US} - CDR_{Mex} = \text{Age effect} + \text{Rate effect} - \text{Interaction}$$

$$0.0088 - 0.0062 = 0.0050 + (-0.0026) - (-0.0002) = 0.0026$$

For Mexico as population of emphasis:

$$\text{Age effect} = CDR_{Mex} - DSDR_{\text{Mex rates, } US \text{ ages}}$$

$$= 0.0062 - 0.0114 = -0.0052$$

$$\text{Rate effect} = CDR_{Mex} - DSDR_{US \text{ rates, } Mex \text{ ages}}$$

$$= 0.0062 - 0.0038 = 0.0024$$

$$\text{Interaction} = CDR_{Mex} + CDR_{US} - DSDR_{\text{Mex rates, } US \text{ ages}}$$

$$- DSDR_{US \text{ rates, } Mex \text{ ages}}$$

$$= 0.0062 + 0.0088 - 0.0114 - 0.0038 = -0.0002$$

$$CDR_{Mex} - CDR_{US} = \text{Age effect} + \text{Rate effect} - \text{Interaction}$$

$$0.0062 - 0.0088 = -0.0052 + 0.0024 - (-0.0002) = -0.0026$$

For the example the age and rate effects are similar using either the United States or Mexico as the population of emphasis. The age effects are particularly pronounced, as we should expect from the difference in age distributions seen in Table 3.1. Rate effects are also strong, at about the same level as the overall difference in the two crude rates. The interaction term is small by comparison, which usually means that there is a consistent pattern of differences in the age distributions and rate distributions for the two countries.

The signs of the age and rate effect terms require comment. With the United States as the population of emphasis, the age term is positive and the rate term negative: if there were no differences in the death rates of the two populations, the U.S. CDR would be higher than Mexico's by 0.0050 (we would have $CDR_{US} - CDR_{Mex}$ = Age effect only = 0.005), while if there were no differences in the age distributions, the U.S. CDR would be lower than Mexico's by 0.0026 (we would have $CDR_{US} - CDR_{Mex}$ = Rate effect only = -0.0026). The same conclusions would follow if Mexico were the population of emphasis. The signs of the age and rate terms are reversed, but that is because $CDR_{Mex} - CDR_{US}$ is opposite in sign from $CDR_{US} - CDR_{Mex}$.

The decomposition can also be performed using the ISDR to substitute for one of the DSDRs: either

$$ISDR_{pop\ i\ rates,\ pop\ j\ ages,\ pop\ i\ CDR} \text{ for } DSDR_{pop\ j\ rates,\ pop\ i\ ages}$$

or

$$ISDR_{pop\ j\ rates,\ pop\ i\ ages,\ pop\ j\ CDR} \text{ for } DSDR_{pop\ i\ rates,\ pop\ j\ ages}$$

With the substitution the interaction term will differ, as will either the age or rate effect term, leaving the other unchanged. The quality of the revised estimates will depend on the appropriateness of the computed ISDR.

Finally, we may note that the crude birth rate and many other measures can be decomposed into age, rate, and interaction effects, or decomposed using other relevant compositional attributes, such as residence or education. For CBR differences, rate effects normally predominate over age effects, but other decompositions are sometimes of interest.

3.6. STATISTICAL TESTS FOR DIFFERENCES BETWEEN RATES *

Most of the statistical tests that are used in demography derive from the variance of the probability of dying in an age interval and the variance in the number of deaths that occur. Assuming that deaths $_nD_x$ are binomially distributed, they will have the probability of occurrence $_nq_x = {_nD_x}/N(x)$, where $N(x)$ is the sample size at exact age x to which the deaths occur. The variance of $_nq_x$ will be:

---

* See also Section 4.8, which introduces variances and statistical tests for life table terms.

$$\text{Var}(_nq_x) = {_np_x}\,{_nq_x}/N(x)$$

$$= \{[N(x) - {_nD_x}]/N(x)\}[_nD_x/N(x)]/N(x) \qquad (3.8)$$

$$= [N(x) - {_nD_x}]_nD_x/N^3(x)$$

The probability of dying can be interpreted as a weighted estimate of the number of deaths that occur, with the weight taken as $1/N(x)$. Using the rule that the variance of a weighted quantity is the weight squared times the variance of the quantity, $\text{Var}(_nq_x)$ is related to $\text{Var}(_nD_x)$ by

$$\text{Var}(_nq_x) = [1/N(x)]^2\,\text{Var}(_nD_x)$$

For the variance of $_nD_x$ we therefore have

$$\text{Var}(_nD_x) = [N(x) - {_nD_x}]_nD_x/N(x) = {_np_x}\,{_nD_x} \qquad (3.9)$$

Like the probability of dying $_nq_x$, the age-specific death rate $_nM_x = {_nD_x}/{_nN_x}$ is a weighted estimate of deaths. Its variance will be (Chiang, 1961)

$$\text{Var}(_nM_x) = (1/_nN_x^2)\text{Var}(_nD_x) = {_np_x}\,{_nD_x}/{_nN_x^2} = {_np_x}\,{_nM_x}/{_nN_x} \qquad (3.10)$$

The CDR is a weighted sum of the age-specific death rates, and its variance can be found using the rule that the variance of a sum or difference is the sum of the variances of the component terms. That is, since

$$\text{CDR} = \sum_x (_nN_x/_\omega N_0)_nM_x$$

for the variance of the CDR we should have

$$\text{Var}(\text{CDR}) = \sum_x (_nN_x/_\omega N_0)^2\,\text{Var}(_nM_x)$$

$$= \sum_x (_nN_x/_\omega N_0)^2{_np_x}\,{_nD_x}/{_nN_x^2} \qquad (3.11)$$

$$= \sum_x (_np_x\,{_nD_x})/_\omega N_0^2$$

More simply,

$$\text{Var}(\text{CDR}) = \sum_x \text{Var}(_nD_x)/_\omega N_0^2 \qquad (3.12)$$

In cases where the ages at death are unknown, the variance of the CDR cannot be estimated with confidence. As an approximation, the rate may be interpreted as a mortality probability, in which case we would have from our original estimate for $\text{Var}(_nq_x)$:

$$\text{Var(CDR)} \simeq \text{CDR}(1 - \text{CDR})/_\omega N_0 \qquad (3.13)$$

This estimate will normally be somewhat high. For human populations the combination of very low death rates at most ages with high death rates toward the end of life reduces variances relative to those of homogeneous samples.

Variances of directly standardized rates are slightly more complex than (3.11) since the weights are taken from the age distributions of the reference population while the variance terms $\text{Var}(_nM_x)$ are those of the source population. That is (Keyfitz, 1966), setting population j as the reference,

$$\text{Var(DSDR}_{\text{rates } i, \text{ ages } j}) = \sum_x (_nN_{x,\,j}/_\omega N_{0,\,j})^2 {}_np_{x,\,i} {}_nD_{x,\,i}/_nN^2_{x,\,i} \qquad (3.14)$$

If the age-specific death rates for the source population are known, the variance of the ISDR can be estimated from the variance of its CDR as

$$\text{Var(ISDR}_{\text{rates } j, \text{ ages } i, \text{ } CDR_j}) = (\text{CDR}_j/\text{DSDR}_{\text{rates } j, \text{ ages } i})^2 \text{ Var(CDR}_i) \qquad (3.15)$$

The expression is derived by interpreting the ISDR as a weighted estimate of the CDR, with the weight

$$W = \text{CDR}_j/\text{DSDR}_{\text{rates } j, \text{ ages } i}$$

Since the number of deaths in the reference population is immaterial to the calculation of the ISDR, the variance of the weight term is 0.

Variances can also be computed for age and rate effects, which represent differences between crude and standardized rates. Given populations i and j, the rate effect for i can be written, from (3.6),

$$\text{Rate effect}_i = \sum_x (_nN_{x,\,i}/_\omega N_{0,\,i}) {}_nM_{x,\,i} - \sum_x (_nN_{x,\,i}/_\omega N_{0,\,i}) {}_nM_{x,\,j}$$

The two age-specific death rates $_nM_{x,\,i}$ and $_nM_{x,\,j}$ are independent, and we apply the rule that the variance of a sum or difference is the sum of the variances of the component terms to find

$$\text{Var(rate effect}_i) = \text{Var(CDR}_i) + \text{Var(DSDR}_{\text{rates } j, \text{ ages } i}) \qquad (3.16)$$

The expression reduces to $\text{Var}(\text{CDR}_i)$ if j is a reference population of arbitrary size, since in that event we may set $\text{Var}(_nM_{x,j}) = 0$.

From (3.5) the age effect for population i can be expressed as

$$\text{Age effect}_i = \sum_x [(_nN_{x,i}/_\omega N_{0,i}) - (_nN_{x,j}/_\omega N_{0,j})]_nM_{x,i}$$

The bracketed term in the expression is the difference of two age weightings, and is therefore also a weight. Following the rule that the variance of a weighted quantity is the weight squared times the variance of the quantity, we will have

$\text{Var}(\text{Age effect}_i)$

$$= \sum_x [(_nN_{x,i}/_\omega N_{0,i}) - (_nN_{x,j}/_\omega N_{0,j})]^2 \, \text{Var}(_nM_{x,i})$$

$$= \sum_x [(_nN_{x,i}/_\omega N_{0,i})^2 + (_nN_{x,j}/_\omega N_{0,j})^2$$

$$- 2(_nN_{x,i}/_\omega N_{0,i})(_nN_{x,j}/_\omega N_{0,j})] \text{Var}(_nM_{x,i}) \tag{3.17}$$

$$= \text{Var}(\text{CDR}_i) + \text{Var}(\text{DSDR}_{\text{rates } i, \text{ ages } j})$$

$$- 2 \sum_x (_nN_{x,i}/_\omega N_{0,i})(_nN_{x,j}/_\omega N_{0,j}) \text{Var}(_nM_{x,i})$$

The reader can use the examples of expressions (3.16) and (3.17) to find the variance of the interaction term (3.7). The expression reduces to $\text{Var}(\text{Age effect}_i)$ if j is a reference population of arbitrary size.

Significance tests of differences between crude and standardized rates can be constructed using the Z scores [see also expression (4.54)]*:

$$Z = (\text{rate}_i - \text{rate}_j)/[\text{Var}(\text{rate}_i) + \text{Var}(\text{rate}_j)]^{1/2} \tag{3.18}$$

Besides rate differences, Z tests can also be used to measure the significance of age, rate, and interaction effects from rate decompositions, since each term is constructed as a difference of crude and directly standardized rates.

---

* Statistical tests can also be performed on differences between the logs of the various rates, where $\text{Var}(\ln X) = \text{Var}(X)/X$. For the properties of log rates see Breslow and Day (1987, pp. 48–79).

A more robust test of the significance of rate differences between two populations is the D statistic, very similar to the Mantel–Haenszel or generalized Wilcoxon test for differences between $_np_x$ distributions (see Section 4.8.2). The test is a chi square with one degree of freedom. Apart from the final age interval, which is sometimes included despite being open-ended, ages for which the variance of $_np_x$ is 0 in both populations do not contribute to the test. D is found from the $_nN_x$ and $_nD_x$ series as

$$D = \left\{ \sum_x [(_nN_{x,\,i} - \tfrac{1}{2}{_n}D_{x,\,i})_nD_{x,\,j} - (_nN_{x,\,j} - \tfrac{1}{2}{_n}D_{x,\,j})_nD_{x,\,i}]/w_x \right\}^2 \Big/$$

$$\sum_x \{ [(_nN_{x,\,i} + \tfrac{1}{2}{_n}D_{x,\,i})(_nN_{x,\,j} + \tfrac{1}{2}{_n}D_{x,\,j})$$

$$\times (_nN_{x,\,i} - \tfrac{1}{2}{_n}D_{x,\,i} + {_n}N_{x,\,j} - \tfrac{1}{2}{_n}D_{x,\,j})(_nD_{x,\,i} + {_n}D_{x,\,j})/ \tag{3.19}$$

$$(_nN_{x,\,i} + \tfrac{1}{2}{_n}D_{x,\,i} + {_n}N_{x,\,j} + \tfrac{1}{2}{_n}D_{x,\,j} - 1)]/w_x^2 \}$$

The test is a summation of 2×2 chi square tests for differences at individual ages, with the substitution

$$\begin{matrix} a & b \\ c & d \end{matrix} = \begin{matrix} {_n}N_{x,\,i} - \tfrac{1}{2}{_n}D_{x,\,i} & {_n}D_{x,\,i} \\ {_n}N_{x,\,j} - \tfrac{1}{2}{_n}D_{x,\,j} & {_n}D_{x,\,j} \end{matrix}$$

The term $_nN_x - \tfrac{1}{2}{_n}D_x$ is an estimate of the population at ages x to $x + n$ surviving to the end of the year, given that $_nN_x$ persons were surviving at midyear and total deaths during the year numbered $_nD_x$. The initial population (the marginal sum $a + b$) is estimated as $_nN_x + \tfrac{1}{2}{_n}D_x$, and comprises the midyear population and persons who died prior to midyear.* In a, b, c, d notation the test becomes

---

* Deaths are distributed toward the beginning of the interval at ages 0 and 1–4. For those intervals the D statistic is estimated using, in a, b notation:

at age 0: $a = {_1}N_0 - 0.15\,{_1}D_0,$ $b = {_1}D_0,$ $a + b = {_1}N_0 + 0.85\,{_1}D_0$

at ages 0–4 or 1–4: $a = {_n}N_x - 0.4\,{_n}D_x,$ $b = {_n}D_x,$ $a + b = {_n}N_x + 0.6\,{_n}D_x$

$$D = \left[\sum_x (ad - bc)/w_x \right]^2 \Bigg/$$

$$\sum_x [(a + b)(c + d)(a + c)(b + d)/(a + b + c + d - 1)]/w_x^2$$

(3.20)

Weights w_x may be set equal to 1 for a sample size weighted test related to the generalized Wilcoxon $_np_x$ distribution test, or to $1/(_nN_{x, i} + \frac{1}{2} _nD_{x, i} + _nN_{x, j} + \frac{1}{2} _nD_{x, j})$ for a uniformly weighted test analogous to the Mantel–Haenszel $_np_x$ test. Depending on the weights selected, the test may favor differences in age-specific death rates at most or relatively few ages. Z tests of differences in age-specific death rates should be computed for the entire age range to determine whether the D statistic is reasonably representative of the age-specific patterns. A point of caution in using the test is that it is sensitive to the number of intervals used and to the concentration of differences into a few intervals.

The reader should note that if the D test is performed using an arbitrary reference population, the reference population should be assigned the same sample size and age distribution as the source population. By that convention, the test will indicate whether the source population event rates and reference rates are statistically distinguishable from each other, without the result being contaminated by structural differences in the two samples. For any other reference population size or age distribution, the significance level of the test will necessarily reflect the distinct characteristics of the two population structures, a compromise that is inappropriate when the reference population is purely one of convenience.

The reader might also note that for differences between national populations, it is rarely necessary to compute statistical significance levels, since large population sizes assure that most differences which are of any interest will be statistically significant. In the example of Table 3.4, a 1/10,000 sample of the data of Table 3.2 is used to avoid wholly trivializing the application of statistical tests to the data.

To estimate variances for the ASDRs and standardized rates, we require the life table survival probabilities $_np_x$, which we may approximate linearly as (see Section 4.3):

$$_np_{x, \text{ linear}} = 1 - _nD_x/(_nN_x/n + \tfrac{1}{2} _nD_x)$$

(3.21)

For the United States at ages 0–14 we will have: $_np_x = 1 - 6/(5130/15 + 3)$ = 0.98261. Other $_np_x$ terms are shown in Table 3.5.

Note in Table 3.5 that the survival probability is 0 at ages 65+ in both populations, as no one survives indefinitely. Because it is 0, however, the

Table 3.4. Mexican and U.S. Populations and Deaths, 1/10,000 Sample, c. 1980

Ages	Mexico			United States		
	Persons $_nN_x$	Deaths $_nD_x$	ASDR $_nM_x$	Persons $_nN_x$	Deaths $_nD_x$	ASDR $_nM_x$
0–14	3464	15	0.0043	5,130	6	0.0012
15–44	3090	9	0.0029	10,520	16	0.0015
45–64	702	8	0.0114	4,450	43	0.0097
65+	244	15	0.0615	2,550	134	0.0525
Total	7500	47	0.0063	22,650	199	0.0088

interval contributes nothing to the sample variance and is essentially lost to the analysis. Introducing additional age intervals after age 65 would reduce the loss, since it is only the final interval that is not used.

Using Tables 3.4 and 3.5, for the variances of the Mexican and U.S. sample CDRs we have:

$$\text{Var}(\text{CDR}) = \sum_x (_np_x \, _nD_x)/_\omega N_0^2$$

$$\text{Var}(\text{CDR}_{\text{Mex}}) = [(0.93709 \times 15) + (0.91628 \times 9) + (0.79540 \times 8)$$

$$+ (0.00000 \times 15)]/7500^2 = 0.00000050962$$

$$\text{Var}(\text{CDR}_{\text{US}}) = [(0.98261 \times 6) + (0.95539 \times 16) + (0.82377 \times 43)$$

$$+ (0.00000 \times 134)]/22,650^2 = 0.00000011033$$

Table 3.5. Life Table Survival Probabilities for Mexico and the United States

Ages	Mexico $_np_x$	U.S. $_np_x$
0–14	0.93709	0.98261
15–44	0.91628	0.95539
45–64	0.79540	0.82377
65+	0.00000	0.00000

Since both age and rate effects contribute to the difference of the CDRs, we would learn little from a Z test for the significance of their difference except to confirm that Mexico's CDR is lower. We would be more interested in knowing whether the rate effect is significant, for which we need the variance of one or both DSDRs. The two variances are

$$\text{Var}(\text{DSDR}_{\text{rates } i, \text{ ages } j}) = \sum_x (_nN_{x,\,j}/_\omega N_{0,j})^2 {}_np_{x,\,i} \, {}_nD_{x,\,i}/_nN^2_{x,\,i}$$

$$\text{Var}(\text{DSDR}_{\text{Mex rates, } US \text{ ages}}) = [0.227^2(0.93709 \times 15)/3464^2]$$

$$+ [0.464^2(0.91628 \times 9)/3090^2] + [0.196^2(0.79540 \times 8)/702^2]$$

$$+ [0.113^2(0.00000 \times 15)/244^2] = 0.00000074235$$

$$\text{Var}(\text{DSDR}_{US \text{ rates, } Mex \text{ ages}}) = [0.462^2(0.98261 \times 6)/5130^2]$$

$$+ [0.412^2(0.95539 \times 16)/10{,}520^2] + [0.094^2(0.82377 \times 43)/4450^2]$$

$$+ [0.032^2(0.00000 \times 134)/2550^2] = 0.000000087068$$

The rate effect using the United States as the source population is CDR_{US} $- \text{DSDR}_{\text{Mex rates, } US \text{ ages}} = 0.0088 - 0.0114 = -0.0026$. It has the variance

$$\text{Var}(\text{Rate effect}) = \text{Var}(\text{CDR}_{US}) + \text{Var}(\text{DSDR}_{\text{Mex rates, } US \text{ ages}})$$

$$= 0.000000011033 + 0.00000074235 = 0.00000085268$$

Using (3.18), $Z = -2.8$ and is significant at about the 0.002 level. The effect is equally significant using Mexico as the source population, despite the difference in age weightings for the two reference populations.

Besides Z statistics, we might also construct confidence intervals for the rate effect. The rate difference has the standard error $[\text{Var}(\text{Rate effect})]^{1/2}$ $= \text{SE}(\text{Rate effect}) = 0.00000085268^{1/2} = 0.000923$. The 95% confidence interval for the rate effect will therefore be $-0.0026 \pm 1.96 \times 0.000923$ $= -0.0044$ to -0.0008.

For the D test, we construct a, b, c, d tables [expression (3.20)] for ages below 65. From our formulas, we have:

$$\begin{matrix} a & b \\ c & d \end{matrix} = \begin{matrix} {}_nN_{x,\,i} - \frac{1}{2}{}_nD_{x,\,i} & {}_nD_{x,\,i} \\ {}_nN_{x,\,j} - \frac{1}{2}{}_nD_{x,\,j} & {}_nD_{x,\,j} \end{matrix}$$

For our data the quantities are:

		Ages: 0–14		15–44		45–64	
a	b	3456.5	15	3,085.5	9	698.0	8
c	d	5127.0	6	10,512.0	16	4428.5	43

Setting the sample weights $w_x = 1$, for D we have:

$$D = \left[\sum_x (ad - bc)/w_x \right]^2 \Bigg/$$

$$\sum_x [(a+b)(c+d)(a+c)(b+d)/(a+b+c+d-1)]/w_x^2$$

$$= [(3456.5 \times 6 - 5127.0 \times 15) + \cdots]^2/$$

$$[(3456.5 + 15)(5127.0 + 6)(3456.5 + 5127.0)(15 + 6)/$$

$$(3456.5 + 15 + 5127.0 + 6 - 1) + \cdots] = 8.479$$

For a chi square of 8.264 with one degree of freedom, the probability is 0.004. The significance level is similar to that for the rate effect.

3.7. ALTERNATIVES TO STANDARDIZATION

Several generalizations of Kitagawa's decomposition will be found in the literature, including hierarchical decompositions [Cho and Retherford (1973), Kim and Strobino (1984)] and purging methods [Clogg and Eliason (1988), Liao (1989), Xie (1989)] that remove part of the effect interaction that limits the precision of (3.5)–(3.7). Besides these methods, several other techniques for analyzing survival differences exist.

One approach that is both simple and widely applicable for human mortality distributions is Schoen's (1970) geometric mean of the age-specific death rates:

$$M_{\text{Schoen}} = \left(\prod_x {}_nM_x \right)^{1/k} \qquad |\,{}_nM_x > 0 \qquad (3.22)$$

where k represents the number of age-specific death rates included in the expression. The restriction ($|$) limits the multiplication to death rates that are not 0.

For the data of Table 3.3, Schoen's estimators are

$$M_{US} = [(0.0013)(0.0015)(0.0096)(0.0526)]^{1/4} = 0.0056$$

$$M_{Mex} = [(0.0044)(0.0028)(0.0112)(0.0611)]^{1/4} = 0.0096$$

The estimators are more representative of mortality differences when age intervals of equal width are used, a restriction that is less important for standardized rates. At the same time, they are less sensitive than standardized rates to the choice of the final age interval (e.g., ages 75+ or ages 85+). For significance testing and for populations that are differentiated on multiple characteristics, Schoen's M can also be estimated using loglinear models, for which the reader should see Teachman (1977).

The most widely used alternative to standardization is the life table, which displays probabilities of surviving from birth to various ages and the mean and median lifetime. The estimates are functions of age-specific death rates, but are independent of the actual age distributions. For the sample of Table 3.4 the life table produces the life expectancy estimates at birth $e_{0, US} = 75.5$ years, $e_{0, Mex} = 68.0$ years. The difference is significant at the 0.001 level ($Z = 3.2$).

Linear modeling is also widely used as an alternative to standardization because of the flexibility it offers in handling multiple variables (Althauser and Wigler, 1972; Breslow and Day, 1975; Page, 1977; Little and Pullum, 1979). It does not handle all problems well. We would rarely use a model of the form $_nM_{x,j} = a + b_n M_{x,i}$ to test for a significant difference in age-specific mortality rates between two populations for example, since the rates do not change linearly with age and those for one population are not typically in fixed ratios to those for another. Additional terms would improve model quality, but for the example either standardized rates or life table measures would serve at least as well. As more variables are entered, and for attributes other than mortality, the attractiveness of linear models becomes greater.

3.8. SUMMARY

Standardization is a technique for calculating summary demographic measures that adjusts for the distorting effects of compositional differences between source populations. Age differences are most commonly adjusted, but sex, education, residence, or other characteristics may also be relevant.

In *direct standardization* the composition-specific rates of each source population are applied to a reference distribution, yielding summary measures that reflect the reference compositional structure. Using age as the compositional variable, we have using j as the reference population:

$$\text{DSDR}_{\text{rates } i, \text{ ages } j} = \sum_x ({}_nD_{x, i}/{}_nN_{x, i})({}_nN_{x, j}/{}_\omega N_{0, j})$$

The quality of the DSDR will depend on relevant compositional variables being selected, and on there being a consistent pattern of differences in the source population rates.

In *indirect standardization,* the composition-specific rates of the source populations, which may be unknown, are replaced with the specific rates of the reference population, creating a directly standardized rate complementary to the usual DSDR. Dividing the summary rate for the source population by the standardized rate produces a *standardized mortality ratio,* which is used to scale the reference crude death rate upward or downward. We have:

$$\text{ISDR}_{\text{rates } j, \text{ ages } i, \text{ } CDR_j} = \text{CDR}_j(\text{CDR}_i/\text{DSDR}_{\text{rates } j, \text{ ages } i})$$

Like the DSDR, the quality of the ISDR will depend on relevant compositional variables being selected, and on there being a consistent pattern of differences in the source population rates. For the ISDR it is also important that the source and reference populations have similar rate patterns.

Besides direct comparisons, the DSDR can be used to decompose differences between the source population summary rates into rate effects and compositional effects, relative to the source compositional distributions. Both effects can exist even in source rates that are identical. Their principal value is as indicators of the relative importance of the two types of effects for the populations being compared.

Statistical tests exist for differences between summary and standardized rates. These derive from the variances of the event rates in the source populations, weighted by the source or reference compositional distribution. Because of the weighting, they are specific for the distributions being used: significance levels will be higher if ages are emphasized at which survival rates in the source populations are most distinct, and lower if ages are emphasized at which the populations are most similar.

For an introduction to medical applications of standardized rates and related measures, with additional statistical tests, the reader should see Breslow and Day (1987).

CHAPTER 4

The Life Table I

Whereas we have found that of 100 quick conceptions about 36 of them die before they be six years old, and that perhaps but one surviveth 76, we, having seven decades between six and 76, we sought six mean proportional numbers between 64, the remainder living at six years, and the one which survives 76, and find that the numbers following are practically near enough to the truth; for men do not die in exact proportions, nor in fractions: from whence arises the Table following:

Viz. of 100 there dies		*The fourth*	*6*
within the first six years	*36*	*The next*	*4*
The next ten years, or decade	*24*	*The next*	*3*
The second decade	*15*	*The next*	*2*
The third decade	*9*	*The next*	*1*

From whence it follows, that of the said 100 conceived there remains alive at six years end 64

At sixteen years end	*40*	*At fifty-six*	*6*
At twenty-six	*25*	*At sixty-six*	*3*
At thirty-six	*16*	*At seventy-six*	*1*
At forty-six	*10*	*At eighty*	*0*

—JOHN GRAUNT (1662)

4.1. INTRODUCTION

The life table shows the proportion of a population or sample who survive at specific durations after exposure to an event risk. We might want, for example, the proportion of women who marry by age 25 (0.65 for U.S. females born in 1940–49) or the proportion expected to survive to their 85th birthday (0.19 for males and 0.39 for females at U.S. 1985 mortality rates). The measures are probabilistic, and can be compared across populations and over time without the adjustments for compositional differences that many crude rates require. The probabilities can also be used to estimate mean survival times—life expectancies—that compactly summarize survival experience.

The key to the life table is estimation of the survival probability $_np_x$ and its complement, the mortality probability $_nq_x = 1 - {_np_x}$, between two age or time points. (As before, the measurement interval is from x to $x + n$, the right subscript indicating the initial point and the left subscript the interval width.) To find the probability, we require two pieces of information: an estimate of the population at risk of the terminating event in the interval $(x, x + n)$, and an estimate of the number of terminations taking place.

The source data for the life table may take different forms, allowing a variety of estimating formulas to be used. We introduce formulas associated with sample surveys first, in Section 4.2, followed by estimators from census and vital statistics information in Section 4.3. The remaining terms of the life table are introduced in Section 4.4. These are followed in Section 4.5 by specialized formulas for national life tables that improve the accuracy of estimates for infancy and old age. We next introduce virtual life tables, which produce what are essentially life table survival estimates by simple techniques. The chapter concludes with variance formulas and statistical tests for life table terms.

The chapter has five appendices. The first discusses data coding for life tables from survey data, and the adjustment of interval units to reflect the level of precision in the source information. Appendix 4A.2 introduces two-census life tables, which form a subset of the virtual life tables in Section 4.7. Appendix 4A.3 elaborates on the text presentation of $_np_x$ estimators with censorship. Appendix 4A.4 outlines the derivation of maximum likelihood survival estimators. Finally, in Appendix 4A.5 we review sample size estimation for the life table.

4.2. 1- AND n-YEAR SURVIVAL PROBABILITIES FROM POPULATION SURVEYS AND EVENT HISTORIES

4.2.1. Nonparametric Estimators

In a survey or panel study, the risk status of members of a population can usually be measured from a specific point, either a birthday or other anniversary, or the time at which the initial event occurred that put each individual at risk. For general mortality, birthdays are particularly useful starting points because deaths are remembered by the decedent's age and the date of death; for many medical studies the initial point will be the date a particular diagnosis was made or a course of treatment was begun.

Beginning with an initial sample $N(0)$ of persons entering a study, or the sample $N(x)$ of persons at risk at their xth birthday or anniversary, the survival probability to time 1 or $x + n$ is estimated by the proportion still surviving as of that point, either $N(1)/N(0)$ or $N(x + n)/N(x)$. Formally, for a sample that is *uncensored in the interval* [that is, a sample $N(x)$ for which the survival status of all individuals is known at the beginning of the interval (x) and at its end $(x + n)$]:

$$_np_{x,\ \text{unadjusted}} = N(x + n)/N(x)$$

$$_nq_{x,\ \text{unadjusted}} = [N(x) - N(x + n)]/N(x) \tag{4.1}$$

$$= {_nD_x}/N(x) = 1 - {_np_{x,\ \text{unadjusted}}}$$

The unadjusted estimator is only used if no observations are censored in the interval. Where individuals have entered or been lost between x and $x + n$, or their status at $x + n$ has not been ascertained, as occurs when the interval is interrupted by study cutoff, the survival probability will require additional terms that allow downward adjustment of the sample and event counts to reflect the actual observation times for the sample.

It is important that the reader understand how interval censorship arises. *Left interval-censorship* occurs when individuals enter observation at a point within an interval and therefore are exposed to the event risk for less than the full interval duration. The most common case is when intervals are delimited by birth dates but persons may enter the study at other times. In that circumstance, the individual is observed for the partial interval between entry and next birthday: if the next birthday is $x + 1$, the initial observation is from a point after x to the point $x + 1$, and will be less than the full 365 days between birthdays. More rarely, individuals may be recruited into a follow-up study at a point between anniversaries as replacements for others who have left.*

Right interval-censorship occurs when an individual leaves observation at a time other than an interval end point. Paralleling the earlier example, a person may be observed at x, the start of an interval, but leave the study before $x + 1$. The reason may be that the study cutoff point finds some

---

* As distinct from interval censorship, *sample censorship* occurs whenever individuals enter observation after the start of risk (left sample-censorship) or leave observation prior to event occurrence (right sample-censorship). The censorship need not occur in every interval, but must occur in at least some: a sample is considered uncensored only if all individuals are followed from the start of risk to a point beyond event occurrence, with no individuals leaving observation who are still at risk. The treatment of interval censorship in survival estimation is discussed in Sections 4.2.1 and 4.2.2. In Section 4.2.3 we consider biases that arise when survival probabilities differ for uncensored and interval-censored samples.

individuals between anniversaries, or that individuals have been lost or dismissed during the interval.

Where interval censorship arises, the researcher may choose to disregard the partial interval and initiate observation at $x + 1$ (or at $x + n$, if the interval width is n), or may use a $_1p_x$ or $_np_x$ formula that allows the partial interval to be included for the limited information it contains.

The simplest option is to estimate $_np_x$ from observations not censored in the interval, using the anniversary or *curtate sample* (CS) estimator:

$$_np_{x, \text{ curtate sample}} = 1 - (_nD_x - _nD_{\text{LC}, x} - _nD_{\text{RC}, x})/$$

$$[N(x) - N_{\text{LC}}(x) - N_{\text{RC}}(x)] \qquad (4.2)$$

$$= 1 - (_nD_x - _nD_{\text{C}, x})/[N(x) - N_{\text{C}}(x)]$$

where $N_{\text{LC}}(x)$ represents all observations left-censored in the interval (those individuals observed from a point after x to the point $x + n$), and $N_{\text{RC}}(x)$ represents all observations right-censored in the interval (individuals observed from x to a point before $x + n$). The terms $_nD_{\text{LC}, x}$ and $_nD_{\text{RC}, x}$ are subsets of $N_{\text{LC}}(x)$ and $N_{\text{RC}}(x)$, respectively, comprising all individuals observed for only part of the interval who experience the terminating event during the time they are observed. The expression is generalized by setting $N_{\text{C}}(x) = N_{\text{LC}}(x) + N_{\text{RC}}(x)$, and $_nD_{\text{C}, x} = _nD_{\text{LC}, x} + _nD_{\text{RC}, x}$.

The reader should find expressions (4.1) and (4.2) intuitive. Both estimate the probability of the event from the proportion of the sample who experience it in the interval. Expression (4.2) is used for intervals in which part of the sample is interval-censored. It deletes the partly observed subset, since the subset does not provide complete information on the event probability.

Where part of a sample is right-censored, (4.2) generalizes to (4.1) if interval widths n are allowed to vary such that a single individual is censored or terminates at each interval end point. In this case, the number of intervals in the table will be the same as the initial sample size $N(0)$. Each $_{n_j}p_x$ term will be 1.0 or $[N(x) - 1]/N(x)$, depending on whether the individual changing status at the interval end point $x + n_j$ is censored or terminated. Survival probabilities $_{n_j}p_x$ satisfying this condition are *product limit* (PL) estimators (Böhmer, 1912; Kaplan and Meier, 1958). They extract all of the information to be had from the source data, but are rarely used where sample sizes are large enough to generate ties between censorship and termination at some durations $x + n_j$.

Both the unadjusted ($_np_x$) and product limit ($_{n_j}p_x$) estimators (4.1) and the curtate sample estimator (4.2) are maximum likelihood estimators (see Appendix 4A.4) and are Fisher consistent: if the probability of censorship is

Table 4.1. Survival Status of Breast Cancer Patients First Seen
between 1956 and 1961. One-Year Intervals.[a]
Source: Drolette (1975)

Start of interval (x)	Total		Right-censored	
	Number at risk	Events	Number at risk	Events
0	350	74	0	0
1	276	48	45	1
2	184	31	50	0
3	103	10	36	1
4	58	4	28	0

[a] Depending on measurement precision, the interval indexes used in life tables may or may not
correspond closely to the exact interval values shown. For a discussion of this point see Appendix
4A.1.

independent of the event risk, samples drawn from a population with the
interval survival probability θ have the expected survival rates $E\,[{}_np_{x,\,\text{unadjusted}}]$
$= \theta$ and $E\,[{}_np_{x,\,\text{curtate sample}}] = \theta$.

Tables 4.1 and 4.2 illustrate calculation of survival probabilities by
expressions (4.1) and (4.2), with a data set from Drolette (1975). In the
initial interval, ${}_np_{x,\,\text{unadjusted}}$ [expression (4.1)] is used as none of the 350 cases
entering the study were observed for less than 1 year. In the second and later
intervals, substantial numbers of cases are right-censored by arrival at the
study cutoff point and the curtate sample estimator ${}_np_{x,\,\text{curtate sample}}$ [expression
(4.2)] is used.

4.2.2. Parametric Estimators

A number of expressions are available that include the incomplete ex-
perience of the censored samples $N_{\text{LC}}(x) + N_{\text{RC}}(x)$ in estimating ${}_np_x$. The
procedures begin by finding the proportion of censored cases in the interval
who survive to their points of censorship, which we may call ${}_np_{x,\,\text{partial}}$. For
right interval-censored observations* these proportions are:

$${}_np_{x,\,\text{right partial}} = 1 - {}_nD_{\text{RC},\,x}/N_{\text{RC}}(x) \qquad (4.3)$$

To relate ${}_np_{x,\,\text{right partial}}$ to ${}_np_x$, the survival distribution needs to be parameterized (that is, assigned a mathematical form). In the simplest case, we
approximate the number of survivors l_x at duration x by the linear function

* Left interval censorship is less often encountered and is discussed in Appendix 4A.3.

Table 4.2. Estimated Proportion of Table 4.1
Sample Surviving Each Interval,
Using CS $_np_x$ Estimator

$_np_{x,\text{ unadjusted}} = 1 - {_nD_x}/N(x)$

$_np_{x,\text{ curtate sample}} = 1 - ({_nD_x} - {_nD_{C,x}})/[N(x) - N_C(x)]$

$_1p_{0,\text{ unadjusted}} = 1 - 74/350 = 0.7886$

$_1p_{1,\text{ curtate sample}} = 1 - (48 - 1)/(276 - 45) = 0.7965$

$_1p_{2,\text{ curtate sample}} = 1 - (31 - 0)/(184 - 50) = 0.7687$

$_1p_{3,\text{ curtate sample}} = 1 - (10 - 1)/(103 - 36) = 0.8657$

$_1p_{4,\text{ curtate sample}} = 1 - (4 - 0)/(58 - 28) = 0.8667$

$l_x = a + bx$. When survival is linear, deaths in the unobserved part of any censored interval will equal deaths in the observed part. For the right interval-censored $_np_x$ estimator, we therefore have:

$$_np_{x,\text{ RC linear}} = 1 - 2{_nD_{\text{RC},x}}/N_{\text{RC}}(x) = 1 - {_nD_{\text{RC},x}}/\tfrac{1}{2}N_{\text{RC}}(x) \quad (4.4)$$

In the expression $_np_x$ is estimated by doubling the number of events $_nD_{\text{RC},x}$ in the partial interval to approximate events in the complete interval. No adjustment is needed in the denominator, since the new deaths imputed to the numerator will be to individuals already counted in $N_{\text{RC}}(x)$ as survivors at censorship.

To estimate $_np_x$ using both the censored and uncensored observations, we may add the numerators and denominators of the curtate sample estimator (4.2) and the estimator under censorship (4.4). Since known events in the censored sample number $_nD_{\text{RC},x}$, and since the observation times for the censored sample are about half those for the uncensored sample, by convention we assign the censored observations one-half the weight of uncensored observations. [Formally, we combine (4.2) with the second form of (4.4).] By that convention, for a linear $_np_x$ estimator incorporating right interval-censored observations we would have:

$$_np_{x,\text{ linear}} = 1 - [({_nD_x} - {_nD_{\text{RC},x}}) + ({_nD_{\text{RC},x}})]/$$

$$\{[N(x) - N_{\text{RC}}(x)] + \tfrac{1}{2}N_{\text{RC}}(x)\}$$

$$= 1 - {_nD_x}/[N(x) - \tfrac{1}{2}N_{\text{RC}}(x)]$$

This expression may take negative values when a high proportion of the censored sample $N_{\text{RC}}(x)$ are terminators. To recognize the estimate range, the expression may be written:

$$_nP_{x, \text{ linear}} = greater\ of\ \{0,\ 1 - {_nD_x}/[N(x) - \tfrac{1}{2}N_{\text{RC}}(x)]\} \qquad (4.5)$$

By (4.5), $_nP_{x, \text{ linear}}$ is set equal to 0 when $_nD_x > [N(x) - \tfrac{1}{2}N_{\text{RC}}(x)]$, since the right-hand expression then becomes negative.

The linear estimator is most appropriate for distributions in which mortality worsens gradually over time. To see that, notice that for equal numbers of events in the observed and unobserved parts of the right-censored interval the event probabilities will be $_nD_{\text{RC}, x}/N_{\text{RC}}(x)$ and $_nD_{\text{RC}, x}/[N_{\text{RC}}(x) - {_nD_{\text{RC}, x}}]$, respectively. The sample size is smaller in the unobserved part of the interval due to the subtraction from $N_{\text{RC}}(x)$ of deaths occurring in the observed part. As a result, the event probability is greater and the survival probability lower.

A formula that is more widely used than (4.5), because it does not require knowledge of events occurring in the censored interval [the subset $_nD_{\text{RC}, x}$ belonging to $N_{\text{RC}}(x)$], is the hyperbolic (or "actuarial") formula.* For samples with right interval-censorship in $(x, x + n)$ the expression is:

$$_nP_{x, \text{ hyperbolic}} = 1 - {_nD_x}/\{N(x) - \tfrac{1}{2}[N_{\text{RC}}(x) - {_nD_{\text{RC}, x}}]\}$$
$$= 1 - {_nD_x}/[N(x) - \tfrac{1}{2}{_nW_{\text{RC}, x}}] \qquad (4.6)$$

In the expression, the term $N_{\text{RC}}(x) - {_nD_{\text{RC}, x}} = {_nW_{\text{RC}, x}}$ represents withdrawals, comprising individuals censored in the interval who were surviving at last contact. The quantity $_nW_{\text{RC}, x}$ will be known even when $_nD_{\text{RC}, x}$ cannot be separated from $_nD_x$. The reader can confirm that the expression is found by adding the numerators and denominators of the curtate sample estimator (4.2) and the right interval-censored hyperbolic estimator:

$$_nP_{x, \text{ RC hyperbolic}} = 1 - {_nD_{\text{RC}, x}}/\{_nD_{\text{RC}, x} + \tfrac{1}{2}[N_{\text{RC}}(x) - {_nD_{\text{RC}, x}}]\}$$
$$= 1 - {_nD_{\text{RC}, x}}/(_nD_{\text{RC}, x} + \tfrac{1}{2}{_nW_{\text{RC}, x}}) \qquad (4.7)$$

In contrast to the linear estimator, the hyperbolic imputes a higher probability of survival to the unobserved part of the interval than to the observed part. It is thus best suited for samples in which the survival probability is

---

* The earliest use of the formula I have found is Ansell (1874), although it may be older. Among modern works, Berkson and Gage (1950) provide an illustration of its computation for medical follow-up studies. The reader should also see Jain and Sivin (1977) and Birnbaum (1979) for critiques of the method.

Table 4.3. Proportion of Table 4.1 Sample
Surviving Each Interval, Using Linear
and Hyperbolic $_np_x$ Estimators

$_1p_{0,\text{ unadjusted}} = 1 - {}_1D_0/N(0) = 1 - 74/350 = 0.7886$

$_np_{x,\text{ linear}} = 1 - {}_nD_x/[N(x) - \frac{1}{2}N_{RC}(x)]$

$_1p_{1,\text{ linear}} = 1 - 48/(276 - 45/2) = 0.8107$

$_1p_{2,\text{ linear}} = 1 - 31/(184 - 50/2) = 0.8050$

$_1p_{3,\text{ linear}} = 1 - 10/(103 - 36/2) = 0.8824$

$_1p_{4,\text{ linear}} = 1 - 4/(58 - 28/2) = 0.9091$

$_np_{x,\text{ hyperbolic}} = 1 - {}_nD_x/\{N(x) - \frac{1}{2}[N_{RC}(x) - {}_nD_{RC,x}]\}$

$_1p_{1,\text{ hyperbolic}} = 1 - 48/[276 - \frac{1}{2}(45 - 1)] = 0.8110$

$_1p_{2,\text{ hyperbolic}} = 1 - 31/[184 - \frac{1}{2}(50 - 0)] = 0.8050$

$_1p_{3,\text{ hyperbolic}} = 1 - 10/[103 - \frac{1}{2}(36 - 1)] = 0.8830$

$_1p_{4,\text{ hyperbolic}} = 1 - 4/[58 - \frac{1}{2}(28 - 0)] = 0.9091$

improving over time. Of necessity, it is also used when interval-censored and uncensored events cannot be separated.*

Table 4.3 displays survival probabilities under $_np_{x,\text{ unadjusted}}$ and the two parametric estimators in this section, for the data of Table 4.1. The reader might also examine Appendix 4A.3 and Table 4A.9 for survival under exponential estimators. My own preference is for the nonparametric CS estimator [$_np_{x,\text{ curtate sample}}$, expression (4.2)], largely through lack of conviction that much is gained from the scraps of information censored observations provide.

4.2.3. Bias

The reader might notice that the parametric survival estimates in Table 4.3, and the additional estimates for the same data set in Table 4A.9, are above the curtate sample estimates of Table 4.2. The comparison suggests that survival probabilities are greater for the censored sample in each interval

---

* Uncertainty as to whether events are interval-censored occurs almost exclusively in human mortality studies when the study samples are compromised by losses to follow-up. In the presence of unscheduled losses, it becomes possible that at least some potential withdrawals are interdicted by death, and therefore that at least *some* deaths assigned to uncensored intervals ($_nD_x - {}_nD_{RC,x}$) might reasonably be considered to belong to the censored subset ($_nD_{RC,x}$). The actuarial accepts interval-censored events, but assigns those and uncensored observations equal weight, which makes the number censored immaterial to the estimation of $_np_x$.

There is less to recommend the actuarial when no losses to follow-up occur or when the terminating event is not death. In these cases, events in the interval are *always* distinguishable as belonging to the censored or uncensored sample and the researcher can apply judgment as to the most appropriate estimating formula.

than for the uncensored sample. The reader may confirm that this is the case by contrasting the proportion of terminators in each uncensored interval sample in Table 4.1 with the proportion of terminators in each censored sample. Interval 1, for example, includes 45 persons but only a single event in the censored sample, as compared with $276 - 45 = 231$ persons and $48 - 1 = 47$ events in the uncensored sample. In a data set as large as this, consistently higher or lower survival in interval-censored samples implies biases in the design or implementation of entry or cutoff decisions. A test for censorship bias (more precisely, for consistency between the curtate and partial $_np_x$ estimators) using the D statistic will be introduced in Section 4.8 [expression (4.55); a version of the test was presented as expression (3.19)].*

Censorship biases can arise through oversights in study design in several ways. First, it is critical that decisions respecting the start and duration of observation on the individuals in the sample precede sample selection, and not be subject to negotiation between the investigator and individual study participants. If study entry or cutoff points are subject to manipulation by participants, durations of observation at censorship become confounding variables in the analysis. (The data of Table 4.1 may have been compromised by release from observation of persons whose cancers were in remission and whose interest in the study had waned. In this case, the losses would contribute to underestimation of the survival probability.) In the same category as confounding effects are losses to follow-up and investigator-instigated dismissals of participants. The bias does not arise in retrospective studies, since the information they contain is historical and observation times are not subject to negotiation or compromised by sample losses.

Other biases exist that do not show up as differences between survival in censored and uncensored samples. Fundamental problems are created by selectivity biases that result from refusals to participate in the study, and from the withholding of information by participants. Other problems arise when there is uncertainty as to the start of risk or time of event occurrence. Medical studies, for example, may follow the progress of an illness from the date of diagnosis unless the date of onset of the disease is known fairly precisely. As an outcome, the occurrence of pregnancies may not be reported until the second or third trimester, when they are evident. (When reporting may be delayed, durations of observation on individuals not reporting an event as of the cutoff date need to be reduced in some measure to preclude misclassifi-

---

* Chiang (1968, pp. 287–288), Mode (Mode *et al.*, 1977), and others have suggested that unscheduled withdrawals be made a subset of the event category $_nD_x$, and that cause-eliminated rates (Section 5.4) be used to estimate survival probabilities as they would appear if no losses occurred. The approach assumes that withdrawals are uncorrelated with survival, and it would not be used if the D statistic indicated that unscheduled withdrawals selected for survival status. For an application of the formula to the data of Table 4.1, see Section 5.4.

cations. There are no formal decision rules for the amount of adjustment the cutoff points might require.)

The survival estimates of the next section, found from midyear populations and annual deaths or other events, become biased when the quality of age or event information is low, or when one data source is substantially more complete than the other. If the data are for national populations, the researcher usually has access to independent commentary on data quality. For smaller data sets, as for survey and follow-up data, the investigator must be on guard for suspect results.

4.3. 1- AND n-YEAR SURVIVAL PROBABILITIES FROM MIDYEAR POPULATION ESTIMATES AND ANNUAL DEATHS

In most national life tables estimation of survival probabilities begins with information on the midyear population by age and on annual deaths rather than information from sample surveys. The population and vital statistics information do not provide survival probabilities directly, but are used to construct age-specific death rates:

$$\text{ASDR}_x = {}_nM_x = {}_nD_x/{}_nN_x$$

The ASDR is not the probability of an individual dying in the course of the year, since the midyear population in an age interval, ${}_nN_x$, is not a count of the persons initially at risk of dying, $N(x)$. For $n > 1$ year, ${}_nN_x$ includes persons at more than one age, and for all intervals n it excludes those who die in the first half of the year, before the population enumeration.*

If the midyear population is a reasonable estimate of the population at risk except for its omission of January–June deaths, we should be able to reconstruct the population initially at risk by adding a fraction of the annual deaths to the midyear count. At most ages the corrections will be about half of annual deaths, giving the estimate (Milne, 1815, pp. 97–100):

---

* The reader might note that the omission of deaths would not be corrected by an enumeration on January 1 or December 31, as the January and December populations are also not the population surviving as of exact age x. Moreover, a January count would exclude any births that occurred during the year, and both January and December counts may err with respect to net migration. The counts might therefore be either larger or smaller than the midyear estimate.

For these reasons, except for the losses due to mortality, a midyear enumeration is more often representative of the average population size than either end point. In effect, it is balanced with respect to the left and right interval-censorship produced through aging across interval categories and through migration.

$$N(x)_{\text{linear}} = {}_1N_x + \tfrac{1}{2}{}_1D_x$$

where ${}_1N_x$ represents the midyear population and ${}_1D_x$ represents annual deaths. As before, we define $N(x)$ to be the population at risk at exact age x.

When wider age intervals are used for the population and death counts, we require a slightly revised formula for $N(x)$:

$$N(x)_{\text{linear}} = {}_nN_x/n + \tfrac{1}{2}{}_nD_x \qquad (4.8)$$

The formula estimates $N(x)$, the population at exact age x, by adjusting from the complete interval population ${}_nN_x$ to the population at the central age in the interval, about ${}_nN_x/n$ for an interval of n years, and adding deaths in the first half of the interval, at most ages about half of total deaths.

Table 4.4 displays the U.S. 1980 census population at ages 0–84 and 85+, and U.S. 1980 deaths from vital statistics. In column 5 of the table the population surviving as of the start of each interval (at xth birthday) is estimated by expression (4.8). As a check on the expression, in column 6 we show the mean annual number of U.S. births ${}_\omega B_0$ during the period each cohort was born. At the younger ages the estimated population surviving at age x exceeds U.S. births x years earlier because of immigration, but both at younger and at older ages the correspondence is adequate to suggest that $N(x)$ is reasonably approximated from the interval population and deaths using (4.8).

Having found the approximate population at risk at the beginning of each age interval and knowing the number of deaths in the interval, the probability of surviving to the start of the next interval is found as the proportion of the risk population not dying, or

Table 4.4. U.S. 1980 Population, Annual Deaths, and Estimated Survivors at xth Birthday

Ages	Int. n	Census population ${}_nN_x$	Deaths ${}_nD_x$	Risk population[a] $N(x)_{\text{linear}}$	Original birth cohort ${}_\omega B_0$
0–4	5	16,348,300	53,713	3,296,500	3,116,000
5–14	10	34,942,100	10,689	3,499,600	3,485,000
15–24	10	42,486,800	49,027	4,273,200	4,195,000
25–44	20	62,716,500	108,658	3,190,200	3,160,000
45–64	20	44,502,600	425,338	2,437,800	2,770,000
65–74	10	15,580,600	466,621	1,791,400	2,760,000
75–84	10	7,728,800	517,257	1,031,500	2,510,000
85+	—	2,240,100	357,970	357,970	—

[a] $N(x)_{\text{linear}} = {}_nN_x/n + \tfrac{1}{2}{}_nD_x$ at ages 0–84. At ages 85+ we set $N(x)$ equal to ${}_nD_x$ since there are no survivors beyond the interval.

$$_1p_{x, \text{ linear}} = 1 - {}_1D_x/N(x) = 1 - {}_1D_x/({}_1N_x + \tfrac{1}{2}{}_1D_x)$$

for single years of age. The probability of surviving n years will be*:

$$_np_{x, \text{ linear}} = 1 - {}_nD_x/N(x) = 1 - {}_nD_x/({}_nN_x/n + \tfrac{1}{2}{}_nD_x)$$

Since the expressions allow negative survival probabilities if deaths at ages x and above exceed the estimated population alive at the xth birthday, we generalize the survival probability as:

$$_np_{x, \text{ linear}} = 1 - {}_nD_x/N(x)$$

$$= \textit{greater of } \{0, 1 - {}_nD_x/({}_nN_x/n + \tfrac{1}{2}{}_nD_x)\}$$

(4.9)

Formally, $_np_{x, \text{ linear}}$ becomes 0 in (4.9) when $_nD_x > 2({}_nN_x/n)$. In words, the proportion surviving the complete interval is set at 0 if more than half die by midinterval.

The approximation, $N(x) = {}_nN_x/n + \tfrac{1}{2}{}_nD_x$, is not satisfactory for infancy and early childhood, where most of the deaths that occur come before the interval midpoint, or for the final age interval, which has no survivors. Conventions for these ages are given in Section 4.5.

Besides the linear formula, the reader will sometimes see the exponential estimator (Gompertz, 1825; Farr, 1864, pp. xxiii–xxiv):

$$_np_{x, \text{ exponential}} = e^{-{}_nnD_x/{}_nN_x}$$

(4.10)

The exponential is widely used in epidemiologic studies where age-specific death rates (incidence densities) can be calculated, but is less accurate for the complete life table than the linear formula. The lower accuracy occurs because the exponential assumes a constant mortality risk in the interval, while the linear formula assumes gradually worsening mortality. After early childhood human mortality worsens slowly with age, at a rate close to that of the linear expression.†

Table 4.5 displays the calculation of the U.S. 1980 life table $_np_x$ terms by the linear and exponential formulas. (We include $_5p_0$ estimates for com-

---

* The numerator and denominator of this expression are sometimes divided by the population $_nN_x$ to produce an alternate form of the expression: $_np_{x, \text{ linear}} = 1 - {}_nM_x/(1/n + \tfrac{1}{2}{}_nM_x)$. We caution that because of rounding of the $_nM_x$ terms to only two or three significant digits in most published sources, the expression may yield poor $_np_x$ estimates.

† U.S. decennial life tables use the linear formula at most single year ages. For the complete methodology underlying the NCHS 1979–1981 life tables, the reader may consult NCHS (1987).

Table 4.5. Linear and Exponential $_np_x$ Estimates
for the Data of Table 4.4

$_5p_{0,\text{ linear}} = 1 - {_5D_0}/({_5N_0}/5 + \frac{1}{2}{_5D_0})$
$\qquad = 1 - 53,713/(16,348,300/5 + 0.5 \times 53,713) = 0.98371$

$_{10}p_{5,\text{ linear}} = 1 - {_{10}D_5}/({_{10}N_5}/10 + \frac{1}{2}{_{10}D_5})$
$\qquad = 1 - 10,689/(34,942,100/10 + 0.5 \times 10,689) = 0.99695$

$_{10}p_{15,\text{ linear}} = 1 - {_{10}D_{15}}/({_{10}N_{15}}/10 + \frac{1}{2}{_{10}D_{15}})$
$\qquad = 1 - 49,027/(42,486,800/10 + 0.5 \times 49,027) = 0.98853$

$_{20}p_{25,\text{ linear}} = 1 - {_{20}D_{25}}/({_{20}N_{25}}/20 + \frac{1}{2}{_{20}D_{25}})$
$\qquad = 1 - 108,658/(62,716,500/20 + 0.5 \times 108,658) = 0.96594$

$_{20}p_{45,\text{ linear}} = 0.82552$

$_{10}p_{65,\text{ linear}} = 0.73952$

$_{10}p_{75,\text{ linear}} = 0.49854$

$_5p_{0,\text{ exp}} = e^{-{_5D_0}/{_5N_0}} = e^{-5\,(53,713/16,348,300)} = 0.98371$

$_{10}p_{5,\text{ exp}} = e^{-10{_{10}D_5}/{_{10}N_5}} = e^{-10\,(10,689/34,942,100)} = 0.99695$

$_{10}p_{15,\text{ exp}} = e^{-10{_{10}D_{15}}/{_{10}N_{15}}} = e^{-10\,(49,027/42,486,800)} = 0.98853$

$_{20}p_{25,\text{ exp}} = e^{-20{_{20}D_{25}}/{_{20}N_{25}}} = e^{-20\,(108,658/62,716,500)} = 0.96594$

$_{20}p_{45,\text{ exp}} = 0.82601$

$_{10}p_{65,\text{ exp}} = 0.74120$

$_{10}p_{75,\text{ exp}} = 0.51209$

$_{\omega-85}p_{85} = 0$

---

pleteness, but will introduce better estimating formulas for these ages in Section 4.5.) Comparing the estimates, they will be seen to be very close at ages under 65, where mortality is low. They begin to diverge after about age 45, from which point the linear estimates would be preferred.

For the final age category, ages 85+, we have set $_{\omega-85}p_{85} = {_\infty}p_{85} = 0$, since no one survives forever.* A higher terminal age category, such as 90+ or 95+, would also be appropriate for the contemporary United States, as about one-fourth of infants will live to age 85 at current mortality rates.

In Table 4.6 we draw together life tables derived using $N(x)$ and using $_nN_x$, by introducing the conversions from one population base to the other. To estimate $N(x)$ from deaths and the survival probability we use:

$$\hat{N}(x) = \begin{cases} {_nN_x}/n & |_nD_x = 0 \\ {_nD_x}/(1 - {_np_x}) & |_nD_x > 0 \end{cases} \qquad (4.11)$$

---

* We use both ω (omega) and ∞ (infinity) to represent the oldest age to which anyone survives. The terms $_\infty p_f$ (ages f to ∞) and $_{\omega-f}p_f$ (ages f to ω, the interval width is $\omega - f$) will both denote the survival probability for the final age interval, always 0. Note that we use $\omega - f$ but not $\infty - f$, since $\infty - f = \infty$.

Table 4.6. $N(x)$ and $_nN_x$ Estimates for the Data of Table 4.1

Start of interval (x)	Curtate estimator				Linear estimator			
	$_np_x$	$_nD_x - {_nD_{C,x}}$	$\hat{N}(x)$	$_n\hat{N}_x$	$_np_x$	$_nD_x$	$\hat{N}(x)$	$_n\hat{N}_x$
0	0.7886	74	350	313.0	0.7886	74	350.0	313.0
1	0.7965	47	231	207.5	0.8107	48	253.5	229.5
2	0.7687	31	134	118.5	0.8050	31	159.0	143.5
3	0.8657	9	67	62.5	0.8824	10	85.0	80.0
4	0.8667	4	30	28.0	0.9091	4	44.0	42.0

Since $_nq_{x,\text{ unadjusted}} = {_nD_x}/N(x)$, the expression can be interpreted as an estimator for $N(x)$ in the absence of censorship, or more broadly, as an estimator equivalent to the unadjusted estimator for samples that merge censored and uncensored observations. [Table 4.4 displays $\hat{N}(x)$ values for the 1980 U.S. population. After completing Section 4.5 the reader can use (4.11) to confirm that $\hat{N}(1) = 3,557,400$.]

The sample sizes $\hat{N}(x)$ of Table 4.6 are the denominators of (4.2) and (4.5). For $_nN_x$ we have used (4.8), rearranged as

$$_n\hat{N}_{x,\text{ curtate sample}} = n[\hat{N}(x) - \tfrac{1}{2}(_nD_x - {_nD_{C,x}})]$$

for the CS estimator (4.2), and as

$$_n\hat{N}_{x,\text{ linear}} = n[\hat{N}(x) - \tfrac{1}{2}{_nD_x}]$$

for the linear estimator (4.5).*

The reader will note that both $\hat{N}(x)$ and $_n\hat{N}_x$ are substantially larger for the linear estimator than for the curtate sample estimator, owing to the high proportion of observations that are censored in each interval.

Table 4.7 describes types of data sets that might be analyzed by the various life table formulas, and also hints at how broadly the concepts of "population" and "death" can be interpreted. The uses span all major demographic events.

---

* Under the actuarial [expression (4.6)] $_nN_x$ is not a linear function of $N(x)$ and $_nD_x$. A closer approximation is provided by the exponential estimator:

$$_n\hat{N}_{x,\text{ exponential}} = \begin{cases} nN(x) & |_nD_x = 0 \\ -n_nD_x/\ln{_np_x} & |_nD_x > 0 \end{cases}$$

For $_nD_x > 0$ the estimator is found by rewriting (4.10).

They have in common that the event itself occurs only once. Ordinary incidence and prevalence rates are more convenient for transitions that may be repeated, such as transitions between health and illness, marital states, migration histories, and cumulative childbearing. Life tables are also not often used to reconstruct observable population characteristics, such as age distributions, or distributions by marital status or family size. Innumerable populations can share the same life table; and therefore to reproduce a particular one will require information beyond what the table contains.

4.4. COMPLETING THE LIFE TABLE

The variety of $_np_x$ formulas available to the researcher results in part from differences in the nature of the source data used for the tables, and in part reflects assumptions external to the data itself. Fewer assumptions are needed for the remainder of the life table, and the reader who is comfortable with the logic underlying $_np_x$ estimates should have no difficulty.

Having found $_np_x$, the next step is to estimate the number of survivors l_x from birth or from the onset of risk to age or duration x. The computation begins with selection of a *radix* l_0, interpreted as the number of births that begin the life table (most often l_0 is 1 or 100,000). l_x is found as l_0 times the product of the individual survival terms $_np_a$ for ages under x. In demographic notation:

$$l_x = l_0 \, (_np_0)(_np_n)(_np_{2n}) \cdots (_np_{x-n}) = l_0 \prod_{a=0}^{x-n} {_np_a} = l_{x-n} \, _np_{x-n} \quad (4.12)$$

The product expression $\prod \, _np_a$ represents the product of all $_np_a$ terms from $a = 0$ to $a = x - n$. The use of the product comes from the fact that the chance of surviving to a given age must equal the chance of surviving to the youngest age $(_np_0)$ times the conditional probability $(_np_n)$ of surviving to the next age after surviving to the first age, and so forth. It is not necessary that all intervals be of the same width: for product limit tables the intervals break at each event or point of censorship. National life tables are constructed for single years of age ("complete" life tables) or using ages 0, 1–4, 5–9, 10–14, . . . , 75–79, 80–84 ("abridged" life tables). The final category is usually 75+ or 85+, although for developed countries higher terminal ages are increasingly needed. Life tables for other events or other types of populations would use other intervals.

We interpret l_x as the number of survivors to age or anniversary x, similar to the quantity $N(x)$ for real populations except that $N(x)$ may be independent

Table 4.7. Examples of Events Measured Using Life Tables

Type of event	Data requirements
Mortality	
Probability of surviving from age x to $x + n$, life expectancy	Central population ($_nN_x$) from census, Deaths ($_nD_x$) from vital statistics
Probability of surviving at various durations from onset or diagnosis of a life-threatening disease	Survivors at x years after onset or diagnosis [$N(x)$] from a survey, Deaths in next n years ($_nD_x$) from same source
Infant mortality rate	Births [$N(0)$] from vital statistics, Deaths ($_1D_0$) from same source; or births [$N(0)$] and deaths ($_1D_0$) from a survey
Morbidity	
Rate of spread of an epidemic	Initial population [$N(0)$] from census or survey, estimated as exposed population less diagnosed cases, Events ($_nD_x$) from vital statistics or surveys. [The subscript x represents the time since start of epidemic, but both population and events may also be broken down by age groups. Since the population is normally far larger than the number of cases, the simple incidence ($_nD_x$) is also a good measure of the epidemic's spread
Rate of recovery from accident or disease	Persons not yet recovered as of duration x from initial event [$N(x)$] from survey, Recoveries between x and $x + n$ ($_nD_x$) from same source
Duration of hospital stays	Persons still in hospital as of duration x from admission [$N(x)$] from hospital records, Discharges ($_nD_x$) from same source
Births and associated events	
Proportion of women reaching ith parity between ages x and $x + n$, cumulative proportion reaching ith parity by age x	Women at parities less than i as of age x [$N(x)$], Births ($_nD_x$) at ith parity between ages x and $x + n$, both from surveys; or Women at parities less than i at central ages ($_nN_x$) from census, Births ($_nD_x$) at parity i from vital statistics. [Rates may also be calculated for males, and can be calculated by duration of marriage or cohabitation from surveys]
Interbirth intervals, proportion of women stopping childbearing at parity i	Women with no further births as of duration x from previous delivery [$N(x)$], Births ($_nD_x$) occurring between x and $x + n$, both from surveys
Duration of lactation	Women lactating at duration x since childbirth [$N(x)$] from a survey, Number stopping breastfeeding between x and $x + n$ ($_nD_x$) from same source

Continued on next page

Table 4.7. Continued

Type of event	Data requirements
Duration of contraceptive use, contraceptive failure rate	Persons continuing contraception at duration x since first use [$N(x)$], Terminations or pregnancies ($_nD_x$) from x to $x + n$, both from surveys
Marriage and divorce	
Proportion marrying between ages x and $x + n$, cumulative proportion married by age x	Persons never married as of xth birthday [$N(x)$] from a survey, First marriages ($_nD_x$) from same source
Proportion of marriages ending in divorce or widowhood	Persons in marriage [$N(x)$] as of duration x since wedding or cohabitation, Dissolutions ($_nD_x$) from ages x to $x + n$ from same source
Labor force	
Age at first entry into labor force	Persons never in labor force as of xth birthday [$N(x)$], Entrants into labor force ($_nD_x$), both from surveys
Job promotion rates, job changes	Persons in same job at duration x from start of employment [$N(x)$], Persons promoted or changing jobs over next n years ($_nD_x$), both from surveys
Migration patterns	
Proportion of population changing residence over n years, proportion who have never moved	Persons [$N(x)$] in location i at time x, Number moving ($_nD_x$) by $x + n$, both from surveys; or Persons born in location i [$N(x)$] from vital statistics or census. Retrospectively, persons in location i at time x by duration since birth or arrival. Movers ($_nD_x$) or nonmovers [$N(x)$] from later censuses. [Distinctions may be made between first-time and repeat migrants, or between migration destinations. Intermediate moves in the interval x to $x + n$ are usually ignored in favor of simple origin–destination patterns.]

of survivors at nearby ages $N(x - n)$, $N(x + n)$, while at all ages $l_x \geq l_{x+n}$. (In real populations each cohort represents a different year's births and each may experience slightly different mortality rates. The life table follows the fixed cohort l_0, which changes only as it is gradually depleted by deaths.)

After finding l_x we calculate $_nd_x$, representing life table deaths in the interval x to $x + n$. Since l_x represents survivors at x and l_{x+n} represents survivors at $x + n$, interval deaths should number:

$$_nd_x = l_x - l_{x+n} \tag{4.13}$$

The $_nd_x$ term is analogous to deaths $_nD_x$ in real populations, just as l_x is analogous to $N(x)$.

We define the life table population to be uncensored, or the subtraction in (4.13) would not always hold. Expression (4.1) is also for uncensored observations. We make use of that fact and the correspondence of $_nd_x$ to $_nD_x$ and l_x to $N(x)$ to equate

$$_np_{x, \text{ unadjusted}} = 1 - _nD_x/N(x)$$

with the life table survival probability:

$$_np_x = 1 - _nd_x/l_x \tag{4.14}$$

To find the probability of surviving from age x to $x + n$ from a census population $_nN_x$ and annual deaths $_nD_x$, in (4.8) we made use of the linear approximation [expression (4.8)]

$$N(x) = _nN_x/n + \tfrac{1}{2}_nD_x$$

The expression can also be used to estimate a census or interval population $_nN_x$ for ages x to $x + n$ from $N(x)$ and $_nD_x$, and to find the life table population $_nL_x$ equivalent to the census population $_nN_x$. We have*:

$$_nN_{x, \text{ linear}} = n[N(x) - \tfrac{1}{2}_nD_x]$$

$$_nL_{x, \text{ linear}} = n(l_x - \tfrac{1}{2}_nd_x) = n[l_x - \tfrac{1}{2}(l_x - l_{x+n})]$$

$$= n(l_x + l_{x+n})/2 \tag{4.15}$$

For the exponential survival distribution (4.10), the life table population ages x to $x + n$ will be [expression (2.7d)]:

---

* Formally, $_nL_x$ is the population or time lived in the interval x to $x + n$:

$$_nL_x = \int_x^{x+n} l(a) \, da$$

If individuals are right-censored at random times during the interval, their survival probability to censorship is given by $_np_{x, \text{ right partial}} = _nL_x/(nl_x)$. The equivalence between right interval-censored observations and the interval population arises from the fact that both represent survivors observed at ages between x and $x + n$, as also does $_nN_x$. In $_np_{x, \text{ right partial}}$ the number surviving is converted to the proportion surviving. If no mortality occurred, the number surviving would be nl_x.

$$_nL_{x, \text{ exponential}} = \begin{cases} 0 & |l_{x+n} = 0 \\ [n(l_x - l_{x+n})]/(\ln l_x - \ln l_{x+n}) & |l_{x+n} > 0 \end{cases} \quad (4.16)$$

The exponential is undefined at $l_{x+n} = 0$, and in (4.16) we have arbitrarily set $_nL_{x, \text{ exponential}}$ to 0 where that occurs. For the interval, either (4.15) or another $_nL_x$ estimator can be substituted for (4.16) provided that the interval width n is known.

The $_nL_x$ term has two interpretations. It is the population that would be found in the age interval x to $x + n$ if annual births numbered l_0 and the survival rates were those given by the $_np_x$ series, and it is a measure of person-time lived in the interval by the l_x individuals alive at its start. The interpretation of $_nL_x$ as a population is brought out in Fig. 1.1, which superimposes the U.S. 1980 $_nL_x$ distribution over the 1980 population.

From the correspondence of $_nL_x$ to $_nN_x$ and $_nd_x$ to $_nD_x$, we can construct a life table age-specific death rate equivalent to the population ASDR,

$$_nM_x = {}_nD_x/{}_nN_x$$

The life table ASDR is

$$_nm_x = {}_nd_x/{}_nL_x \quad (4.17)$$

For most populations the actual and life table ASDRs will be virtually identical since the life table is constructed directly from the population and event counts at each age. The actual and life table ASDRs will also be near $_nq_x/n$ at most ages, since $_nq_x$ and $_nm_x$ differ in the ratio of their denominators, l_x and $_nL_x$. At ages of low mortality $_nL_x \simeq nl_x$.

Interpreting the $_nL_x$ series as a population age distribution, we may also construct survival estimates across age intervals, by the formula

$$_nS_{x+(1/2)n} = {}_nL_{x+n}/{}_nL_x \quad (4.18)$$

The survival terms $_nS_{x+(1/2)n}$ are distinct from the $_np_x$ terms from which the life table is constructed. Whereas $_np_x$ survives individuals from exact age x to exact age $x + n$, $_nS_{x+(1/2)n}$ survives the population initially ages x to $x + n$ into the next age interval, $x + n$ to $x + 2n$. The survival probability roughly corresponds to survival from the interval midpoint $x + \frac{1}{2}n$ to the point $x + 1\frac{1}{2}n$. It is used principally for population projections, where an observed population $_nN_x^{(t)}$ at time t is projected forward n years to become $_nN_{x+n}^{(t+n)}$ at time $t + n$.

For an initial population of $l_0 = 1$ or 100,000, $_nL_x$ also represents the amount of time lived in the interval x to $x + n$. If no mortality occurs, the amount of person-time lived in an interval of n years will be nl_x; with low mortality, the time lived will be near nl_x; at ages where almost no one survives, $_nL_x$ will be near 0.

As a measure of time lived in an interval, $_nL_x$ is the basis for an important life table summary indicator, the mean future lifetime or life expectancy (e_x), defined as:

$$e_x = \sum_{a=x}^{\omega-n} {}_nL_a \bigg/ l_x \qquad (4.19)$$

The summation $\sum_a {}_nL_a$ represents the sum of all $_nL_a$ terms from $a = x$ to $a = \omega - n$. The final interval, $_nL_{\omega-n}$, terminates at ω, the oldest age to which anyone survives. Hence, (4.19) is the ratio of persons ages x and above in the life table to persons reaching age x, or time lived after age x per survivor at x. The expression only sometimes holds in real populations. Fluctuations in actual births and deaths over time disturb both the numerator and denominator of the equivalent real population estimator,

$$e_x \simeq \sum_{a=x}^{\omega-n} {}_nN_a \bigg/ N(x) \qquad (4.20)$$

To facilitate calculation of e_x, the term T_x is commonly included in life tables. T_x is the sum of the population ages x and older:

$$T_x = \sum_{a=x}^{\omega-n} {}_nL_a \qquad (4.21)$$

T_0 represents the complete life table population. It can be used to calculate the life table crude birth rate or death rate, which are both l_0/T_0. Note also that $e_0 = T_0/l_0$: in the life table the crude birth and death rates are simply the inverse of the life expectancy. (The 1980 U.S. life expectancy of 74 implies that 1/74 of the population, or 1.4% should die and be replaced by new entrants each year. The actual 1980 birth rate was 1.6% and the death rate 0.9%.)

For some distributions the life expectancy e_x cannot be estimated, either because the life table spans only part of the survival distribution or because no satisfactory estimate of $_{\omega-f}L_f$, the time lived in the final age or duration interval, is available. In that event, in place of e_x the partial life expectancy to age f may be used. The partial life expectancy is given by:

$$f_{-x}e_x = \sum_{a=x}^{f-n} {}_nL_a \, / \, l_x = (T_x - T_f)/l_x \qquad (4.22)$$

A measure that combines death rates and life expectancies is population *entropy*, or the rate at which lives are lost relative to life expectancy, approximately:

$$H_{\text{linear}} = \sum_x {}_nd_x \, e_{x+(1/2)n} \, / \, ({}_\omega d_0 \, e_0) = \sum_x {}_nd_x \, e_{x+(1/2)n} \, / \, (l_0 \, e_0) \qquad (4.23)$$

The expression sums the product of deaths in each interval times the midinterval life expectancy, and divides the result by the estimate as it would appear if all deaths occurred at the single age e_0. (Where all deaths occur at age e_0 entropy $= 0$; it rises to 1.0 in life tables with a constant survival probability p independent of age. See Fig. 6A.1.)

Entropy is most often seen in an incomplete form as *Years of Potential Life Lost* (Centers for Disease Control, 1986) which multiplies the observed number of deaths for one or more causes at each age by the life expectancy at the middle of the age interval (or by the partial life expectancy to age 65, for estimates of years of potential working life lost). The sum across all ages becomes a crude estimator of the overall cost in lives of the causes of death of interest, either

$$\text{YPLL}_j = \sum_x {}_nD_{x,\,j} \, e_{x+(1/2)n} \qquad (4.24)$$

or, for the working ages,

$$\text{YPWL}_j = \sum_{x \le 65-n} {}_nD_{x,\,j \; 65-[x+(1/2)n]} e_{x+(1/2)n} \qquad (4.25)$$

In the expression, j denotes the selected cause or causes of death. [The reader should note that the measure is approximate, since the life expectancy that is used incorporates the effects of cause j deaths at ages $x + n$ and above. Substitution of cause-eliminated life expectancies $e_{x+(1/2)n,\,-j}$ for $e_{x+(1/2)n}$ would better estimate the cost in lives associated with cause j. See Section 5.4.]

In some works the linear ${}_np_x$ formula (4.9) is generalized by substituting $(1 - {}_na_x/n)_nD_x$ for $\frac{1}{2}{}_nD_x$ in the denominator, using ${}_na_x$ to represent the mean number of years lived in the interval x to $x + n$ by those who die in it.* (If the mean lifetime is $_na_x$ years, the proportion dying in the first half of the interval is $1 - _na_x/n$.) With the change we have

$$N(x) = [_nN_x/n + (1 - _na_x/n)_nD_x]$$
$$= [_nN_x + (n - _na_x)_nD_x]/n \tag{4.26}$$

$$_np_{x,\text{ linear }a} = 1 - n_nD_x/[_nN_x + (n - _na_x)_nD_x] \tag{4.27}$$

Since $_nL_x$ is the number of years lived by all persons in the interval and nl_{x+n} is the number lived by the survivors, the number of years lived by those dying will be $_nL_x - nl_{x+n}$. Dividing this quantity by the number who die, $_nd_x$, we find that

$$_na_x = (_nL_x - nl_{x+n})/_nd_x \tag{4.28}$$

and that

$$_nL_x = nl_{x+n} + _na_x\,_nd_x \tag{4.29}$$

Although (4.29) suggests that the $_na_x$ terms may be used to estimate $_nL_x$ in place of (4.15), the $_na_x$ terms do not follow a simple pattern from one age group to another, probably because of the heterogeneity in causes of death. As a result, $_na_x$ terms are usually calculated after $_nL_x$, using (4.28).†

Figure 4.1 illustrates the principal life table terms using the 1980 U.S. life table.

Of the formulas we have introduced, we emphasize that those for $_np_x$ using (4.5), (4.6), (4.9), and (4.10), and those for $_nL_x$ using (4.15) and (4.16) incorporate simple linear or exponential approximations and are often replaced by other estimating formulas. Formulas (4.12)–(4.14), (4.17), (4.19)–(4.22), (4.28), and (4.29) define relationships among life table terms.

Table 4.8 illustrates the calculation of the life table using $_np_x$, curtate sample

---

* Formally, $1 - _na_x/n$ also represents the life table *separation factor*, identifying the proportion of deaths at ages x through $x + n - 1$ that occur in the calendar year of the birthday, if birthdays are distributed uniformly during the year. The complement, $_na_x/n$, is the proportion occurring in the subsequent year. Separation factors are discussed briefly in Section 1.5.

† An exception is Schoen (1978; 1988, pp. 13–15), who finds $_na_x$ by a quadratic fitting to the $_nM_x$ distribution. Schoen's method yields $_np_x$ estimates that are less precise than Keyfitz–Frauenthal estimates (Section 6.2) but competitive with other formulas.

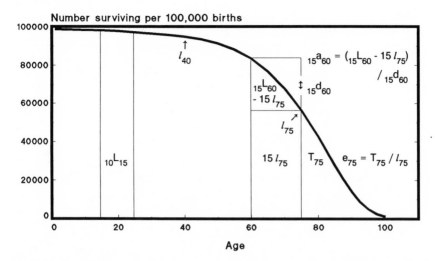

Figure 4.1. U.S. 1980 life table, with selected demographic terms. *Source:* National Center for Health Statistics (1985).

from Table 4.1 and estimating the life table population $_nL_x$ linearly, using $_nL_{x,\text{linear}} = n(l_x + l_{x+n})/2$. Beginning from $_np_x$, and setting the radix of the table to $l_0 = 10,000$, we have:

$$l_1 = l_0 \, _1p_0 = 10,000 \times 0.7886 = 7886$$

$$l_2 = l_1 \, _1p_1 = 7886 \times 0.7965 = 6281$$

$$\cdots$$

$$l_5 = l_4 \, _1p_4 = 4180 \times 0.8667 = 3623$$

$$_1d_0 = l_0 - l_1 = 10,000 - 7886 = 2114$$

$$_1d_1 = l_1 - l_2 = 7886 - 6281 = 1605$$

$$\cdots$$

$$_1d_4 = l_4 - l_5 = 4180 - 3623 = 557$$

$$_1L_0 = (1)(l_0 + l_1)/2 = (10,000 + 7886)/2 = 8943$$

Table 4.8. Life Table for Breast Cancer Patients First Seen between 1956 and 1961, Using $_np_{x, \text{curtate sample}}$ and $_nL_{x, \text{linear}}.$[a] *Source:* Drolette (1975)

Int. (x)	Uncensored Number at risk	Events	Probability of survival from x to $x+1$ $_1p_x$	Number alive at x l_x	Deaths between x and $x+1$ $_1d_x$	Population age x $_1L_x$	Partial life exp. $_{5-x}e_x$
0	350	74	0.7886	10,000	2114	8943	3.00
1	231	47	0.7965	7,886	1605	7083	2.67
2	134	31	0.7687	6,281	1453	5554	2.22
3	67	9	0.8657	4,828	648	4504	1.74
4	30	4	0.8667	4,180	557	3901	0.93
5	26			3,623			

Formulas

$$_np_{x, \text{curtate sample}} = 1 - (_nD_x - _nD_{C,x})/[N(x) - N_C(x)]$$

$$l_x = l_0 \prod_{a=0}^{x-n} {_np_a} = l_{x-n}\, _np_{x-n}$$

$$_nd_x = l_x - l_{x+n}$$

$$_nL_{x, \text{linear}} = n(l_x + l_{x+n})/2$$

$$_{f-x}e_x = \sum_{a=x}^{f-n} {_nL_a} \Big/ l_x = (T_x - T_f)/l_x$$

[a] The radix $l_0 = 10,000$ is used to allow four-digit precision as an aid to readers working the example. A more appropriate choice would have been $l_0 = 1000$ given the small initial sample size.

$$_1L_1 = (1)(l_1 + l_2)/2 = (7886 + 6281)/2 = 7083$$

$$\cdots$$

$$_1L_4 = (1)(l_4 + l_5)/2 = (4180 + 3623)/2 = 3901$$

Since the life table stops before all individuals have died, the complete life expectancy for the cancer sample cannot be calculated, but we can find years lived during the first 5 years after diagnosis. We have:

$$_5e_0 = (_1L_0 + {_1L_1} + \cdots + {_1L_4})/l_0$$

$$= (8943 + 7083 + \cdots + 3901)/10,000 = 3.00$$

$$_4e_1 = (_1L_1 + {_1L_2} + \cdots + {_1L_4})/l_1$$

$$= (7083 + 5554 + \cdots + 3901)/7886 = 2.67$$

. . .

$$_1e_4 = {}_1L_4/l_4 = 3901/4180 = 0.93$$

These terms show the number of years lived from each anniversary to duration 5.0. For the complete life expectancy e_x we would add $_{\omega-5}L_5/l_x$ (or $_\infty L_5/l_x$) to each of the $_{5-x}e_x$ terms.

4.5. AGES 0–4 AND 85+ IN HUMAN MORTALITY TABLES

While the approximation $_np_x = 1 - {}_nD_x/({}_nN_x/n + \frac{1}{2}{}_nD_x)$ is satisfactory at most ages, deaths in the first years of life are concentrated toward the beginning of the intervals and require special conventions. At age 0 about 90% of deaths occur in the first half of the interval, with a mean age at death of $_1a_0 = 0.125$ year,* and therefore for $N(0)$ we have:

$$N(0) \simeq {}_1N_0 + 0.875\,{}_1D_0 \tag{4.30}$$

This expression will not be highly accurate unless the midyear population $_1N_0$ is estimated from vital statistics, as very small children are usually undercounted in censuses. If vital statistics are well reported, a simpler and better estimate for $N(0)$ is the birth count itself:

$$N(0) = {}_\omega B_0$$

Using births to estimate $N(0)$, the probability of surviving from birth to age 1 is given by:

$$_1p_0 = greater \ of \ \{0, \ 1 - {}_1D_0/{}_\omega B_0\} \tag{4.31}$$

The estimate omits some deaths to infants born during the year, but includes about as many deaths to infants born the previous year. Owing to the partial independence of the numerator and denominator of (4.31), for rare data sets

---

* The mean age at death for infants dying in their first year of life increases with increasing infant mortality. Preston *et al.* (1972) suggest the approximate relationship

$$_1a_0 \simeq 0.07 + 1.7\,{}_1M_0$$

$_1D_0$ may exceed $_\omega B_0$, requiring the upward correction of $_1p_0$ to 0. In that event, the birth and death samples should be redrawn from a single cohort.*

For $_1L_0$ we also require information on the distribution of deaths in the interval. Using the estimate $_1a_0 = 0.125$ year for the mean age at death among infants dying in their first year of life, we have from (4.29):

$$_1L_0 = l_1 + {}_1a_0\,{}_1d_0 = l_1 + 0.125\,{}_1d_0 = 0.125l_0 + 0.875l_1 \qquad (4.32)$$

At ages 1–4 about 60% of deaths occur in the first 2 years of the interval, with a mean age at death of 2.6 (from which $_4a_1 = 1.6$ years), and we may estimate $N(1)$ as:

$$N(1) \simeq {}_4N_1/4 + 0.6\,{}_4D_1 \qquad (4.33)$$

For $_4p_1$ and $_4L_1$ we have

$$_4p_1 = 1 - {}_4D_1/N(1)$$
$$= \textit{greater of } \{0,\, 1 - {}_4D_1/({}_4N_1/4 + 0.6\,{}_4D_1)\} \qquad (4.34)$$

$$_4L_1 = 4l_5 + {}_4a_1\,{}_4d_1 = 4l_5 + 1.6(l_1 - l_5) = 1.6l_1 + 2.4l_5 \qquad (4.35)$$

The correction to (4.34) for negative $_np_x$ values follows from the correction on (4.9).

At the upper end of the life table, $_{\omega-85}p_{85}$ or $_\infty p_{85}$ is 0 as no one survives indefinitely. For $_\infty L_{85}$ it is customary to invert (4.17), giving $_\infty L_{85} = {}_\infty d_{85}/{}_\infty m_{85}$. If the observed age-specific death rate $_\infty M_{85}$ is substituted for the life table death rate $_\infty m_{85}$, we then have

$$_\infty p_{85} = 0 \qquad (4.36)$$

$$_\infty L_{85} = {}_\infty d_{85}/{}_\infty M_{85} = {}_\infty d_{85}({}_\infty N_{85}/{}_\infty D_{85})$$
$$= l_{85}({}_\infty N_{85}/{}_\infty D_{85}) \qquad (4.37)$$

---

* Where information for infants and small children is limited, $_np_x$ terms can be estimated from the ratios of surviving children to children ever born for women at successively older ages. The methodology is due to Brass (Brass and Coale, 1968, pp. 104–122; Brass, 1975, pp. 50–59; Trussell, 1975).

The expression imputes the same ratio of deaths to population in the life table as in the observed population. Since $l_{85} = {}_{\infty}d_{85}$, life expectancy at ages above 85 $({}_{\infty}L_{85}/l_{85})$ can be estimated as ${}_{\infty}N_{85}/{}_{\infty}D_{85}$ by the formula. In other words, the life expectancy at 85 is the inverse of the proportion of individuals 85 and over who die during the year:

$$e_{85} = {}_{\infty}L_{85}/{}_{\infty}d_{85} = {}_{\infty}N_{85}/{}_{\infty}D_{85} \qquad (4.38)$$

4.6. THE U.S. 1980 LIFE TABLE

Using these formulas for infancy and old age, and the earlier formulas for intermediate ages, the U.S. 1980 life table is completed in Table 4.9. Appendix 6A.2 reproduces 1980 U.S. population estimates and deaths and the National Center for Health Statistics 1980 life table. The method of estimation used by NCHS is more complex than the linear model we have introduced, but the difference in life expectancies in the two tables, about 1/2 year at age 0, is due more to the wide age groupings in Table 4.9 than to the choice of formulas.* We also note for the reader that the NCHS 1979–81 decennial life table, completed after the 1980 life table, has somewhat higher life expectancies (about 0.2 year at birth for the white population and 0.5 year for the black population). The decennial table is constructed by graduating the midyear 1980 population (Miller, 1984) and 1979–1981 deaths from 5-year to single year ages using Beers multipliers (Section 2.3). After graduating the source data, the survival probabilities ${}_1p_x$ are estimated linearly, except in infancy and at the oldest ages.

From Table 4.9b we may estimate both entropy, the relative loss of life from early deaths, and years of potential life lost. We have [expression (4.23)]

---

* For U.S. life tables between censuses, the National Center for Health Statistics (NCHS) estimates ${}_np_x$ terms from a census year reference series that uses single year ages and deaths in the census year and one year each side of the census to find ${}_nM_x$, ${}_np_x$, and ${}_nq_x$. For later years it sets;

$${}_nf_x^{(\text{census})} = {}_nq_x^{(\text{census})}/{}_nM_x^{(\text{census})}$$

$${}_np_x^{(t)} = 1 - {}_nM_x^{(t)} \, {}_nf_x^{(\text{census})} = 1 - {}_nq_x^{(\text{census})} \left({}_nM_x^{(t)}/{}_nM_x^{(\text{census})} \right)$$

The expression adjusts ${}_np_x$ terms each year in proportion to changes in annual age-specific death rates ${}_nM_x$, which both simplifies table construction and helps to maintain consistency in the tables from year to year. The life table ${}_nL_x$ terms are found by (4.29) using ${}_na_x$ values from the same reference table. The method is due to Greville (1947). For 1979–1981 decennial life tables the reader may see NCHS (1985). The methodology is presented in NCHS (1987).

Table 4.9. Life Table for the 1980 U.S. Population, by Text Formulas

Ages $(x, x+n-1)$	Int. (n)	Census population[a]	Deaths	Prob. of death between x and $x+n$ $_nq_x$	Prob. of survival from x to $x+n$ $_np_x$	Number alive at x l_x	Deaths between x and $x+n$ $_nd_x$	Pop. ages x to $x+n$ $_nL_x$	Life exp. e_x
Births:		3,596,100							
0	1	3,556,300	45,526	0.01266	0.98734	100,000	1,266	98,892	
1–4	4	12,814,600	8,187	0.00255	0.99745	98,734	252	394,331	
5–14	10	34,942,100	10,689	0.00305	0.99695	98,482	301		
15–24	10	42,486,800	49,027	0.01147	0.98853	98,181	1,126		
25–44	20	62,716,500	108,658	0.03406	0.96594	97,055	3,306		
45–64	20	44,502,600	425,338	0.17448	0.82552	93,749	16,357		
65–74	10	15,580,600	466,621	0.26048	0.73952	77,392	20,159		
75–84	10	7,728,800	517,257	0.50146	0.49854	57,233	28,700		
85+	—	2,240,100	357,970	1.0	0.0	28,533	28,533	178,554	6.3

a. Preliminary table with completed $_np_x$, l_x, and $_nd_x$ series and with $_1L_0$, $_4L_1$, $_{\omega-85}L_{85}$, and e_{85}.

b. Completed life table

Age	n	$_nN_x$	$_nD_x$	$_nq_x$	$_np_x$	l_x	$_nd_x$	$_nL_x$	e_x
Births: 3,596,100									
0	1	3,556,300	45,526	0.01266	0.98734	100,000	1,266	98,892	73.5
1–4	4	12,814,600	8,187	0.00255	0.99745	98,734	252	394,331	73.5
5–14	10	34,942,100	10,689	0.00305	0.99695	98,482	301	983,317	69.7
15–24	10	42,486,800	49,027	0.01147	0.98853	98,181	1,126	976,181	59.9
25–44	20	62,716,500	108,658	0.03406	0.96594	97,055	3,306	1,908,039	50.5
45–64	20	44,502,600	425,338	0.17448	0.82552	93,749	16,357	1,711,412	31.9
65–74	10	15,580,600	466,621	0.26048	0.73952	77,392	20,159	673,125	16.5
75–84	10	7,728,800	517,257	0.50146	0.49854	57,233	28,700	428,829	10.6
85+	—	2,240,100	357,970	1.0	0.0	28,533	28,533	178,554	6.3

Formulas

$$_1p_0 = 1 - {_1D_0}/{_\omega B_0}$$

$$_4p_1 = 1 - {_4D_1}/({_4N_1}/4 + 0.6\,{_4D_1})$$

$$_np_{x,\text{linear}} = 1 - {_nD_x}/({_nN_x}/n + \tfrac{1}{2}{_nD_x})$$

$$_{\omega-x}p_x = 0$$

$$l_x = l_0 \prod_{a=0}^{x-n} {_np_a} = l_{x-n}\,{_np_{x-n}}$$

$$_nd_x = l_x - l_{x+n}$$

$$_1L_0 = l_1 + 0.125\,{_1d_0}$$

$$_4L_1 = 4l_5 + 1.6(l_1 - l_5)$$

$$_nL_{x,\text{linear}} = n(l_x + l_{x+n})/2$$

$$_{\omega-x}L_x = l_x({_{\omega-x}N_x}/{_{\omega-x}D_x})$$

$$e_x = \sum_{a=x}^{\omega-x} {_nL_a}/l_x$$

[a] $_1N_0$ has been estimated by expression (4.30), to be consistent with recorded births. The census estimate for the age interval is 3,533,700 (see Table 6A.1a).

$$H_{\text{linear}} = \sum_x {}_nd_x \, e_{x+(1/2)n} \, / \, (l_0 \, e_0)$$

$$= \tfrac{1}{2}[1266(73.5 + 73.5) + 252(73.5 + 69.7) + \cdots$$

$$+ \, 28{,}533(6.3 + 0)]/(100{,}000 \times 73.5) = 0.18$$

where we have estimated $e_{x+(1/2)n}$ as $\tfrac{1}{2}(e_x + e_{x+n})$. The low value for H suggests that our current life table is close to one in which all mortality occurs at age 73.5, our life expectancy at birth. For the actual years of potential life lost we find

$$\text{YPLL}_j = \sum_x {}_nD_{x,\,j} \, e_{x+(1/2)n}$$

$$= 45{,}526(73.5 + 73.5)/2 + 8187(73.5 + 69.7)/2$$

$$+ \cdots + 357{,}970(6.3 + 0)/2 = 33{,}900{,}000$$

or about 17 years for each of the 2 million persons dying during the year if we accept e_{85} as fixed. The reader might note that substituting terms in ${}_nD_x$ for ${}_nd_x$ in (4.23) yields the approximate value $H_{\text{linear}} \simeq 33{,}900{,}000/(1{,}990{,}000 \times 73.5) = 0.23$. Because of the concentration of deaths at the oldest ages, the ${}_nD_x$ distribution is currently relatively close to the life table ${}_nd_x$ distribution. That is not true of the age distributions ${}_nN_x$ and ${}_nL_x$: using (4.20) in place of (4.19) gives the life expectancy $e_0 \simeq 226{,}545{,}800/3{,}596{,}100 = 63.0$ years.

Several of the relationships between life table terms that were noted earlier are brought out in Tables 4.9 and 4.10. Comparing first the population $({}_nM_x)$ and life table $({}_nm_x)$ death rates of Table 4.10, we find them to be virtually the same owing to the closeness with which the life table follows its source data.

Comparing the ${}_nM_x$ series of Table 4.10 with the ${}_nq_x$ series of Table 4.9 and ${}_nq_x/n$ in Table 4.10, ${}_nq_x$ is seen to be about n times ${}_nM_x$. The relationship is expected, since ${}_nM_x$ is the death rate for members of the age interval for one year and ${}_nq_x$ is the probability that death occurs over the n years the interval spans. The quantities diverge at the older ages because ${}_nM_x$ has a lower bound (0) but no upper bound (annual deaths may exceed the number of survivors at midyear, in which case ${}_nM_x > 1.0$) while ${}_nq_x$ must lie in the range 0 to 1. (The reader might also note from the tables that mortality is substantially higher in infancy than at ages 1–39. Combining the sexes, the age at which adult mortality passed infant mortality was near 80 in 1900, when infant mortality was over 15%, and about 40 in 1985, when infant mortality was 1.1%. At ages 80–84 the death rate is now about 8.4% per year, about half the 1900 level.)

Table 4.10 also compares the l_x series with $_nL_x/n$, representing the life table population at about age $x + \frac{1}{2}n$. The absence of a pattern in the $_nL_x$ series of Table 4.9 will be seen to be due to the shifting interval widths that were used: after adjustment to single year ages it is always the case that $l_x \geq (_nL_x/n) \geq l_{x+n}$. In the e_x column, note that life expectancy always falls by less than n years between any age x and $x + n$, and may increase. Each death in the interval $(x, x + n)$ contributes a short lifetime $(_na_x \leq n$ years) to e_x, with the consequence that e_x is less than $(e_{x+n} + n)$. The exact equality is

$$e_x = {_np_x}(e_{x+n} + n) + {_nq_x}\,{_na_x} \qquad (4.39)$$

The U.S. life table is a *synthetic* life table, as are other life tables constructed from period data. It describes mortality experience for the calendar period, but with distortions wherever the current mortality of a cohort reflects past experiences peculiar to itself. The 1980 life table, for example, displays current mortality associated with past and present smoking behavior, and is not representative of survival probabilities as they will appear in cohorts with other smoking patterns, even if no other changes in mortality occur.

The table is approximate for another reason. For most causes of death, susceptibility differs among individuals for both biological and behavioral reasons. Most national life tables are computed separately by sex, and those in the United States by ethnicity, because of the identifiability of gender and

Table 4.10. Comparisons among Population and Life Table Estimators

Ages $(x, x + n - 1)$	n	Census population	Deaths	Age-specific death rate $_nM_x$	Life table ASDR $_nm_x$	Approx. proportion dying each year $_nq_x/n$	Number alive at x l_x	Approx. no. age $x + \frac{1}{2}n$ $_nL_x/n$
Births:		3,596,100	45,526	0.01280	0.01280	0.01266	100,000	98,892
0	1	3,556,300						
1–4	4	12,814,600	8,187	0.00064	0.00064	0.00064	98,734	98,583
5–14	10	34,942,100	10,689	0.00031	0.00031	0.00031	98,482	98,332
15–24	10	42,486,800	49,027	0.00115	0.00115	0.00115	98,181	97,618
25–44	20	62,716,500	108,658	0.00173	0.00173	0.00170	97,055	95,402
45–64	20	44,502,600	425,338	0.00956	0.00956	0.00872	93,749	85,571
65–74	10	15,580,600	466,621	0.02995	0.02995	0.02605	77,392	67,313
75–84	10	7,728,800	517,257	0.06693	0.06693	0.05015	57,233	42,883
85+	—	2,240,100	357,970	0.15980	0.15980		28,533	

ethnic groups and the sharpness of their survival differentials (Table 6A.2). The distinctions are aspects of population heterogeneity, introduced in Section 1.3 in connection with fecundability, and explored in works by Vaupel and Yashin (1985; Vaupel, 1986) and Manton and Stallard (1984). (The limitations imposed by period analysis and population heterogeneity are common to all national life tables, and are not severe. The reader should be aware that they exist, and that they may influence the interpretability of fine differences between life tables for national populations and over time.)

4.7. VIRTUAL LIFE TABLES

The correspondence between real populations and events $[N(x), {}_nN_x, {}_nD_x]$ and the life table population and events $(l_x, {}_nL_x, {}_nd_x)$ will sometimes permit direct estimation of the life table terms from population terms. Expression (4.38) is an example. The expression, $e_f = {}_\infty N_f / {}_\infty D_f$, estimates life expectancy at the final age f in the life table as the population ages f and above divided by annual deaths at ages f and above. In the final interval of the life table $l_f = {}_\infty d_f$, hence (4.38) is the real population equivalent to the ordinary life expectancy (4.19), which for the final age interval will be $e_f = {}_\infty L_f / l_f = {}_\infty L_f / {}_\infty d_f$.

Since real populations experience changing numbers of births over time and changing survival rates, the use of ${}_\infty N_f / {}_\infty D_f$ to estimate ${}_\infty L_f / {}_\infty d_f$ in (4.38) is not necessarily satisfactory. If the final age interval is very old, however, the changes in population size with age due to current mortality (in the United States, 10% per year at age 85) are substantially greater than changes due to past birth and death rates. As a result, late in life the population age distribution comes close to a life table distribution.*

Other types of distributions may be close to their life table equivalents at nearly all ages or durations, in which case (4.38) generalizes to the *virtual life expectancy estimator* [introduced earlier as expression (4.20)]:

---

* For populations in which age exaggeration is suspected in the oldest intervals, Horiuchi and Coale (1982) suggest the approximation

$$e_f = \{({}_\infty D_f / {}_\infty N_f) \exp[0.0951 r(f+)({}_\infty D_f / {}_\infty N_f)^{-1.4}]\}^{-1} \qquad |f \geq 65$$

where $r(f+)$ represents the annual rate of increase of the population ages f and above. The expression is derived by regression fitting to a Gompertz (1825) curve representing mortality at ages $f+$, with allowance for different rates of population increase (r). The age f is selected to be younger than the ages at which exaggeration is a problem, to avoid bias in ${}_\infty D_f / {}_\infty N_f$.

On the problem of age misstatement late in life, the reader should see Rosenwaike (1979, 1981), Rosenwaike and Logue (1983), and Coale and Kisker (1986, 1990). A valuable comment on centenarians in the Soviet Union will be found in Bennett and Garson (1983).

$$e_{0,\,j,\text{ virtual}} = \sum_{x=0}^{\infty} {}_{n}N_{x,\,j} / N(0) = {}_{\infty}N_{0,\,j} / N(0) \qquad (4.40)$$

The estimator finds the life expectancy for the attribute j as the number with the attribute divided by the initial risk population.

Expression (4.40) has been used by Mosley *et al.* (1982) and Ferry and Smith (1983) to estimate the mean duration of breastfeeding from the number of mothers breastfeeding at a given time ${}_{\infty}N_{0,\,j}$ divided by annual births $N(0)$ or infants ever breastfed $N^*(0)$. The expression is applied to U.S. data from the 1976 National Survey of Family Growth in Table 4.11. The estimate denominators (annual births, or annual births of infants ever breastfed) are derived from 1974–1975 births because interviews took place over a number of weeks in 1976. Using ordinary life tables, the means for the 1974–1976 birth sample are 1.8 and 5.5 months, for all births and for children ever breastfed, respectively.

When cohort sizes fluctuate across age or duration intervals, the radix $N(0)$ in (4.40) is replaced by $N_x(0)$, the radix for the xth cohort. Alternatively, to remove the effects of different cohort sizes, for ${}_{n}N_{x,\,j}/N_x(0)$ we may substitute ${}_{n}N_{x,\,j}/({}_{n}N_x/n) = n{}_{n}N_{x,\,j}/{}_{n}N_x$, where ${}_{n}N_x$ is the population ages x to $x + n$ and ${}_{n}N_{x,\,j}$ is the subset sharing the attribute j. In the alternate form, the expression equates $N_x(0)$ with $({}_{n}N_x/n)$, in effect disregarding mortality between 0 and the xth interval. With the change, the virtual life expectancy becomes:

$$e_{0,\,j,\text{ virtual}} = n \sum_{x=0}^{\infty} {}_{n}N_{x,\,j} / {}_{n}N_x \qquad (4.41)$$

Table 4.11. U.S. 1974–1976 Births and Children Breastfed, 1976 National Survey of Family Growth

Year	Births	Infants ever breastfed
1974–1975		
Total	1719.0	559.0
Mean	859.5	279.5
1976 (part)	301.0	115.0

Infants breastfed at survey: 138.0

Formulas
$e_{0,\,j,\text{ virtual}} = {}_{\omega}N_{0,\,j}/N(0) = 138/859.5 = 0.16$ year, or 1.9 months
$e_{0^*,\,j,\text{ virtual}} = {}_{\omega}N_{0,\,j}/N^*(0) = 138/279.5 = 0.49$ year, or 5.9 months

Table 4.12. Proportion of Women 15–44 Remaining Single and Life Table Mean Age at Marriage $_{45}a_0$. *Source:* Glick and Norton (1976)

Ages	Number of women $_nN_x$	Proportion never married $_nN_{x,j}/_nN_x$
0–4	—	1.000
5–9	—	1.000
10–14	—	1.000
15–19	10,275	0.839
20–24	9,276	0.376
25–29	8,334	0.128
30–34	6,906	0.069
35–39	5,870	0.045
40–44	5,805	0.042
Proportion single at age 45:		0.040

$$_{45}a_{0,f} = [5(1.000 + 1.000 + \cdots + 0.045 + 0.042) - 45\,(0.040)]/(1 - 0.040) = 21.6$$

Expression (4.41) is related to the ordinary life expectancy (4.19) by the substitution of $_nN_{x,j}/_nN_x$ for $_nL_x$, where $l_0 = 1$. Because $_nL_x/n$ approximates the life table population surviving at the midpoint of the interval, $l_{x+(1/2)n}$, for $l_0 = 1$ we also have:

$$l_{x+(1/2)n,\text{ virtual}} \simeq {}_nL_{x,\text{ virtual}}/n = {}_nN_{x,j}/_nN_x \qquad |\,l_0 = 1.0 \qquad (4.42)$$

In words, the proportion in an age or duration interval x to $x + n$ who have attribute j may be taken to represent the life table population with the attribute, or the proportion with the attribute who survive at the midpoint of the interval.*

An important distinction between (4.42) and the ordinary life table terms l_x and $_nL_x$ is that each of the virtual life table terms reflects the experience of a different sample $_nN_x$, and is independent of earlier terms. As a result, it is possible that $l_{x+n,\text{ virtual}} \gtrless l_{x,\text{ virtual}}$ and that $_nL_{x+n,\text{ virtual}} \gtrless {}_nL_{x,\text{ virtual}}$. The conditions $l_{x+n} > l_x$ and $_nL_{x+n} > {}_nL_x$ are anomalous, since they imply the interval survival probability $_np_x > 1$. Although usually a nuisance, anomalous $_np_x$ values are of practical interest in *two-census life tables* (Appendix 4A.2), where $_np_{x,\text{ virtual}}$ estimates serve as measures of intercensal population migration and census quality.

---

* The relationship $l_{x+(1/2)n} \simeq {}_nL_x/n$ is exact for $_nL_{x,\text{ linear}}$, expression (4.15).

If an attribute is shared by only some of the population, in place of the life expectancy $e_{0,j}$ we may substitute $_fa_{0,j}$, the mean age at event occurrence among individuals experiencing the event by age f:

$$_fa_{0,\,j,\text{ virtual}} = \left[n \sum_{x=0}^{f-n} (_nL_{x,\text{ virtual}}) - fl_f \right] \bigg/ (1 - l_f)$$

$$= \left\{ n \sum_{x=0}^{f-n} (_nN_{x,\,j}/_nN_x) - f[N_j(f)/N(f)] \right\} \bigg/ \quad (4.43)$$

$$[1 - N_j(f)/N(f)]$$

The expression removes the proportion of the population, $l_f = N_j(f)/N(f)$, not experiencing the event by age f from $_nL_x$ and l_0. It was introduced by Hajnal (1947), who used proportions of women 15–49 who were ever married to estimate the mean age at marriage. Hajnal used a cutoff age of $f = 50$ to limit analysis to marriages during the childbearing years.

Table 4.12 uses Hajnal's expression to estimate the mean age at first marriage for U.S. women married by age 45. For the proportion single at 45,

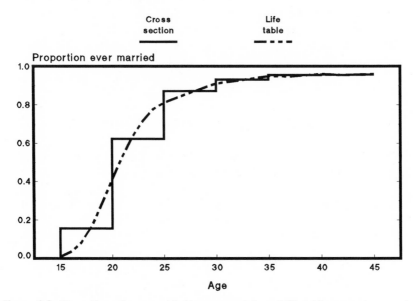

Figure 4.2. Proportion of women 15–44 ever married, and life table proportion married $(1 - l_x)$, June 1975 Current Population Survey. *Source:* Glick and Norton (1976).

$N_j(45)/N(45)$, we have substituted the proportion single at ages 45–49. In Fig. 4.2 the proportions ever married by age are graphed with the life table proportions $1 - l_x$. The value of Hajnal's formula will be apparent from the closeness of the two series.

4.8. STATISTICAL ANALYSIS OF THE LIFE TABLE

The data of Tables 4.13 and 4.14 are a subsample of the Current Population Survey for June 1975 and fairly closely approximate a simple random sample owing to the large number of sample areas (461) from which the data were drawn. Deaths reported in the vital statistics also constitute a random sample drawn from a superpopulation of deaths that occur over many years and deaths that might occur. In comparing marriage rates for different cohorts or national life tables for different years, there are clear advantages to knowing something about the magnitude of sampling variability that influences them. Especially when sample sizes are small, it is easy to be misled in the absence of robust statistical tests.

4.8.1. Variances of Life Table Terms

The life table derives from deaths or events $_nD_x$ in observed populations $N(x)$ or $_nN_x$. If events are binomially distributed,* with each event in the interval x to $x + n$ having the fixed occurrence probability $_nq_x$, then the expected number of events at ages x to $x + n$ in a sample of size $N(x)$ will be $_nD_x = N(x)_nq_x$. The variance of $_nD_x$ will be given by

$$\text{Var}(_nD_x) = N(x)_np_x {}_nq_x \tag{4.44}$$

The sample probabilities $_nq_x = {}_nD_x/N(x)$ are interpretable as weighted estimates of $_nD_x$, with weights $1/N(x)$. Applying the rule that the variance of a weighted estimate is the square of the weight times the variance of the unweighted estimate, we have for $\text{Var}(_nq_x)$ and $\text{Var}(_np_x)$

$$\text{Var}(_nq_x) = \text{Var}(_np_x) = [1/N(x)]^2 \, \text{Var}(_nD_x) = {}_np_x {}_nq_x/N(x) \tag{4.45}$$

or, substituting $_nD_x/_nq_x$ for $N(x)$,

$$\text{Var}(_nq_x) = \text{Var}(_np_x) = \begin{cases} 0 & \mid {}_nD_x = 0 \\ {}_np_x {}_nq_x^2/_nD_x & \mid {}_nD_x > 0 \end{cases} \tag{4.46}$$

---

* The reader should also see Brillinger (1986), for variance estimation using the Poisson distribution.

Table 4.13. Age at First Marriage Life Table for U.S. Female Cohorts 1925–29 and 1950–54. *Sources:* Glick (1972), Glick and Norton (1976)

		Observed				Life table	
						Cumulative proportion	
Age interval (years) x to $x+n$	n	Population single at start of interval $N(x)$	Marriages during interval $_nD_x$	Proportion marrying in interval $_nq_x$	Proportion remaining single $_nP_x$	Remaining single l_x	Marrying $l_0 - l_x$
			a. 1925–29 cohort				
0–14.5	$14\frac{1}{2}$	6046	26	0.004	0.996	1.000	0.000
14.5–15.5	1	6020	101	0.017	0.983	0.996	0.004
15.5–16.5	1	5919	213	0.036	0.964	0.979	0.021
16.5–17.5	1	5706	381	0.067	0.923	0.944	0.056
17.5–18.5	1	5325	598	0.112	0.888	0.881	0.119
18.5–19.5	1	4727	684	0.145	0.855	0.782	0.218
19.5–20.5	1	4043	734	0.182	0.818	0.669	0.331
20.5–21.5	1	3309	758	0.229	0.771	0.547	0.453
21.5–22.5	1	2551	552	0.216	0.784	0.422	0.578
22.5–23.5	1	1999	411	0.206	0.794	0.331	0.669
23.5–24.5	1	1588	295	0.186	0.814	0.263	0.737
24.5–29.5	5	1293	696	0.538	0.462	0.214	0.786
29.5–34.5	5	597	237	0.397	0.603	0.099	0.901
34.5–39.5	5	360	67	0.186	0.814	0.060	0.940
39.5–44.5	5	293	33	0.113	0.887	0.048	0.952
44.5+	—	263	—	—	—	0.043	0.957
			b. 1950–54 cohort				
0–14.5	$14\frac{1}{2}$	9276	22	0.002	0.998	1.000	0.000
14.5–15.5	1	9254	101	0.011	0.989	0.998	0.002
15.5–16.5	1	9153	231	0.025	0.975	0.987	0.013
16.5–17.5	1	8922	528	0.059	0.941	0.962	0.038
17.5–18.5	1	8394	884	0.105	0.895	0.905	0.095
18.5–19.5	1	7510	1175	0.156	0.844	0.810	0.190
19.5–20.5	1	6335	1132	0.179	0.821	0.683	0.317
20.5+	—	5203	—	—	—	0.561	0.439

These expressions will be used to estimate the variances of l_x and e_x, both of which are functions of $_nP_x$ (l_x is the product of the $_nP_a$ terms from duration $a = 0$ to $a = x - n$, while e_x is a function of $_nP_a$ from $a = x$ to $a = \omega$, the end of life).

The variance estimates given by (4.46) hold with minor changes for both the nonparametric and parametric $_nP_x$ estimators introduced in this chapter. The complete series of estimators and their variances are presented in Table 4.15.

Table 4.14. Standard Errors and 95% Confidence Intervals (1.96 SE)
for the Data of Table 4.13b

Start of age interval x	Proportion marrying in interval			Cumulative proportion marrying		
	Prop. marrying $_nq_x$	Stnd. error SE $(_nq_x)$	Confidence interval $_nq_x \pm 1.96$ SE	Prop. marrying $1 - l_x$	Stnd. error SE (l_x)	Confidence interval $(1 - l_x) \pm 1.96$ SE
0.0	0.00237	0.00051	0.00137–0.00337	0.00000	0.00000	0.00000–0.00000
14.5	0.01091	0.00108	0.00879–0.01303	0.00237	0.00051	0.00137–0.00337
15.5	0.02524	0.00164	0.02203–0.02845	0.01326	0.00119	0.01093–0.01559
16.5	0.05918	0.00250	0.05428–0.06408	0.03816	0.00199	0.03426–0.04206
17.5	0.10531	0.00335	0.09874–0.11188	0.09508	0.00305	0.08910–0.10106
18.5	0.15646	0.00419	0.14825–0.16467	0.19038	0.00408	0.18238–0.19838
19.5	0.17869	0.00481	0.16926–0.18812	0.31705	0.00483	0.30758–0.32652
20.5				0.43909	0.00515	0.42900–0.44918

The variance of the age-specific death rate $_nM_x = {}_nD_x/{}_nN_x$ is also found by interpreting the term as a weighted estimate of $_nD_x$, with the weight $1/{}_nN_x$. From (4.44):

$$\text{Var}(_nM_x) = (1/{}_nN_x)^2 \, \text{Var}(_nD_x) = {}_nM_x \, {}_np_x/{}_nN_x \qquad (4.47)$$

When mortality is low, $_nM_x \simeq {}_nq_x/n$, implying that $\text{Var}(_nM_x) \simeq (1/n^2) \times \text{Var}(_nq_x)$. Readers may confirm this approximate equality by substituting $nN(x)$ for $_nN_x$ and $_nq_x/n$ for $_nM_x$ in (4.47). Both $_nM_x$ and $_nq_x$ and their variances gradually diverge as mortality becomes high. The reader might note, incidentally, that although $_nN_x$ is about n times as large as $N(x)$ the coefficients of variation of the survival probabilities (4.46) and (4.47), SE $(_nM_x)/{}_nM_x$ and SE $(_nq_x)/{}_nq_x$, are of similar magnitudes. The advantage of the larger sample size $_nN_x$ in (4.47) is lost in the estimation of the n-year survival probability $_np_x$ from a single year death count $_nD_x$ or death rate $_nM_x$. The use of expression (4.47) is largely restricted to analysis of standardized rates, introduced in Chapter 3.

The variance of l_x in the absence of censorship is found by setting $l_0 = 1$ and equating l_x with $_xp_0$. Whence,

$$\text{Var}(l_x) = \text{Var}(_xp_0) = l_x(1 - l_x)/N(0) \qquad |l_0 = 1.0 \qquad (4.48)$$

More commonly, l_x is found as the product of an $_np_x$ series with censorship occurring in some intervals. Its variance is given by (Greenwood, 1926)

$$\text{Var}(l_x) = l_x^2 \sum_{a=0}^{x-n} \text{Var}(_np_a)/_np_a^2 \tag{4.49}$$

The expression is derived by writing l_x as a weighted estimate of $_np_a$. That is, $l_x = (l_x/_np_a)_np_a$. Its variance is then $(l_x/_np_a)^2 \text{Var}(_np_a)$, contributed by $_np_a$. Summing across $_np_a$ terms for all ages younger than x yields (4.49). * [The expression and those that follow omit *covariance terms* $\text{Cov}(l_i, l_j)$ that arise under some sample designs (Chiang, 1967; Lawless, 1982, pp. 59–64).] Using (4.45) to estimate $\text{Var}(_np_x)$, expression (4.49) becomes

$$\text{Var}(l_x) = l_x^2 \sum_{a=0}^{x-n} {_nq_a}/[_np_a N(a)] \tag{4.50}$$

$$= l_x^2 \sum_{a=0}^{x-n} {_nq_a^2}/(_np_a \, _nD_a) \tag{4.51}$$

The reader is referred to Table 4.15 for $\text{Var}(_np_x)$ terms for (4.49) appropriate to specialized $_np_x$ formulas.

The variance of life expectancy (e_x) is given by (Wilson, 1938; Chiang, 1960)†

---

* Expression (4.49) can be derived as an expansion of (4.48) for samples with no censorship prior to x. Setting $l_0 = 1$ and making the substitutions $l_x = N(x)/N(0)$, $l_x/N(0) = N(x)/N(0)^2 = l_x^2/N(x)$ and $1 - l_x = [N(0) - N(x)]/N(0)$ we have:

$$\text{Var}(l_x) = l_x (1 - l_x)/N(0)$$

$$= [l_x^2/N(x)][N(0) - N(x)]/N(x)$$

$$= l_x^2 [1/N(x) - 1/N(0)]$$

$$= l_x^2 [1/N(n) - 1/N(0) + 1/N(2n) - 1/N(n) + 1/N(3n) - 1/N(2n) + \cdots]$$

$$= l_x^2 \{1/[N(0)_np_0] - 1/N(0) + 1/[N(n)_np_n] - 1/N(n) + 1/$$

$$[N(2n)_np_{2n}] - 1/N(2n) + \cdots\}$$

$$= l_x^2 \{_nq_0/[N(0)_np_0] + _nq_n/[N(n)_np_n] + _nq_{2n}/[N(2n)_np_{2n}] + \cdots\}$$

$$= l_x^2 \sum_a {_np_a} \, {_nq_a}/[N(a)_np_a^2] = l_x^2 \sum_a \text{Var}(_np_a)/_np_a^2$$

† For the life table crude death rate $\text{CDR}_{lt} = 1/e_0$, Chiang (1961) suggests rewriting the CDR_{lt} as $(1/e_0^2)e_0$, which provides the approximate variance

$$\text{Var}(\text{CDR}_{lt}) = (1/e_0^4)\text{Var}(e_0)$$

$$\text{Var}(e_x) = (1/l_x)^2 \sum_{a=x}^{\omega-n} l_a^2 [e_{a+n} + n - {}_n a_a]^2 \, \text{Var}({}_n p_a) \qquad (4.52)$$

The expression exploits the relationship of e_x to e_{x+n} given in (4.39)

$$e_x = {}_n p_x (e_{x+n} + n) + {}_n q_x \, {}_n a_x$$

$$= {}_n p_x (e_{x+n} + n - {}_n a_x) + {}_n a_x$$

Table 4.15. Variance Formulas for Selected Life Table Estimators[a]

---

a. ${}_n p_x$

(4.1) ${}_n p_{x,\text{ unadjusted}} = 1 - {}_n D_x / N(x)$
  $\text{Var} = {}_n p_x \, {}_n q_x / N(x) = {}_n p_x \, {}_n q_x^2 / {}_n D_x$

(4.2) ${}_n p_{x,\text{ curtate sample}} = 1 - ({}_n D_x - {}_n D_{C,x}) / [N(x) - N_C(x)]$
  $\text{Var} = {}_n p_x \, {}_n q_x / [N(x) - N_C(x)] = {}_n p_x \, {}_n q_x^2 / ({}_n D_x - {}_n D_{C,x})$

(4.5) ${}_n p_{x,\text{ linear}} = 1 - {}_n D_x / [N(x) - \frac{1}{2} N_{\text{RC}}(x)]$
  $\text{Var} = {}_n p_x \, {}_n q_x / [N(x) - \frac{1}{2} N_{\text{RC}}(x)] = {}_n p_x \, {}_n q_x^2 / {}_n D_x$

(4.6) ${}_n p_{x,\text{ hyperbolic}} = 1 - {}_n D_x / [N(x) - \frac{1}{2} {}_n W_{\text{RC},x}]$
  $\text{Var} = {}_n p_x \, {}_n q_x / [N(x) - \frac{1}{2} {}_n W_{\text{RC},x}] = {}_n p_x \, {}_n q_x^2 / {}_n D_x$

(4.9) ${}_n p_{x,\text{ linear}} = 1 - {}_n D_x / ({}_n N_x / n + \frac{1}{2} {}_n D_x)$
  $\text{Var} = {}_n p_x \, {}_n q_x / ({}_n N_x / n + \frac{1}{2} {}_n D_x) = {}_n p_x \, {}_n q_x^2 / {}_n D_x$

(4.10) ${}_n p_{x,\text{ exponential}} = \exp[-n \, {}_n D_x / {}_n N_x]$
  $\text{Var} = {}_n p_x \, {}_n q_x^2 / {}_n D_x$

(4.27) ${}_n p_{x,\text{ linear } a} = 1 - n \, {}_n D_x / [{}_n N_x + (n - {}_n a_x) {}_n D_x]$
  $\text{Var} = n \, {}_n p_x \, {}_n q_x / [{}_n N_x + (n - {}_n a_x) {}_n D_x] = {}_n p_x \, {}_n q_x^2 / {}_n D_x$

${}_n p_{x,\text{ NCHS}} = 1 - {}_n M_x / [{}_n q_x^{(\text{ref})} / {}_n M_x^{(\text{ref})}]$
  $\text{Var} = {}_n p_x \, {}_n q_x^2 / {}_n D_x$

(4A.2) ${}_j p_{x+(1/2)n,\text{ linear}} = {}_n N_{x+j}^{(t+j)} / {}_n N_x^{(t)}$
  $\text{Var} = {}_j p_{x+(1/2)n} \, {}_j q_{x+(1/2)n} / [{}_n N_x^{(t)} / n]$

(5.1) ${}_n p_{x,j,\text{ linear}} = 1 - {}_n q_x ({}_n D_{x,j} / {}_n D_x)$
  $\text{Var} = {}_n p_{x,j} \, {}_n q_{x,j} / N(x) = {}_n p_{x,j} \, {}_n q_{x,j}^2 / {}_n D_{x,j}$

(5.16) ${}_n p_{x,j,\text{ Greville}} = {}_n p_x^{D_{x,j} / {}_n D_x}$
  $\text{Var} = {}_n p_{x,j,\text{ Gre}} \, {}_n q_{x,j,\text{ Gre}}^2 / {}_n D_{x,j}$

b. Other life table terms

(3.10) ${}_n M_x$ $\text{Var} = {}_n M_x \, {}_n p_x / {}_n N_x$

(4.12) l_x $\text{Var} = \sum_{a=0}^{x-n} (l_x / {}_n p_a)^2 \text{Var}({}_n p_a)$

(4.19) e_x $\text{Var} = (1/l_x)^2 \sum_{a=x}^{\omega-n} l_a^2 [e_{a+n} + n - {}_n a_a]^2 \text{Var}({}_n p_a)$

(4.43) ${}_x a_{0,\text{ virtual}}$ $\text{Var} = {}_x a_0 (x - {}_x a_0) / (x^2 {}_x N_0)$

---

[a] These variance estimates are approximate. The reader should also see Littell (1952), Gail (1975), Elandt-Johnson and Johnson (1980, pp. 128, 171), and Chiang (1985, pp. 193–243) for other formulas.

Using this relationship the variance of e_x is a function of the variance of $_np_x$, weighted by $e_{x+n} + n - {_na_x}$, and of the variance of $_na_x$ (trivially). It depends as well on life expectancy at higher ages by the presence of e_{x+n}. The contribution at the later ages is weighted both by $e_{a+n} + n - {_na_a}$ and by $l_a/l_x = {_{a-x}p_x}$. [Compare (4.52) with Var (l_x) in (4.49), which is a function of the same form but sums over $_np_a$ value at ages below x.] At most ages (4.52) can be slightly simplified by the substitution $_na_a = n/2$.

We note for the reader that the variance of e_x can also be written

$$\text{Var}(e_x) = (l_{x+n}/l_x)^2 [e_{x+n} + n - {_na_x}]^2 \, \text{Var}(_np_x)$$

$$(4.53)$$

$$+ (l_x/l_{x+n})^2 \, \text{Var}(e_{x+n})$$

When mortality is largely confined to old age, as in human populations, at younger ages $_np_x \simeq 1$ and $l_x \simeq l_{x+n}$ with the result that the variances of e_x and e_{x+n} will also be approximately equal. The concentration of mortality in old age also implies that at the younger ages, differences in life expectancy between populations will also be relatively constant. This combination of relatively constant life expectancy differences and constant variances suggests that the significance level of a difference in life expectancy between two populations will be largely independent of the age at which the test is made, at least to middle life. The property does not hold for nonhuman populations.

Table 4.14 displays standard errors SE $(_nq_x)$ and SE $(1 - l_x)$ for the 1950–1954 female birth cohort age at first marriage life table (Table 4.13). All are small, the largest being SE $(_1q_{19.5}) = 0.005$. It will be seen from (4.48) and (4.50) that Var$(_nq_x)$ terms vary inversely with sample sizes, and SE $(_nq_x)$ inversely with their square roots. A sample half as large as the 6335 persons at age $19\frac{1}{2}$ in the table would thus have produced an error SE $(_1q_{19.5}) = 0.01$. The reader may estimate the sample size for which the standard error of the proportion remaining single at $20\frac{1}{2}$, $1 - l_{20.5}$, would reach 5%.

4.8.2. Significance Tests of Life Table Differences

The final columns of the $_nq_x$ and l_x series of Table 4.14 show the confidence intervals $_nq_x \pm 1.96$ SE $(_nq_x)$ and $(1 - l_x) \pm 1.96$ SE $(1 - l_x)$ under simple random sampling. Intervals are only slightly wider for the actual sample design. The reader should note that none of the ranges overlap for the different $_nq_x$ and l_x estimates, suggesting that at every age changes occur in the probabilities of marrying as well as in the overall proportion still single.

A more rigorous test of the significance of changes across age groups or between different samples than the simple overlap of confidence bands is to use the normally distributed test statistic for $_np_x$ and $_np_y$ or $_nq_x$ and $_nq_y$

$$Z_p = \frac{|_np_x - _np_y| - \frac{1}{2}[1/N(x) + 1/N(y)]}{[\text{Var}(_np_x) + \text{Var}(_np_y)]^{1/2}} \qquad (4.54)$$

provided that $_np_x \neq _np_y$. The sample size correction $\frac{1}{2}[1/N(x) + 1/N(y)]$ is commonly omitted when it is small in comparison with $_np_x - _np_y$. The expression may be used to compare any two age groups (x, y) and/or samples, and for l_x and l_y values satisfying (4.48). {A close approximation for $_np_x$ estimates satisfying (4.9), where samples are enumerated in age intervals, is to calculate an adjusted sample base from the $_nD_x$ and $_nq_x$ terms by the formula $N(x) = _nD_x/_nq_x$. For $_nD_x = 0$, $N(x) = _nN_x/n$ [expression (4.11)].}

Table 4.16 displays proportions married by age 20.5 for 1925–54 female birth cohorts from the 1975 survey and for an earlier survey in 1971 with a nonoverlapping sample. For the two youngest cohorts shown in the table (1940–44 and 1945–49), differences in proportions married by age 20+ are significant at the 0.05 level, indicating that a change in reported marriage frequencies may have occurred between the two surveys. For the 1945–49 cohort, however, differences at 19+ were significant only at the 0.13 level and at 21+ only at the 0.27 level (table not shown). As sometimes happens, we have evidently picked an atypical age for the comparison. The 1940–44 cohort difference is significant at all ages above 18.

When differences at single ages are unrepresentative of overall differences between life tables, or there is no particular advantage to testing the tables only at a single point, a test of differences between two or more series of proportions can be used. Two that are relatively simple are the generalized Wilcoxon and Mantel–Haenszel tests. For the tests, differences between observed and expected numbers of events at each duration are summed. Dividing the square of the summed differences by the sample variance yields the test

Table 4.16. Proportion of Women Born during 1925–54 Who Married by Age $20\frac{1}{2}$ from Surveys in 1971 and 1975. *Sources:* Glick (1972), Glick and Norton (1976)

Birth cohort	Sample size		Proportion married			Z score	$p(Z)$
	1971	1975	1971	1975	Diff.		
1925–29	6114	6046	0.457	0.453	0.004	0.4	0.337
1930–34	5615	5805	0.510	0.503	0.007	0.7	0.232
1935–39	5722	5870	0.551	0.544	0.007	0.7	0.233
1940–44	5863	6906	0.522	0.495	0.027	3.1	0.001
1945–49	8376	8334	0.474	0.458	0.016	2.0	0.021
1950–54	—	9276	—	0.439	—		

statistic D, which is asymptotically (i.e., for large samples) distributed as a chi square with $k - 1$ degrees of freedom, where k is the number of samples being compared. For two-sample tests (d.f. = 1):

$$D = \left\{ \sum_x [N_1(x)_nD_{x,\,2} - N_2(x)_nD_{x,\,1}]/w_x \right\}^2 \Bigg/$$

$$\left\{ \sum_x \{ N_1(x)N_2(x)[N_1(x) - {}_nD_{x,\,1} + N_2(x) - {}_nD_{x,\,2}] \right. \qquad (4.55)$$

$$\left. \times ({}_nD_{x,\,1} + {}_nD_{x,\,2})/[N_1(x) + N_2(x) - 1]\}/w_x^2 \right\}$$

where $w_x = 1$ for the generalized Wilcoxon sample size weighted test and $w_x = 1/[N_1(x) + N_2(x)]$ for the uniformly weighted Mantel–Haenszel test (Lagakos, 1982). Expression (4.55), like (3.19), is a sum of chi square tests for 2×2 tables with entries

$$\begin{array}{cc} a & b \\ c & d \end{array} \;=\; \begin{array}{cc} N_1(x) - {}_nD_{x,\,1} & {}_nD_{x,\,1} \\ N_2(x) - {}_nD_{x,\,2} & {}_nD_{x,\,2} \end{array}$$

with

$$D = \left[\sum_x (ad - bc)/w_x \right]^2 \Bigg/$$

$$\left\{ \sum_x [(a + b)(c + d)(a + c)(b + d)/(a + b + c + d - 1)]/w_x^2 \right\}$$

The Mantel–Haenszel test converts the table entries to proportions by dividing by the sample size. The test can be used with cross-sectional data, as in Table 4.16, with the substitution

$$N(x) = {}_nN_x/n + \tfrac{1}{2}{}_nD_x$$

The D statistic can also be used as a test for consistency between ${}_nP_x$ estimates from censored and uncensored observations in sample surveys (see Section 4.2.3). The test uses the terms

$$\begin{array}{cc} a & b \\ c & d \end{array} = \begin{array}{cc} N(x) - N_C(x) - {}_nD_x & {}_nD_x - {}_nD_{C,\,x} \\ \left\{ \begin{array}{l} \frac{1}{2}N_C(x)\,|\,{}_nq_{x,\,\text{censored sample}} = 0 \\ {}_nD_{C,\,x}/{}_nq_{x,\,\text{cen}} - {}_nD_{C,\,x}\,|\,{}_nq_{x,\,\text{cen}} > 0 \end{array} \right\} & {}_nD_{C,\,x} \end{array}$$

where $\frac{1}{2}N_C(x)$ or ${}_nD_{C,\,x}/{}_nq_{x,\,\text{censored sample}}$ estimates $N^*_C(x)$, the effective sample size for the observations under censorship, depending on whether ${}_nq_{x,\,\text{cen}}$ is 0 or greater than 0.

Table 4.17 shows the calculation of the D statistic for the data of Table 4.1, using the linear estimator for right-censored samples:

$${}_np_{x,\,\text{linear}} = greater\ of\ \{0,\ 1 - {}_nD_x/[N(x) - \tfrac{1}{2}N_{RC}(x)]\}$$

for which the censored sample estimator is

$${}_np_{x,\,\text{RC linear}} = 1 - {}_nD_{C,\,x}/\tfrac{1}{2}N_C(x)$$

$${}_nq_{x,\,\text{RC linear}} = {}_nD_{C,\,x}/\tfrac{1}{2}N_C(x)$$

The chi square probability for these data is found to be $p = 0.0014$. That level of significance implies that the censored and uncensored samples represent

Table 4.17. Estimation of D for the Data of Table 4.1, Using ${}_np_{x,\,\text{linear}}$

Start of interval (x)	Total		Right-censored		Uncensored			Censored
	Number at risk	Events	Number at risk	Events d	Number at risk $a + b$	Events b	${}_nq_{x,\,\text{cen}}$	Effective number at risk $c + d$
0	350	74	0	0	350	74	0.0000	0.0
1	276	48	45	1	231	47	0.0111	22.5
2	184	31	50	0	134	31	0.0000	25.0
3	103	10	36	1	67	9	0.0556	18.0
4	58	4	28	0	30	4	0.0000	14.0
Interval:	1		2		3			4
$\begin{array}{cc} a & b \\ c & d \end{array} =$	$\begin{array}{cc} 231 - 47 & 47 \\ 22.5 - 1 & 1 \end{array}$		$\begin{array}{cc} 134 - 31 & 31 \\ 25 - 0 & 0 \end{array}$		$\begin{array}{cc} 67 - 9 & 9 \\ 18 - 1 & 1 \end{array}$			$\begin{array}{cc} 30 - 4 & 4 \\ 14 - 0 & 0 \end{array}$

$D = [(184 \times 1 - 21.5 \times 47) + (103 \times 0 - 25 \times 31) + (58 \times 1 - 17 \times 9)$
$+ (26 \times 0 - 14 \times 4)]^2/[(231 \times 22.5 \times 205.5 \times 48)/252.5 + (134 \times 25 \times 128 \times 31)/158$
$+ (67 \times 18 \times 75 \times 10)/84 + (30 \times 14 \times 40 \times 4)/43] = 10.25$, with 1 df

populations with dissimilar survival experience, and that sample $_np_x$ estimates, by whatever formulas they are generated, will be of uncertain quality.

For survival differences in human populations, where mortality is concentrated at relatively few ages near the end of life, Z tests for life expectancy differences will usually outperform Mantel–Haenszel and related tests. For two populations or samples i, j the test for a difference in life expectancy at age x is

$$Z_e = \frac{e_{x,\,i} - e_{x,\,j}}{[\mathrm{Var}(e_{x,\,i}) + \mathrm{Var}(e_{x,\,j})]^{1/2}} \tag{4.56}$$

The power of the Z test arises from the fact that a difference in survival probabilities at one age impacts on the life expectancy at all younger ages, and is thus likely to be identified. A difference in $_np_x$ at a single age has less effect on D, which essentially tests for a pattern of differences between the distributions.

In general, the Z_e test is appropriate to rectangular survival distributions and Mantel–Haenszel and related tests to linear and exponential distributions. Using the concept of entropy (H) introduced as expression (4.23) and in Fig. 6A.1, the distinction is between populations whose mortality is low until near the end of life $(H < 0.25)$ and those with significant losses at most ages $(H \geq 0.5)$.

4.9. SUMMARY

The life table is made by following a population or sample from one exact age or exact duration of exposure to a later exact age or duration. Depending on the type of information given, one of four formulas, (4.1), (4.2), (4.9), or (4.10), will usually estimate the interval survival probability $_np_x$. The remaining terms of the life table—the radix l_0 and cumulative survival probabilities l_x/l_0, the estimated number of persons or the person time lived in each interval $_nL_x$ and events occurring in the interval $_nd_x$, and the life expectancy e_x—embody the principal contributions of the life table to population analysis.

The life table terms contain two distinct types of information. The $_np_x$, l_x, and e_x terms are probabilistic measures that permit precise and intuitive comparisons between populations. By contrast, the $_nL_x$ and $_nd_x$ terms have a cross-sectional focus that makes them analogous to observed populations $_nN_x$ and numbers of deaths or events $_nD_x$. They describe the age structure as it would appear if births and deaths always numbered l_0 and death rates were frozen at the levels from which the life table was generated.

The similarities between life table and real population terms sometimes allow life tables to be constructed by direct substitution of population for life table terms. With direct substitution it is possible for some values l_{x+n} to exceed earlier l_x terms due to sample errors or differences between the cohorts from which the rates are estimated, but apart from such errors the overall quality of the approximations can be high.

The chapter has not emphasized the limits to life table analysis. The most critical is the need for complete population and event counts. Populations can be standardized (Chapter 3) using subsets of events, such as deaths for one cause, but the life table is a table of probabilities and requires completeness. The life table is also not calculable for repeated terminating events. That is, for $y > x$, no individuals in $_nD_x$ are retained in $N(y)$ or $_nD_y$. Finally, the life table translates poorly to calendar events. It is tedious to attempt to estimate events in a given month or year, such as the marriages and deaths of the chapter examples, or annual numbers of births at various parities, from the event probabilities that form the life table.* The reader should be alert to these limits, and to other applications for which life tables are not well suited.

Readers desiring additional information on life table construction may consult a number of other texts. At an elementary level, Barclay (1958, pp. 93–122), Pollard (1973, pp. 3–21), Pollard *et al.* (1981, pp. 26–47), and Newell (1988, pp. 63–81) introduce life tables by the linear formulas (4.9) and (4.15). Pressat (1972, pp. 107–152) and Wunsch and Termote (1978, pp. 79–105) should also be reviewed, particularly for their attention to cohort and period distinctions. More comprehensive texts are Namboodiri and Suchindran (1987) and Chiang (1984), and for follow-up study data Elandt-Johnson and Johnson (1980). The reader should also see DeGruttola and Lagakos (1989) on the analysis of data with both left and right censorship.

We close the chapter with a selection of problems in life table analysis, using the U.S. 1980 census population and deaths and NCHS 1980 life tables (Appendix 6A.2). The chapter appendices continue the discussion of life tables with comments on data coding for life table analysis, formulas for construction of life tables from census data, and further remarks on parametric estimators and maximum likelihood.

4.9.1. Applications of the Life Table to Survival at Exact and Interval Ages

The life table allows survival to be estimated between exact ages, using the $_np_x$ and l_x series, and interval ages, using $_nL_x$. This section introduces several problems that bring out the distinctions between the two types

---

* An example of the estimation of annual deaths from survival probabilities is given in Section 5.5.

of estimates, using the NCHS 1980 life table, reproduced as Appendix Table 6A.2.

1. Using exact ages, find the proportion of the total population (Table 6A.2a) surviving from birth to age 20 and to age 65. Find the proportion of 20-year-olds who survive to 65.

Answer: The proportion surviving from birth to age 20 is given by the $_np_x$ series, as the product $_1p_0 \times {}_4p_1 \times {}_5p_5 \times {}_5p_{10} \times {}_5p_{15} = l_{20}/l_0$. For survival to age 65 we have $_1p_0 \times {}_4p_1 \times \cdots \times {}_5p_{60} = l_{65}/l_0$. Survival from 20 to 65 is estimated as $_5p_{20} \times {}_5p_{25} \times \cdots \times {}_5p_{60} = l_{65}/l_{20}$. For the total population the needed l_x terms are $l_0 = 100,000$, $l_{20} = 97,700$, $l_{65} = 76,944$. We have $l_{20}/l_0 = 0.97700$, $l_{65}/l_0 = 0.76944$, $l_{65}/l_{20} = 76,944/97,700 = 0.78755$.

2. Given that the sex ratio at birth is about 105 males to 100 females in the white population, what proportion of white infants survive to age 20? Of black infants, whose sex ratio at birth is about 102:100?

Answer: From Table 6A.2, $l_0 = 100,000$, $l_{20, \text{wm}} = 97,461$, and $l_{20, \text{wf}} = 98,346$. Weighting these terms by the ratio of births, we will have $l_{20, \text{w}} = (105 \times 0.97461 + 100 \times 0.98346)/205 = 0.97893$. For black infants, $l_{20, \text{b}} = (102 \times 0.96127 + 100 \times 0.97183)/202 = 0.96650$.

3. At birth, what is the complete life expectancy for the total U.S. population? If we define the working ages as 15–65, what is the working life expectancy?

Answer: The complete life expectancy $e_0 = T_0/l_0$ is given as 73.7 in Table 6A.2a. It is decomposable as life expectancy from birth to age 15, from age 15 to age 65 and at age 65 as $(T_0 - T_{15})/l_0$, $(T_{15} - T_{65})/l_0$, and $(T_{65} - T_\infty)/l_0$. The estimates become $(7,371,986 - 5,895,364)/100,000 = 14.8$ years, $(5,895,364 - 1,261,626)/100,000 = 46.3$ years, and $(1,261,626 - 0)/100,000 = 12.6$ years.

Comment: The reader will note that these quantities add to the complete life expectancy of 73.7 years. Formally, the first quantity is the partial life expectancy $_{15}e_0 = 14.8$ years (out of 15.0 years that would be lived if no deaths occurred). The second and third terms are future life expectancies as assessed at birth. Out of the 50 years that would be lived between 15 and 65 in the absence of mortality, at birth we expect to live 46.3, and from age 65 onward we expect to live 12.6 years. The dependency ratio [expression (1.9)] as assessed from the life table is $(14.8 + 12.6)/46.3 = 0.59$, which suggests that we spend about 60% as much time at the nonworking ages as at the working ages, or $100 \times (14.8 + 12.6)/73.7 = 37\%$ of our expected lifetimes.

The reader might also note that at age 15 our working life expectancy is $_{50}e_{15} = (T_{15} - T_{65})/l_{15} = (5,895,364 - 1,261,626)/98,182 = 47.2$ years. The expectancy is nearly a year greater than the 46.3 years expected at birth, since mortality from birth to age 15 is no longer taken into account. Similarly, the life expectancy at 65 is e_{65} = 16.4 years, almost 4 years greater than the 12.6 years assessed at birth.

4. Working with grouped ages, what is the probability that an individual aged between 20 and 25 will live 50 more years?

Answer: In the life table the $_nL_x$ series represents both time lived between ages x and $x + n$, and the population we would have at those ages if births and mortality probabilities remained constant at the life table levels. Under those assumptions for Table 6A.2a the proportion surviving 50 years from ages 20–24 will be $_5L_{70}/_5L_{20}$ = 312,015/486,901 = 0.64082. Note that the figure will be between the 50-year survival probability at exact age 20 (l_{70}/l_{20} = 0.69579) and the probability at exact age 25 (l_{75}/l_{25} = 0.58177), since the population $_5L_{20}$ comprises individuals between those two ages.

Comment: This is a problem in population projection, in that if mortality remained constant we would be surviving persons ages 20–24 in 1980 to ages 70–74 in 2030, at which point about 64% would still be living. For an actual projection we would want to separate males from females and blacks from whites, since survival probabilities differ substantially for the four groups (75% of females would survive versus 56% of males in the white population, and 60% versus 40% in the black population, Tables 6A.2d–6A.2g).

5. Find the probability that a couple, both white, who married when they were ages 20–24, will be living 50 years later, when they are 70–74.

Answer: Using interval ages ($_nL_x$) the probability both will survive is the product of the individual probabilities. We therefore need to find $(_5L_{70, wm}/_5L_{20, wm})(_5L_{70, wf}/_5L_{20, wf})$ = (272,110/484,997)(367,579/491,029) = (0.56106)(0.74859) = 0.42. The remaining probabilities will be (1 − 0.56106)(0.74859) = 0.33 that the female partner alone survives, (0.56106)(1 − 0.74859) = 0.14 that the male partner alone survives, and (1 − 0.56106)(1 − 0.74859) = 0.11 that neither survives.

6. A white female age 25 has just given birth to a son. At 1980 survival rates, find the probability that she will outlive him.

Answer: Using exact ages (l_x) we need to compute joint survival and mortality probabilities at all ages to the end of the mother's life. For the first interval, to her age 30, we have the joint probability ($l_{5, wm}/l_0$)($l_{30, wf}/l_{25, wf}$) = (98,508/100,000)(97,776/98,063) = 0.98220 that both survive, the probability [(100,000 − 98,508)/100,000](97,776/98,063) = 0.01488 that she alone survives, and the probability [(100,000 − 98,508)/100,000] × [(98,063 − 97,776)/98,063] = 0.00004 that neither survives. If we assume that where both die the mother survives her son half of the time, the probability that she outlives him in the first 5 years becomes 0.01488 + 0.00002 = 0.01490.

During the next 5 years the survival probabilities are conditional on both surviving the initial period. For the joint probabilities we therefore have

$0.98220(l_{10,\,wm}/l_{5,\,wm})(l_{35,\,wf}/l_{30,\,wf})$ = $0.98220(98{,}348/98{,}508)(97{,}420/$ $97{,}776)$ = 0.97703 that both survive, the probability $0.98220[(98{,}508 - 98{,}348)/98{,}508](97{,}420/97{,}776)$ = 0.00159 that she alone survives, and the probability $0.98220[(98{,}508 - 98{,}348)/98{,}508][(97{,}776 - 97{,}420)/ 97{,}776]$ = 0.000006 that neither survives. The cumulative probability that she outlives her son now becomes $0.01490 + 0.00159 + 0.000006/2 = 0.01649$.

Continuing through the rest of the life table, the probability ultimately reaches 0.156 or about $1/6$, treating the final interval $85+$ as 85–89 to be the same width as earlier intervals. In the black population the probability is 0.237 or about $1/4$ for a mother the same age at the birth of her son. Both females have a probability of 0.64 of surviving a husband of their same age.

Formally, the cumulative probability an individual at age y outlives another individual age x is given by

$$\sum_{j=0}^{\infty} (l_{x+j}/l_x)(l_{y+j}/l_y)[(1 - l_{x+j+n}/l_{x+j})(l_{y+j+n}/l_{y+j})$$

$$+ (1 - l_{x+j+n}/l_{x+j})(1 - l_{y+j+n}/l_{y+j})/2]$$

where the durations j, x, y are integer multiples of n, the interval width in the life table.

APPENDIX 4A.1. DATE CODING FOR LIFE TABLE ANALYSIS

a. Coding by Duration of Exposure

Population and event data for national life tables are usually taken from census and vital statistics estimates, as were the data of Table 4.4, or from samples tabulated in the same format. The researcher may want to adjust the data for distortions or omissions in reported ages and deaths by age, but the information is otherwise useable as presented. The life table methodology addresses problems of left and right censorship and incomplete overlap between numerators and denominators.

By contrast, in sample surveys population and event data are normally coded as the dates of entry into risk, event if it has occurred, and latest contact or study cutoff. The data need to be recoded as intervals and summed before life tables can be constructed.

As an example, we might have a sample that includes the cases shown in Table 4A.1. The cases are observed from start of risk, and are right-censored at cutoff: left censorship, affecting cases that are first observed after the start of risk, will be introduced below. All dates are calendar 1980, so we may convert from the day and month to 1980 calendar day, for which $1/1/1980 = 1$, $1/20/1980 = 20$, and so forth, as shown in columns 4–6.

The durations to event and cutoff are found by date subtraction in the final columns of the table. Grouping the durations into 30-day intervals ("months") and summing, we have the life table sample shown in Table 4A.2. Beginning with five cases at risk, in the initial interval case d experiences the terminating event but not cutoff, and e reaches cutoff. The remaining three cases begin interval 1. In that interval case b experiences the event but none in the sample reach cutoff. Cases a and c begin interval 2, where case a reaches cutoff. Case c begins intervals 3 and 4, reaching cutoff in interval 4.

It is possible that all of the durations in the example are coded incorrectly, and that one individual, case d, is mislocated in Table 4A.2. For case d, the duration from exposure on $4/15/1980$ to cutoff on $5/15/1980$ may be 29.01 to 30.99 complete days. It is under 30 complete days, and case d belongs in the right-censored subsets $N_C(0)$ and $_1D_{C,0}$, if exposure began at a later time during the day on $4/15/1980$ than the cutoff time point on $5/15/1980$. With the correction, the entries in the first row of Table 4A.2 would be 5, 1, 2, 1 and not 5, 1, 1, 0.

The potential error is significant because it is directional: durations can be overestimated by one unit of measure (here, one day) but not underestimated. The error can be corrected in large measure by a $\frac{1}{2}$-unit downward recalibration of the interval indexes. If, for example, we locate the start of interval 1 at $29\frac{1}{2}$ days rather than 30 days, we will overestimate interval lengths only for those whose actual durations are 29.01 to 29.49 days. At the same time, we will underestimate interval lengths for those whose true intervals are between 59.50 and 59.99 days [these are persons coded as 59 days who should fall into recoded interval 2 ($59\frac{1}{2}$ days to $89\frac{1}{2}$ days) but are in interval 1]. By recalibrating the interval indexes we replace the unidirectional errors that may arise by bidirectional errors that are largely offsetting.

Table 4A.1. Dates of Start of Risk, Event, and Cutoff (Hypothetical Cohort)

Case	Date of start of risk (1)	Date of event (2)	Date of cutoff (3)	Date—12/31/1979 Risk (4)	Event (5)	Cutoff (6)	Duration from risk to Event (7) = (5) − (4)	Cutoff (8) = (6) − (4)
a	1/20/1980	—	4/15/1980	20	—	106	—	86
b	1/20/1980	3/5/1980	5/5/1980	20	65	126	45	106
c	2/10/1980	—	6/20/1980	41	—	172	—	131
d	4/15/1980	5/10/1980	5/15/1980	106	131	136	25	30
e	4/15/1980	—	4/15/1980	106	—	106	—	0

Table 4A.2. Survival Status for the Sample in Table 4A.1

Start interval (x)	Recalibrated interval[a] x-1/2 u	Total		Right-censored	
		Number at risk	Events	Number at risk	Events
0	0.0	5	1	1	0
1	0.983	3	1	0	0
2	1.983	2	0	1	0
3	2.983	1	0	0	0
4	3.983	1	0	1	0

[a] Recalibrated by subtracting 1/2 unit (1/2 day or 1/60 month) from each indexed interval. See text.

If in place of the year, month, and day at start of risk, event, and cutoff, dates are given only by year and month, we would have the date codes and intervals shown in Table 4A.3, and the life table entries of Table 4A.4. With the change in interval units, cases a, b, and d are followed at longer index durations than earlier. The greater recalibration, 1/2 month rather than 1/2 day, corrects for the apparent difference in observation times.*

Our example has not yet dealt with left censorship. To introduce left censorship, we may suppose that cases b and c in Table 4A.1 entered observation on 2/25/1980 (calendar day 56). For b, the initial observation date is 36 days after start of risk, which places b in the second interval at first contact. The case is therefore omitted from the initial interval and introduced as a left-censored case in the second interval. The event date for case b also

---

* The effects of misstatement of the interval widths are illustrated using the example of fecundability in Goldman *et al.* (1984). The authors include formulas for estimating $_nq_x$ terms from $_nq_{x-1/2}$ for the hyperbolic distribution (Section 4.2.2 and Appendix 4A.3), which are:

$$_1q_{0,\text{ hyperbolic}} = {}_{1/2}q_0 + (1 - {}_{1/2}q_0)(\tfrac{1}{2}{}_1q_{1/2})/(1 - \tfrac{1}{2}{}_1q_{1/2})$$

$$_1q_{x,\text{ hyperbolic}} = \tfrac{1}{2}{}_1q_{x-1/2} + (1 - \tfrac{1}{2}{}_1q_{x-1/2})(\tfrac{1}{2}{}_1q_{x+1/2})/(1 - \tfrac{1}{2}{}_1q_{x+1/2})$$

The expressions are best suited to distributions in which mortality hazards are decreasing. For constant or increasing mortality, the researcher may use the quadratic fitting

$$_1q_{0,\text{ quadratic}} = \begin{cases} {}_{1/2}q_0 + (1 - {}_{1/2}p_0\,{}_1p_{1/2})/3 & |(1 - {}_{1/2}p_0\,{}_1p_{1/2}) < 3{}_{1/2}p_0 \\ 1 - {}_{1/2}p_0\,{}_1p_{1/2}^{1/2} & |(1 - {}_{1/2}p_0\,{}_1p_{1/2}) \geq 3{}_{1/2}p_0 \end{cases}$$

where the restrictions avoid $_1q_0$ estimates greater than 1. Besides the hyperbolic, for later intervals either exponential interpolation [expression (2.3d)] or linear or cubic interpolation [expressions (2.3a), (2.3b)] may be used to estimate $_1q_x$ from the midinterval series $_1q_{x-1/2}, {}_1q_{x+1/2}, \ldots,$.

Table 4A.3. Dates of Start of Risk, Event, and Cutoff
for the Sample of Table 4A.1

Case	Date of start of risk (1)	Date of event (2)	Date of cutoff (3)	Duration from risk to	
				Event $(7) = (5) - (4)$	Cutoff $(8) = (6) - (4)$
a	1/1980	—	4/1980	—	3
b	1/1980	3/1980	5/1980	2	4
c	2/1980	—	6/1980	—	4
d	4/1980	5/1980	5/1980	1	1
e	4/1980	—	4/1980	—	0

falls in the second interval and is left-censored. The cutoff point for b occurs in the fourth interval and is not of concern. For case c entry into observation occurs in the initial interval, 15 days after start of risk. The case is thus left-censored in the initial interval. Case c remains in the sample as an uncensored observation in each of the next three intervals, and is right-censored in the fifth interval. With the changes to b and c, Table 4A.2 is revised as shown in Table 4A.5.

b. Coding by Age Interval

Besides life tables coded by exposure and event durations, tables are sometimes required in which intervals are grouped by the ages at which individuals were at risk. In medical studies, for example, survival may depend as strongly on the age at which an individual is diagnosed or treated for disease as on the nature of the disease and the efficacy of the treatment offered. To determine whether treatment has influenced survival, the appropriate com-

Table 4A.4. Survival Status for the Sample in Table 4A.3

Start of interval (x)	Recalibrated interval[a] x-1/2 u	Total		Right-censored	
		Number at risk	Events	Number at risk	Events
0	0.0	5	0	1	0
1	0.5	4	1	1	1
2	1.5	3	1	0	0
3	2.5	2	0	1	0
4	3.5	1	0	1	0

[a] Recalibrated by subtracting 1/2 unit (1/2 month) from each indexed interval. See text.

Table 4A.5. Survival Status for the Sample in Table 4A.1, with Left Censorship of Cases b and c

Start of interval (x)	Recalibrated interval[a] x-1/2 u	Total		Left-censored		Right-censored	
		Number at risk	Events	Number at risk	Events	Number at risk	Events
0	0.0	4	1	1	0	1	0
1	0.983	3	1	1	1	0	0
2	1.983	2	0	0	0	1	0
3	2.983	1	0	0	0	0	0
4	3.983	1	0	0	0	1	0

[a] Recalibrated by subtracting 1/2 unit (1/2 day or 1/60 month) from each indexed interval. See text.

parison may be to the mortality rates of individuals not receiving the treatment, or individuals drawn at random from the general population, whose ages and durations of observation compare to those of the study sample.

To construct life tables by age, we begin by replacing the dates of start of risk, event, and cutoff for the sample with their ages at start of risk, event, and cutoff. The five individuals in Table 4A.1, for example, might be infants with the dates of birth and ages shown in Table 4A.6.

Using Table 4A.6 we find the exposure time accrued in each age interval, essentially equivalent to the sample ($_nN_x$) that would be expected to be counted if a census were taken at midinterval. These exposure times are shown in Table 4A.7.

Examining the table, for case a, we find 0.5 month of actual exposure during the first month of life, 1.0 month of risk in months 1 and 2, and 0.33 month of risk in month 3. These estimates derive from an age at entry into risk of 15 days (born 1/5/1980, entered into risk 1/20/1980) and continuation

Table 4A.6. Dates of Birth and Ages at Start of Risk, Event, and Cutoff for the Example of Table 4A.1 (Ages in Months[a])

Case	Date of birth	Age at start of risk	Age at event	Age at cutoff
a	1/5/1980	0.50	—	3.33
b	1/10/1980	0.33	1.83	3.83
c	1/15/1980	0.83	—	5.17
d	1/15/1980	3.00	3.83	4.00
e	3/5/1980	1.33	—	1.33

[a] For ease of calculation, each month has been set to 30 days.

Table 4A.7. Exposure Time to Event Occurrence at Ages 0–5 Months for the Sample of Table 4A.6

Case	Interval						
	0	1	2	3	4	5	Total
a	0.50	1.00	1.00	0.33	0	0	2.83
b	0.67	0.83	0	0	0	0	1.50
c	0.17	1.00	1.00	1.00	1.00	0.17	4.33
d	0	0	0	0.83	0	0	0.83
e	0	0	0	0	0	0	0
No. at risk	1.33	2.83	2.00	2.17	1.00	0.17	9.50
Events	0	1	0	1	0	0	2

at risk until age 3 months and 10 days (cutoff 4/15/1980). The reader may confirm the exposure times shown for cases b–e.

Summing vertically, the table shows the number of person months at risk during each month of age and the number of events. The two rows are the interval population $_nN_x$ and events $_nD_x$ for life tables using events and person months of exposure [expression (4.9)] or age-specific event rates [expression (4.10)].

Defining the events as infant deaths, we might want to compare the survival of the sample with the survival of a random subset of infants of the same ages. For the random subset, we require the exposure durations and numbers of events the sample infants would accrue at the ordinary survival probabilities for their ages.

If no deaths occurred, which is what we expect at 1980 U.S. survival rates to the two- or three-digit precision we are using, the comparison sample would have the observation times of the study infants, shown in Table 4A.8, with no events. At higher mortality rates, or using greater estimate precision, the sample sizes would be smaller than in Table 4A.8, due to occasional infant deaths. If, for example, l_x decreased exponentially at the rate $\mu = 0.05$ per month, or from $l_{0.5} = 1.00$ to $l_{3.33} = 0.868$, using expression (2.7d) to estimate exposure times for the sample, the observation time and event count for the comparison infant a' would be:

in interval 0: $(0.5)(0.975 - 1.00)/(\ln 0.975 - \ln 1.00)$
$$= 0.494 \text{ month and } (1.00 - 0.975) = 0.025 \text{ death}$$

in interval 1: $(1.0)(0.928 - 0.975)/(\ln 0.928 - \ln 0.975)$
$$= 0.951 \text{ month and } (0.975 - 0.928) = 0.047 \text{ death}$$

in interval 2: $(1.0)(0.883 - 0.928)/(\ln 0.883 - \ln 0.928)$
$$= 0.905 \text{ month and } 0.045 \text{ death}$$

in interval 3: $(0.33)(0.868 - 0.883)/(\ln 0.868 - \ln 0.883)$
$$= 0.292 \text{ month and } 0.015 \text{ death}$$

For the same mortality pattern, comparison infant b' entering at $l_{0.33} = 1.00$ would have the observation times and events:

in interval 0: $(0.67)(0.967 - 1.00)/(\ln 0.967 - \ln 1.00)$
$$= 0.656 \text{ month and } 0.033 \text{ event}$$

in interval 1: 0.943 month and 0.047 event

in interval 2: 0.897 month and 0.045 event

in interval 3: 0.714 month and 0.036 event

The reader may complete the example for infants c', d', and e', to find the total exposure times and events 1.315 months and 0.066 event in interval 0, 2.862 months and 0.143 event in interval 1, 2.722 months and 0.136 event in interval 2, and 2.857 months and 0.143 event in interval 3.

The reader might note that since the reference survival distribution is exponential, the event rate $_nM_x = {_nD_x}/{_nN_x}$ will be $_nM_x = \mu = 0.05$ in all intervals and will serve as a check on the $_nD_x$ and $_nN_x$ estimates. Under other survival distributions the rates would be sensitive to the left and right interval censorship observed in Tables 4A.7 and 4A.8.

Table 4A.8. Hypothetical Exposure Times at Ages 0–5 Months for the Sample of Table 4A.6, in the Absence of Terminating Events

Case	\multicolumn{7}{c}{Interval}
	0	1	2	3	4	5	Total
a	0.50	1.00	1.00	0.33	0	0	2.83
b	0.67	1.00	1.00	0.83	0	0	3.50
c	0.17	1.00	1.00	1.00	1.00	0.17	4.33
d	0	0	0	1.00	0	0	1.00
e	0	0	0	0	0	0	0
Total	1.33	3.00	3.00	3.17	1.00	0.17	11.67

Omitting the censored intervals, the life tables would be constructed using the observations in months 1 and 2 for infants a and b, months 1 through 4 for c, and month 3 for d (Table 4A.8). Matching observation times, the comparison sample would enter at $l_1 = 1.0$ for a', b', and c', and at $l_3 = 1.0$ for d', and continue to l_3 for a' and b', l_5 for c', and l_4 for d'.

APPENDIX 4A.2. TWO-CENSUS LIFE TABLES

The relatively high level of annual immigration into the United States (about 0.3% of total population) and a 2% difference in completeness of coverage between the 1970 and 1980 censuses limit them as a source of information about mortality patterns. In much of the developing world, age misstatements contribute an additional element of uncertainty to census figures. When they exist, however, reasonably good censuses can be used to construct life tables, and when reasonably good life tables exist they provide a useful check on census quality.

The reason this is so is that in the absence of migration the population counted in a census at time t represents the survivors of earlier censuses plus the survivors of births in the intervening years. If j years elapse between censuses, then the population between $x + j$ and $x + j + n$ at time $t + j$ should number

$$_nN_{x+j}^{(t+j)} = {_nN_x^{(t)}}({_nL_{x+j}}/{_nL_x})$$
(4A.1)

Together with independent estimates of births and net migration, (4A.1) is used in the United States to project the expected population count at succeeding censuses.

To construct a life table from (4A.1) it is necessary to convert the terms in $_nL_x$ to terms in $_np_x$. For linear survival distributions we make the substitution

$$l_{x+(1/2)n,\ \text{linear}} = {_nL_x}/n$$

which uses the mean single year population in the interval as an estimate of survival at the interval midpoint $x + \frac{1}{2}n$. The expression does not provide an estimate of the number of individuals starting the life table, the radix l_0, but since $_nN_x^{(t)}$ and $_nN_{x+j}^{(t+j)}$ are the survivors at t and at $t + j$ of the same birth cohort, we do not require the radix to find

$$_jp_{x+(1/2)n,\ \text{linear}} = l_{x+j+(1/2)n,\ \text{linear}}/l_{x+(1/2)n,\ \text{linear}}$$

$$= {_nL_{x+j}}/{_nL_x} = {_nN_{x+j}^{(t+j)}}/{_nN_x^{(t)}}$$
(4A.2)

The terms in $_jp_{x+(1/2)n}$ can be fitted to model life tables to generate a complete l_x series or, if a life table is already available, they may be matched against it to estimate the relative quality of coverage of the two censuses. When the enumeration is better in one census than the other, (4A.2) will produce improbable survival estimates. In or out migration also has that effect.

An alternative to (4A.1) and (4A.2), due to Preston and Bennett (1983), is to use the census populations at time t and $t + j$, $_nN_x^{(t)}$ and $_nN_x^{(t+j)}$, to estimate the intercensal growth rates and midperiod age distributions:

$$e^{jnr_x} = {_nN_x^{(t+j)}}/{_nN_x^{(t)}}$$

$$_nr_x = (1/j)[\ln_nN_x^{(t+j)} - \ln_nN_x^{(t)}] \tag{4A.3}$$

$$_nN_x^{[t+(1/2)j]} = [_nN_x^{(t+j)} - {_nN_x^{(t)}}]/[\ln_nN_x^{(t+j)} - \ln_nN_x^{(t)}] \tag{4A.4}$$

where (4A.4) is an exponential interpolation formula related to (2.7d).

If mortality is constant, the population $_nN_x^{[t+(1/2)j]}$ will differ from any younger population $_nN_{x-k}^{[t+(1/2)j]}$ in proportion to survival and to the changes in birth rates over the k year interval, which are estimated from the $_nr_x$ terms. A consistent series of $_nL_x$ estimators can therefore be constructed as

$$_nL_x = \exp\left[n\left(\sum_{a=0}^{x-n} {_nr_a} + \tfrac{1}{2}{_nr_x}\right)\right]_nN_x^{[t+(1/2)j]} \tag{4A.5}$$

Except at age 0, l_x terms can be found from $_nL_x$ by derivative estimators [expression (2.8)], of which the simplest is the linear function

$$l_{x,\text{ linear}} = (_nL_{x-n} + {_nL_x})/(2n)$$

Like (4A.2), (4A.5) will produce improbable survival estimates in the presence of migration and when the source censuses differ in quality or completeness. These points are discussed and applications of the method presented in Preston and Bennett (1983). A general introduction to age-specific growth rates will be found in Horiuchi and Preston (1988).

Life tables constructed using (4A.2) or (4A.5) belong to the set of virtual life tables introduced in Section 4.7, in which the nature of the source data and methods of table construction allow terms $(_np_x = l_{x+n}/l_x) > 1$.

APPENDIX 4A.3. PARAMETRIC $_np_x$ ESTIMATES

Samples that are left- or right-censored in an interval $[N_{LC}(x), N_{RC}(x)]$ are of limited value for survival estimation, since the relationship between observed and unobserved segments of the interval is problematic. Given the interval survival probability $_np_x$ and the proportions surviving at censorship in the censored samples,

$$_np_{x,\ \text{left partial}} = 1 - {}_nD_{\text{LC},\ x}/N_{\text{LC}}(x) \qquad (4A.6)$$

$$_np_{x,\ \text{right partial}} = 1 - {}_nD_{\text{RC},\ x}/N_{\text{RC}}(x) \qquad (4A.7)$$

the investigator can make an informed judgment as to the concentration of mortality in its early and later segments. Alternatively, the $_np_x$ distribution may be expressible as a mathematical function in a region encompassing $(x, x + n)$, which would allow the function to determine the relationship of the partial intervals to the full interval.

The latter approach, involving parameterization of the survival distribution, is widely used for exploiting partial interval survival. In the simplest case, discussed in Section 4.2, the number or proportion of survivors at duration x is estimated by the linear function $l_x = a + bx$. When the survival distribution is linear, deaths in the unobserved part of any censored interval will equal deaths in the observed part. For $_np_x$ were therefore have:

$$_np_{x,\ \text{LC linear}} = 1 - 2_nD_{\text{LC},\ x}/[N_{\text{LC}}(x) + {}_nD_{\text{LC},\ x}]$$

$$= 1 - {}_nD_{\text{LC},\ x}/\tfrac{1}{2}[N_{\text{LC}}(x) + {}_nD_{\text{LC},\ x}] \qquad (4A.8)$$

$$_np_{x,\ \text{RC linear}} = 1 - 2_nD_{\text{RC},\ x}/N_{\text{RC}}(x) = 1 - {}_nD_{\text{RC},\ x}/\tfrac{1}{2}N_{\text{RC}}(x) \qquad (4A.9)$$

Expressions (4A.8) and (4A.9) differ only slightly. In (4A.8), $_np_x$ is estimated by doubling the number of events $_nD_{\text{LC},\ x}$ in the partial interval to represent events in the complete interval, and adding the extra events to the sample base $N_{\text{LC}}(x)$, where they would not have been counted since they left the sample before the initial observation. In (4A.9), the numerator is doubled to include the additional $_nD_{\text{RC},\ x}$ events occurring after censorship. The denominator is not adjusted, since the cases are already included in $N_{\text{RC}}(x)$ as individuals surviving at censorship.

Substituting (4A.6) and (4A.7) into (4A.8) and (4A.9), the relationship between $_np_x$ and the partial interval estimators becomes:

$$_np_{x,\ \text{linear}} = {}_np_{x,\ \text{left partial}}/(2 - {}_np_{x,\ \text{left partial}})$$

$$_np_{x,\ \text{left partial}} = 2_np_{x,\ \text{linear}}/(1 + {}_np_{x,\ \text{linear}}) \qquad (4A.10)$$

$$_np_{x,\ \text{linear}} = 2_np_{x,\ \text{right partial}} - 1$$

$$_np_{x,\ \text{right partial}} = (1 + {}_np_{x,\ \text{linear}})/2 \qquad (4A.11)$$

To estimate $_np_x$ using both censored and uncensored observations, we combine the numerators and denominators of the curtate sample estimator [expression (4.2)] and the estimators under censorship, (4A.8) and (4A.9). Since known events in the censored samples number $_nD_{C,x}$, and since the observation times for the censored samples are about half those for the uncensored sample, we will assign the censored observations 1/2 unit weight. [That is, we will combine (4.2) with the second form of (4A.8) and (4A.9).] By that convention, for a linear $_np_x$ estimator incorporating left- and right-censored observations in the interval we would have:

$$_np_{x,\text{ linear}} = 1 - _nD_x/[N(x) - \tfrac{1}{2}N_{\text{LC}}(x) - \tfrac{1}{2}N_{\text{RC}}(x) + \tfrac{1}{2}_nD_{\text{LC},x}]$$

If the data set contains no left-censored observations $N_{\text{LC}}(x)$, the expression reduces to $1 - _nD_x/[N(x) - \tfrac{1}{2}N_{\text{RC}}(x)]$. In either form it may take negative values when a high proportion of the censored sample $N_C(x)$ are terminators. To control the estimate range, the expression with right censorship is written:

$$_np_{x,\text{ linear}} = \textit{greater of }\{0,\ 1 - _nD_x/[N(x) - \tfrac{1}{2}N_{\text{RC}}(x)]\} \quad (4A.12)$$

By (4A.12), $_np_{x,\text{ linear}}$ is reset to 0 when $_nD_x > [N(x) - \tfrac{1}{2}N_{\text{RC}}(x)]$, as the right-hand expression becomes negative.

If the survival distribution is exponential ($l_x = ae^{bx}$), the event risk is constant in the interval and the survival probability $_np_x$ is related to the partial probability $_np_{x,\text{ right partial}}$ by (Chiang, 1984, p. 225):

$$_np_{x,\text{ right partial}} = (_np_{x,\text{ exp}} - 1)/\ln_np_{x,\text{ exp}} \quad (4A.13)$$

$$_np_{x,\text{ exp}} = 1 + _np_{x,\text{ right partial}}\ln_np_{x,\text{ exp}} \quad (4A.14)$$

where $\ln_np_{x,\text{ exp}}$ is the natural logarithm of the survival probability. After substituting (4A.7) for $_np_{x,\text{ right partial}}$, (4A.14) can be solved for $_np_{x,\text{ exp}}$ by Newton–Raphson iteration, outlined in Appendix 4A.4.

Assigning 1/2 weight to censored observations as in (4A.12), (4A.14) can be merged with the curtate sample estimator (4.2) to yield, for samples with right-censored observations,

$$_np_{x,\text{ exp1}} = 1 - [_nD_x - _nD_{\text{RC},x} + \tfrac{1}{2}(1 - _np^*_{x,\text{ exp}})N_{\text{RC}}(x)]/$$
$$[N(x) - \tfrac{1}{2}N_{\text{RC}}(x)] \quad (4A.15)$$

where $_np^*_{x,\text{ exp}}$ is the solution to (4A.14). For $_nD_{\text{RC},x} > 0$ the numerator of this expression will be smaller than the numerator of the linear estimator (4A.12), yielding a higher estimate of the survival probability.

An alternative to (4A.12) and (4A.15) is to incorporate the curtate sample estimator (4.2) with the linear (4A.9) or exponential (4A.14) in a maximum likelihood estimator. For the exponential, the MLE estimator is Chiang's A. In samples with right-censored observations it is:

$$_np_{x,\ \text{exp2}} = S(x)/\{[N_{\text{RC}}(x) + {_nD_x} - 2{_nD_{\text{RC},\ x}}]/{_nq_x}$$

$$+ N_{\text{RC}}(x)/({_np_x}\ln{_np_x}) - {_nD_{\text{RC},\ x}}\,{_nq_x}/[{_np_x}({_nq_x} + \ln{_np_x})]\} \qquad (4A.16)$$

[where $S(x) = [N(x) - N_{\text{RC}}(x)] - ({_nD_x} - {_nD_{\text{RC},x}})$. For readers familiar with calculus, Chiang's expression is derived in Appendix 4A.4.

Expressions (4A.15) and (4A.16) produce identical $_np_x$ estimates only when the curtate sample (4.2) and right partial (4A.14) estimates are identical, or when $N_{\text{RC}}(x) = 0$. When $N_{\text{RC}}(x) > 0$ and (4.2) $\neq$ (4A.14), Chiang's estimator is biased downward, at times falling below the linear estimator (4A.12).

In samples with improving survival in each interval, and samples in which censored $({_nD_{\text{RC},x}})$ and uncensored $({_nD_x} - {_nD_{\text{RC},x}})$ events in the interval cannot be clearly distinguished (see Section 4.2.2), the hyperbolic (or "actuarial") formula is commonly used. For right-censored samples the expression is:

$$_np_{x,\ \text{hyperbolic}} = 1 - {_nD_x}/\{N(x) - \tfrac{1}{2}[N_{\text{RC}}(x) - {_nD_{\text{RC},\ x}}]\}$$

$$= 1 - {_nD_x}/[N(x) - \tfrac{1}{2}{_nW_{\text{RC},\ x}}] \qquad (4A.17)$$

In (4A.17) the term $N_{\text{RC}}(x) - {_nD_{\text{RC},x}} = {_nW_{\text{RC},x}}$ represents individuals surviving at censorship, who can be counted without distinguishing $_nD_{\text{RC},x}$ from $_nD_x$.

The hyperbolic estimate is derived by setting $l_x = 1/(a + bx)$, making the probability of surviving in the subinterval from $x + k$ to $x + n$ a linear function of the time remaining in the interval. That is (Batten, 1978, pp. 5–6):

$$_{n-k}p_{x+k} = l_{x+n}/l_{x+k} = \frac{a + b(x + k)}{a + b(x + n)} = a' + b'(x + k) \qquad \text{for } 0 \le k \le n$$

The survival distribution is a hyperbola within the interval. It estimates $_np_x$ from right-censored observations as:

$$_np_{x,\ \text{RC hyperbolic}} = 1 - {_nD_{\text{RC},\ x}}/\tfrac{1}{2}[N_{\text{RC}}(x) + {_nD_{\text{RC},\ x}}]$$

Table 4A.9. Estimated Proportion of Table 4.1 Sample
Surviving, by Selected $_np_x$ Formulas

$$_1p_{0,\,\text{unadjusted}} = 1 - {}_1D_0/N(0)$$
$$= 1 - 74/350 = 0.78857$$

$$_1p_{1,\,\text{exp 1}} = 0.81068$$
$$_1p_{2,\,\text{exp 1}} = 0.80503$$
$$_1p_{3,\,\text{exp 1}} = 0.88246$$
$$_1p_{4,\,\text{exp 1}} = 0.90909$$

$$_1p_{1,\,\text{exp 2}} = 0.81033$$
$$_1p_{2,\,\text{exp 2}} = 0.80391$$
$$_1p_{3,\,\text{exp 2}} = 0.88231$$
$$_1p_{4,\,\text{exp 2}} = 0.90863$$

For the hyperbolic, the numerator and denominator of the estimate are added to the numerator and denominator of the curtate sample estimator.

Table 4A.9 displays survival probabilities under the two parametric estimators in this section, for the data of Table 4.1. The reader may compare these estimates with those of the curtate sample, linear, and hyperbolic estimators in Tables 4.2 and 4.3.

APPENDIX 4A.4. MAXIMUM LIKELIHOOD ESTIMATION OF $_np_x$

In data sets with right censorship but not left censorship, the maximum likelihood estimator is derived from the probability of drawing $S(x) = [N(x) - N_{\text{RC}}(x)] - (_nD_x - {}_nD_{\text{RC},\,x})$ survivors and $(_nD_x - {}_nD_{\text{RC},\,x})$ nonsurvivors in a sample of $[N(x) - N_{\text{RC}}(x)]$ uncensored observations at the survival probability $_np_x$, which is given by the binomial:

$$\binom{S(x) + {}_nD_x - {}_nD_{\text{RC},\,x}}{S(x)} {}_np_x^{S(x)} \left(1 - {}_np_x\right)^{(_nD_x - {}_xD_{\text{RC},\,x})}$$

and of drawing $S_{\text{RC}}(x) = N_{\text{RC}}(x) - {}_nD_{\text{RC},\,x}$ survivors and $_nD_{\text{RC},\,x}$ nonsurvivors among $N_C(x)$ censored observations at the survival probability $_np_{x,\,\text{partial}}$, given by the binomial:

$$\binom{S_{\text{RC}}(x) + {}_nD_{\text{RC},\,x}}{S_{\text{RC}}(x)} {}_np_{x,\,\text{partial}}^{S_{\text{RC}}(x)} \left(1 - {}_np_{x,\,\text{partial}}\right)^{{}_nD_{\text{RC},\,x}}$$

The likelihood function is the product of these two probabilities, omitting constant terms. Using $\propto$ to represent proportionality, we have:

$$L(x;\, _np_x) \propto\, _np_x^{S(x)} (1 - \, _np_x)^{(_nD_x - _nD_{RC,x})}$$

$$\times\, _np_{x,\,\text{partial}}^{S_{RC}(x)} (1 - \, _np_{x,\,\text{partial}})^{_nD_{RC,x}} \quad (4A.18)$$

To find the survival probabilities $_np_x$ and $_np_{x,\,\text{partial}}$ for which the observed sample of $S(x)$, $S_{RC}(x)$, $_nD_x$, and $_nD_{RC,x}$ would be likely to be drawn, we replace $_np_{x,\,\text{partial}}$ by its estimating function and set the derivative of the likelihood function (dL/d_np_x) or its logarithm $(d\ln L/d_np_x)$ equal to 0.

The unadjusted and curtate sample estimators are the solution to $(d\ln L/d_np_x) = 0$ with censored observations omitted. For the curtate sample estimator in samples with right censorship we will have:

$$L(x;\, _np_x) \propto\, _np_x^{S(x)}(1 - \, _np_x)^{(_nD_x - _nD_{RC,x})}$$

$$\ln L(x;\, _np_x) \propto S(x)\ln_np_x + (_nD_x - _nD_{RC,\,x})\ln(1 - \, _np_x)$$

$$d\ln L/d_np_x = S(x)/_np_x - (_nD_x - _nD_{RC,\,x})/(1 - \, _np_x) = 0$$

$$_np_{x,\,\text{curtate sample}} = S(x)/[S(x) + _nD_x - _nD_{RC,x}]$$

Chiang's exponential estimator (4A.16) is found by substitution of (4A.13) in the derivative of the log likelihood function. Both Chiang's estimator and (4A.14) are solved for $_np_x$ by iteration, most easily by using the Newton–Raphson formula:

$$_np_x^* = \, _np_x - f(_np_x)/f'(_np_x) \quad (4A.19)$$

where an initial $_np_x$ estimate is inserted on the right-hand side of (4A.19) and the expression is solved to yield a better estimate $_np_x^*$ on the left. The new estimate is inserted on the right and the expression again solved, continuing until $f(_np_x) \simeq 0$ and $_np_x^*$ stabilizes. Convergence is faster if the initial $_np_x$ estimate is nearly correct, which suggests using $_np_{x,\,\text{curtate sample}}$ for the initial approximation.†

† The Newton–Raphson formula generalizes as $x^* = x - f(x)/f'(x)$. It is satisfactory for distributions whose derivative $f'(x)$ is large relative to $f(x)$ near the point $f(x) = 0$ and approximately constant. It may converge slowly or not at all if this condition is not met. For polynomial expressions a formula that converges more rapidly and for a broader range of functions is the Laguerre (1880) formula [Householder (1970, pp. 176–179)]:

$$x^* = x - nf(x)/(f'(x) \pm \{[(n-1)f'(x)]^2 - n(n-1)f(x)f''(x)\}^{1/2})$$

Because of its complexity, Chiang's expression will not always converge using Newton–Raphson. Expression (4A.14) is more easily solved. It has the terms

$$f(_np_x) = 1 + [1 - _nD_{RC,\,x}/N_{RC}(x)]\ln_np_x - _np_x$$

$$f'(_np_x) = [1 - _nD_{RC,\,x}/N_{RC}(x)]/_np_x - 1$$

As in Chiang's exponential, the CS estimator $_np_{x,\,\text{curtate sample}}$ may be used in (4A.13) as an initial approximation to $_np_{x,\,\text{exp}}$. After finding the value $_np^*_{x,\,\text{exp}}$ for which $f(_np_x) \simeq 0$, it is substituted on the right side of (4A.15) and the expression is solved for $_np_{x,\,\text{exp1}}$.

Inserting the linear estimator $_np_{x,\,\text{right partial}}$ [expression (4A.11)] in (4A.18) and setting $(d\ln L/d_np_x) = 0$ produces Elveback's estimator (Elveback, 1958):

$$_np_{x,\,\text{ML linear}} = \left(\frac{-\frac{1}{2}_nD_{RC,\,x} + \{\frac{1}{4}_nD^2_{RC,\,x} + 4[N(x) - \frac{1}{2}N_{RC}(x)] \times [S(x) + \frac{1}{2}(N_{RC}(x) - _nD_{RC,\,x})]\}^{1/2}}{2[N(x) - \frac{1}{2}N_{RC}(x)]} \right)^2$$

(4A.20)

This estimator is not Fisher consistent in the presence of censorship within the interval. That is, for a sample drawn from a population with the survival rate θ, the estimator satisfies only the approximate equality $E[_np_{x,\,\text{Elveback}}] \simeq \theta$.

The reader may consult Elveback (1958, p. 431), Elandt-Johnson (1977, p. 252), or Chiang (1984, p. 227) for the variance of Elveback's estimator.

---

where the sign of the square root term is taken so as to minimize the absolute value $|x^* - x|$, and n is the order of the polynomial. The function converges from real to both real and complex values: in Newton–Raphson, convergence is from real to real values or from complex to either real or complex values.

When several roots are sought, the researcher can use root sweeping to avoid convergence to roots already found. Rewriting $f(x)$ as $(x - x_0)(x - x_1) \cdots (x - x_n)$, after finding the root x_j we remove it by the division $f_{-j}(x) = f(x)/(x - x_j)$. The procedure is outlined in Keyfitz and Flieger (1971, pp. 202–203).

If all roots are distinct, a simpler method of root sweeping can be used in Newton–Raphson iteration. For the solution to the jth root we may set

$$x^*_j = x_j - [f'(x)/f(x) - 1/(x_j - x_0) - 1/(x_j - x_1) - \cdots - 1/(x_j - x_{j-1})]^{-1}$$

where the terms $x_0, x_1, \ldots, x_{j-1}$ are roots already found and x_j is the current estimate of the jth root.

APPENDIX 4A.5. SAMPLE SIZE ESTIMATION FOR LIFE TABLES

The sampling error formulas introduced in Section 4.8.1 can be inverted to provide estimates of the sample sizes needed to establish statistical significance for selected differences between survival distributions. The exercise is an important one: much of the value of a research project may be forfeited through inadequate sample sizes or, more rarely, unnecessary costs may be incurred through overestimation of sample size needs. Using a two-tailed test, the relationship between the difference of two proportions, the sample variance, and the significance level desired leads to the approximate equality, assuming no sample losses occur in the interval j to $j + n$,

$$N_2(j) \simeq \left[\frac{(_np_{j,\,1} - {}_np_{j,\,2})^2}{Z^2_{(1/2)\alpha}\,{}_np_j\,{}_nq_j} - \frac{1}{N_1(j)} \right]^{-1} \quad (4A.21)$$

for unequal sample sizes $N_1(j)$ and $N_2(j)$, and

$$N_1(j) = N_2(j) = Z^2_{(1/2)\alpha}\,{}_np_j\,{}_nq_j/(_np_{j,\,1} - {}_np_{j,\,2})^2 \quad (4A.22)$$

for two equal samples. In the expressions $Z_{(1/2)\alpha}$ is the normal deviate corresponding to the significance level α, $_np_{j,\,1} - {}_np_{j,\,2}$ is the anticipated difference between the proportions surviving from j to $j + n$ in samples 1 and 2, and $_np_j$ is the proportion surviving in the combined samples. The expressions omit a continuity correction, which requires the addition of approximately W cases to $N_1(j)$ and $W[N_1(j)/N_2(j)]$ cases to $N_2(j)$, where

$$W = [N_2(j)/N_1(j) + 1]/[(_np_{j,\,1} - {}_np_{j,\,2})N_2(j)/N_1(j)] \quad (4A.23)$$

For $N_1(j) = N_2(j)$, W reduces to $2/(_np_{j,\,1} - {}_np_{j,\,2})$.

These expressions may also be used for survival differences between durations 0 and x by the substitution $l_x = {}_xp_0$ as in (4.48), for samples in which no losses occur prior to x.*

As an example, suppose we want to select two samples of equal size that are large enough for an absolute difference of 0.025 to be significant at the 5% level. (That is, if the rates in the interval j to $j + n$ were further apart, we would want that finding to be statistically significant.) If the combined sample survival probability in the interval is $_np_j = 0.5$ (which suggests that $_np_{j,\,1}$ and $_np_{j,\,2}$ not be closer than about 0.4875 and 0.5125), at the 5% level of significance

---

* The condition is met when $N(x) = N(0) - {}_xD_0$.

$(Z = 1.96)$, the required sample sizes from expression (4A.22) with continuity correction (4A.23) are

$$N_1(j) = N_2(j) \simeq (1.96)^2(0.5)(1 - 0.5)/(0.025)^2 + 2/0.025 = 3200$$

For a similar difference to be significant near $_np_j = 0.25$ or $_np_j = 0.75$, the sample sizes would need to be about 2400, or one-fourth less.

When unequal sample sizes are used, the overall numbers needed are increased. If at $_np_j = 0.5$ we desire that $N_1(j)$ be no larger than 2000, $N_2(j)$ would need to be about 7500. This estimate is derived by initially setting $N_1(j) = 1950$ in (4A.21), yielding $N_2(j) = 7300$ and $W = 50$. The final sample sizes become $N_1(j) = 1950 + 50 = 2000$, and $N_2(j) = 7300 + 50$ $(7300/1950) = 7500$ after the W adjustment. [The initial estimate $N_1(j) = 1950$ was determined by testing $N_1(j) = 2000$ and finding W to be about 50.]

Larger sample sizes than those estimated by (4A.21)–(4A.23) allow the researcher to control at a preselected level for the risk of not finding significant differences between samples when they are present in the initial populations, as well as for the risk of finding significant sample differences when there are no population differences. The modification of (4A.22) that satisfies both conditions for samples of equal sizes is

$$N_1(j) = N_2(j)$$

$$= \frac{\{Z_{(1/2)\alpha}(2_np_j\,_nq_j)^{1/2} - Z_{1-\beta}[_np_{j,\,1}\,_nq_{j,\,1} + _np_{j,\,2}\,_nq_{j,\,2}]^{1/2}\}^2}{(_np_{j,\,1} - _np_{j,\,2})^2} \qquad (4A.24)$$

In the expression, $Z_{1-\beta}$ is the normal deviate corresponding to the (one-tailed) probability of accepting the observed sample difference as significant when a population difference of the magnitude $_np_{j,\,1} - _np_{j,\,2}$ exists. As before, an additional W cases are required for continuity correction. [The reader may consult Fleiss (1981, pp. 44–48) for estimation formulas for unequal sample sizes, which are far more complex.]

Suppose, as before, we want to select equal samples such that a difference of 0.025 in survival rates near $_np_j = 0.5$ would be significant at the 5% level, and we also want the probability to be no more than 5% of not finding a significant difference if the populations do actually differ by 0.025. Then from (4A.24) and (4A.23) the samples would need to be of sizes $N_1(j) = N_2(j) = 7400$, using $Z_{(1/2)\alpha} = 1.96$ and $Z_{1-\beta} = 1.645$. In samples this large, a difference of only 0.01 would be significant at the 5% level; and we would be 95% certain of finding a difference of that magnitude or greater in the samples if in fact they were drawn from populations which differed by at least 0.025 at that duration.

In our example of ages at first marriage (Table 4.16), we observed that surveys in 1971 and 1975 produced estimates of the proportion of women born in 1940–44 who married by age $20\frac{1}{2}$ that differed by about 0.027, the reported proportions being 0.522 in the 1971 survey and 0.495 in the 1975 survey. The difference was significant at the 0.001 level. Among other birth cohorts the reporting was more consistent between the two surveys, although all gave lower figures in 1975 than in 1971. Sample sizes for the 1940–44 birth cohort were 5863 in the 1971 survey and 6906 in the later survey.

These numbers accord nicely with our previous example, and suggest that the samples drawn were about the right size for reasonably assuring that we would find a significant difference if one existed, as well as reasonably assuring that we would not find a significant difference if there was none.*

We refer the reader to George and Desu (1973), Wu *et al.* (1980), and Lachin (1981) for formulas for sample size estimation when cumulative survival differences (l_x) rather than single interval differences ($_np_j$) are to be tested. If interval sample sizes vary and l_x is estimated as the product of a series of $_np_j$ terms [expression (4.12)] not reducible to l_0 $_xp_0$, sample size estimation becomes complex. Lachin suggests the crude adjustment $N(0)_{adj} = N(0)/(1 - r)^2$ for testing significance of l_x differences in samples in which the proportion r leave observation prior to x. In the expression, $N(0)$ is the initial sample size that would be required in the absence of losses.

---

* Explaining the difference in the two survey results is another matter. Within the population the proportion ever-married could not have changed, although the quality of reporting may have, or changes in the sampling frame between the two surveys may have altered the representativeness of the samples. [The overall age distributions of respondents in the 1925–29 through 1945–49 birth cohorts (columns 1 and 2 of Table 4.16) were not significantly different in the two surveys ($p = 0.34$), but that does not preclude other types of compositional changes which might account for the drop in reported proportions ever married at all ages over 20 in every cohort.]

CHAPTER 5

The Life Table II

In composing this Memoir, . . . I was above all concerned to display in a single table the two conditions of mankind, the one as it actually is and the other as it would be if we were able to rid the whole human race of smallpox. I had in mind that the comparison of these two conditions would explain the difference and the contrast between them better than the most ample commentary; but I had in mind, too, the difficulty of the enterprise and the defective nature of the Bills of Mortality, which do not give the age of those carried off by smallpox and were bound to be a serious obstacle to my purpose. I could see immediately that to carry out such a design demands two items of elementary information: what is the risk, at various ages, of being caught by smallpox, for those who have not already had it, and what is the risk, for those who are attacked by it, of dying of it?

—DANIEL BERNOULLI (1766)
Translated by Leslie Bradley (1971)

5.1. INTRODUCTION

Besides total deaths or events, life tables can be disaggregated to provide information on subsets of events that together comprise the total. Two different approaches are used. In *multiple decrement* tables, the number or proportion dying at each age is distributed into categories according to cause of death. By summing across ages, the total population eventually dying of each cause, and their mean age at death, can be estimated.

The multiple decrement table can be extended to states other than death, such as rural and urban residence with migration, or labor force status, in which the number or proportion surviving (l_x) in a given state may either increase or decrease with age. *Increment–decrement* or *multistate* tables are of this type. They largely follow multiple decrement formulas, but with additional terms to allow transitions between attribute states.

Cause-eliminated and *cause-substituted* life tables resolve an important problem in multiple decrement analysis, the effects of competing causes of death on mortality for each single cause. By controlling for competing risks, the tables improve the quality of comparisons across populations where survival differences may be attributable to several causes of death. The tables are also valuable in mortality projections, where they allow the user to specify anticipated changes in single causes of death and to trace their effects on mortality rates for other causes.

The chapter has one appendix, which introduces procedures for data regrouping for the life table. The problem arises in the context of the text example for multistate rates, which is condensed from 5-year interval data in the source article (Tabah, 1968) to 15-year intervals to permit readers to more easily work the example.

Much of the discussion of the chapter will refer to deaths, since that is the context in which multiple decrement and cause-eliminated life tables are most commonly used. The methods apply equally to all other types of terminating events for which life tables are constructed.

5.2. MULTIPLE DECREMENT LIFE TABLES

The life tables considered in the previous chapter were constructed for total deaths or events enumerated by age or by duration of exposure. To separate multiple causes requires that the $_nd_x$ term, life table deaths at ages x to $x + n$, be partitioned into subcategories $_nd_{x,1}, _nd_{x,2}, \ldots, _nd_{x,j}$. That is most often done by distributing the $_nq_{x,j}$ and $_nd_{x,j}$ terms linearly in proportion to observed deaths for each cause, $_nD_{x,j}$. That is,

$$_nq_{x, j, \text{ linear}} = {}_nq_x(_nD_{x, j}/_nD_x) \qquad (5.1)$$

$$_nd_{x, j, \text{ linear}} = l_x\, _nq_{x, j} = {}_nd_x(_nD_{x, j}/_nD_x) \qquad (5.2)$$

The variance of (5.1) is found from the variance of the source $_nq_x$ distribution (Table 4.15) with the substitution of $_np_{x,j}, _nq_{x,j}$ for $_np_x, _nq_x$ in the pq/N form of the expression. In the pq^2/D form, the terms become $_np_{x,j}\, _nq_{x,j}\, _nq_x/_nD_x$.

Table 5.1 illustrates the estimation of $_nd_{x,j}$ terms for the U.S. 1980 life table, using 1980 deaths for neoplasms, major cardiovascular diseases, and all other causes, and the life table $_nd_x$ estimates of Table 4.9.* Beginning at age 0, we have:

---

* The causes of death used are, for neoplasms, codes 140–239, and for major cardiovascular diseases, codes 390–448, from the Ninth Revision, International Classification of Diseases (1975).

Table 5.1. Deaths and Multiple Decrement Life Table Deaths for Neoplasms, Major Cardiovascular Diseases, and Other Causes, United States, 1980

Ages	Deaths				Life table			
	$_nD_x$	$_nD_{x,\,neop}$	$_nD_{x,\,cvd}$	$_nD_{x,\,other}$	$_nd_x$	$_nd_{x,\,neop}$	$_nd_{x,\,cvd}$	$_nd_{x,\,other}$
0	45,526	180	984	44,362	1,266	5	27	1,234
1–4	8,187	611	407	7,169	252	19	12	221
5–14	10,689	1,601	450	8,638	301	45	13	243
15–24	49,027	2,813	1,750	44,464	1,126	65	40	1,021
25–44	108,658	18,010	18,360	72,288	3,306	548	559	2,199
45–64	425,338	137,273	174,585	113,480	16,357	5,279	6,714	4,364
65–74	466,621	128,999	235,800	101,822	20,159	5,573	10,187	4,399
75–84	517,257	96,769	310,704	109,784	28,700	5,369	17,240	6,091
85+	357,970	36,418	245,331	76,221	28,533	2,903	19,555	6,075
Total (l_0, $l_{0,j}$)					100,000	19,806	54,347	25,847

$$_1 d_{0, \text{ neoplasms}} = {}_1 d_0({}_1 D_{0, \text{ neop}} / {}_1 D_0) = 1266(180/45{,}526) = 5.0$$

$$_1 d_{0, \text{ cvd}} = {}_1 d_0({}_1 D_{0, \text{ cvd}} / {}_1 D_0) = 1266(984/45{,}526) = 27.4$$

$$_1 d_{0, \text{ other}} = {}_1 d_0({}_1 D_{0, \text{ other}} / {}_1 D_0) = 1266(44{,}362/45{,}526) = 1233.6$$

The reader may check the ${}_n d_{x, j}$ estimates at other ages. Since the example includes all causes of death, the reader can confirm that ${}_n d_x = \Sigma_j \, {}_n d_{x, j}$.

The ${}_n d_{x, j}$ terms are used to estimate the proportion of the life table population that dies from each cause of death at ages up to age x and at ages after x. For ages up to x we have,

$$_x d_{0, j} = \sum_{a=0}^{x-n} {}_n d_{a, j} \tag{5.3}$$

and for ages x and above,

$$_{\omega-x} d_{x, j} = \sum_{a=x}^{\omega-n} {}_n d_{a, j} \tag{5.4}$$

Expression (5.4) uses ω (the term ∞ is also used) to represent the oldest age to which anyone lives in the life table.

The sum of the ${}_n d_{x, j}$ terms across all ages, found by adding (5.3) and (5.4), represents all life table deaths for the jth cause. It is also the number of persons who eventually die of cause j from among the l_0 births that begin the life table. The probability that an individual dies of the jth cause is therefore

$$_\omega q_{0, j} = \sum_{a=0}^{\omega-n} {}_n d_{a, j} \Big/ l_0 = {}_\omega d_{0, j} / l_0 \tag{5.5}$$

The ${}_n d_{x, j}$ series can also be used to construct a conditional life table, showing the survival distribution for individuals who eventually die of one cause, by defining the initial population $l_{0, j}$ to be

$$l_{0, j} = {}_\omega d_{0, j} = \sum_{a=0}^{\omega-n} {}_n d_{a, j} \tag{5.6}$$

Table 5.1 displays the summations of the ${}_n d_{x, j}$ terms, which yield the totals: $l_{0, \text{ neop}} = 19{,}806$, $l_{0, \text{ cvd}} = 54{,}347$, and $l_{0, \text{ other}} = 25{,}847$. The reader can confirm that ${}_\omega d_0 = l_0 = 100{,}000 = \Sigma_j \, l_{0, j}$. The $l_{0, j}$ estimates inform us that of 100,000 persons born, 20% would eventually die from neoplasms, 54% from cardiovascular diseases, and 26% from other causes at 1980 survival probabilities. [At age 65 the proportions become 18%, 61%, and 21%. The proportions at the two ages are similar, since only about one-fourth of deaths ($_{65}q_0 = 0.22608$) occur before age 65.]

Having found $l_{0,j}$, the life table population eventually dying of the jth cause, we estimate the number of survivors for the cause at subsequent ages $l_{x,j}$ by subtraction of the $_nd_{x,j}$ terms. That is,

$$l_{x+n,j} = l_{x,j} - {_nd_{x,j}} \qquad (5.7)$$

The $l_{x,j}$ series is exactly like the l_x series of the ordinary life table, except that it describes the survival experience of persons eventually dying of a particular cause j.

For the conditional table, the life table population in the age interval x to $x + n$, $_nL_{x,j}$, can be constructed from the $l_{x,j}$ series using (4.15), (4.16), or one of the $_nL_x$ formulas of Section 6.2.* A problem arises in estimating the final $_nL_x$ term $_{\omega-f}L_{f,j}$, since the proportion of deaths due to each cause is known, but not the ages within the interval at which deaths for each cause peak.

One possibility for the final interval is to let the conditional life expectancy at f, $e_{f,j}$, be the same for all causes. In that event,

$$_{\omega-f}L_{f,j,\text{ linear}} = l_{f,j}\, e_f \qquad (5.8)$$

Expression (5.8) will usually be adequate when the proportion surviving at the final age f is small. It may not be when the proportion is high, since for many causes of death it is manifestly wrong. An alternative solution is to assume that deaths for the jth cause in the final interval follow the age pattern of deaths in the preceding interval, given by $_na_{f-n,j}$. We set:

---

* Since $_nL_{x,j}$ represents individuals at ages x to $x + n$ who will die of the jth cause at some point, the sum of the $_nL_{x,j}$ terms for all causes will be the complete life table population in the interval, $_nL_x$. That is:

$$_nL_x = \sum_j {_nL_{x,j}}$$

The equality will be exact if $_nL_x$ and all $_nL_{x,j}$ terms are estimated linearly, but will only be approximate for most other $_nL_x$ formulas. If the error is nontrivial, the $_nL_{x,j}$ terms should be rescaled to sum to $_nL_x$, and the adjusted $_nL_{x,j}$ terms checked to ensure that $l_{x,j} \geq ({_nL_{x,j}}/n) \geq l_{x+n,j}$. [Rescaling the terms $(nl_{x,j} - {_nL_{x,j}})$, which represent the time lived in the interval by individuals dying between x and $x + n$, to sum to $(nl_x - {_nL_x})$ will assure that the inequality is satisfied.]

$$_{\omega-f}L_{f,\ j,\ n}a_x = k l_{f,\ j\ n}a_{f-n,\ j} \tag{5.9}$$

where k is estimated as

$$k = {}_{\omega-f}L_f \Big/ \Big[\sum_j l_{f,\ j\ n}a_{f-n,\ j} \Big]$$

Expression (5.9) reduces to (5.8) when the terms $_nL_{f-n,j}$ are estimated linearly using (4.15).

When the user is unsure as to an appropriate estimate for $_{\omega-f}L_{f,j}$, he or she may omit $_{\omega-f}L_{f,j}$ and construct the partial life expectancy $_{f-x}e_{x,j}$ for ages x to f in place of the complete life expectancy $e_{x,j}$.

Construction of the life expectancy is by the formulas of Chapter 4, with the substitution of the conditional terms $l_{x,j}$ and $_nL_{x,j}$ for the ordinary life table quantities l_x and $_nL_x$.

Table 5.2 displays multiple decrement survival distributions for neoplasms, major cardiovascular diseases, and other causes for the United States in 1980, using the $_nd_{x,j}$ series of Table 5.1. [The table is constructed by the linear formulas of Chapter 4, and therefore uses (5.8) to estimate $_{\omega-f}L_{f,j}$.] We have added the term $l^*_{x,\ j} = l_{x,j}(100{,}000/l_{0,j})$, which rescales the $l_{x,j}$ series to the radix 100,000. The rescaling is not necessary to the table, but simplifies comparison of rates of population attrition for each cause.

Since the multiple decrement life table is a device for partitioning the ordinary life table into component tables for various causes of death, a number of relationships link the two types of tables. At all ages $l_x = \sum_j l_{x,j}$ and $_nL_x = \sum_j {_nL_{x,j}}$. From these relationships, for the total life expectancy and jth cause life expectancy we have:

$$e_x = \sum_j (l_{x,j}\ e_{x,\ j})/l_x$$

In words, the life expectancy for a population is the average of the multiple decrement life expectancies for the separate causes of death, weighted by the proportions $(l_{x,j}/l_x)$ dying of each cause. Thus, the life expectancies at birth for those dying of the three groups of causes in Table 5.2 are 70.5, 78.5, and 65.4 years. For the overall life expectancy we have:

$$e_0 = \sum_j (l_{0,j}\ e_{0,j})/l_0$$

$$= [(19{,}806)(70.5) + (54{,}347)(78.5)$$

$$+ (25{,}847)(65.4)]/100{,}000 = 73.5$$

Table 5.2. Multiple Decrement Life Table for Neoplasms, Major Cardiovascular Diseases, and Other Causes, United States 1980

a. Neoplasms

Multiple decrement

Ages	$_nd_{x,\,neop}$	$l_{x,\,neop}$	$_nL_{x,\,neop}$	$e_{x,\,neop}$	$l^{*}_{x,\,neop}$
0	5	19,806	19,802	70.5	100,000
1–4	19	19,801	79,158	69.5	99,975
5–14	45	19,782	197,595	65.6	99,879
15–24	65	19,737	197,045	55.7	99,652
25–44	548	19,672	387,960	45.9	99,323
45–64	5279	19,124	329,690	26.9	96,557
65–74	5573	13,845	110,585	13.3	69,903
75–84	5369	8,272	55,875	9.0	41,765
85+	2903	2,903	18,289	6.3	14,657

b. Cardiovascular diseases

Multiple decrement

Ages	$_nd_{x,\,cvd}$	$l_{x,\,cvd}$	$_nL_{x,\,cvd}$	$e_{x,\,cvd}$	$l^{*}_{x,\,cvd}$
0	27	54,347	54,323	78.5	100,000
1–4	12	54,320	217,251	77.6	99,950
5–14	13	54,308	543,015	73.6	99,928
15–24	40	54,295	542,750	63.6	99,904
25–44	559	54,255	1,079,510	53.6	99,831
45–64	6,714	53,696	1,006,780	34.1	98,802
65–74	10,187	46,982	418,885	17.5	86,448
75–84	17,240	36,795	281,750	11.0	67,704
85+	19,555	19,555	123,196	6.3	35,982

c. All other causes

Multiple decrement

Ages	$_nd_{x,\,other}$	$l_{x,\,other}$	$_nL_{x,\,other}$	$e_{x,\,other}$	$l^{*}_{x,\,other}$
0	1234	25,847	24,767	65.4	100,000
1–4	221	24,613	97,922	67.7	95,226
5–14	243	24,392	242,705	64.3	94,371
15–24	1021	24,149	236,385	54.9	93,431
25–44	2199	23,128	440,570	47.1	89,480
45–64	4364	20,929	374,940	31.0	80,973
65–74	4399	16,565	143,655	16.5	64,089
75–84	6091	12,166	91,205	10.6	47,069
85+	6075	6,075	38,272	6.3	23,504

Continued on next page

Table 5.2. Continued

Formulas:

$$_n d_{x,j,\text{linear}} = {}_n d_x \left({}_n D_{x,j} / {}_n D_x \right)$$

$$l_{0,j} = {}_\omega d_{0,j} = \sum_{a=0}^{\omega-n} {}_n d_{a,j} / l_0$$

$$l_{x+n,j} = l_{x,j} - {}_n d_{x,j}$$

$$l^*_{x,j} = l_{x,j} \left(100{,}000 / l_{0,j} \right)$$

$$_n L_{x,j,\text{linear}} = n \left(l_{x,j} + l_{x+n,j} \right) / 2$$

$$_{\omega-f} L_{f,j,\text{linear}} = l_{f,j}\, e_f$$

$$e_{x,j} = \left(\sum_{a \geq x} {}_n L_{a,j} \right) / l_{x,j}$$

Figure 5.1 displays the multiple decrement $l_{x,j}$ distributions as they appear in Table 5.2 and rescaled to the radix $l_{0,j} = 100{,}000$. In the rescaled series the differences in ages at death for the three groups of causes are pronounced. The long life expectancies of persons dying of cardiovascular diseases (78.5 years) and neoplasms (70.5 years) will be seen to be due to the rarity of deaths for these causes before about age 40, in contrast to the fairly steady losses that occur from birth onward for other causes ($e_0 = 65.4$ years). If the other cause group were disaggregated, life expectancies would be about 40 years for accidental deaths and homicides, only a few months for causes of death associated with infancy, and 65 or more years for most other causes.

To this point our discussion of multiple decrement life tables has been restricted to populations followed to age or duration ω (in Table 5.1 the open-ended interval 85+), beyond which no individuals survive. The researcher will sometimes need tables truncated at an earlier duration f, as in the single decrement examples of Tables 4.1 and 4.8 (breast cancer) and Table 4.13 (first marriage). No problems arise in such tables if the ultimate distribution of events by cause is known and the terms $_{\omega-f} d_{f,j} = l_{f,j}$ can be estimated, but where information is incomplete the user is at a loss.

In that circumstance, the table can be constructed only by defining a new event category $_{\omega-f} D_{f,u} = N(f) - \sum_j {}_{\omega-f} D_{f,j}$, comprising events in (f, ω) unassigned by cause. The *incomplete multiple decrement life table* that is then constructed will have initial terms $l_{0,j-}$ distributing attributable events, and the residual $l_{0,u}$ comprising deaths for which the cause is undetermined. The correct initial values $l_{0,j}$ remain unknown, but satisfy the equality $\sum_j l_{0,j} = l_0$ and the inequalities $l_{0,j-} \leq l_{0,j} \leq (l_{0,j-} + l_{0,u})$. That is, the correct initial terms will not be less than the values estimated in the table, nor can any be greater than its estimated value plus the unattributed residual. The reader can confirm the inequality by assigning deaths after age 75 in Tables 4.9 and 5.1 to the category $_{\omega-75} d_{75,\text{unattrib}} = l_{75} = 57{,}233$. He or she will then find $l_{0,\text{neop}-} = 11{,}534$;

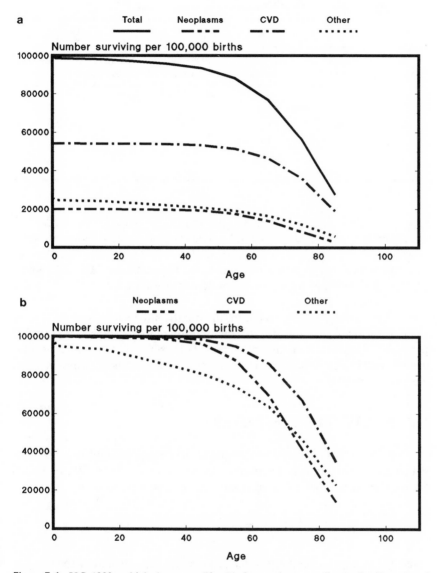

Figure 5.1. U.S. 1980 multiple decrement life table for neoplasms, cardiovascular diseases, and all other causes of death: (a) cause-specific survival distribution and (b) rescaled single cause estimates.

Table 5.3. Survival Status of Breast Cancer Patients First Seen between 1956 and 1961, with Inclusion of Unattributable Deaths. *Source:* Drolette (1975)

Start of interval (x)	Total			Right-censored	
	Number at risk	Recorded deaths	Subsequent deaths	Number at risk	Recorded deaths
0	350	74	0	0	0
1	276	48	0	45	1
2	184	31	0	50	0
3	103	10	0	36	1
4	58	4	26	28	0
ω	0				

$l_{0, \text{cvd}-} = 17,552$; $l_{0, \text{other}-} = 13,681$; and $l_{0, \text{unattrib}} = 57,233$. The reader will note from the example that if we did not have cause of death information for ages beyond 75, over half of life table deaths would be unattributable. The incomplete multiple decrement life table for breast cancer (Table 4.1) with unattributed mortality after year 4 is presented as Tables 5.3 and 5.4. In Table 5.4, unattributed mortality is set equal to the number of survivors at study completion (time 5.0). By its nature the unattributed event count is uncensored. From Table 5.4, the life table distribution of total deaths becomes 6377 per 10,000 diagnosed patients, with 0 to 3623 possible additional breast cancer deaths, and 3623 to 0 possible deaths for other causes. These numbers might have been found directly from Table 4.8.

5.3. MULTISTATE LIFE TABLES

For events other than death, multiple decrement life tables can be constructed that allow transfers between attribute states. In the *multistate* model the number of survivors with attribute j at age $x + n$ is given by

$$l_{x+n, j} = \sum_i l_{x, i} \, {}_np_{x, i \to j} \, {}_nt_{x, i \to j} \tag{5.10}$$

where ${}_nt_{x, i \to j}$ represents the transfer probability from all states i to state j as indicated by the direction arrow, and ${}_np_{x, i \to j}$ is the associated survival probability. As in the ordinary multiple decrement table, $l_{x+n} = \sum_j l_{x+n, j}$. However, with the occurrence of transfers, $l_{x+n, j}$ may be greater or smaller than $l_{x, j}$.

The transfer probabilities ${}_nt_{x, i \to j}$ are estimated from available data sources, usually censuses or surveys, or from model distributions. All are *restricted*

Table 5.4. Life Table for the Data of Table 5.3, Using $_np_{x, \text{curtate sample}}$

Int. (x)	Uncensored Number at risk	Uncensored Events	Probability of survival from x to $x+1$ $_1p_x$	Number alive at x l_x	Deaths between x and $x+1$ $_1d_x$	Neoplasms $_1d_{x,\text{neop}-}$	Neoplasms $l_{x,\text{neop}-}$	Unattributed $_1d_{x,\text{un}}$	Unattributed $l_{x,\text{un}}$
0	350	74	0.7886	10,000	2114	2114	6377	0	3623
1	231	47	0.7965	7,886	1605	1605	4263	0	3623
2	134	31	0.7687	6,281	1453	1453	2658	0	3623
3	67	9	0.8657	4,828	648	648	1205	0	3623
4	30	4	0.8667	4,179	557	557	557	0	3623
5	26			3,623	3623	0	0	3623	3623

probabilities in the important sense that they estimate the proportion of the population observed at one location at time t and observed at the same or a different location at time $t + n$, using the survival terms $_np_x$ to adjust for mortality. Intermediate transfers, as $i \rightarrow k \rightarrow j$, are subsumed into the general category of $i \rightarrow j$ transfers, with the result that only part of the population flow is recorded in the model. The reader will recognize that information is lost whenever interval widths n are wide enough to encompass multiple moves.

The method may be illustrated by a simplified version of a model by Tabah (1968), in which he projected transfers between economic activity and inactivity and between rural and urban residence for Mexico, using 1960 population estimates. Tabah's source data are displayed in Appendix Table 5A.1 and are regrouped from 5-year to 15-year ages in Table 5.5 to simplify calculations for readers wanting to work the example. Appendix 5A.1 discusses the methodology for the regroupings.

The data in Table 5A.1 include 1960 census distributions for the urban and rural economically inactive and active male populations ($_5N_x$). These are recentered from ages 0–4, 5–9, 10–14, . . . , to ages 0–$7\frac{1}{2}$, $7\frac{1}{2}$–$22\frac{1}{2}$, $22\frac{1}{2}$–$37\frac{1}{2}$, . . . , in Table 5.5 to facilitate calculation of labor force transfer probabilities. (The initial interval 0–$7\frac{1}{2}$ represents ages near birth, for which the proportion economically active is 0. Later intervals are centered at exact ages 15, 30, 45, 60 and 75.) The source table also displays net migration estimates from rural (r) and urban (u) residential distributions in the 1950 and 1960 censuses ($_5t_{x+2.5,\, r \rightarrow u}$), and survival estimates ($_5S_{x+2.5}$) for 1960–1964 from life tables computed by Benitez and Cabrera (1966). The latter terms are estimated as

Table 5.5. Mexican 1960 Male Population by Residence; Ages Grouped for Estimating Life Table Labor Force Transitions

	1960 urban population			1960 rural population		
Ages	Inactive $_nN_{x,\,u,\,i}$	Active $_nN_{x,\,u,\,a}$	Proportion active[a] $_n\nu_{x,\,u,\,a}$	Inactive $_nN_{x,\,r,\,i}$	Active $_nN_{x,\,r,\,a}$	Proportion active[a] $_n\nu_{x,\,r,\,a}$
0–$7\frac{1}{2}$	2,373,800	0	0.0000	2,446,150	0	0.0000
$7\frac{1}{2}$–$22\frac{1}{2}$	1,993,450	951,650	0.3231	1,745,250	1,367,000	0.4392
$22\frac{1}{2}$–$37\frac{1}{2}$	119,400	1,622,650	0.9315	114,150	1,602,550	0.9335
$37\frac{1}{2}$–$52\frac{1}{2}$	44,850	988,100	0.9566	49,550	942,350	0.9500
$52\frac{1}{2}$–$67\frac{1}{2}$	61,150	495,050	0.8901	39,400	533,000	0.9312
$67\frac{1}{2}$–$82\frac{1}{2}$	135,950	94,350	0.4097	97,800	123,800	0.5587
$82\frac{1}{2}$+	0	0	0.0000	26,100	0	0.0000

[a] $_n\nu_{x,\,u,\,a} = {_nN_{x,\,u,\,a}}/({_nN_{x,\,u,\,i}} + {_nN_{x,\,u,\,a}})$.

$_5S_{x+2.5} = {}_5L_{x+5}/{}_5L_x$ [expression (4.18)], and represent life table survival from the age interval $(x, x + 5)$ to the interval $(x + 5, x + 10)$.

Table 5.6 displays survival and migration probabilities for the example, also from Appendix 5A.1. For the transfer probabilities between activity (a) and inactivity (i) in the table we adopt the conventions suggested by Tabah:

$$
_nl_{x,\ i\to a} = \begin{cases} 0 \\ \quad |\, x \geq \mu_x \quad or \quad {}_n\nu_{x+(1/2)n,\ a} \leq {}_n\nu_{x-(1/2)n,\ a} \\ \left({}_n\nu_{x+(1/2)n,\ a} - {}_n\nu_{x-(1/2)n,\ a}\right)/\left(1 - {}_n\nu_{x-(1/2)n,\ a}\right) \\ \quad |\, x < \mu_x \quad and \quad {}_n\nu_{x+(1/2)n,\ a} > {}_n\nu_{x-(1/2)n,\ a} \end{cases}
$$

$$(5.11)$$

$$
_nl_{x,\ a\to i} = \begin{cases} 0 \\ \quad |\, x < \mu_x \quad or \quad {}_n\nu_{x+(1/2)n,\ a} \geq {}_n\nu_{x-(1/2)n,\ a} \\ \left({}_n\nu_{x-(1/2)n,\ a} - {}_n\nu_{x+(1/2)n,\ a}\right)/\left({}_n\nu_{x-(1/2)n,\ a}\right) \\ \quad |\, x \geq \mu_x \quad and \quad {}_n\nu_{x+(1/2)n,\ a} < {}_n\nu_{x-(1/2)n,\ a} \end{cases}
$$

$$_nl_{x,\ i\to i} = 1 - {}_nl_{x,\ i\to a}$$

$$_nl_{x,\ a\to a} = 1 - {}_nl_{x,\ a\to i}$$

In the expression, the terms $_n\nu_{x,j} = {}_nN_{x,j}/{}_nN_x$ are the proportions of the population ages x to $x + n$ with attribute j, and the term μ_x is the mean age in

Table 5.6. 15-Year $_np_x$ Terms and Transfer Probabilities for the Data of Tables 5.5 and 5A.1

	Urban population			Rural population			
	Life table	Probability of remaining		Life table	Probability of remaining		Net out migration
Ages	$_np_{x,\,u}$	Inactive $_nl_{x,\,u,\,i\to i}$	Active $_nl_{x,\,u,\,a\to a}$	$_np_{x,\,r}$	Inactive $_nl_{x,\,r,\,i\to i}$	Active $_nl_{x,\,r,\,a\to a}$	$_nl_{x,\,r\to u}$
0–14	0.9582	0.6769	1.0000	0.9056	0.5608	1.0000	0.2172
15–29	0.9479	0.1013	1.0000	0.9138	0.1186	1.0000	0.2390
30–44	0.9007	0.6335	1.0000	0.8408	0.7513	1.0000	0.2137
45–59	0.7584	1.0000	0.9305	0.7125	1.0000	0.9801	0.1835
60–74	0.4000	1.0000	0.4603	0.4101	1.0000	0.6000	0.1619
75+	0.0000	1.0000	0.0000	0.0000	1.0000	0.0000	0.0279

the population. [It is used to differentiate between conventions at young and old ages. For the inactive population, the probability of becoming active is set to 0 at ages $x \geq \mu_x$, since at these ages the proportion active is constant or decreasing. For the active population, the probability of becoming inactive is set to 0 at young ages ($x < \mu_x$), where the proportion active would be expected to be increasing.]

Applying (5.11), for the urban population the activity transition probabilities from birth to age 15 are given by

$$_{15}t_{0, \text{ u, i}\to\text{a}} = \left(_{15}\nu_{7.5, \text{ u, a}} - _{7.5}\nu_{0, \text{ u, a}}\right)/\left(1 - _{7.5}\nu_{0, \text{ u, a}}\right)$$

$$= (0.3231 - 0)/(1 - 0) = 0.3231$$

$$_{15}t_{0, \text{ u, a}\to\text{i}} = 0$$

$$_{15}t_{0, \text{ u, i}\to\text{i}} = 1 - 0.3231 = 0.6769$$

$$_{15}t_{0, \text{ u, a}\to\text{a}} = 1 - 0 = 1$$

The labor force transition probabilities at ages 15 to 30 are shown in Appendix 5A.1. The reader may calculate the estimates for the older urban population and the rural population, which should agree with Table 5.6.

Using the Table 5.6 estimates for survival, migration, and labor force transitions, the construction of multistate life tables for urban and rural Mexico follows easily using (5.10). Since urban and rural survival probabilities and labor force activity rates differ, however, we will need to make a judgment as to whether migrants should share the survival and activity probabilities of their rural origin or urban destination for the interval in which they migrate.*

For survival an intermediate probability may be reasonable, of which the simplest will be the geometric mean of the two probabilities:

$$_{n}p_{x, \text{ r}\to\text{u, exp}} = \left(_{n}p_{x, \text{ r}} \, _{n}p_{x, \text{ u}}\right)^{1/2} \tag{5.12}$$

For labor force activity we will follow Tabah in using the probabilities of the sending area (here, rural probabilities) for the interval of migration.

With these conventions and setting† $l_{0, \text{u,i}} = l_{0, \text{r,i}} = 10{,}000$ we have the urban and rural life table distributions of Table 5.7. (The nonmigrant and

---

* Additional life tables will be needed if migrants are assumed to remain distinct from other urban residents beyond the interval in which they migrate.

† We select 10,000 rather than 100,000 for the radix for consistency with the three- to four-digit precision of the survival and migration probabilities in the source article.

migrant distributions are estimated separately, since the increment added to the urban population by migration from rural areas will depend on the number of life table births in each area. Actual urban and rural births were approximately equal in 1960, but the life table is not restricted to that circumstance, and rescaling the proportions is tedious once the tables are merged.)

Table 5.7 displays the $l_{x,j}$ series for the example. Checking a few entries more or less at random, we have:

(Table 5.7b) $l_{30,\,r,\,a} = l_{15,\,r,\,a}\ _{15}p_{15,\,r}\ _{15}t_{15,\,r,\,a\to a}\ _{15}t_{15,\,r\to r}$

$+\ l_{15,\,r,\,i}\ _{15}p_{15,\,r}\ _{15}t_{15,\,r,\,i\to a}\ _{15}t_{15,\,r\to r}$

$= (3114)(0.9138)(1.0000)(0.7610)$

$+\ (3976)(0.9138)(0.8814)(0.7610)$

$= 4602.5 \to 4602$

(Table 5.7a) $l_{45,\,u,\,i} = l_{30,\,u,\,i}\ _{15}p_{30,\,u}\ _{15}t_{30,\,u,\,i\to i}$

$+\ l_{30,\,u,\,a}\ _{15}p_{30,\,u}\ _{15}t_{30,\,u,\,a\to i}$

$= (623)(0.9007)(0.6335)$

$+\ (8460)(0.9007)(0.0000)$

$= 355.5 \to 355$

(Table 5.7c) $l_{45,\,u,\,i} = l_{30,\,u,\,i}\ _{15}p_{30,\,u}\ _{15}t_{30,\,u,\,i\to i}$

$+\ l_{30,\,r,\,i}\ _{15}p_{30,\,r\to u}\ _{15}t_{30,\,r,\,i\to i}\ _{15}t_{30,\,r\to u}$

$+\ l_{30,\,r,\,a}\ _{15}p_{30.\,r\to u}\ _{15}t_{30,\,r,\,a\to i}\ _{15}t_{30,\,r\to u}$

$+\ l_{30,\,u,\,a}\ _{15}p_{30,\,u}\ _{15}t_{30,\,u,\,a\to i}$

$= (214)(0.9007)(0.6335)$

$+\ (328)(0.8702)(0.7513)(0.2137)$

$+\ (4602)(0.8702)(0.0000)(0.2137)$

Table 5.7. Multistate Life Tables for the Data of Tables 5.5 and 5.6

a. Resident urban population

Age	Inactive population $l_{x,u,i}$	Survivors remaining inactive	Transfers from active population	Active population $l_{x,u,a}$	Survivors remaining active	Transfers from inactive population
0	10,000	6486	0	0	0	3096
15	6,486	623	0	3096	2935	5525
30	623	355	0	8460	7620	206
45	355	269	412	7826	5523	0
60	681	272	1192	5523	1017	0
75	1,464	0	0	1017	0	0

Formulas:

Survivors remaining inactive $= l_{x,u,i}\ {}_nP_{x,u}\ {}_nl_{x,u,i\to i}$

Transfers from active $= l_{x,u,a}\ {}_nP_{x,u}\ {}_nl_{x,u,a\to i}$

Survivors remaining active $= l_{x,u,a}\ {}_nP_{x,u}\ {}_nl_{x,u,a\to a}$

Transfers from inactive $= l_{x,u,i}\ {}_nP_{x,u}\ {}_nl_{x,u,i\to a}$

b. Resident rural population

Age	Inactive population $l_{x,r,i}$	Survivors remaining inactive	Transfers from active population	Active population $l_{x,r,a}$	Survivors remaining active	Transfers from inactive population
0	10,000	3976	0	0	0	3114
15	3,976	328	0	3114	2165	2437
30	328	163	0	4602	3042	54
45	163	95	36	3096	1765	0
60	131	45	243	1765	364	0
75	288	0	0	364	0	0

Formulas:

Survivors remaining inactive $= l_{x,r,i} \, _np_{x,r} \, _n t_{x,r,i\to i} \, _n t_{x,r\to r}$

Transfers from active $= l_{x,r,a} \, _np_{x,r} \, _n t_{x,r,a\to i} \, _n t_{x,r\to r}$

Survivors remaining active $= l_{x,r,i} \, _np_{x,r} \, _n t_{x,r,a\to a} \, _n t_{x,r\to r}$

Transfers from inactive $= l_{x,r,i} \, _np_{x,r} \, _n t_{x,r,i\to a} \, _n t_{x,r\to r}$

c. Rural-to-urban migrant population

Age	Inactive pop. $l_{x,u,i}$	Survivors remaining inactive	Transfers from Rural Inact.	Transfers from Rural Act.	Urban act.	Active pop. $l_{x,u,a}$	Survivors remaining active	Transfers from Rural Inact.	Transfers from Rural Act.	Urban inact.
0	0	0	1135	0	0	0	0	889	0	0
15	1135	109	105	0	0	889	843	780	693	967
30	214	122	46	0	0	3283	2957	15	856	71
45	168	127	22	8	206	3899	2751	0	409	0
60	363	145	9	46	682	3160	582	0	69	0
75	882	0	0	0	0	651	0	0	0	0

Formulas:

$_np_{x,r\to u} = (_np_{x,r} \, _np_{x,u})^{1/2}$

Urban inactive population:

Survivors remaining inactive $= l_{x,u,i} \, _np_{x,u} \, _n t_{x,u,i\to i}$

Transfers from rural inactive $= l_{x,r,i} \, _np_{x,r\to u} \, _n t_{x,r,i\to i} \, _n t_{x,r\to u}$

Transfers from rural active $= l_{x,r,a} \, _np_{x,r\to u} \, _n t_{x,r,a\to i} \, _n t_{x,r\to u}$

Transfers from urban active $= l_{x,u,a} \, _np_{x,u} \, _n t_{x,u,a\to i}$

Urban active population:

Survivors remaining active $= l_{x,u,a} \, _np_{x,u} \, _n t_{x,u,a\to a}$

Transfers from rural inactive $= l_{x,r,i} \, _np_{x,r\to u} \, _n t_{x,r,i\to a} \, _n t_{x,r\to u}$

Transfers from rural active $= l_{x,r,a} \, _np_{x,r\to u} \, _n t_{x,r,a\to a} \, _n t_{x,r\to u}$

Transfers from urban inactive $= l_{x,u,i} \, _np_{x,u} \, _n t_{x,u,i\to a}$

$$+ (3283)(0.9007)(0.0000)$$

$$= 167.9 \rightarrow 168$$

For a life table population with $l_{0, u, i} = 10,000$ and $l_{0, r, i} = 6000$ entrants, Table 5.7a and 5.7c produce the combined estimate $l_{45, u, i} = 364.7 + (6000/10,000)(169.8) = 466.6 \rightarrow 467$ males surviving and in the inactive urban population at age 45.0.

To estimate the life table population $_nL_{x, j}$ from the $l_{x, j}$ series we may use (4.15) or (4.16), or one of the formulas of Section 6.2.*

Alternatively, we may estimate $_nL_x$ and use the proportion of the source population in the attribute state j, $_nN_{x, j}/_nN_x$, to partition $_nL_x$ into attribute subgroups $_nL_{x, j}$. We exploit the approximate equality

$$_nL_{x, j} \simeq {_nL_x}(_nN_{x, j}/_nN_x) \qquad (5.13)$$

[We note for the reader that using the linear relationship $l_{x+(1/2)n, j, \text{linear}} = {_nL_{x, j}}/n$, we also have the virtual life table estimator, expression (4.42),

$$l_{x+(1/2)n, j, \text{linear}} = {_nL_{x, j}}/n \simeq {_nL_x}(_nN_{x, j}/_nN_x)/n$$

The expression might be used to construct conventional multiple decrement life tables, except that the population $_nN_{x, j}$ eventually dying or terminating due to cause j is rarely known before the fact.]

After calculating the $_nL_{x, j}$ terms they should be checked for consistency with $l_{x, j}$. If the interval $(x, x + n)$ does not contain a distribution peak or minimum, the unit population $_nL_{x, j}/n$ should satisfy the inequality

$$greater\ of\ \{l_{x, j}, l_{x+n, j}\} \geq {_nL_{x, j}}/n \geq lesser\ of\ \{l_{x, j}, l_{x+n, j}\} \qquad (5.14)$$

In conventional (decrement) life tables the constraint holds for all $_nL_{x, j}$.

Table 5.8 displays the residence and occupation distribution of Table 5A.1, grouped into 15-year ages for use with (5.13). The regrouping in Table 5.8 is conventional, since we do not require estimates of transfers across in-

---

* Land and Schoen (1982, pp. 285–290) also find $_nL_x$ by fitting a quadratic through l_x, $l_{x+(1/2)n}$, and l_{x+n}, where $l_{x+(1/2)n}$ is estimated nonlinearly. The integral of the quadratic gives their expression (2.26):

$$_nL_{x, \text{quadratic}} = n(l_x + 4l_{x+(1/2)n} + l_{x+n})/6$$

We have introduced other polynomial estimators in Section 2.2.

Table 5.8. Mexican 1960 Male Population by Residence, with Ages Grouped for $_nL_{x,j}$ Estimation

Ages	1960 urban population			1960 rural population		
	Inactive $_nN_{x,u,i}$	Active $_nN_{x,u,a}$	Proportion active	Inactive $_nN_{x,r,i}$	Active $_nN_{x,r,a}$	Proportion active
0–14	4,015,000	73,800	0.0180	4,035,000	250,900	0.0585
15–29	428,100	1,780,400	0.8062	228,500	2,022,200	0.8985
30–44	69,600	1,288,400	0.9487	70,600	1,239,900	0.9461
45–59	44,900	742,300	0.9430	40,200	721,300	0.9472
60–74	74,500	266,900	0.7818	39,300	334,400	0.8948
75+	96,500	0	0.0000	104,800	0	0.0000

tervals to partition $_nL_x$. In Table 5.9 we construct $_nL_x$ and complete the partitioning into $_nL_{x,j}$. We also find $_nL_{x,j}$ by (4.15) for comparison with the source table estimates. [We omit $_\infty L_{75}$, for which an estimate of annual deaths is required. See expression (4.38).]

In comparing the two $_nL_{x,j}$ series, the source data estimate is seen to be out of the range given by (5.14) in one case (nonmigrant active rural population ages 15–29), where the estimate using (5.13), $_{15}L_{15, r, a, source}/15$, exceeds both $l_{15, r, a}$ and $l_{30, r, a}$. The interval may be a distribution peak, but is not necessarily one. If we decide it is not, we correct $_{15}L_{15, r, a}$ to a value no greater than the larger of the boundary values $l_{15, r, a}$, $l_{30, r, a}$. The larger term is $l_{30, r, a}$ = 4602, which limits $_{15}L_{15, r, a}$ to no more than 15 × 4602 = 69,030. Since $_{15}L_{15, r}$ = 90,150, for the limiting value $_{15}L_{15, r, a}$ = 69,030, $_{15}L_{15, r, i}$ will equal 21,120, which is within the correct range for the inactive population. For

Table 5.9. Linear and Source Data $_nL_{x,j}$ Estimates for the Data of Tables 5.5–5.8[a]

Ages	l_x	$_nL_{x, linear}$	$_nL_{x, i, linear}$	$_nL_{x, i, source}$	$_nL_{x, a, linear}$	$_nL_{x, a, source}$
		a. Resident urban population				
0–14	10,000	146,865	123,645	144,221	23,220	2,644
15–29	9,582	139,987	53,317	27,129	86,670	112,858
30–44	9,083	129,480	7,335	6,642	122,145	122,838
45–59	8,181	107,887	7,770	6,150	100,117	101,737
60–74	6,204	65,137	16,087	14,213	49,050	50,924
75+	2,481	(20,657)				
		b. Resident rural population				
0–14	10,000	128,175	104,820	120,677	23,355	7,498
15–29	7,090	90,150	32,280	9,150	57,870	81,000[b]
30–44	4,930	61,417	3,682	3,310	57,735	58,107
45–59	3,259	38,662	2,205	2,041	36,457	36,621
60–74	1,896	19,110	3,142	2,010	15,968	17,100
75+	652	(5,429)				
		c. Rural-to-urban migrant population				
0–14	0	15,180	8,513	14,907	6,667	273
15–29	2,024	41,407	10,117	8,025	31,290	33,382
30–44	3,497	56,730	2,865	2,910	53,865	53,820
45–59	4,067	56,925	3,982	3,245	52,943	53,680
60–74	3,523	37,920	9,337	8,274	28,583	29,646
75+	1,533	(12,764)				

[a] The tables include the estimates $_{\omega-75}L_{75} = l_{75} e_{75} = 8.326 \, l_{75}$, from Keyfitz and Flieger (1968, p. 118).
[b] This estimate is outside the expected range for increment–decrement life tables: *greater of* $\{l_{x,j}, l_{x+n,j}\} \geq {}_nL_{x,j}/n \geq$ *lesser of* $\{l_{x,j}, l_{x+n,j}\}$. See text.

other ages and other subpopulations, both sets of $_nL_{x,j}$ estimates are within range. Other estimating formulas for $_nL_x$ might result in more or fewer $_nL_{x,j}$ terms being out of the expected range.

We note that except for $_{15}L_{15,\,r,\,a}$, the $_nL_{x,j,\,source}$ estimates are at least equal to $_nL_{x,j,\,linear}$ estimates in quality: at the youngest ages in particular, the linear estimates probably assign too few person years to the nonlabor force $_nL_{x,i}$ and too many to the active labor force $_nL_{x,a}$. The proportions inactive and active in the source populations are also biased with respect to the life table since they are more heavily weighted toward young ages owing to population growth, about 3% annually at that time.

The value of multistate life tables is contributed both by the $l_{x,j}$ estimates, which display proportions in each attribute state as of age or duration x, and by the $_nL_{x,j}$ estimates, which display person-time spent in each state. Had the source data included annual deaths at age 75+ we could also have found the expected lifetime $e_{x,j}$ spent in each attribute state: here, the number of years spent in the labor force, spent in childhood before labor force entry, and spent in retirement.

Besides the formulas presented here, a number of others have been introduced for multistate tables. As a starting point, the reader is referred to Schoen and Nelson (1974), Rogers (1975), Schoen (1975, 1978, 1988), Hoem (1975), Krishnamoorthy (1979), Willekens et al. (1982), Land and Rogers (1982), Land et al. (1986), and Land and Hough (1989). Readers should also see Keyfitz (1985, pp. 350–367) and the comment by Nour and Suchindran (1984), who emphasize that common estimating formulas may yield multistate transition probabilities that are suspect or out of range for at least some data sets. An application of the transition probabilities of Table 5.9 to population projection is presented in Section 9.3.

5.4. CAUSE-ELIMINATED AND CAUSE-SUBSTITUTED LIFE TABLES; COMPETING RISKS

Since multiple decrement rates correspond to the observed rates of occurrence of different causes of death, it may not be obvious that they can be improved upon. In fact they sometimes can be. Whenever two populations have an equal risk of death from a particular cause, but one has a greater risk from other causes, the actual occurrence rates for the equal risk cause will differ between the populations. The problem is one of competing risks: in the population with higher overall mortality rates, some people die of other causes who in the lower mortality population would have survived those and ultimately died of the cause of interest. To find the actual risk for any one cause, tables are needed in which the distorting effects of other causes of death are eliminated.

For projections of future mortality and life expectancy, the same consideration applies. Because observed rates are affected by competing risks, the past patterns of individual mortality rates are not a reliable indicator of changes occurring in underlying survival probabilities. In consequence, they are also relatively poor guides to the possible course of future mortality. Rates that more nearly reflect the underlying probabilities are a better base from which to extrapolate.

To develop cause-eliminated life tables, we need a means of estimating survival probabilities for individual causes of death as they would appear if no other causes operated. The actual survival probability $_np_x$ over the age interval x to $x + n$ would be the product of these rates. For example, if the chance of surviving cardiovascular risks is $_np_{x,\,\text{cvd}}$, the chance of surviving the various cancers is $_np_{x,\,\text{neoplasms}}$, and the chance of surviving other risks is $_np_{x,\,\text{other}}$, the probability of surviving the combined risks for all factors should be

$$_np_x = \left(_np_{x,\,\text{cvd}}\right)\left(_np_{x,\,\text{neop}}\right)\left(_np_{x,\,\text{other}}\right) = \prod_j {}_np_{x,\,j}$$

We implicitly assume that the causes of death are independent.*

The elimination of one cause is equivalent to setting the survival rate for that cause to 1.0. For example, the survival probability $_np_{x,\,-\text{cvd}}$, representing the probability of surviving through the interval if cardiovascular deaths were eliminated, is $(1.0)\left(_np_{x,\,\text{neop}}\right)\left(_np_{x,\,\text{other}}\right)$. Elimination of all causes but one would set $_np_x$ to the rate for that cause.

A simple approach to the estimation of the $_np_{x,\,j}$ terms is to suppose that the risk of mortality is constant over the age interval and equal to the multiple decrement death rate $_nM_{x,\,j} = {}_nD_{x,\,j}/{}_nN_x$. We might then estimate $_np_{x,\,j}$ using the exponential†:

$$_np_{x,\,j,\,\text{exp}} = e^{-n_nM_{x,\,j}} \tag{5.15}$$

More generally, for $_nM_{x,\,j}$ we can substitute $_nM_x({}_nD_{x,\,j}/{}_nD_x)$, which allows us to rewrite the survival probability as

$$_np_{x,\,j} = e^{-n_nM_x({}_nD_{x,\,j}/{}_nD_x)}$$

---

* If causes are not independent, they can be handled in cause-eliminated life tables only to the extent that their interconnectedness can be modeled explicitly. The issue is raised forcefully in Prentice *et al.* (1978), and in works by Manton and others (Manton *et al.,* 1976; Manton and Stallard, 1984; Manton and Myers, 1987) on underlying causes of mortality.

† The expression is shown in $_nM_{x,\,j}$ form for continuity with the discussion that follows. When (5.15) is used, $_nD_{x,\,j}/{}_nN_x$ should be substituted for $_nM_{x,\,j}$ to preserve accuracy.

If we then substitute $_np_x$ for $e^{-_nn_Mx}$ we have

$$_np_{x,\,j,\,\text{Greville}} = \begin{cases} 1 & |\,_nD_x = 0 \\ _np_x{}^{nD_{x,\,j}/_nD_x} & |\,_nD_x > 0 \end{cases} \qquad (5.16)$$

This expression was introduced by Greville (1948).* When $_np_x$ is estimated by the exponential, the equivalence of (5.15) and (5.16) is exact. Under all $_np_x$ formulas it produces cause-elminated rates whose product $\prod_j {}_np_{x,j} = {}_np_x$.

Examining (5.16), $_np_{x,j}$ takes the value $_np_x$ when all deaths in the age interval are due to cause j, and the value 1.0 when no deaths in the interval are due to j. These are correct limits. The chance of surviving for a single risk j cannot be lower than the chance of surviving for all risks combined; nor can it be above 1.

The elimination of a cause of death is found by setting all of the $_np_{x,j}$ terms for that cause to 1.0, the value they would take if the cause produced no fatalities, and recalculating $_np_x$ as the product of the survival rates for the remaining causes. Alternatively, the new survival estimate can be found from the initial $_np_x$ and $_np_{x,j}$ values using

$$_np_{x,\,-j} = \prod_{i \neq j} {}_np_{x,\,i} = {}_np_x/_np_{x,\,j} \qquad (5.17)$$

where $_np_{x,\,-j}$ is the survival probability with cause j eliminated.† If $_np_{x,j}$ is estimated by (5.16), the expression simplifies to

---

* Readers will also often see the hyperbolic ("actuarial") single cause survival probability:

$$_np_{x,\,j,\,\text{hyperbolic}} = 1 - {}_nD_{x,\,j}/[N(x) - \tfrac{1}{2}{}_nW_x - \tfrac{1}{2}{}_nD_{x,\,-j}]$$

where $_nW_x = N_C(x) - {}_nD_{C,\,x}$, representing individuals censored in the interval who were surviving at the point of loss of contact. The formula assigns fractional observation times to these individuals, and in the cause-eliminated rates, to individuals dying of causes other than j in the interval $(_nD_{x,\,-j})$ and therefore exposed to the risk of dying of cause j for only part of the interval. Although widely used, in most applications the hyperbolic single cause survival probabilities are of lower quality than Greville's $_np_{x,\,j}$ estimates (Smith, 1985a). On the estimation of survival probabilities with competing risks the reader should also see Pollard (1982, 1988) and Hsieh (1989).

† In studies with censorship due to unscheduled sample losses or to arrivals at study cutoff, (5.16) and (5.17) may be used to estimate survival in the absence of the losses. Following Chiang (1968, pp. 287–288) and Mode (Mode et al., 1977), we treat the loss subset $N_C(x) - {}_nD_{C,\,x}$ as an event subset, say $_nD_{W,\,x}$. We then estimate $_np_x$ by the unadjusted sample formula

$$_np_{x,\,\text{unadjusted}} = 1 - (_nD_x + {}_nD_{W,\,x})/N(x)$$

$$_nP_{x, -j, \text{ Greville}} = {}_nP_x{}^{(1-{}_nD_{x, j}/{}_nD_x)} \tag{5.18}$$

Partial rather than complete elimination of a cause of death can also be investigated, most simply by setting

$$_nP_{x, -j, (1-\alpha)j} = {}_nP_x/({}_nP_{x, j})^\alpha \tag{5.19}$$

After finding $_nP_x$, we estimate the survival probability in the absence of withdrawal as

$$_nP_{x, -W} = {}_nP_x{}^{[1-{}_nD_{W, x}/({}_nD_x + {}_nD_{W, x})]}$$

The reader can confirm that for the data of Table 4.1, treating sample losses as a competing risk will yield the survival probabilities in the absence of losses:

$$_1P_{1, -W, \text{ Greville}} = (1 - 92/276)^{(1-44/92)} = 0.80933$$

$$_1P_{2, -W, \text{ Greville}} = (1 - 81/184)^{(1-50/81)} = 0.80087$$

$$_1P_{3, -W, \text{ Greville}} = (1 - 45/103)^{(1-35/45)} = 0.88019$$

$$_1P_{4, -W, \text{ Greville}} = (1 - 32/58)^{(1-28/32)} = 0.90454$$

These rates will be found to fall near or within the range of the Table 4.2 and 4.3 estimates. Although not widely used, the formula is competitive with conventional estimators.

We might also distinguish censorship by losses (CL) from censorship by arrival at study cutoff (CC). Restricting analysis to right-censored samples, we would have the subsets

$$N_C(x) = N_{CL}(x) + N_{CC}(x)$$

$$_nD_{C, x} = {}_nD_{CL, x} + {}_nD_{CC, x}$$

$$_nD_{W, x} = N_{CL}(x) - {}_nD_{CL, x}$$

Defining only the unscheduled losses as events in competition with other causes of termination, total events in the interval will number $_nD_x + {}_nD_{W, x}$. By this convention, the censored subset is restricted to persons censored by study cutoff, $N_{CC}(x)$ and $_nD_{CC, x}$. A curtate survival probability for the sample would be found as:

$$_nP_{x, \text{ curtate sample}} = 1 - [{}_nD_x + {}_nD_{W, x} - {}_nD_{CC, x}]/[N(x) - N_{CC}(x)]$$

The survival probability in the absence of sample losses is then

$$_nP_{x, -\text{loss, Greville}} = {}_nP_x{}^{1-{}_nD_{W, x}/[{}_nD_x + {}_nD_{W, x} - {}_nD_{CC, x}]}$$

In the absence of unscheduled losses the expression reduces to the curtate estimator, (4.2). The reader may find survival probabilities under other $_nP_x$ formulas where assignment of the censored sample is partly to losses and partly to censorship by arrival at study cutoff.

We caution that treatment of losses as a competing risk is not a way of removing the biases arising when the losses are nonrandom. A test for bias is presented in Section 4.8.

In the expression α represents the proportion of the jth cause that has been removed. (α can also be assigned negative values, to show the impact of an increase in mortality for cause j.)

A different approach to the partial elimination or augmentation of causes of death is to substitute the $_np_{x,j}$ terms of one life table for those of another. Using j and j^* to represent cause j in the source and alternate tables, respectively, the original and revised survival probabilities at ages x to $x + n$ become

$$_np_x = (_np_{x,j})(_np_{x,-j})$$

and

$$_np_{x,-j,j^*} = (_np_{x,j^*})(_np_{x,-j}) = \,_np_x \,_np_{x,j^*}/_np_{x,j} \tag{5.20}$$

Any of the series of terms $_np_{x,j}$, $_np_{x,-j}$, $_np_{x,-j,(1-\alpha)j}$, or $_np_{x,-j,j^*}$ can be substituted for $_np_x$ to construct a life table displaying the effect of the change on l_x, $_nL_x$, and life expectancy to the start of the final age interval $_{f-x}e_x$, using the same radix as the ordinary life table, commonly either 1 or 100,000.

In the final age category (f, ω) of cause-eliminated and cause-subsituted tables, no satisfactory conventions exist for estimating person years lived $_{\omega-f}L_{f,j}$ or life expectancy $e_{f,j}$. For the trivial case where j contributes no deaths in the final interval, we may set $_{\omega-f}L_{f,-j} = \,_{\omega-f}L_f$, but the example is of limited interest. We also expect that with the reduction or elimination of causes producing some deaths, the time lived in the interval will increase—that is, for $0 < \alpha < 1$, $_{\omega-f}L_{f,-j,(1-\alpha)j} > \,_{\omega-f}L_f$—but the inequality does not yield exact $_{\omega-f}L_{f,-j,(1-\alpha)j}$ estimates. For other changes the relationship of $_{\omega-f}L_{f,-j,j^*}$ to $_{\omega-f}L_f$ will depend on the intensity and age pattern of deaths in the source (j) and substituted (j^*) tables. That information is unlikely to be known. In the final interval the population $_{\omega-f}N_f$ and deaths by cause $_{\omega-f}D_{f,j}$ are given, but not the ages at which the deaths occur.[†]

[†] The reader is cautioned that for cause-eliminated rates the life expectancy for the terminal category is sometimes estimated as $e_{f,j} = \,_{\omega-f}N_f/_{\omega-f}D_{f,j}$, or population ages f and over divided by cause j deaths. The life expectancy for all other causes becomes $e_{f,-j} = \,_{\omega-f}N_f/(_{\omega-f}D_f - \,_{\omega-f}D_{f,j})$.
The first expression is correct for $_{\omega-f}D_{f,j} = \,_{\omega-f}D_f$ (that is, if all deaths are due to cause j) but is undefined for $_{\omega-f}D_{f,j} = 0$; the opposite conditions hold for the second expression. At intermediate $_{\omega-f}D_{f,j}$ values the expressions produce life expectancy estimates between the source life table e_f and ∞, with $e_{f,j}$ becoming increasingly implausible as $(_{\omega-f}D_{f,j}/_{\omega-f}D_f) \to 0$ and $e_{f,-j}$ becoming increasingly implausible as $(_{\omega-f}D_{f,j}/_{\omega-f}D_f) \to 1$.
Since everyone dies, the identity $N(f) = \,_{\omega-f}D_f$ must continue to hold as deaths for cause j or deaths for other causes approach 0, implying that $_{\omega-f}D_{f,-j}$ or $_{\omega-f}D_{f,j}$ converges to $N(f)$ and that all effects of cause elimination are expressed as increases in the population (or amount of time lived) beyond f, $_{\omega-f}N_f$. For the two life expectancies $e_{f,-j}$ and $e_{f,j}$, we therefore have $e_{f,-j} = k_{\omega-f}N_f/_{\omega-f}D_f = ke_f$, and $e_{f,j} = k'_{\omega-f}N_f/_{\omega-f}D_f = k'e_f$, where it is known only that $k > 1$ and $k' > 1$. Historically, the gains at the oldest ages have been small (Fries, 1980; Fries and Crapo, 1981) but even that does not tell us much about k and k'.

Table 5.10. Cause-Eliminated Survival Distributions for Neoplasms, Major Cardiovascular Diseases, and Other Causes, U.S. 1980 Life Table

a. Neoplasms

Ages	$_nP_x$	$_nd_{x,\,neop}/_nd_x$	$_nP_{x,\,neop}$	$l_{x,\,neop}$	$_nL_{x,\,neop}$	$_{85-x}e_{x,\,neop}$	$l_{x,\,-neop}$	$_{85-x}e_{x,\,-neop}$
					Cause eliminated			
0	0.98734	0.00395	0.99995	100,000	99,996	81.2	100,000	74.1
1–4	0.99745	0.07540	0.99981	99,995	399,934	80.2	98,739	74.1
5–14	0.99694	0.14950	0.99954	99,976	999,530	76.2	98,506	70.3
15–24	0.98853	0.05773	0.99933	99,930	998,965	66.2	98,250	60.4
25–44	0.96594	0.16576	0.99427	99,863	1,991,540	56.3	97,188	51.0
45–64	0.82552	0.32274	0.94000	99,291	1,926,240	36.5	94,418	32.2
65–74	0.73952	0.27645	0.91996	93,333	895,980	18.2	82,920	15.3
75–84	0.49854	0.18707	0.87791	85,863	806,215	9.4	66,656	7.8
85+	0.00000	0.10174	0.00000	75,380	0	0.0	37,852	0.0

b. Cardiovascular diseases

Ages	$_nP_x$	$_nd_{x,\,cvd}/_nd_x$	$_nP_{x,\,cvd}$	$l_{x,\,cvd}$	$_{85-x}e_{x,\,cvd}$	$l_{x,\,-cvd}$	$_{85-x}e_{x,\,-cvd}$
				Cause eliminated			
0	0.98734	0.02133	0.99973	100,000	79.1	100,000	75.8
1–4	0.99745	0.04762	0.99988	99,973	78.1	98,761	75.7
5–14	0.99694	0.04319	0.99987	99,961	74.1	98,521	71.9
15–24	0.98853	0.03552	0.99959	99,947	64.1	98,233	62.1
25–44	0.96594	0.16909	0.99416	99,907	54.2	97,146	52.8
45–64	0.82552	0.41047	0.92432	99,323	34.4	94,388	34.0
65–74	0.73952	0.50533	0.85857	91,806	16.4	84,300	16.9
75–84	0.49854	0.60070	0.65828	78,822	8.3	72,611	8.8
85+	0.00000	0.68535	0.00000	51,887	0.0	54,991	0.0

c. All other causes

Ages	$_np_x$	$_nd_{x,\,other}/_nd_x$	$_np_{x,\,other}$	$l_{x,\,other}$	Cause eliminated $_{85-x}e_{x,\,other}$	$l_{x,\,-other}$	$_{85-x}e_{x,\,-other}$
0	0.98734	0.97472	0.98766	100,000	78.9	100,000	76.2
1–4	0.99745	0.87698	0.99776	98,766	78.9	99,968	75.3
5–14	0.99694	0.80731	0.99753	98,545	75.1	99,936	71.3
15–24	0.98853	0.90675	0.98960	98,301	65.3	99,877	61.3
25–44	0.96594	0.66515	0.97721	97,279	55.9	99,770	51.4
45–64	0.82552	0.26680	0.95013	95,062	37.0	98,619	31.9
65–74	0.73952	0.21822	0.93627	90,321	18.4	85,685	15.2
75–84	0.49854	0.21223	0.86267	84,565	9.3	67,679	7.9
85+	0.00000	0.21291	0.00000	72,952	0.0	39,112	0.0

Omitting the terminal age category from analysis, for cause-eliminated and cause-substituted rates the life expectancy is replaced by the partial life expectancy to the start of the final age interval (f, ω),

$$_{f-x}e_x = \sum_{a=x}^{f-n} {}_nL_a \bigg/ l_x$$

Table 5.10 and Figs. 5.2 and 5.3 display cause-eliminated survival rates for the United States in 1980 for neoplasms, major cardiovascular diseases, and other causes. The example uses $_np_x$ terms from Table 4.9 and the proportional distribution of deaths $_nD_{x,j}/_nD_x$ found from Table 5.1. After estimating $_np_{x,j}$ by (5.16), $l_{x,j}$, $_nL_{x,j}$, and $_{f-x}e_{x,j}$ distributions are computed by standard formulas. The table also displays $l_{x,-j}$ and $_{f-x}e_{x,-j}$, estimating $_np_{x,-j}$ by (5.17). [The reader might note that after interpolating from initial (x) to midinterval $(x + \frac{1}{2}n)$ ages, the terms $_{f-x}e_{x,-j}$ can be substituted for the ordinary life table terms $e_{x+(1/2)n}$ in (4.24) or (4.25), to estimate years of potential life lost. In their original formulation the expressions do not incorporate the effects of competing risks.]

At age 0 the single cause probabilities are

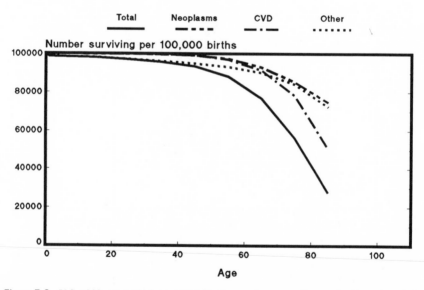

Figure 5.2. U.S. 1980 cause-eliminated life table for neoplasms, cardiovascular diseases, and all other causes of death.

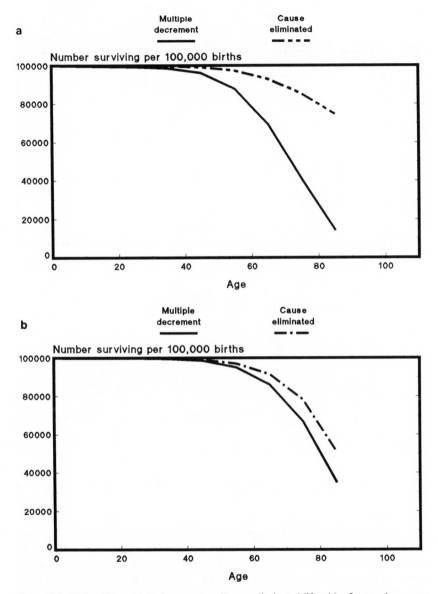

Figure 5.3. U.S. 1980 multiple decrement and cause-eliminated life tables for neoplasms, cardiovascular diseases, and all other causes of death: (a) neoplasms, (b) major cardiovascular diseases, and (c) all other causes.

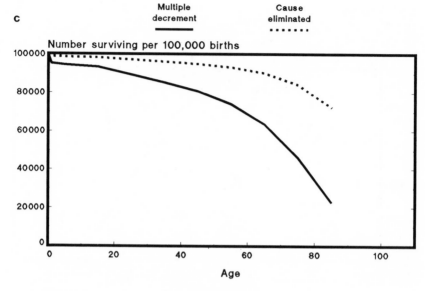

Figure 5.3. Continued

$$_1p_{0,\text{ cvd}} = 0.98734^{0.00395} = 0.99995, \qquad _1q_{0,\text{ cvd}} = 0.00005$$

$$_1p_{0,\text{ neop}} = 0.98734^{0.02133} = 0.99973, \qquad _1q_{0,\text{ neop}} = 0.00027$$

$$_1p_{0,\text{ other}} = 0.98734^{0.97472} = 0.98766, \qquad _1q_{0,\text{ other}} = 0.01234$$

The product of the survival terms is

$$\prod_j {}_1p_{0,\,j} = (0.98734^{0.00395})(0.98734^{0.02133})(0.98734^{0.97472}) = 0.98734 = {}_1p_0$$

For all three causes the single cause probabilities of dying $_1q_{0,j}$ agree closely with the $_1q_{0,j}$ terms of the multiple decrement table (Table 5.1: the table displays $_1d_{0,j} = l_0 \, _1q_{0,j} = 100,000 \, _1q_{0,j}$). The terms diverge at older ages where the proportions dying of each cause are more nearly equal.

The single cause and overall l_x distributions are graphed in Fig. 5.2. At young ages, neoplasms and cardiovascular deaths are rare, and l_x is only slightly lower than $l_{x,\text{ other}}$. At the oldest ages, where cardiovascular deaths predominate, the l_x distribution closely parallels $l_{x,\text{ cvd}}$. In Fig. 5.3 the multiple decrement and cause-eliminated distributions are superimposed. For all three causes the survival patterns are similar, since at most ages mortality is low and the adjustment for competing risks in the cause-eliminated tables is small.

Variances for the cause-eliminated survival probabilities of (5.16), (5.19), and (5.20) are similar to those for multiple decrement rates, with the substitutions $_np_{x,j,\text{Greville}}$, $_nq_{x,j,\text{Greville}}$, $_np_{x,-j,(1-\alpha)j}$, $_nq_{x,-j,(1-\alpha)j}$, and $_np_{x,-j,j^*}$, $_nq_{x,-j,j^*}$ for terms in $_np_x$, $_nq_x$, respectively.

5.5. EFFECTS OF CHANGING SURVIVAL RATES ON THE RISK POPULATION $_nN_x$, DEATHS $_nD_x$, AND DEATH RATES $_nM_x$

We measure the effects of a change in the probability of survival on the interval population, deaths, and age-specific death rates by inverting standard life table formulas. Restricting analysis to ages $(x, x + n)$ below f, the start of the final age interval, and letting $_np_{x,j}$ and $_np^*_{x,j}$ represent the initial and changed survival probabilities for the jth cause of death, and $_np_x$ and $_np^*_x$ represent the corresponding probabilities for all causes combined, for total deaths before and after the change in the survival probability we will have

$$_nD_x = N(x)(1 - _np_x)$$

$$_nD^*_x = N(x)(1 - _np^*_x) = _nD_x(1 - _np^*_x)/(1 - _np_x)$$

(5.21)

$N(x)$ does not itself change, since it represents survivors at the start of the interval.

For the jth cause, the change in the number of deaths is found by solving Greville's expression (5.16) for $_nD^*_{x,j}$, after substituting $_np^*_x$, $_np^*_{x,j}$, and $_nD^*_x$ for $_np_x$, $_np_{x,j}$, and $_nD_x$. With the substitutions the expression becomes

$$_np^*_{x,\,j,\,\text{Greville}} = _np^{*\,(_nD^*_{x,\,j}/_nD^*_x)}$$

(5.22)

whence

$$_nD^*_{x,\,j,\,\text{Greville}} = _nD^*_x \ln_np^*_{x,\,j}/\ln_np^*_x$$

(5.23)

A change in the survival rate for cause j changes the interval population $_nN_x$ as well as deaths $_nD_x$. With the change in deaths from $_nD_x$ to $_nD^*_x$ the population size becomes

$$_nN^*_{x,\,\text{linear}} = n[N(x) - \tfrac{1}{2}_nD^*_x] = _nN_x + (n/2)(_nD_x - _nD^*_x)$$

(5.24)

The expression is derived from the linear estimator [expression (4.8)] $N(x)_{\text{linear}}$ $= {}_nN_x/n + \frac{1}{2}{}_nD_x$.

Using (5.21) and (5.24), for the age-specific death rate we have

$${}_nM^*_{x,\,\text{linear}} = {}_nD^*_x/{}_nN^*_{x,\,\text{linear}} = {}_nD^*_x/[{}_nN_x + (n/2)({}_nD_x - {}_nD^*_x)] \quad (5.25)$$

[Where fewer or more than half of interval deaths fall before the interval midpoint, the estimate $n(1 - {}_na_x/n)$ may be substituted for $n/2$ in (5.24) and (5.25).]

Using (5.21)–(5.25) and Tables 5.1 and 5.2, we will illustrate the effect of changes in survival probabilities on ${}_nN_x$, ${}_nD_x$, ${}_nD_{x,j}$, ${}_nM_x$, and ${}_nM_{x,j}$, by letting ${}_{10}p_{75,\,\text{neop}}$ increase from 0.87791 to $0.87791^{0.80915} = 0.90000$ and letting ${}_{10}p_{75,\,\text{cvd}}$ increase from 0.65828 to $0.65828^{0.85303} = 0.70000$. With the changes, we have, omitting the subscripted identifiers, Greville and linear,

$${}_{10}p^*_{75} = \prod_j {}_{10}p_{75,\,j} = (0.90000)(0.70000)(0.86267) = 0.54348$$

$${}_{10}D^*_{75} = {}_{10}D_{75}(1 - {}_{10}p^*_{75})/1 - {}_{10}p_{75})$$

$$= 517{,}257(1 - 0.54348)/(1 - 0.49854) = 470{,}901$$

$${}_{10}D^*_{75,\,j} = {}_{10}D^*_{75}\ln{}_{10}p^*_{75,\,j}/\ln{}_{10}p^*_{75}$$

$${}_{10}D^*_{75,\,\text{neop}} = 470{,}901(\ln 0.90000)/(\ln 0.54348) = 81{,}367$$

$${}_{10}D^*_{75,\,\text{cvd}} = 470{,}901(\ln 0.70000)/(\ln 0.54348) = 275{,}449$$

$${}_{10}D^*_{75,\,\text{other}} = 470{,}901(\ln 0.86267)/(\ln 0.54348) = 114{,}082$$

The revised numbers of deaths can be compared with the earlier values ${}_{10}D_{75,\,\text{neop}} = 96{,}769$, ${}_{10}D_{75,\,\text{cvd}} = 310{,}704$, and ${}_{10}D_{75,\,\text{other}} = 109{,}784$. The changes represent a 16% decline for neoplasms, an 11% decline for cardio-vascular diseases, and a 4% increase for other causes.

The example brings out the effects of competing risks on numbers of deaths and mortality rates. With improvements in survival rates for two causes and no change for the third cause, numbers of deaths for the third cause increase. What has happened is that the improvements increase the number at risk for the third cause. Competing risks also impact on the improved causes. If survival had increased only for neoplasms, we would have $_{10}D^*_{75, \text{ neop}} = 79,162$, out of a total ($_{10}D^*_{75}$) of 504,312 deaths. The number of deaths for neoplasms with no other mortality changes is slightly smaller than is found when survival improves for both neoplasms and cardiovascular deaths.

The increase in persons at risk $_{10}N^*_{75}$ with changes in survival probabilities can be estimated by (5.24):

$$_{10}N^*_{75} = {}_{10}N_{75} + (10/2)({}_{10}D_{75} - {}_{10}D^*_{75})$$

$$= 7,728,800 + (10/2)(517,257 - 470,901) = 7,960,600$$

The reader should note that although $_{10}N^*_{75}$ is estimated from the 1980 census population $_{10}N_{75}$, it represents a hypothetical population. The new population estimate and the changes in deaths by cause are for the population $N(75)$ who survive to their 75th birthday. The changes in $_{10}p_{75, j}$ do not affect $N(75)$, or we would be unable to generate estimates of the interval population and deaths that would follow from changes in survival.

For the revised population, the age-specific death rates become:

$$_nM^*_x = {}_nD^*_x / {}_nN^*_x = 470,901 / 7,960,600 = 0.05915$$

$$_nM^*_{x, j} = {}_nD^*_{x, j} / {}_nN^*_x$$

$$_nM^*_{x, \text{ neop}} = 0.01022$$

$$_nM^*_{x, \text{ cvd}} = 0.03460$$

$$_nM^*_{x, \text{ other}} = 0.01433$$

For comparison, the initial age-specific death rate was 0.06693, and the rates by cause were 0.01252, 0.04020, and 0.01420 for neoplasms, cardiovascular diseases, and other causes, respectively. The reader can work backward through the example to confirm that the interval survival probability $_np_{x, \text{ other}}$ remains 0.86267 and that the difference in the age-specific death rates $_nM_{x, \text{ other}}$ and $_nM^*_{x, \text{ other}}$ is wholly attributable to the changes in the competing causes $_np_{x, \text{ neop}}$ and $_np_{x, \text{ cvd}}$.

We note for the reader that of the three terms $_nN^*_x$, $_nD^*_x$, and $_nM^*_x$, the first two are changes specific to the source estimates $_nN_x$ and $_nD_x$. For another source population $_n\mathcal{N}_x$ with the same initial age-specific death rate $_nM_x$ and deaths $_n\mathcal{D}_x = {}_n\mathcal{N}_x \, {}_nM_x$, the revised population and death terms would become

$_nN^*_x = {_nN_x}(_nN^*_x / _nN_x)$ and $_n\mathcal{D}^*_x = {_n\mathcal{D}_x}(_n D^*_x / _nD_x)$. The age-specific death rates, being ratios of deaths to population, would be the same for the two cohorts. That is, given $_n\mathcal{M}_x = {_nM_x}$ we will also have $_n\mathcal{M}^*_x = {_nM^*_x}$.

5.6. DECOMPOSITION OF CHANGES IN LIFE EXPECTANCY

Differences in life expectancy between populations and changes over time are wholly explained by the differences in the survival probabilities for each cause of death. If a single cause is responsible for the difference, (5.20) will generate either life table from the other, up to the start of the final age interval (f, ω) or (f, ∞). We may also have the population and death estimates $_{\omega-f}N_f$, $_{\omega-f}D_f$ for both populations, which would allow complete life expectancies to be found by the formulas of Chapter 4. The difference in life expectancies $_{f-x}e_x$ or e_x measures the contribution of j and j^* to survival at ages x and above.

When life expectancy differences are due to several causes of death, the apportionment of the differences by cause is no longer unambiguous. Constructing a series of life tables, each with a single cause substituted from the other table, will provide a series of differences

$$c_{x, j, \text{ forward}} = {_{f-x}e_{x, -j, j^*}} - {_{f-x}e_x} \tag{5.26}$$

that sum more or less to the overall difference $_{f-x}e^*_x - {_{f-x}e_x}$. The summation will usually be inexact, since competing risks operate differently in each of the calculated life tables. The equality can be made exact by distributing the error proportionately among the causes, for which we set:

$$\hat{c}_{x, j, \text{ forward}} = g_{j, \text{ forward}} \, c_{x, j, \text{ forward}} \tag{5.27}$$

where

$$g_{j, \text{ forward}} = 1 + \text{sign}(c_{x, j, \text{ forward}}) \left(e_{\text{forward}} \Big/ \sum_j |c_{x, j, \text{ forward}}| \right)$$

and e is the error term

$$e_{\text{forward}} = ({_{f-x}e^*_x} - {_{f-x}e_x}) - \sum_j c_{x, j, \text{ forward}}$$

In $g_{j, \text{ forward}}$ the quantities within verticals ($|\ \ |$) are absolute values. (The complexity of these expressions arises from the necessity of adjusting the absolute magnitudes of the $c_{x,j}$ terms. For the individual terms the corrections will be greater or less than 1.0 depending on their signs and the sign of the error term e.)

Besides forward differences we may also estimate the backward differences

$$c_{x,j,\text{ backward}} = {}_{f-x}e_x^* - {}_{f-x}e_{x,-j^*,j}^* \tag{5.28}$$

$$\hat{c}_{x,j,\text{ backward}} = g_{j,\text{ backward}}\, c_{x,j,\text{ backward}} \tag{5.29}$$

where

$$g_{j,\text{ backward}} = 1 + \text{sign}(c_{x,j,\text{ backward}})\left(e_{\text{backward}}\left/\sum_j |c_{x,j,\text{ backward}}|\right.\right)$$

$$e_{\text{backward}} = ({}_{f-x}e_x^* - {}_{f-x}e_x) - \sum_j c_{x,j,\text{ backward}}^*$$

For Table 4.9b the life expectancy to age 85 is $_{85}e_0 = 71.1$ years. We also have, from Table 5.10, the life expectancies to age 85 with single causes eliminated $_{85}e_{0,-\text{neop}} = 74.1$ years, $_{85}e_{0,-\text{cvd}} = 75.8$ years, $_{85}e_{0,-\text{other}} = 76.2$ years. The gains in life expectancy following elimination of each cause are thus

$$c_{0,-\text{neop, forward}} = 74.1 - 71.7 = 2.4 \text{ years}$$

$$c_{0,-\text{cvd, forward}} = 75.8 - 71.7 = 4.1 \text{ years}$$

$$c_{0,-\text{other, forward}} = 76.2 - 71.7 = 4.5 \text{ years}$$

The differences sum to $\sum_j c_{0,j} = 11.0$ years, less than the $85.0 - 71.7 = 13.3$ years that would actually be gained if all three causes (that is, all causes of death) were eliminated at ages below 85. Using (5.27), the scale adjustments we require to correct $\sum_j c_{0,j}$ will be

$$\hat{c}_{x,j,\text{ forward}} = g_{j,\text{ forward}}\, c_{x,j,\text{ forward}}$$

$$= \left[1 + \text{sign}(c_{x,j,\text{ forward}})\left(e_{\text{forward}}\left/\sum_j |c_{x,j,\text{ forward}}|\right.\right)\right]$$

$$\times ({}_{f-x}e_{x,-j,j^*} - {}_{f-x}e_x)$$

$$\hat{c}_{0,\text{ neop, forward}} = g_{\text{neop, forward}}\, c_{x,\text{ neop, forward}}$$

$$= [1 + (+)(2.3/11.0)](2.4) = (1.21)(2.4) = 2.9$$

$$\hat{c}_{0,\text{ cvd, forward}} = (1.21)(4.1) = 5.0$$

$$\hat{c}_{0,\text{ other, forward}} = (1.21)(4.5) = 5.4$$

(Note that all of the changes are positive, since they arise through elimination of causes of death. For mixed changes some terms g_j will be greater than 1.0 and some less than 1.0.)

The reader may use the single cause survival probabilities $_{85}e_{0,j}$ from Table 5.10 to find adjusted backward survival changes using (5.28) and (5.29) from the unadjusted changes $85.0 - 81.2 = 3.8$ years, $85.0 - 79.1 = 5.9$ years, and $85.0 - 78.9 = 6.1$ years for neoplasms, cardiovascular diseases, and other causes, respectively. He or she might also average the unadjusted forward and backward differences, to produce estimates (3.1, 5.0, and 5.3 years, respectively) that are usually closer to the correct difference, and therefore need less adjustment than forward or backward estimates taken separately.

5.7. MORTALITY PROJECTION

In addition to past and current mortality, problems of competing risks also arise in projections of future mortality. Projections typically assume increasing longevity, but they are rarely specific as to the causes of death contributing to the gains. By extrapolating from past changes in cause-eliminated $l_{x,j}$ rates, it is possible to construct life table survival estimates for future years based on clearer assumptions about mortality trends.

For the projection let $_np_{x,j}^{(0)}$ represent the cause-eliminated survival rate for the jth cause at time 0, and let $_np_{x,j}^{(1)}$ represent the rate at time 1. The relationship between the two rates can be expressed by a variety of functions. We will use*:

---

* An alternative to (5.30) suggested by Keyfitz (1977a) is to fit the survival probabilities $_np_{x,j}$ for two or more periods to a reference distribution using the Brass logit (Section 6.3). Survival probabilities for future periods are found from the reference distribution by extrapolation from the fitted coefficients $\hat{a}$, $\hat{b}$ for the source periods. Like (5.30), the logit fitting constrains $_np_{x,j}$ values to the range (0, 1). It also smooths the projected mortality changes at the various ages, helpful principally when source distributions display erratic patterns due to small sample sizes or small numbers of events. The reader is cautioned that neither (5.30) nor the logit is intended to substitute for insight.

$$
{}_np_{x,j}^{(t)} = \begin{cases} 0 & |_n p_{x,j}^{(1)} = 0 \\ 1 & |_n p_{x,j}^{(1)} = 1 \\ [_n p_{x,j}^{(1)}]^t & |_n p_{x,j}^{(0)} = 0,\ 1;\ {}_np_{x,j}^{(1)} \neq 0,\ 1 \\ [_n p_{x,j}^{(t-1)}]^h & |0 < [_n p_{x,j}^{(0)},\ {}_np_{x,j}^{(1)}] < 1 \end{cases}
\tag{5.30}
$$

where h is estimated as:

$$
h = \ln {}_np_{x,j}^{(1)}/\ln {}_np_{x,j}^{(0)}
$$

The first three ${}_np_{x,j}^{(t)}$ estimators in (5.30) address cases in which either ${}_np_{x,j}^{(0)}$ or ${}_np_{x,j}^{(1)}$ is 0 or 1 and h is 0 or is undefined. The final expression, for intermediate values of ${}_np_{x,j}$, generates future mortality changes with two useful properties: ${}_np_{x,j}^{(t)}$ is bounded between 0 and 1 at all durations t; and mortality at times 0 and 1 can be reproduced by backward projection from future values provided ${}_np_{x,j}^{(t)} \neq 0$ *or* 1. The estimator can be generalized as an average of $\ln {}_np_{x,j}$ ratios over several past intervals.

A limitation of (5.30) is that if two causes are combined, the joint estimate $({}_np_{x,1}\ {}_np_{x,2})^{(t)}$ may differ from the product of the separate cause estimates $[_n p_{x,1}^{(t)}][_n p_{x,2}^{(t)}]$. Additionally, future changes in the intensity of mortality or mortality hazard* are made proportional to the change from time 0 to time 1. Proportional intensities capture ceiling effects well (that is, the slowing of gains as ${}_np_{x,j} \rightarrow 1.0$), but where an initially high survival probability decreases from time 0 to time 1, the rate of worsening accelerates in future projections. If the user is willing to establish upper and lower asymptotes for ${}_np_{x,j}^{(\infty)}$, changes can be controlled by rescaling ${}_np_{x,j}$ values near or outside the asymptotic limits to bring them into range.

Expression (5.30) is not used for the final age interval in the life table (f, ω), since ${}_{\omega-f}p_{f,j} = 0$ for all causes of death j.

Table 5.11 displays the projection of mortality for neoplasms, cardiovascular diseases, and other causes of death to 1985, from (5.30) and 1975 and 1980 cause-eliminated ${}_np_{x,j}$ values.

The reader may note in Table 5.11c that the coefficients $h = \ln[_n p_{x,j}^{(1980)}]/\ln[_n p_{x,j}^{(1975)}]$ take values greater than 1 when survival rates are worsening and values less than 1 when survival is improving. In the example, survival probabilities for neoplasms are found to have improved from 1975 to 1980 at ages under 50 but to have worsened thereafter, controlling for the

---

* The intensity of mortality (μ_x) is related to ${}_np_x$ by the equality ${}_np_x = \exp[-\int_0^n \mu(x+a)da]$. From (4.10) we have the approximate equality $\mu_{x+(1/2)n} \simeq {}_nM_x$. See Appendix 6A.1 for the calculus of the life table.

Table 5.11. U.S. 1975 and 1980 Life Tables, and NCHS and Projected 1985 Life Tables

Ages	Estimated population $_nN_x$	Deaths				Survival probability			
		$_nD_x$	$_nD_{x,neop}$	$_nD_{x,cvd}$	$_nD_{x,other}$	$_nP_x$	$_nP_{x,neop}$	$_nP_{x,cvd}$	$_nP_{x,other}$
a. U.S. 1975 life table (linearly interpolated)									
Births:	3,146,203								
0	3,103,254	50,525	184	814	49,527	0.98394	0.99994	0.99974	0.98426
1–4	12,969,000	9,060	752	338	7,970	0.99721	0.99977	0.99990	0.99755
5–14	38,240,000	13,479	1,937	576	10,966	0.99648	0.99949	0.99985	0.99714
15–24	40,812,000	47,545	2,836	1,741	42,968	0.98842	0.99931	0.99957	0.98953
25–44	54,302,000	104,732	17,096	19,576	68,060	0.96216	0.99372	0.99282	0.97524
45–64	43,801,000	450,066	130,000	193,758	126,308	0.81364	0.94217	0.91504	0.94377
65–74	13,917,000	442,496	108,784	238,149	95,563	0.72566	0.92419	0.84149	0.93309
75–84	6,958,000	489,458	82,190	310,607	96,661	0.47959	0.88392	0.62731	0.86492
85+	1,821,000	285,077	26,846	205,338	52,893	0.00000	0.00000	0.00000	0.00000
b. U.S. 1980 life table (linearly interpolated)									
Births:	3,596,100								
0	3,556,300	45,526	180	984	44,362	0.98734	0.99995	0.99973	0.98766
1–4	12,814,600	8,187	611	407	7,169	0.99745	0.99981	0.99988	0.99776
5–14	34,942,100	10,689	1,601	450	8,638	0.99694	0.99954	0.99987	0.99753
15–24	42,486,800	49,027	2,813	1,750	44,464	0.98853	0.99933	0.99959	0.98960
25–44	62,716,500	108,658	18,010	18,360	72,288	0.96594	0.99427	0.99416	0.97721
45–64	44,502,600	425,338	137,273	174,585	113,480	0.82552	0.94000	0.92432	0.95013
65–74	15,580,600	466,621	128,999	235,800	101,822	0.73952	0.91996	0.85857	0.93627
75–84	7,728,800	517,257	96,769	310,704	109,784	0.49854	0.87791	0.65828	0.86267
85+	2,240,100	357,970	36,418	245,331	76,221	0.00000	0.00000	0.00000	0.00000

c. Mortality projection to 1985 and NCHS 1985 life table

	$_nh_{x,\text{neop}}$	$_np_{x,\text{neop}}$	$_nh_{x,\text{cvd}}$	$_np_{x,\text{cvd}}$	$_nh_{x,\text{other}}$	$_np_{x,\text{other}}$	l_x	NCHS l_x
0	0.83333	0.99996	1.03847	0.99972	0.78264	0.99033	100,000	100,000
1–4	0.82607	0.99984	1.20001	0.99986	0.91419	0.99795	99,001	98,931
5–14	0.90194	0.99959	0.86666	0.99989	0.86347	0.99787	98,769	98,731
15–24	0.97100	0.99935	0.95348	0.99961	0.99328	0.98967	98,507	98,473
25–44	0.91217	0.99477	0.81282	0.99525	0.91951	0.97902	97,388	97,542
45–64	1.03871	0.93775	0.88635	0.93262	0.88395	0.95579	94,396	94,311
65–74	1.05819	0.91550	0.88357	0.87395	0.95087	0.93930	78,905	78,678
75–84	1.05529	0.87161	0.89666	0.68735	1.01795	0.86039	59,300	58,699
85+	0.00000	0.00000	0.00000	0.00000	0.00000	0.00000	30,567	29,283

effects of competing risks for other causes of death. Survival rates for cardiovascular diseases and other causes improved at most ages. These patterns are continued to 1985 in the mortality projection. The reader might note that the National Center for Health Statistics 1985 life table l_x estimates (NCHS, 1985) are near the projected series at most ages. The series diverge at about age 75, but would be closer if for 1980 we had used NCHS l_x estimates (Table 6A.2) in place of the linear estimates of Tables 4.9 and 5.11. That is not to say they would have been correct. The advantage in projection by cause-eliminated rates is that we are clear as to the assumptions being made, a criterion only marginally met in examples that include few age categories and that fail to distinguish between males and females, for whom patterns of mortality change are dissimilar.

We refer the reader to McNown and Rogers (1989) for newer formulas and ongoing research in mortality projection.

5.8. SUMMARY

Multiple decrement, cause-eliminated, and cause-substituted tables were developed to disentangle the effects of competing causes of death on overall mortality. All depend on the researcher's ability to distinguish clearly between the various causes: where there is uncertainty or where causes are only partly separable, the methods may seriously distort the actual survival patterns. Unfortunately, that qualification is almost a description of our current understanding of mortality in extreme old age. It argues powerfully for truncating cause-eliminated life tables at ages under 100.

The essential distinction between the methods is that cause-eliminated and cause-substituted tables take into account competing risks from other causes of death, while multiple decrement rates reflect the patterns as they are observed. The distinction is important for comparisons between populations whose overall mortality levels differ markedly, or whose patterns differ sharply for single causes. In these cases multiple decrement tables may give misleading impressions. Where the researcher is in doubt, both types of tables may be constructed to check their consistency.

In mortality projection, cause-substituted rates allow the user to explore the effects of changes in one or several causes of death on overall deaths and life expectancy. We no longer look to changes as dramatic as the elimination of smallpox would have been in Bernoulli's time, or as the control of major infectious diseases became in the postwar period. But our need for informed analysis is not less, particularly in the United States where more than 5 years separates the life expectancies of black and white populations. The projection formula we have introduced as (5.30) allows reasonable near-term projections to be made by extrapolation from past changes. The reader may choose other assumptions or other formulas. As in ordinary population projections (Chapter 8), our confidence in more distant projections will be lower.

Multistate life tables were developed to relate life table analysis to survival models with repeated events, initially marriages and geographic migration. The transition probabilities for these events are analogous to conventional life table interval survival estimates $_nS_{x+(1/2)n} = {}_nL_{x+n}/{}_nL_x$, but with both entry and exit possible $_nS_{x+(1/2)n}$ becomes a *ratio* estimator. For individual states j we have $_nL_{x+n,j} = (\sum_i {}_nL_x \, {}_n t_{x, i \to j}) \gtrless {}_nL_{x,j}$, and therefore $_nS_{x+(1/2)n,j} \gtrless 1.0$. The computation of the transition ratios is not difficult, but more care is needed than in conventional life tables to ensure that $_nL_{x,j}$ estimates remain correctly bounded [expression (5.14)].

APPENDIX 5A.1. REGROUPING INTERVAL DATA FOR LIFE TABLE CONSTRUCTION

The source data for the multistate life table of Section 5.3 included 1960 census population estimates by residence and labor force status in 5-year age intervals, life table survival estimates [expression (4.18)] $_5S_{x+2.5} = {}_5L_{x+5}/{}_5L_x$, and estimates of rural-to-urban migration probabilities $_5t_{x+2.5, r \to u}$. The data for the male population are presented in Table 5A.1. To construct life tables in 15-year age intervals for these data requires both data recentering (from $_5S_{x+2.5}$, $_5t_{x+2.5}$ to $_5S_x$, $_5t_x$) and regrouping (from $_5p_x$, $_5S_x$, $_5t_x$ to $_{15}p_x$, $_{15}S_x$, $_{15}t_x$).

Regrouping is straightforward. For survival terms, probabilities or their complements are produced as in (4.12):

$$_{15}p_x = ({}_5p_x)({}_5p_{x+5})({}_5p_{x+10}) \tag{5A.1}$$

$$_{15}t_x = 1 - (1 - {}_5t_x)(1 - {}_5t_{x+5})(1 - {}_5t_{x+10}) \tag{5A.2}$$

where we interpret transfer probabilities $_nt_x$ as analogues to conventional mortality probabilities $_nq_x = 1 - {}_np_x$.

To estimate transfers $_{15}t_x$ from $_5t_{x+2.5}$ we also require the half-interval transition probabilities $_{2.5}t_{x+2.5}$, $_{2.5}t_{x+5}$. If we assume a constant transfer probability in the interval $(x + \frac{1}{2}n, x + 1\frac{1}{2}n)$, the partial probabilities become

$$_{2.5}t_{x+2.5, \, \text{exp}} = {}_{2.5}t_{x+5, \, \text{exp}} = 1 - (1 - {}_5t_{x+2.5})^{1/2} \tag{5A.3}$$

Combining (5A.2) and (5A.3), for the 15-year transition probabilities $_{15}t_x$ we have:

$$_{15}t_{x,\,exp} = 1 - (1 - {}_5t_{x-2.5})^{1/2}(1 - {}_5t_{x\,+\,2.5})$$

$$\times\,(1 - {}_5t_{x+7.5})(1 - {}_5t_{x+12.5})^{1/2} \qquad (5A.4)$$

We will also require

$$_5p_{x,\,exp} = ({}_5L_x/{}_5L_{x-5})^{1/2}({}_5L_{x+5}/{}_5L_x)^{1/2} = ({}_5S_{x-2.5})^{1/2}({}_5S_{x+2.5})^{1/2}$$

$$_{15}p_{x,\,exp} = ({}_5S_{x-2.5})^{1/2}({}_5S_{x+2.5})({}_5S_{x+7.5})({}_5S_{x+12.5})^{1/2}$$

To fit probabilities at ages 0–14, we substitute Tabah's $_{2.5}S_0$ for $({}_5S_{x-2.5})^{1/2}$ and approximate the migration probability from birth to age $2\frac{1}{2}$ as $_{2.5}t_0 = 1 - (1 - {}_5t_{2.5})^{1/2}$.

These conventions yield survival and transfer probabilities

$$_{15}p_{0,\,u} = (0.9772)(0.9945)(0.9923)(0.9874^{1/2}) = 0.9582$$

$$_{15}p_{0,\,r} = (0.9481)(0.9811)(0.9833)(0.9803^{1/2}) = 0.9056$$

$$_{15}t_{0,\,r\rightarrow u} = 1 - (0.93^{1/2})(0.93)(0.915)(0.91^{1/2}) = 0.2172$$

$$_{15}p_{15,\,u} = (0.9874^{1/2})(0.9839)(0.9809)(0.9770^{1/2}) = 0.9479$$

$$_{15}p_{15,\,r} = (0.9803^{1/2})(0.9748)(0.9671)(0.9584^{1/2}) = 0.9138$$

$$_{15}t_{15,\,r\rightarrow u} = 1 - (0.91^{1/2})(0.91)(0.915)(0.918^{1/2}) = 0.2390$$

The reader may compute the survival and transfer probabilities for other ages, which should agree with the entries in Table 5.6.

Transfers between inactivity and activity can be estimated from the proportions inactive and active in Table 5A.1, with survival being defined to mean remaining inactive at ages under 45 and remaining active at older ages, since the data do not allow estimates of the two-way flows. We apply (5.11) to adjust from proportions economically active to transition probabilities.

Using 5-year age intervals, the initial transfer probabilities from inactivity to activity for urban males will be given by

$$_5t_{x+2.5,\,i\rightarrow a} = \begin{cases} 0 & |_5\nu_{x+5,\,a} \leq {}_5\nu_{x,\,a} \\ ({}_5\nu_{x+5,\,a} - {}_5\nu_{x,\,a})/(1 - {}_a\nu_{x,\,a}) & |_5\nu_{x+5,\,a} > {}_5\nu_{x,\,a} \end{cases}$$

where $_n\nu_{x,a} = {_n}N_{x,a}/{_n}N_x$ is the proportion active at ages x to $x + n$. For the data of Table 5A.1 we have

$$_{2.5}t_{0,\,u,\,i\to a} = 0$$

$$_5t_{2.5,\,u,\,i\to a,\,exp} = 0$$

$$_5t_{7.5,\,u,\,i\to a,\,exp} = (0.22 - 0)/(1 - 0) = 0.22$$

$$_5t_{12.5,\,u,\,i\to a,\,exp} = (0.86 - 0.22)/(1 - 0.22) = 0.8205$$

$$_{15}t_{0,\,u,\,i\to a,\,exp} = 1 - (1 - 0)(1 - 0)(1 - 0.22)(1 - 0.8205)^{1/2} = 0.6695$$

The reader can confirm that for the later ages of labor force entry we will have $_{15}t_{15,\,u,\,i\to a,\,exp} = 0.8039$, and $_{15}t_{30,\,u,\,i\to a,\,exp} = 0.2285$, if we let $_5t_{37.5,\,u,\,i\to a} = {_5}t_{42.5,\,u,\,i\to a} = {_5}t_{47.5,\,u,\,i\to a} = 0$.

The transition probabilities can also be estimated by recentering and regrouping ages, from 0–4, 5–9, ... to $0–7\frac{1}{2}$, $7\frac{1}{2}–22\frac{1}{2}$, $22\frac{1}{2}–37\frac{1}{2}$, ... Note that the initial interval is arbitrarily $0–7\frac{1}{2}$, representing time near birth, for which the transition probability for labor force entry is 0. Using linear estimation for the partial intervals, we will have

$$_{7.5}N_{0,\,linear} = {_5}N_0 + \tfrac{1}{2}{_5}N_5$$

$$_{15}N_{x+7.5,\,linear} = \tfrac{1}{2}{_5}N_{x+5} + {_5}N_{x+10} + {_5}N_{x+15} + \tfrac{1}{2}{_5}N_{x+20}$$

Thus, $_{7.5}N_{0,\,u,\,i} = 1{,}712{,}700 + \frac{1}{2}(1{,}322{,}200)$, $_{15}N_{7.5,\,u,\,i} = \frac{1}{2}(1{,}322{,}200) + 980{,}100 + 319{,}200 + \frac{1}{2}(66{,}100)$, and so forth.

After recentering and regrouping ages the proportions inactive and active are estimated as

$$_{15}\nu_{x+7.5,\,j} = {_{15}}N_{x+7.5,\,j}/{_{15}}N_{x+7.5}$$

These terms are entered into expression (5.11). For urban males ages 0–14 and 30–44, they yield the transition probabilities for labor force entry

$$_{15}t_{0,\,u,\,i\to a,\,exp} = (0.3231 - 0)/(1 - 0) = 0.6769$$

$$_{15}t_{30,\,u,\,i\to a} = (0.9315 - 0.3231)/(1 - 0.3231) = 0.8988$$

Table 5.A1. Mexican 1960 Male Population, Life Table $_np_x$, and
Net Migration Probabilities. *Source:* Tabah (1968)

a. 1960 urban population

Ages	Inactive $_5N_{x,u,i}$	Active $_5N_{x,u,a}$	Proportion active $_5\nu_{x,u,a}$	Life table $_5S_{x+2.5,u}$
$_{2.5}S_0$				0.9772
0–4	1,712,700	0	0.000	0.9945
5–9	1,322,200	0	0.000	0.9923
10–14	980,100	73,800	0.070	0.9874
15–19	319,200	543,600	0.630	0.9839
20–24	66,100	668,500	0.910	0.9809
25–29	42,800	568,300	0.930	0.9770
30–34	32,300	506,800	0.940	0.9717
35–39	22,500	426,600	0.950	0.9627
40–44	14,800	355,000	0.960	0.9488
45–49	12,200	294,000	0.960	0.9309
50–54	13,200	251,600	0.950	0.9028
55–59	19,500	196,700	0.910	0.8582
60–64	22,600	128,300	0.850	0.7953
65–69	24,900	88,500	0.780	0.7066
70–74	27,000	50,100	0.650	0.5904
75–79	96,500	0	0.000	0.3774
80+	0	0	0.000	0.0000

b. 1960 rural population

Ages	Inactive $_5N_{x,r,i}$	Active $_5N_{x,r,a}$	Proportion active $_5\nu_{x,r,a}$	Life table $_5S_{x+2.5,r}$	Migrants $_5l_{x+2.5,r\rightarrow u}$
$_{2.5}S_0$				0.9481	
0–4	1,746,700	0	0.000	0.9811	0.070
5–9	1,398,900	0	0.000	0.9833	0.085
10–14	889,400	250,900	0.220	0.9803	0.090
15–19	127,400	782,600	0.860	0.9748	0.090
20–24	58,000	667,000	0.920	0.9671	0.085
25–29	43,100	572,600	0.930	0.9584	0.082
30–34	31,000	486,400	0.940	0.9496	0.080
35–39	22,100	420,100	0.950	0.9395	0.075
40–44	17,500	333,400	0.950	0.9268	0.070
45–49	14,600	277,400	0.950	0.9094	0.067
50–54	12,800	243,000	0.945	0.8846	0.064
55–59	12,800	200,900	0.940	0.8463	0.060
60–64	13,700	157,900	0.920	0.7914	0.058
65–69	13,000	105,400	0.890	0.7167	0.056
70–74	12,600	71,100	0.850	0.6177	0.055
75–79	52,600	0	0.000	0.4212	0.000
80+	52,200	0	0.000	0.0000	0.000

These probabilities may be compared to the corresponding probabilities 0.6695 and 0.8039 found using 5-year age intervals. Other transitions at ages 30–44 are estimated as

$$_{15}t_{30, \, u, \, a \to i} = (0.9315 - 0.9566)/0.9315 = -0.0269 \to 0$$

$$_{15}t_{30, \, u, \, i \to i} = 1 - 0.8988 = 0.1012$$

$$_{15}t_{30, \, u, \, a \to a} = 1 - 0 = 1$$

These estimates are used in Table 5.5 for their ease of calculation. The reader should recognize, however, that they are less accurate than probabilities found from 5-year age intervals.

CHAPTER 6

The Life Table III

. . . it is plain that the Purchaser *ought to pay only for such a part of the value of the* Annuity, *as he has Chances that he is living; and this ought to be computed yearly, and the Sum of all those yearly Values being added together, will amount to the value of the* Annuity *for the* Life *of the Person proposed. Now the present value of Money payable after a term of years, at any given rate of Interest, either may be had from Tables already computed; or almost as compendiously, by the Table of Logarithms: For the Arithmetical Complement of the Logarithm of Unity and its yearly Interest (that is, of 1.06 for Six per Cent. being 9.974694.) being multiplied by the number of years proposed, gives the present value of One Pound payable after the end of so many years. Then by the foregoing Proposition, it will be as the number of Persons living after that term of years, to the number dead; so are the Odds that any one person is Alive or Dead. And by consequence, as the Sum of both or the number of Persons living of the Age first proposed, to the number remaining after so many years, (both given by the [life] Table) so the present value of the yearly Sum payable after the term proposed, to the Sum which ought to be paid for the Chance the person has to enjoy such an Annuity after so many Years. And this being repeated for every year of the persons Life, the Sum of all the present Values of those Chances is the true Value of the Annuity. This will without doubt appear to be a most laborious Calculation, but it being one of the principal Uses of this Speculation, and having found some* Compendia *for the Work, I took the pains to compute the following Table, being the short Result of a not ordinary number of Arithmetical Operations; It shews the Value of Annuities for every Fifth Year of Age, to the Seventieth, as follows.*

Age	Years purchase	Age	Years purchase	Age	Years purchase
1	10.28	25	12.27	50	9.21
5	13.40	30	11.72	55	8.51
10	13.44	35	11.12	60	7.60
15	13.33	40	10.57	65	6.54
20	12.78	45	9.91	70	5.32

This shews the great Advantage of putting Money into the present Fund *lately granted to their Majesties* [*William and Mary*], *giving 14* per Cent. per Annum, *or at the rate of 7 years purchase for a Life; when young Lives, at the usual rate of Interest, are worth above 13 years Purchase. It shews likewise the Advantage of young Lives over those in Years; a life of Ten Years being almost worth 13½ years purchase, whereas one of 36 is worth but 11 . . . .*

—EDMUND HALLEY (1693)

6.1. INTRODUCTION

This chapter introduces one of the earliest contributions to life table analysis and three relatively recent developments. The first of the recent contributions, due to Keyfitz and Frauenthal (1975), is a series of $_np_x$ and $_nL_x$ formulas which permit construction of life tables that use 5-year age intervals, but are virtually indistinguishable from life tables using single year ages. The formulas have not replaced the NCHS reference series formulas for constructing intercensal life tables (Section 4.6), but could.

The second topic we address is the fitting of life table survival probabilities to model schedules using Berkson's (1944, 1951) logits, introduced in demographic modeling by Brass (Brass and Coale, 1968, pp. 127–135; Brass, 1975, pp. 85–105) and extended to model tables for amenorrhea and breast-feeding by Lesthaeghe and Page (1980). The method is used to smooth and adjust distributions where small sample sizes or age heaping in the source data limit the quality of direct estimates.

The third development is the adaptation of linear models to life tables, allowing the researcher to examine covariates of survival differences between populations. The most respected of the models is the Cox (1972; Cox and Oakes, 1984, pp. 91–141) proportional hazards model, whose coefficients represent the relative mortality risks associated with various attributes of the populations or samples being compared.

Besides these methods, the chapter includes life table formulas for insurance and annuities, the essential concerns that motivated early life table work. In the 20th century the focus of demography has expanded so dramatically that they are not now routinely studied except in advanced courses. The basic formulas are not difficult and should be understood.

The chapter includes two appendices. The first presents the life table columns and related terms in continuous notation, which allows the relationships between them to be expressed more compactly than in the discrete formulations presented in the main text. The discussion is abbreviated, but may help clarify a few points for readers familiar with calculus. Appendix

6A.2 displays the 1980 U.S. population and NCHS life tables by age, sex, and ethnicity, used in the text to illustrate life table construction.

6.2. HIGHER PRECISION LIFE TABLE FORMULAS FOR LARGE DATA SETS

When mortality tables are constructed from initial or interval population and death estimates for single year ages, the $_np_x$ and $_nL_x$ formulas introduced in Chapter 4 provide as much precision as investigators are likely to need. With wider age intervals, however, $_np_x$ estimates by those formulas tend to drift noticeably at the older ages, where mortality rates are high.

Efforts to produce 5- and 10-year rates that very closely duplicate single year rates have continued for more than a century. Old formulas exist that are fairly good, but during the Second World War they were eclipsed by new estimating formulas due to Reed and Merrell (1939) and Greville (1943). Part of Greville's contribution was a derivation for the Reed–Merrell $_np_x$ formula, which they had developed empirically. Reed and Merrell's estimator

$$_np_{x,\,RM} = \exp[-n_nM_x - (n/5)^3{}_nM_x^2] \qquad (6.1)$$

and Greville's

$$_np_{x,\,Greville} = lesser\ of\,\{\,1,$$

$$\exp[-n_nM_x - (n^2/24)(_nM_{x+n} - {}_nM_{x-n})_nM_x]\} \qquad (6.2)$$

continue to be widely respected for their good fit at the oldest ages. A range restriction is applied to Greville's estimator, since for rare survival distributions the sign of the bracketed term may be positive, with the result that $_np_x$ exceeds 1.0. Readers using either expression are reminded that estimate precision will normally be higher if terms in $_nD_x/_nN_x$ are substituted for $_nM_x$, due to aggressive rounding of $_nM_x$ in most sources.

In 1975, expanding on Greville's methodology, Keyfitz and Frauenthal introduced a series of formulas for life table terms that offer higher precision for a wider range of populations and mortality distributions than do any of their predecessors'. For $_np_x$ they have suggested

$$_np_{x,\,KF} = lesser\ of\,\{\,1,$$

$$\exp[-n_nM_x - (n/48)(_nM_{x+n} - {}_nM_{x-n})(_nN_{x-n} - {}_nN_{x+n})/_nN_x]\} \qquad (6.3)$$

As in (6.2), terms in $_nD_x/_nN_x$ should be substituted for terms in $_nM_x$ whenever the precision of the $_nM_x$ terms is low due to rounding.

All three of these $_np_x$ formulas have as their first term the simple exponential [expression (4.10)], $_np_x = \exp[-n_nM_x]$, which overestimates $_np_x$ at the older, high-mortality ages. (The exponential assumes constant mortality within intervals. The actual pattern is one of worsening mortality.) To reduce $_np_x$, in Reed and Merrell survival is adjusted downwards in proportion to $_nM_x^2$, which locates the adjustment at the ages it is most needed. In Greville, $_np_x$ is reduced in proportion both to $_nM_x$ and to the rate at which $_nM_x$ is changing (the derivative of $_nM_x$) at ages x to $x + n$, which is on the order of $d/dx \,_nM_x = (_nM_{x+n} - {_nM_{x-n}})/2n$. Greville's is the more general of the two approaches and produces $_np_x$ rates that are usually a little closer to those of life tables with single year ages. In Keyfitz and Frauenthal an additional adjustment is made for population composition. It is introduced because populations with different age distributions but identical mortality probabilities not only have different crude death rates but also slightly different age-specific death rates. The derivative $1/_nN_x \, d/dx \,_nN_x = (_nN_{x-n} - {_nN_{x+n}})/(2n^2{_nN_x})$ in (6.3) takes these effects into account.* The residual quantities in the three formulas are introduced by the estimation procedures.

Table 6.1 displays $_np_x$ and l_x values at selected ages for 1980 U.S. NCHS life tables and by linear, Reed–Merrell, and Keyfitz–Frauenthal formulas. (The table sets $l_{65} = 100,000$ for all formulas, since estimate differences at younger ages are not of great interest. The source data are from Table 6A.1.) Even at the oldest ages the differences are uniformly small. Changes in the U.S. age distribution will favor Keyfitz–Frauenthal estimates somewhat more in the 1990s (Smith, 1984).

In addition to $_np_x$, linear and exponential $_nL_x$ estimates [(4.15) and (4.16)] also tend to drift at the older ages when intervals as wide as 5 or 10 years are used. Fitting a cubic through the values $l_{x-n}, l_x, l_{x+n}, l_{x+2n}$ allows $_nL_x$ to be estimated as

$$_nL_{x, \text{ cubic}} = median \text{ } of \{ nl_x, nl_{x+n}, $$

$$(6.4)$$

$$(n/24)[13(l_x + l_{x+n}) - (l_{x-n} + l_{x+2n})] \}$$

---

* All three formulas are derived by expanding the survival probability $_np_x = \exp[-\int_0^n \mu(x + t)$ $\times \, dt]$ as a Taylor series, and expressing the derivatives of the function by linear terms in $_nM_x$ and $_nN_x$. The reader should consult Keyfitz and Frauenthal (1975) for the derivation of the expressions.

Table 6.1. U.S. 1980 Life Table $_np_x$ and l_x Values by Selected Formulas, for $l_{65} = 100,000$

Ages	NCHS 1979–1981		NCHS 1980		Linear	
	$_np_x$	l_x	$_np_x$	l_x	$_np_x$	l_x
20–24	0.99354		0.99340		0.99342	
40–44	0.98602		0.98610		0.98614	
60–64	0.92094		0.92060		0.92127	
65–69	0.88511	100,000	0.88350	100,000	0.88433	100,000
70–74	0.83224	88,511	0.83060	88,349	0.83245	88,433
75–79	0.76022	73,663	0.75730	73,381	0.75996	73,616
80–84	0.64752	56,000	0.64460	55,573	0.64684	55,945
85+	0.00000	36,261	0.00000	35,822	0.00000	36,188

Ages	Reed–Merrell		Keyfitz–Frauenthal	
	$_np_x$	l_x	$_np_x$	l_x
20–24	0.99341		0.99341	
40–44	0.98613		0.98607	
60–64	0.92107		0.92095	
65–69	0.88393	100,000	0.88377	100,000
70–74	0.83177	88,393	0.83137	88,377
75–79	0.75900	73,522	0.75813	73,474
80–84	0.64646	55,804	0.64242	55,703
85+	0.00000	36,075	0.00000	35,785

with four-digit precision to age 70 or 75 in the U.S. life table.* The limiting values, $_nL_{x,\,\text{cubic}} = nl_x$ and $_nL_{x,\,\text{cubic}} = nl_{x+n}$, are used in the rare cases when the principal estimator is out of range. [The corresponding estimate for l_x from $_nL_x$ terms is:

$$l_{x,\,\text{cubic}} = \text{median of } \{_nL_{x-n}/n,\ _nL_x/n,$$
$$[7(_nL_{x-n} + {}_nL_x) - (_nL_{x-2n} + {}_nL_{x+n})]/(12n)\} \tag{6.5}$$

The two expressions differ because the $_nL_x$ series represents survivors in intervals and l_x represents survivors at exact ages. Section 2.4 discusses their derivation.]

* The cubic can also be written

$$_nL_{x,\,\text{cubic}} = n[(1/2)(l_x + l_{x+n}) + (1/24)(_nd_{x-n} + {}_nd_{x+n})]$$

An expression that is competitive with (6.4) at the older ages is the Keyfitz–Frauenthal estimator

$$
_nL_{x,\ KF} = \begin{cases} 0\ or\ nl_x/2 & |\,l_{x+n} = 0 \\[2mm] median\ of\,\{\,nl_x,\ nl_{x+n}, \\[2mm] \dfrac{n(l_x - l_{x+n})}{\ln l_x - \ln l_{x+n}}\,[1 + (n/24)(_nM_{x+n} - _nM_{x-n})]\,\} & |\,l_{x+n} > 0 \end{cases}
$$

$$(6.6)$$

The formula adjusts the exponential $_nL_x$ estimator [(4.16)] upwards in proportion to the rate at which mortality is changing over the interval, as is done in the Greville and Keyfitz–Frauenthal $_np_x$ estimators. The user should substitute terms in $_nD_x/_nN_x$ for terms in $_nM_x$ whenever the two choices yield different $_nL_x$ estimates due to rounding of the $_nM_x$ terms.

Keyfitz and Frauenthal have also introduced a generalization of Greville's formula [(5.16)] that adjusts cause-eliminated survival rates to take into account changing mortality patterns and population size across age groups.* They suggest the estimator

$$
_np_{x,\ j,\ KF} = \begin{cases} _np_x & |\,_nD_x = 0 \\[2mm] _np_x^{(_nD_{x,\ j}/_nD_x)} & |\,_nD_x > 0,\ R\ undefined \\[2mm] _np_x^{R} & |\,_nD_x > 0,\ _nD_{x,\ j} > 0,\ R\ defined \end{cases}
$$

$$(6.7)$$

where, if its terms are defined,

$$
R = \frac{_nD_{x,\ j}}{_nD_x}\left\{1 + (1/48)\ln\left[\frac{_nN_{x+n}}{_nN_{x-n}}\right]\ln\left[\frac{_nD_{x+n}\ _nD_{x-n,\ j}}{_nD_{x-n}\ _nD_{x+n,\ j}}\right]\right\}
$$

$$(6.8)$$

The expression is undefined when any of the terms in D or N other than $_nD_{x,\ j}$ is 0.

In applying the formulas of this section, readers should note that the key expressions are out of range or undefined only for markedly irregular age and survival distributions, or when numbers of deaths are too small to display consistent patterns by age. Other formulas can be substituted whenever problems occur, or for $_nL_x$, if the estimates lead to questionable $_na_x$ values. We

---

* We omit the Keyfitz–Frauenthal expression for multiple decrement rates, which they found to differ only trivially from (5.2) (Keyfitz and Frauenthal, 1975, pp. 897–898).

also stress that the formulas are intended for use with large data sets, as in constructing national life tables. They will not improve small sample estimates.

Variances for (6.3) and (6.7) may be estimated as

$$\text{Var}_n p_{x,\ \text{KF}} = {}_n p_x\ {}_n q_x^2 / {}_n D_x \tag{6.9}$$

$$\text{Var}_n p_{x,\ j,\ \text{KF}} = {}_n p_{x,\ j}\ {}_n q_{x,\ j}\ {}_n q_x / {}_n D_x \tag{6.10}$$

6.3. LOGIT FITTING TO REFERENCE LIFE TABLES

When survival rates are estimated using relatively poor age information, errors may occur in the count of deaths by age or age group sizes. The result will be to produce uneven or erratic ${}_n q_x$, ${}_n p_x$, and l_x distributions. The same may happen when life tables are produced from sample data in which the number of events reported is small. To the extent that biases at adjacent ages offset each other, relatively robust estimates of life expectancy (e_x) may still be produced. What is most critical for life expectancy estimation is that the overall counts of deaths and population be roughly correct, and that the age shifting is not largely in one direction.

If these conditions are met, it is possible to smooth the estimated ${}_n q_x$, ${}_n p_x$, or l_x distributions by regressing either series on the ${}_n q_x$, ${}_n p_x$, or l_x distribution of a reference life table. Relatively simple models, such as the linear $l_x = a + b l_x^{(\text{ref})}$, are not especially helpful, in part because the distributions are nonlinear across ages, and also because the models may produce estimated proportions surviving that are greater than 1 or less than 0. Brass (Brass and Coale, 1968, pp. 127–135; Brass, 1975, pp. 85–105) has suggested a transform of the l_x distribution that resolves these two problems, the logit model

$$\ln[(l_0 - l_x)/l_x] = a + b \ln[(l_0 - l_x^{(\text{ref})})/l_x^{(\text{ref})}] \tag{6.11}$$

After estimating the constants a, b by ordinary or weighted linear regression, smoothed l_x values are found from the inverse of (6.11):

$$\hat{l}_x = l_0 / \{1 + e^{\hat{a}}[(l_0 - l_x^{(\text{ref})})/l_x^{(\text{ref})}]^{\hat{b}}\} \tag{6.12}$$

Weights for (6.11) should be inversely proportional to the variances of the logit terms, which are found as

$$\text{Var}(\text{logit } l_x) = [l_x^2(1 - l_x)^2]^{-1} \text{Var}(l_x) \tag{6.13}$$

Where $l_x = {}_x p_0$ the expression reduces to

$$\text{Var(logit } l_x) = [N(x)l_x(1 - l_x)]^{-1} \qquad (6.14)$$

The regression constants in (6.11) and (6.12) have an intuitive interpretation, a being loosely associated with life expectancy and b with the distribution of mortality between younger and older ages, relative to the reference table. The constants do not allow the user unlimited scope in the selection of the reference life table, however. Certain ratios in the reference table—mortality at ages 1–4 and later in life relative to infant mortality, and the rate at which mortality worsens in old age—will be preserved in the smoothed l_x rates. If these ratios are inappropriate for the population whose rates are being smoothed, the fitted estimates might be less informative than the initial values.

The reference tables most commonly used for fitting developing country data to the Brass logit are the Brass (Brass and Coale, 1968, p. 133) and Coale *et al.* (1983) model life tables. Other valuable sources are national life tables for countries or subpopulations with mortality experience similar to the population being investigated, where the tables derive from original data and have not themselves been smoothed by (6.11) or other techniques. Besides mortality, the logit is also used to fit the Lesthaeghe and Page (1980) model amenorrhea and breastfeeding distributions.

For nonhuman populations and most events other than death, the choice of reference tables is usually restricted to simple linear or exponential models. The linear model is $l_x^{(\text{ref})} = a + bx$; the exponential is $l_x^{(\text{ref})} = ae^{bx}$, or taking logarithms, $\ln l_x^{(\text{ref})} = \ln a + bx$. The fitting of the models is restricted to l_x and $l_x^{(\text{ref})}$ values in the range $0 < [l_x, l_x^{(\text{ref})}] < l_0$.

Whenever the logit is used, the researcher should examine the residuals $l_x - \hat{l}_x$ to ensure that no systematic differences between the source and fitted l_x estimates arise. A test for autocorrelation—the tendency for positive or negative differences to be grouped in particular age ranges—is the Durbin–Watson statistic (Durbin and Watson, 1950, 1951, 1971; Judge *et al.*, 1980, pp. 216–217):

$$D_{\text{DW}} = \sum_{i=2}^{k} (\mathbf{e}_i - \mathbf{e}_{i-1})^2 \Bigg/ \sum_{i=1}^{k} \mathbf{e}_i^2 \qquad (6.15)$$

where

$$\mathbf{e}_i = l_i - \hat{l}_i$$

and k is the number of age intervals in the life table. The logit fitting and Durbin–Watson test can also be used to fit $_np_x$ or $_nq_x$.

The distribution of the D_{DW} statistic is given in statistics and econometrics textbooks. For the $_nq_x$, l_x, and logit l_x distributions of most abridged life tables, the critical value at the 0.05 level falls between 1.3 (for intervals 0, 1–4, and 5-year intervals to ages 60–64) and 1.4 (for intervals to ages 80–84): smaller values of D_{DW} are significant (Smith, 1983). The Durbin–Watson test should always be used when estimated life tables are fitted to reference tables, as a check on the appropriateness of the reference table selected.

Table 6.2 and Fig. 6.1 illustrate the application of the logit regression and Durbin–Watson statistics, using mortality estimates ($_nq_x$) from the 1971 Liberian Population Growth Survey. The life expectancy at birth was found to be near 45 for both sexes in the survey, an estimate that is probably of the right order of magnitude. The survey $_nq_x$ distribution, however, displays sharp fluctuations at individual ages.

The dotted lines in the figure show fitted $_nq_x$ estimates using Coale–Demeny West Level 12 model life tables as a reference. The level selected produces life expectancies at birth of about 45 years, close to those found from the survey.

Neither Durbin–Watson statistic is significant at the 0.05 level, although for females the level is close to its critical value (1.30). Readers will note from the table that the estimate error terms (e_i) for females are positive at the youngest and oldest ages and negative at central ages, accounting for the near significance of the statistic. The male error term distribution displays less pattern.

The reader may construct $\hat{l}_x$ distributions from the fitted $_n\hat{q}_x$ terms. He or she will find that for both males and females the fitted distributions produce higher proportions surviving at most ages and higher life expectancies than the source distributions. The intent of fittings to model tables is to impose reasonable age patterns of mortality on defective samples, and not to preserve the sample life tables unchanged. It is left to the user to judge whether the given result is satisfactory.

An application of the Brass logit model to migration flows will be found in Rogers and Castro (1982). Comments on the quality of fit of the logit transform and two others, $\ln[-\ln l_x]$ and $\ln[-\ln(1 - l_x)]$, for historical data will be found in Barrett (1976).

6.4. LINEAR MODELS FOR LIFE TABLE ANALYSIS

Mortality tables and life tables for other events constructed from sample survey data can be analyzed in greater detail than the decompositions by cause of death in Chapter 5, by using each individual's survivorship status as the dependent variable in one of several linear models. All code survivorship status at age or duration x in one of the forms

Table 6.2. 1970 Mortality Probabilities $_nq_x$ from the Liberian Population Growth Survey, Coale–Demeny Model West 12 Mortality Probabilities, and Fitted Probabilities. Sources: Coale et al. (1983), Massalee (1974)

Start of age interval	Females				Males			
	$_nq_{x,\,LPGS}$	$_nq_{x,\,CD\ West\ 12}$	$_nq_{x,\,fitted}$	e_i	$_nq_{x,\,LPGS}$	$_nq_{x,\,CD\ West\ 12}$	$_nq_{x,\,fitted}$	e_i
0	0.1831	0.1317	0.1220	0.0611	0.1372	0.1554	0.1379	−0.0007
1	0.0898	0.0826	0.0815	0.0083	0.0747	0.0835	0.0761	−0.0014
5	0.0300	0.0242	0.0284	0.0016	0.0373	0.0235	0.0228	0.0145
10	0.0310	0.0189	0.0230	0.0080	0.0065	0.0171	0.0169	−0.0104
15	0.0188	0.0254	0.0297	−0.0109	0.0349	0.0243	0.0236	0.0113
20	0.0218	0.0323	0.0364	−0.0146	0.0606	0.0345	0.0328	0.0278
25	0.0383	0.0365	0.0404	−0.0021	0.0286	0.0379	0.0359	−0.0073
30	0.0198	0.0413	0.0450	−0.0252	0.0114	0.0435	0.0409	−0.0295
35	0.0540	0.0461	0.0494	−0.0046	0.0512	0.0515	0.0480	0.0032
40	0.0232	0.0512	0.0540	−0.0308	0.0884	0.0635	0.0586	0.0298
45	0.1260	0.0585	0.0606	0.0654	0.0690	0.0777	0.0710	−0.0020
50	0.1172	0.0775	0.0772	0.0400	0.1176	0.1023	0.0923	0.0253
55	0.0971	0.1022	0.0979	−0.0008	0.1451	0.1331	0.1188	0.0263
60	0.2031	0.1495	0.1362	0.0669	0.1639	0.1848	0.1631	0.0008
65	1.0000	1.0000	1.0000	1.0000	1.0000	1.0000	1.0000	1.0000

Coefficients:

	Females	Males
e^a	1.424	1.262
b	0.859	0.945
D_{DW}	2,222,318/1,616,329 = 1.375	752,593/437,963 = 1.718

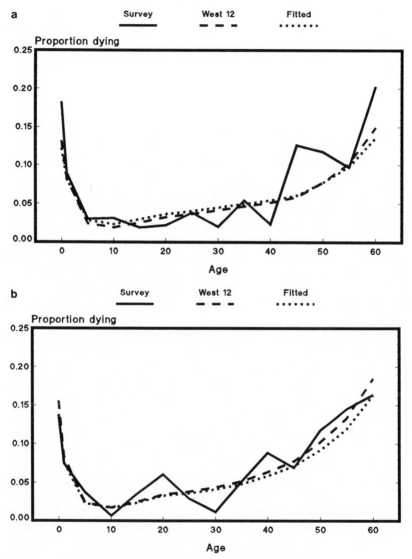

Figure 6.1. Logit fitting of Liberia 1970 $_nq_x$ estimates to Coale–Demeny model West 12 estimates. *Sources:* Coale *et al.* (1983), Massalee (1974): (a) females and (b) males.

$$f(l_x) = \begin{cases} 0, & \text{for individuals experiencing the terminating event prior to } x \\ 1, & \text{for individuals not experiencing the event as of } x \end{cases}$$

$$(6.16)$$

$$f(_np_x) = \begin{cases} 0, & \text{for individuals experiencing the event in } x \text{ to } x + n \\ 1, & \text{for individuals not experiencing the event as of } x + n \end{cases}$$

$$(6.17)$$

The analysis omits individuals with exposure times less than x in (6.16), and those with exposure times less than $x + n$ or terminations prior to x in (6.17).

The terms $f(l_x)$ and $f(_np_x)$ can be regressed on ordinal scale attributes of the sample (e.g., age, education, income) using discriminant or probit analysis, or on mixed nominal scale (e.g., sex, ethnicity) and ordinal scale attributes using logistic regression or other categorical models (Freeman, 1987; Hosmer and Lemeshow, 1989). Changes in significance levels, magnitudes, and signs of the regression coefficients for different observation intervals give the researcher an indication of the relative explanatory power of the regressor variables that have been used. They indicate as well which variables are significant at most ages or durations, and which are only locally significant (for example, significant in the early part of the l_x or $_np_x$ series but not the later part).

The researcher also has the option of combining some or all of the observation intervals in a single model, with dependent variables $f(l_x) - l_x$ or $f(_np_x) - _np_x$. In this form the dependent variables measure the difference between the individual's survival status at x, or in the interval x to $x + n$, and that of the sample as a whole. When intervals are combined, observations at each duration x or interval x to $x + n$ are weighted in proportion to the inverse of the variance of l_x or $_np_x$, which can be found by the formulas of Section 4.8. Alternatively, (6.16) or (6.17) may be used, but with the inclusion of duration (x) as a regressor variable.

The discriminant and difference models have the limitation that they may produce survival estimates $\hat{f}(l_x)$ or $\hat{f}(_np_x)$ outside the range 0 to 1 [or the range 0 to l_0 for $f(l_x)$ when $l_0 \neq 1$], especially for individuals with rare attributes. That is avoided in logistic regression, which fits the distribution

$$f(l_{x, x}) = \{1 + e^{\Sigma\, bX}\}^{-1} \qquad | l_{0,\, x} = 1.0 \qquad (6.18)$$

where $l_{x, x}$ is the proportion surviving at duration x among individuals with attributes X, and b is the set of regression coefficients associated with X.

More widely used than (6.18) is the Cox (1972) proportional hazards model

$$l_{x,\,X} = (l_{x,\,0})^{e^{\sum bX}} \qquad |\, l_{0,\,X} = 1.0 \qquad (6.19)$$

As with discriminant analysis, both models may be fitted either to the complete survival distribution or separately to subintervals by the introduction of time-dependent terms, according to the researcher's interpretation of the effects of the regressor variables at different durations. For the Cox model the coefficients b are estimates of the relative risk of mortality associated with the attributes X.

To understand the ability of the logistic and Cox model to control the range of fitted l_x values, the reader should note that for all values of the sum $\sum bX$, the exponential $\exp[\sum bX] > 0$. The exponential term contributes to the denominator of (6.18), which fixes its range to the interval $(0, 1)$. In the Cox model the range is fixed to the $(0, 1)$ interval by raising the fractional value $l_{x,\,0}$ to the power $\exp[\sum bX]$.

A linear analogue to (6.19) exists that can be fitted by ordinary or weighted least squares. On taking the log minus log transform $[\ln(-\ln\alpha)]$ of $l_{x,\,X}$, we have

$$\ln(-\ln l_{x,\,X}) = \ln(-\ln l_{x,\,0}) + \sum bX \qquad |\, l_{0,\,X} = 1.0 \qquad (6.20)$$

Some readers will recognize (6.20) as a variant of the Brass (United Nations, 1983, pp. 25–26) relational Gompertz function used to smooth or *graduate* fertility distributions:

$$\ln\left[-\ln\left({}_n f_x / \sum_x {}_n f_x\right)\right] = a + b \ln\left[-\ln\left({}_n f_x^{\,(\mathrm{ref})} / \sum_x {}_n f_x^{\,(\mathrm{ref})}\right)\right] \qquad (6.21)$$

In the Brass expression ${}_n f_x / \sum_x {}_n f_x$ is the proportion of total fertility achieved by ages x to $x + n$, and ${}_n f_x^{\,(\mathrm{ref})} / \sum_x {}_n f_x^{\,(\mathrm{ref})}$ is the proportion achieved by the same age in a model fertility schedule. The Brass logit fitting to model life tables $[(6.11)]$ is essentially similar, but with the substitution of the odds of an event, $(l_0 - l_x)/l_x$, for the log proportion $-\ln({}_n f_x / \sum_x {}_n f_x)$ in (6.21). The term *relational* is a descriptor for fittings to a reference series.

The transform given by (6.21) is essentially linear in l_x, and provides a link between ordinary or weighted least squares regressions using (6.16) and (6.17) and the proportional hazards model (6.19). To a close approximation, we have (Smith, 1985b)*:

$$b_{\mathrm{PH}} \simeq -3 b_{\mathrm{OLS}}$$

---

* The estimate is found from the derivative $d/dx \ln(-\ln x) = 1/(x \ln x)$. The derivative at $x = 0.5$ is -2.9.

Table 6.3. Difference and Proportional Hazards Coefficients for Duration of Breastfeeding, Bahia State, Brazil, 1980. *Source:* Anderson *et al.* (1984)

Variable	Difference regression [a]	−3 (diff.)	Prop. hazards [b]
Constant	0.096	−0.288	−1.131
Urban residence	−0.050	0.150	0.158
Education	−0.123 [c]	0.369	0.365 [c]
Age of woman	0.030	−0.090	−0.122
Place of last live birth	−0.099 [c]	0.297	0.335 [c]

[a] $f(l_x) - l_x = \Sigma\, bX$.
[b] $l_{x,x} = (l_{x,0})^{\exp(\Sigma\, bX)}$.
[c] Significant at 0.05 level.

The two models are compared in an analysis of breastfeeding durations in Bahia State, Brazil, in Anderson *et al.* (1984). Table 6.3 displays the coefficient estimates for their model.

An excellent introduction to the properties of the logistic and proportional hazards models is given in Manton and Stallard (1988, pp. 69–74, 79–87). Applications of proportional hazards models to conventional life tables include Trussell and Hammerslough (1983) on child mortality, Trussell *et al.* (1985) on interbirth intervals, and Menken *et al.* (1981) on marriage dissolution. An application to virtual life tables (Section 4.7) for breastfeeding distributions will be found in Diamond *et al.* (1986). On possible limitations of the model the reader should see Aalen (1989). Valuable general introductions to linear models in demography include Namboodiri and Suchindran (1987) and Halli and Rao (1991).

6.5. INSURANCE AND ANNUITIES

When Edmund Halley invented the life table in 1693, one of his first interests was to address problems in individual and joint survivorships that had arisen with the popularization of insurance and annuity plans in the late 17th century. Both types of plans represent wagers between a subscriber and an issuing provider as to how long the subscriber will live. Under an insurance plan the subscriber's estate benefits if he or she dies earlier than the provider anticipates. Annuities provide lifetime pensions that begin at a stated age, and benefit subscribers surviving longer than the number of years anticipated by the provider.

In current practice, providers cover themselves generously for overhead, risk, and profit. (The provider's *risk* is the prospect of a run on reserves through investment losses and through random fluctuations and unanticipated secular changes in subscriber mortality.) Until Halley's life table became available, providers had not begun to resolve even the basic question of how long subscribers might reasonably be expected to live.

Ignoring interest for the present, at a fixed annual insurance premium K_s a provider can expect revenues A_s to total*

$$A_s = K_s \sum_{a=x}^{\omega-n} {}_nL_a/l_x = K_s e_x \tag{6.22}$$

dollars accrued over the lifetimes of subscribers joining the plan at age x. In the expression, l_x is the life table population surviving at exact age x, ${}_nL_x$ is the life table population or person years lived in the interval x to $x + n$, and e_x is the life expectancy at x, found as years lived after x divided by survivors at x. [The summation is from ${}_nL_x$ to ${}_nL_{\omega-n}$, where ω represents the oldest age to which anyone survives.] From the expression, the number of years an average individual will pay into the fund is the same as his or her life expectancy.†

The amount $K_s e_x$ constitutes the provider's reserve from which to pay insurance benefits. Assuming the provider withdraws a proportion α of each payment to cover operating costs and risk, the insurance benefit paid at the subscriber's death would be

$$B_s = (1 - \alpha)A_s = (1 - \alpha)K_s e_x \tag{6.23}$$

For a fixed benefit B_s the premium will therefore be

$$K_s = B_s/[(1 - \alpha)e_x] \tag{6.24}$$

Straight life insurance is of this form, but with provisions for the subscriber's recovery of part of the benefit in the event of withdrawal from the plan.

Since the young earn lower incomes than their seniors, and are at a very small risk of imminent death, annual premiums as high as K_s dollars for an eventual return to their estates of $(1 - \alpha)K_s e_x$ dollars are not necessarily

---

* For ease of interpretation, the notation of this section differs from current actuarial usage. We use A to represent the present value of accruals to an insurance or annuity account, B to represent benefits paid from the account, and K to represent annual premiums. Subscripts a, s, and t refer to annuities, straight life insurance, and term insurance, respectively.

† Payments might also be made from the subscriber's age x to a later age f, at which time the policy will be paid up. In place of $K_s e_x$, revenues will total $A_s = K_s(T_x - T_f)/l_x$ in that event, again omitting interest. Allowing interest, revenues will be found from (6.28), with substitution of the age limit $f - n$ for $\omega - n$ in the summation Σ_x.

appealing. An alternative to straight life insurance that defers payments from the present to the future is *term insurance*. Term insurance fixes the payment K_t for n years only, accumulating revenues of

$$A_t = K_t \, {}_nL_x/l_x \tag{6.25}$$

dollars per subscriber over the n year period. The accrued revenue equals the annual premium times the number of years on average lived in the interval.

Since the proportion of subscribers dying in the intervals is $(l_x - l_{x+n})/l_x = {}_nd_x/l_x$, the individual death benefit will be

$$B_t = (1 - \alpha)K_t({}_nL_x/l_x)/({}_nd_x/l_x)$$

$$= (1 - \alpha)K_t \, {}_nL_x/{}_nd_x \tag{6.26}$$

[Note in comparing term insurance (6.26) with straight life (6.23), that (6.23) has the denominator $l_x/l_x = 1$, since all subscribers die while the policies are in effect.] Fixing the death benefit at B_t, the annual premium becomes

$$K_t = B_t \, {}_nd_x/[(1 - \alpha)_nL_x] \tag{6.27}$$

For the same death benefit, $B_s = B_t = (1 - \alpha)K_se_x = (1 - \alpha)K_t {}_nL_x/{}_nd_x$, the annual premiums at ages x to $x + n$ for policies entered into at age x are in the proportion

$$K_t/K_s = e_x \, {}_nd_x/{}_nL_x \le 1$$

The advantage of the lower initial premium for term insurance relative to straight life insurance is made up in higher future premiums. At ages $x + j$ to $x + j + n$ the ratio of term to straight life premiums for the same benefit payment becomes

$$K_t/K_s = e_x \, {}_nd_{x+j}/{}_nL_{x+j} \gtrless 1$$

The expression reflects a change in the term premium with age, and no change in the straight life premium.

As an example, in the 1980 U.S. life table (Table 4.9) at age 15 ${}_{10}d_{15}$ = 1126, ${}_{10}L_{15}$ = 976,181, and e_{15} = 59.9; at age 65 ${}_{10}d_{65}$ = 20,159, ${}_{10}L_{65}$ = 673,125, and e_{65} = 16.5; and at age 75 ${}_{10}d_{75}$ = 28,700, ${}_{10}L_{75}$ = 428,829, and e_{75} = 10.6 years.

For a premium of K_s = \$1000 per year to a provider retaining $\alpha = 1/4$ of receipts, a 15-year-old could buy a straight life policy paying (1

$-\frac{1}{4}$)(1000)(59.9) = \$44,925 at his death. The same death benefit would cost (1000)(59.9)(1126)/(976,181) = \$69 if bought at 10-year term. At ages 65–74 the annual premium for \$44,925 in 10-year term insurance would be (1000)(59.9)(20,159)/(673,125) = \$1794, or nearly double the annual \$1000 fixed premium for the straight life policy. By ages 75–84 the premium for the term policy would have risen to \$4009, or about four times the annual premium for straight life insurance and over the 10 years of the policy nearly the value of the benefit. In old age, as the proportion of the age group expected not to survive through the interval becomes high, the cost of term insurance rises prohibitively.

If the provider is able to invest the premiums at a fixed real rate of interest r (interpreting r as the difference between the rate of interest actually paid r_1 and the rate of inflation r_2—a distinction insurance salespersons do not emphasize), the cost ratio between term and straight life insurance changes.

As before, a straight life policy with an annual premium K_s taken out at age x will yield $K_s e_x$ dollars to the provider in actual payments. At any interest rate $r > 0$, the provider gains an additional sum through interest: in t years an immediate payment of K_s dollars will be worth $K_s(1 + r)^t$ dollars, or in continuous notation, $K_s e^{rt}$ dollars. A payment made next year will be worth $K_s e^{r(t-1)}$ dollars in year t, and so forth. Inverting the fractions, we can interpret a premium of K_s dollars paid next year as equivalent to $K_s e^{-r}$ dollars paid immediately, or a premium of K_s dollars paid in t years as equivalent to an immediate premium of $K_s e^{-rt}$ dollars.

To measure the ratio of premiums to benefits that is required to ultimately balance the fund, we may suppose that all premiums are paid immediately, and therefore at their current value; and are deposited in a fund from which benefits can be withdrawn as they come due. The present value of the annual premiums K_s will be

$$A_{s,\,r} = K_s \sum_{a=x}^{\omega-n} e^{-r[a-x+(1/2)n]} {}_nL_a \Big/ l_x \qquad (6.28)$$

where the term $e^{-r[a-x+(1/2)n]}$ measures the duration to the midpoint of the payment interval. [For example, premiums paid between x and $x + n$ have the present value $e^{-r[a-x+(1/2)n]} = e^{-r[(1/2)n]}$, premiums paid between $x + n$ and $x + 2n$ have the value $e^{-r(1.5n)}$, and so forth.*]

Reserving a proportion α of each premium to cover costs, in terms of their present values death benefits $B_{s,\,r}$ will be paid out at the rate

---

* The width of the final interval, from age 85 to ω in Table 4.9, can be estimated linearly as twice the life expectancy e_{85}, making the life expectancy the interval midpoint.

$$(1 - \alpha)A_{s, r} = B_{s, r} \sum_{a=x}^{\omega-n} e^{-r[a-x+(1/2)n]} {}_n d_a / l_x$$

The individual benefit is therefore:

$$B_{s, r} = (1 - \alpha)K_s \left(\sum_{a=x}^{\omega-n} e^{-r[a-x+(1/2)n]} {}_n L_a \right) \Big/ \left(\sum_{a=x}^{\omega-n} e^{-r[a-x+(1/2)n]} {}_n d_a \right) \qquad (6.29)$$

and for a benefit of $B_{s, r}$ the premium will be

$$K_s = B_{s, r} \left(\sum_{a=x}^{\omega-n} e^{-r[a-x+(1/2)n]} {}_n d_a \right) \Big/ \left[(1 - \alpha) \sum_{a=x}^{\omega-n} e^{-r[a-x+(1/2)n]} {}_n L_a \right] \qquad (6.30)$$

Continuing with our earlier example, if the real rate of interest is 3%, the straight life insurance premium for a policy begun at age 15 and paying \$44,925 becomes

$$K_s = (44,925)[e^{-(0.03)(5)}1126 + e^{-(0.03)(20)}3306 + e^{-(0.03)(40)}16,357$$

$$+ e^{-(0.03)(55)}20,159 + e^{-(0.03)(65)}28,700 + e^{-(0.03)(76.3)}28,533]/$$

$$\{(1 - \tfrac{1}{4})[e^{-(0.03)(5)}976,181 + e^{-(0.03)(20)}1,908,039$$

$$+ e^{-(0.03)(40)}1,711,412 + e^{-(0.03)(55)}673,125$$

$$+ e^{-(0.03)(65)}428,829 + e^{-(0.03)(76.3)}178,554]\}$$

$$= \$426$$

as against \$1000 if the fund is simply hoarded. (The example uses the life expectancy at 85, $e_{85} = 6.3$ years, to approximate the interval midpoint.) Taking interest into account, the individual will pay about \$25,500 over his expected lifetime ($e_{15} = 59.9$ years), which is much less than the death benefit his estate receives. If interest was not being earned on the principal, the expected premiums would total \$59,900, of which $\alpha = 1/4$, or \$14,975, is retained by the provider.

Term policies gain little of the benefit of interest rates, since each policy remains in effect only n years. (At the level of aggregation we have used, both premiums and benefits are paid at the same time point $x + \tfrac{1}{2}n$ and no effects of interest are felt. With finer measurement of the ages at payment and at death, a small interest contribution would be seen.) If interest makes no contribution, by about age 50 the premium on 10-year term insurance exceeds that on a straight life policy entered into age 15 and earning 3% interest.

Term policies have two advantages over straight life policies that these numbers do not address. First, the amount of insurance an individual might reasonably want is not constant throughout life. The claims on the subscriber's estate will be greater when he or she is married than when single, greater when a home is being purchased on mortgage than when it is rented or owned outright, and greater in the presence of minor dependents, especially older adolescents, than in their absence. Straight life policies typically accommodate such changing needs by including provisions for termlike adjustment of premiums and benefits.

A more important distinction between the two types of policies is the risk inherent in projecting lifetime returns on the basis of historical or current experience. Projections over a few years are not normally hazardous, but as intervals lengthen they may become so. The U.S. inflation of the 1970s, for example, sharply diminished the real value of straight life insurance policies that had been entered into in the 1950s and 1960s.

Annuity plans charge their subscribers a fixed annual premium K_a from initiation of the policy to a specified age, typically 65, after which the subscriber begins drawing an annual pension. Disregarding interest, the provider accumulates premiums in proportion to the expected lifetimes of the subscribers up to age 65, and therefore

$$A_a = K_a \sum_{a=x}^{65-n} {}_nL_a/l_x = K_a(T_x - T_{65})/l_x \qquad (6.31)$$

where T_x represents persons ages x and over in the life table. If a proportion α of each premium is retained, the fund becomes $(1 - \alpha)A_a$ out of which benefits totaling

$$B_a \sum_{a=65}^{\omega-n} {}_nL_a/l_x = B_a(l_{65}/l_x)e_{65}$$

are to be returned to the subscriber. [The benefits are drawn for the rest of their lives (e_{65}) by the proportion of subscribers (l_{65}/l_x) who survive to age 65.] Setting the reserve fund equal to benefits: $(1 - \alpha)A_a = B_a(l_{65}/l_x)e_{65}$, the annual pension becomes

$$B_a = (1 - \alpha)K_a(T_x/T_{65} - 1) \qquad (6.32)$$

Inverting (6.32), the annual premium on a pension plan subscribed at age x and paying B_a dollars from age 65 will be

$$K_a = B_a/[(1 - \alpha)(T_x/T_{65} - 1)]$$

Using the 1980 U.S. life table (Table 4.9), a pension plan absorbing $\alpha = 1/4$ of each premium, and paying a benefit of $1000 per year after age 65, would need to charge premiums of $K_a = (1000)/[(1 - \frac{1}{4})(5,876,140/1,280,508 - 1)] = \$372$ to subscribers entering at age 15. The premium is about $1/3$ of the expected annual pension. The reader can confirm that a person joining at age 45 would pay premiums of $998 for the same benefit, or very nearly the amount he or she would annually draw out.

If the provider earns interest on the premiums at the real rate r, the amount accumulated by age 65 will have the present value

$$A_{a,\,r} = K_a \sum_{a=x}^{65-n} e^{-r[a-x+(1/2)n]} {}_nL_a/l_x \tag{6.33}$$

Benefits will have the present value

$$B_{a,\,r} \sum_{a=65}^{\omega-n} e^{-r[a-x+(1/2)n]} {}_nL_a/l_x = (1 - \alpha)A_{a,\,r}$$

from which the value of $B_{a,\,r}$ at the time of payment is found to be

$$B_{a,\,r} = (1 - \alpha)K_a\left(\sum_{a=x}^{65-n} e^{-r[a-x+(1/2)n]} {}_nL_a\right) \bigg/ \left(\sum_{a=65}^{\omega-n} e^{-r[a-x+(1/2)n]} {}_nL_a\right) \tag{6.34}$$

The premium will equal

$$K_a = B_{a,\,r}\left(\sum_{a=65}^{\omega-n} e^{-r[a-x+(1/2)n]} {}_nL_a\right) \bigg/ \left[(1 - \alpha)\left(\sum_{a=x}^{65-n} e^{-r[a-x+(1/2)n]} {}_nL_a\right)\right] \tag{6.35}$$

Setting $\alpha = 1/4$, and $B_{a,\,r} = \$1000$ per year, and assuming a real interest rate of 3%, the annual premium for an individual joining the plan at age 15 will be

$$K_a = (1000)[e^{-(0.03)(55)}673,125 + e^{-(0.03)(65)}428,829$$
$$+ e^{-(0.03)(76.3)}178,554]/\{(1 - \tfrac{1}{4})[e^{-(0.03)(5)}976,181$$

$$+ e^{-(0.03)(20)}1,908,039 + e^{-(0.03)(40)}1,711,412]\}$$

$$= \$116$$

The reader can confirm that for a person joining the fund at age 45 the premium is $539.

Differences in life expectancy between males and females, and between whites and nonwhites, create fairly large differences in life insurance and annuity costs. From the 1980 NCHS life tables, an annual premium of $1000 would buy the straight life insurance and annuity benefits shown in Table 6.4 for white and black males and females entering the plans at age 25. (The table assumes $\alpha = 1/4$ in provider overhead and real interest = 3%.) At the extremes, the estate of the nonwhite male would receive only 60% as large a death benefit as that of a white female. A white female would receive lower annuity benefits than a nonwhite male in roughly the same proportion.

Like straight life insurance policies, annuities with fixed benefit payments can be severely eroded by inflation. With the relatively high inflation rates of the 1970s, they have been superceded by variable annuities, whose reserve funds fluctuate with current market conditions. A variety of hybrid policies are also offered for annuities and life insurance that preserve features of both fixed and variable benefit plans.

We caution the reader that insurance and annuity plans are more complex than our remarks may suggest. A critical dimension is the treatment of risk, particularly as it relates to the probability of declines in portfolio values or of runs on reserves for which the provider is unprepared. Accessible introductions to insurance and annuity calculations include Jordan (1975) and Beard *et al.* (1984). At a higher mathematical level the reader may see Beekman (1974) and Slud and Hoesman (1989). Keyfitz (1985) develops matrix analogues of actuarial formulas. An overview of the insurance industry is available in Huebner and Black (1982).

6.6. SUMMARY

The Keyfitz–Frauenthal estimators of Section 6.2 were developed to closely replicate life tables for single years of age using 5-year or wider intervals. At ages beyond infancy their high accuracy makes it unlikely they will be superceded by other $_np_x$ formulas. Greater potential exists for new formulas to fit real data to model life tables, especially as model tables of greater generality are developed. For analysis of the correlates of mortality, proportional hazards models and logistic regression are also a major advance over traditional regression methods. Here too, the scope for improvement is broad, as computer

Table 6.4. Life Insurance and Annuity Benefits per $1000 Annual Premium,
U.S. Black and White Males and Females, 1980[a]

Type of policy/age entered	Females		Males	
	White	Black	White	Black
Insurance:				
Age 0	192,600	148,300	146,600	109,500
25	92,100	73,400	70,200	52,400
50	34,300	27,900	25,200	20,000
75	9,500	8,700	7,000	6,600
Annuity:				
Age 0	12,900	16,200	18,400	25,600
25	4,900	6,000	6,800	9,000
50	1,100	1,300	1,500	1,800

[a] In the table, provider overhead is assumed to be 25% and annual interest on the fund is set at 3%.

technology removes barriers to the testing of new methodologies that were once formidable.

Among topics we have not addressed, the most important may be the analysis of mortality due to multiple or overlapping causes, and the implications of heterogeneity of risk. For an introduction to these issues the reader should see Manton and Stallard (1984, 1988), Keyfitz (1985, pp. 385–399), and shorter papers by Keyfitz and Littman (1979), Vaupel et al. (1979), Vaupel and Yashin (1985), and Trussell and Rodríguez (1990). In many respects, heterogeneity remains both a challenge and an enigma. There exists a broad consensus that individuals are at unequal risk for many causes of illness and death, but the differences are unquantifiable where underlying survival distributions are nonparametric in form. Parametric forms can be imposed on the survival distribution, or on the distribution of heterogeneity, but the implications of each model cannot be divorced from the choices the researcher makes (Trussell and Richards, 1985). The heterogeneity of fecundability, introduced in Section 1.3 in connection with the Pearl Index, is more tractable only because conception probabilities may be assumed constant over intervals of a few years or so, a period long enough for distribution moments to be estimated.

APPENDIX 6A.1. THE LIFE TABLE IN CONTINUOUS NOTATION

Applications of the life table to real data always require discrete analysis and the formulas appropriate to it, but in the theoretical models that underlie life table construction continuous notation is a simpler medium with which to work. An easy entry into continuous analysis is provided by the l_x term, the number surviving at exact age x from among l_0 births. In continuous notation l_x becomes $l(x)$; for convenience we will set the radix $l_0 = 1.0$.

The number surviving in an age interval, $_nL_x$, can be decomposed into the sum of the numbers of survivors in a series of smaller intervals of width k. For $n = 5$ the sum may be over the five single year intervals

$$_nL_x = {_1L_x} + {_1L_{x+1}} + \cdots + {_1L_{x+4}} = \sum_{a=x}^{x+n-1} {_1L_a}$$

or the sum over the 10 half-year intervals

$$_nL_x = {_{1/2}L_x} + {_{1/2}L_{x+1/2}} + \cdots + {_{1/2}L_{x+n-1/2}} = \sum_{a=x}^{x+n-1/2} {_{1/2}L_a}$$

and so forth. The limit of the decomposition substitutes a continuous summation ($\int$) across $l(a)$ terms for the discrete summation ($\sum$) across $_kL_a$ to yield

$$_nL_x = \lim_{k \downarrow 0} \sum_{a=x}^{x+n-k} {_kL_a} = \int_{a=x}^{x+n} l(a)\, da \qquad (6A.1)$$

Both the discrete and continuous terms represent the sum of all persons in the age interval from x to $x + n$. The transition from $_kL_a$ to $l(a)$ occurs as the age interval narrows to widths at which the distinction between an interval and a point largely disappears.

The life expectancy, in discrete notation

$$e_x = \sum_{a=x}^{\omega-n} {_nL_a}/l_x$$

becomes in continuous notation

$$e_x = \int_{a=x}^{\omega} l(a)\, da / l_x \qquad (6A.2)$$

At birth the life expectancy is $\int_0^\omega l(a)\, da / l_0$, and since $\int_0^\omega l(a)\, da$ represents the total population the birth rate is $b = l_0 / \int_0^\omega l(a)\, da = 1/e_0$. The life table death rate is also $1/e_0$ since the number in the life table birth cohort is also the number of deaths.

The proportional rate at which the population is dying at age x is given by the derivative of l_x over l_x, or $(1/l_x)\, d/dx\, l_x$, which from elementary calculus is also $d/dx\, \ln l_x = \mu(x)$. The rate $\mu(x)$ represents the *hazard* or *force of mortality*. We can define l_x in terms of the integral of its hazard function: if $\mu(x)$ is the derivative of the logarithm of $l(x)$, then $\ln l(x) = -\int_{-\infty}^{x} \mu(a)\, da = -\int_0^x \mu(a)\, da$, since μ is undefined for negative ages. Setting $l_0 = 1$, $l(x)$ is found as

$$l(x) = \exp\left[-\int_0^x \mu(a)\, da \right] \qquad | l_0 = 1 \qquad (6A.3)$$

Over smaller age intervals we define $_np_x = \exp[\int_x^{x+n} \mu(a)\, da]$.

The reader may think of the integral $\int_0^x \mu(a)\, da$ as summing the rates at which the population is being depleted by deaths over the age intervals from birth to x, for which a reasonable approximation is the sum of the age-specific death rates $_nM_a$ to age x. For example, in the U.S. 1980 life table (Table 4.9), the sum of the mortality rates up to age 25 is $0.01280 + 4(0.00063) + 10(0.00031 + 0.00115) = 0.02992$. The life table estimate is

$$\int_0^{25} \mu(a)\, da = -\ln l_{25} = 0.02989 \qquad (6A.4)$$

When the hazard μ is constant over an age interval, as in our example, the integral $\int_x^{x+n} \mu(a)\, da$ reduces to $\mu \int_x^{x+n} da = n\mu$, and $_np_x = e^{-n\mu}$. Substituting $_nM_x$ for μ produces the familiar exponential $_np_x$ formula [(4.10)]

$$_np_{x;\ \text{exponential}} = e^{-n\,_nM_x}$$

We used this expression to find (6A.4). Approximate formulas for finding $\mu(x)$ from the l_x distribution are given in the footnote on p. 38.

For most of life the rate of population depletion is low and the sum of the increments $\mu(a)$ or $n\,_nM_a$ remains small. Near the end of life $\mu(a)$ rises sharply, in 1980 reaching about 0.07 by ages 80–84. Only about two-thirds of those alive at 80 survive to 85, and fewer to 90 or beyond.

The curvature of the l_x distribution is measured by $H(x)$, defined for $l_0 = 1.0$ as

$$H(x) = -\int_x^{\omega} l(a)\ln l(a)\, da / e_x \qquad | l_0 = 1.0 \qquad (6A.5)$$

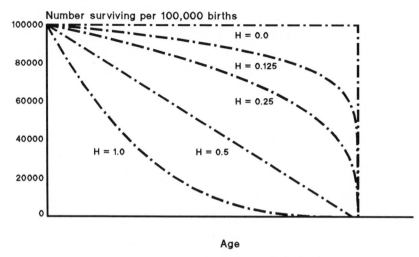

Figure 6A.1. Values of *H* for selected l_x distributions.

$$= \int_x^\omega d(a)e(a) \, da/e_x \qquad (6A.6)$$

where $d(a) = -l'(a)$ is the number of deaths in the interval $(a, a + da)$. H has two equivalent interpretations. The first, due to Keyfitz (1977a; 1985, pp. 62–72), presents it as a measure of the rate at which the population is depleted, or population entropy, over its lifetime. The second, due to Goldman and Lord (1986), sees it as the average years of future life lost by observed deaths, divided by life expectancy. A linear approximation to the Goldman and Lord expression was introduced as (4.23), in connection with measures of potential years of life lost.

For ages at which all persons survive, $l_a = 1$ and $\ln l_a = 0$. When the l_x distribution is rectangular (that is, when all deaths occur at the single age ω), $H(x) = 0$, as both the Keyfitz and Goldman and Lord interpretations will suggest. When survival falls linearly by age, $H(x) = 1/2$, representing the loss of half of the potential life span; and when the decline is exponential, $H(x) = 1$, indicating that the loss is equal to the life expectancy. For the United States, $H(0)$ is about 0.18 (see Section 4.6). The relationship between the slope of l_x and $H(x)$ for selected survival distributions is shown in Fig. 6A.1.

The essential source for readers interested in mathematical demography is Keyfitz (1977b). Readers should also see Keyfitz (1985), both for its introduction to entropy and for its many extensions of Keyfitz (1977b).

APPENDIX 6A.2. U.S. 1980 POPULATION, DEATHS, AND NATIONAL CENTER FOR HEALTH STATISTICS LIFE TABLES BY AGE, SEX, AND ETHNICITY

Table 6.A1. 1980 Census Population and Deaths, and Age-Specific Death Rates, for Total, Male, and Female Populations by Race. (Population Estimates are for the Resident Population, and Omit Overseas U.S. Military.)
Source: National Center for Health Statistics (1984–1985)

a. Total population

Age interval x to $x + n$	Census population $_nN_x$	1980 deaths $_nD_x$	Age-specific death rate $_nM_x$
0–1	3,533,692	45,526	0.012 883
1–5	12,814,562	8,187	0.000 639
5–10	16,699,956	5,075	0.000 304
10–15	18,242,129	5,614	0.000 979
15–20	21,168,124	20,733	0.000 979
20–25	21,318,704	28,294	0.001 327
25–30	19,520,919	25,732	0.001 318
30–35	17,560,920	24,508	0.001 396
35–40	13,965,302	25,656	0.001 837
40–45	11,669,408	32,762	0.002 808
45–50	11,089,755	49,787	0.004 489
50–55	11,710,032	83,370	0.007 120
55–60	11,615,254	126,016	0.010 849
60–65	10,087,621	166,165	0.016 472
65–70	8,782,481	216,277	0.024 626
70–75	6,798,124	250,344	0.036 825
75–80	4,793,722	263,611	0.054 991
80–85	2,935,033	253,646	0.086 420
85 and over	2,240,067	357,970	0.159 803
Unknown		568	
Total	226,545,805	1,989,841	0.008 783

Continued on next page

b. Total males and females

Age interval x to $x+n$	Males			Females		
	Census population $_nN_{x,M}$	1980 deaths $_nD_{x,M}$	Age-specific death rate $_nM_{x,M}$	Census population $_nN_{x,F}$	1980 deaths $_nD_{x,F}$	Age-specific death rate $_nM_{x,F}$
0–1	1,806,338	25,804	0.014 285	1,727,354	19,722	0.011 417
1–5	6,555,671	4,761	0.000 726	6,258,891	3,426	0.000 547
5–10	8,539,080	2,989	0.000 350	8,160,876	2,086	0.000 256
10–15	9,316,221	3,571	0.000 383	8,925,908	2,043	0.000 229
15–20	10,755,409	15,207	0.001 414	10,412,715	5,526	0.000 531
20–25	10,663,231	21,696	0.002 035	10,655,473	6,598	0.000 619
25–30	9,705,107	19,037	0.001 962	9,815,812	6,695	0.000 682
30–35	8,676,796	17,003	0.001 960	8,884,124	7,505	0.000 845
35–40	6,861,509	16,822	0.002 452	7,103,793	8,834	0.001 244
40–45	5,708,210	20,790	0.003 642	5,961,198	11,792	0.001 978
45–50	5,388,249	31,469	0.005 840	5,701,506	18,318	0.003 213
50–55	5,620,670	53,003	0.009 430	6,089,362	30,367	0.004 987
55–60	5,481,863	80,075	0.014 607	6,133,391	45,941	0.007 490
60–65	4,669,892	104,187	0.022 310	5,417,729	61,978	0.011 440
65–70	3,902,955	132,459	0.033 938	4,879,526	83,818	0.017 177
70–75	2,853,547	144,912	0.050 783	3,944,577	105,432	0.026 728
75–80	1,847,661	138,208	0.074 802	2,946,061	125,403	0.042 566
80–85	1,019,227	114,557	0.112 416	1,915,806	139,089	0.072 601
85 and over	681,525	128,134	0.188 011	1,558,542	229,836	0.147 469
Unknown		394			174	
Total	110,053,161	1,075,078	0.009 769	116,492,644	914,583	0.007 851

Continued on next page

Table 6.A1. Continued

c. White males and females

Age interval x to x + n	Males			Females		
	Census population $_nN_{x,M}$	1980 deaths $_nD_{x,M}$	Age-specific death rate $_nM_{x,M}$	Census population $_nN_{x,F}$	1980 deaths $_nD_{x,F}$	Age-specific death rate $_nM_{x,F}$
0–1	1,486,617	18,290	0.012 303	1,411,942	13,590	0.009 625
1–5	5,402,382	3,573	0.000 661	5,127,023	2,526	0.000 493
5–10	7,038,966	2,285	0.000 325	6,688,217	1,613	0.000 241
10–15	7,734,050	2,891	0.000 374	7,369,190	1,612	0.000 219
15–20	9,013,319	12,866	0.001 427	8,677,221	4,664	0.000 537
20–25	9,109,473	17,391	0.001 909	8,975,451	5,139	0.000 573
25–30	8,369,837	14,618	0.001 747	8,299,991	4,851	0.000 584
30–35	7,569,880	12,685	0.001 676	7,596,100	5,544	0.000 730
35–40	6,016,948	12,559	0.002 087	6,110,694	6,607	0.001 081
40–45	4,992,983	15,785	0.003 161	5,120,900	8,913	0.001 741
45–50	4,756,856	24,816	0.005 217	4,939,612	14,070	0.002 848
50–55	5,017,149	43,490	0.008 668	5,345,469	24,258	0.004 538
55–60	4,929,331	67,809	0.013 756	5,466,745	38,043	0.006 959
60–65	4,221,379	90,363	0.021 406	4,858,423	52,430	0.010 792
65–70	3,517,450	116,502	0.033 121	4,375,819	71,892	0.016 429
70–75	2,578,300	129,502	0.050 228	3,575,510	92,430	0.025 851
75–80	1,668,496	124,611	0.074 685	2,683,070	112,386	0.041 887
80–85	931,993	105,008	0.112 756	1,773,837	128,362	0.072 364
85 and over	620,764	118,549	0.190 973	1,439,899	215,691	0.149 796
Unknown		285			108	
Total	94,976,173	933,878	0.009 833	99,835,113	804,729	0.008 061

d. Black males and females

0–1	268,994	6,958	0.025 867	265,806	5,645	0.021 237
1–5	967,347	1,069	0.001 105	950,534	802	0.000 844
5–10	1,262,180	627	0.000 497	1,242,096	417	0.000 336
10–15	1,351,353	613	0.000 454	1,335,911	370	0.000 277
15–20	1,497,744	2,015	0.001 345	1,504,109	757	0.000 503
20–25	1,308,760	3,854	0.002 945	1,433,135	1,315	0.000 918
25–30	1,091,202	4,020	0.003 684	1,243,992	1,648	0.001 325
30–35	875,932	3,993	0.004 559	1,023,162	1,752	0.001 712
35–40	665,779	3,906	0.005 867	799,636	2,015	0.002 520
40–45	569,477	4,615	0.008 104	688,176	2,804	0.004 075
45–50	517,667	6,219	0.012 014	630,617	3,952	0.006 267
50–55	506,443	8,937	0.017 647	626,921	5,708	0.009 105
55–60	467,930	11,498	0.024 572	572,215	7,472	0.013 058
60–65	386,011	13,036	0.033 771	487,119	9,064	0.018 607
65–70	332,379	14,904	0.044 840	446,264	11,328	0.025 384
70–75	234,651	14,191	0.060 477	329,821	12,400	0.037 596
75–80	152,950	12,377	0.080 922	234,964	12,321	0.052 438
80–85	75,029	8,669	0.115 542	125,154	10,050	0.080 301
85 and over	53,010	8,534	0.160 988	106,047	13,115	0.123 672
Unknown		103			62	
Total	12,584,838	130,138	0.010 341	14,045,679	102,997	0.007 333

Table 6.A2. 1980 NCHS Life Tables for Total, Male, and Female Populations by Race.
Source: National Center for Health Statistics (1984–1985)

Age interval	Proportion dying	Of 100,000 born alive		Stationary population		Average remaining lifetime
Period of life between two exact ages stated in years x to $x+n$	Proportion of persons alive at beginning of age interval dying during interval $_nq_x$	Number living at beginning of age interval l_x	Number dying during age interval $_nd_x$	In the age interval $_nL_x$	In this and all subsequent age intervals T_x	Average number of years of life remaining at beginning of age interval e_x
			a. Total population			
0–1	0.01266	100,000	1,266	98,901	7,371,986	73.7
1–5	0.00253	98,734	250	394,355	7,273,085	73.7
5–10	0.00152	98,484	150	492,017	6,878,730	69.8
10–15	0.00155	98,334	152	491,349	6,386,713	64.9
15–20	0.00491	98,182	482	489,817	5,895,364	60.0
20–25	0.00663	97,700	648	486,901	5,405,547	55.3
25–30	0.00657	97,052	638	483,665	4,918,646	50.7
30–35	0.00697	96,414	672	480,463	4,434,981	46.0
35–40	0.00914	95,742	875	476,663	3,954,518	41.3
40–45	0.01392	94,867	1,321	471,250	3,477,855	36.7
45–50	0.02222	93,546	2,079	462,857	3,006,605	32.1
50–55	0.03508	91,467	3,209	449,811	2,543,748	27.8
55–60	0.05298	88,258	4,676	430,230	2,093,937	23.7
60–65	0.07942	83,582	6,638	402,081	1,663,707	19.9
65–70	0.11651	76,944	8,965	363,181	1,261,626	16.4
70–75	0.16942	67,979	11,517	312,015	898,445	13.2
75–80	0.24268	56,462	13,702	248,534	586,430	10.4
80–85	0.35540	42,760	15,197	175,192	337,896	7.9
85 and over	1.00000	27,563	27,563	162,704	162,704	5.9

b. Male population

Age						
0–1	0.01400	100,000	1,400	98,787	6,995,933	70.0
1–5	0.00287	98,600	283	393,749	6,897,146	70.0
5–10	0.00176	98,317	173	491,124	6,503,397	66.1
10–15	0.00192	98,144	188	490,340	6,012,273	61.3
15–20	0.00710	97,956	695	488,224	5,521,933	56.4
20–25	0.01014	97,261	986	483,870	5,033,709	51.8
25–30	0.00975	96,275	939	478,990	4,549,839	47.3
30–35	0.00978	95,336	932	474,430	4,070,849	42.7
35–40	0.01217	94,404	1,149	469,323	3,596,419	38.1
40–45	0.01803	93,255	1,681	462,351	3,127,096	33.5
45–50	0.02883	91,574	2,640	451,697	2,664,745	29.1
50–55	0.04621	88,934	4,110	435,061	2,213,048	24.9
55–60	0.07070	84,824	5,997	409,935	1,777,987	21.0
60–65	0.10612	78,827	8,365	374,082	1,368,052	17.4
65–70	0.15708	70,462	11,068	325,406	993,970	14.1
70–75	0.22595	59,394	13,420	263,862	668,564	11.3
75–80	0.31487	45,974	14,476	193,303	404,702	8.8
80–85	0.43542	31,498	13,715	121,742	211,399	6.7
85 and over	1.00000	17,783	17,783	89,657	89,657	5.0

Continued on next page

Table 6.A2. Continued

c. Female population

Age interval	Proportion dying	Of 100,000 born alive		Stationary population		Average remaining lifetime
Period of life between two exact ages stated in years x to $x + n$	Proportion of persons alive at beginning of age interval dying during interval $_nq_x$	Number living at beginning of age interval l_x	Number dying during age interval $_nd_x$	In the age interval $_nL_x$	In this and all subsequent age intervals T_x	Average number of years of life remaining at beginning of age interval e_x
0–1	0.01126	100,000	1,126	99,021	7,748,490	77.5
1–5	0.00217	98,874	215	394,990	7,649,469	77.4
5–10	0.00128	98,659	126	492,954	7,254,479	73.5
10–15	0.00115	98,533	113	492,411	6,761,525	68.6
15–20	0.00265	98,420	261	491,492	6,269,114	63.7
20–25	0.00311	98,159	305	490,045	5,777,622	58.9
25–30	0.00341	97,854	334	488,463	5,287,577	54.0
30–35	0.00422	97,520	412	486,634	4,799,114	49.2
35–40	0.00619	97,108	601	484,140	4,312,480	44.4
40–45	0.00998	96,507	963	480,283	3,828,340	39.7
45–50	0.01595	95,544	1,524	474,143	3,348,057	35.0
50–55	0.02470	94,020	2,322	464,624	2,873,923	30.6
55–60	0.03687	91,698	3,381	450,481	2,409,299	26.3
60–65	0.05583	88,317	4,931	429,930	1,958,818	22.2
65–70	0.08277	83,386	6,902	400,651	1,528,888	18.3
70–75	0.12608	76,484	9,643	359,605	1,128,237	14.8
75–80	0.19374	66,841	12,950	303,049	768,632	11.5
80–85	0.30875	53,891	16,639	228,072	465,583	8.6
85 and over	1.00000	37,252	37,252	237,511	237,911	6.4

d. White male population

0–1	0.01233	100,000	1,233	98,928	7,068,892	70.7
1–5	0.00262	98,767	259	394,478	6,969,964	70.6
5–10	0.00162	98,508	160	492,116	6,575,486	66.8
10–15	0.00187	98,348	184	491,369	6,083,370	61.9
15–20	0.00716	98,164	703	489,235	5,592,001	57.0
20–25	0.00951	97,461	927	484,997	5,102,766	52.4
25–30	0.00867	96,534	837	480,529	4,617,769	47.8
30–35	0.00836	95,697	800	476,553	4,137,240	43.2
35–40	0.01037	94,897	984	472,195	3,660,687	38.6
40–45	0.01565	93,913	1,470	466,164	3,188,492	34.0
45–50	0.02579	92,443	2,384	456,675	2,722,328	29.4
50–55	0.04256	90,059	3,833	441,382	2,265,653	25.2
55–60	0.06673	86,226	5,754	417,577	1,824,271	21.2
60–65	0.10205	80,472	8,212	382,727	1,406,694	17.5
65–70	0.15363	72,260	11,101	334,374	1,023,967	14.2
70–75	0.22371	61,159	13,682	272,110	689,593	11.3
75–80	0.31451	47,477	14,932	199,743	417,483	8.8
80–85	0.43629	32,545	14,199	125,737	217,740	6.7
85 and over	1.00000	18,346	18,346	92,003	92,003	5.0

Continued on next page

Table 6.A2. Continued

| Age interval | Proportion dying | Of 100,000 born alive | Number dying during age interval | Stationary population | | Average remaining lifetime |
Period of life between two exact ages stated in years x to $x + n$	Proportion of persons alive at beginning of age interval dying during interval nq_x	Number living at beginning of age interval l_x	nd_x	In the age interval nL_x	In this and all subsequent age intervals T_x	Average number of years of life remaining at beginning of age interval e_x
			e. White female population			
0–1	0.00969	100,000	969	99,156	7,812,718	78.1
1–5	0.00195	99,031	193	395,676	7,713,562	77.9
5–10	0.00120	98,838	119	493,868	7,317,886	74.0
10–15	0.00109	98,719	108	493,350	6,824,018	69.1
15–20	0.00269	98,611	265	492,434	6,330,668	64.2
20–25	0.00288	98,346	283	491,029	5,838,234	59.4
25–30	0.00293	98,063	287	489,619	5,347,205	54.5
30–35	0.00364	97,776	356	488,043	4,857,586	49.7
35–40	0.00538	97,420	524	485,886	4,369,543	44.9
40–45	0.00863	96,896	836	482,541	3,883,657	40.1
45–50	0.01413	96,060	1,357	477,123	3,401,116	35.4
50–55	0.02246	94,703	2,127	468,520	2,923,993	30.9
55–60	0.03423	92,576	3,169	455,395	2,455,473	26.5
60–65	0.05267	89,407	4,709	435,930	2,000,078	22.4
65–70	0.07919	84,698	6,707	407,755	1,564,148	18.5
70–75	0.12199	77,991	9,514	367,579	1,156,393	14.8
75–80	0.19071	68,477	13,059	311,089	788,814	11.5
80–85	0.30752	55,418	17,042	234,762	477,725	8.6
85 and over	1.00000	38,376	38,376	242,963	242,963	6.3

f. Black male population

Age						
0–1	0.02335	100,000	2,335	97,987	6,366,187	63.7
1–5	0.00429	97,665	419	389,668	6,268,200	64.2
5–10	0.00249	97,246	242	485,569	5,878,532	60.5
10–15	0.00228	97,004	221	484,569	5,392,963	55.6
15–20	0.00678	96,783	656	482,506	4,908,394	50.7
20–25	0.01472	96,127	1,415	477,300	4,425,888	46.0
25–30	0.01827	94,712	1,730	469,268	3,948,588	41.7
30–35	0.02257	92,982	2,099	459,833	3,479,320	37.4
35–40	0.02893	90,883	2,629	448,122	3,019,487	33.2
40–45	0.03973	88,254	3,506	432,856	2,571,365	29.1
45–50	0.05841	84,748	4,950	411,834	2,138,509	25.2
50–55	0.08469	79,798	6,758	382,683	1,726,675	21.6
55–60	0.11598	73,040	8,471	344,578	1,343,992	18.4
60–65	0.15593	64,569	10,068	298,103	999,414	15.5
65–70	0.20189	54,501	11,003	245,198	701,311	12.9
70–75	0.26321	43,498	11,449	188,676	456,113	10.5
75–80	0.33508	32,049	10,739	132,368	267,437	8.3
80–85	0.44378	21,310	9,457	81,589	135,069	6.3
85 and over	1.00000	11,853	11,853	53,480	53,480	4.5

Continued on next page

Table 6.A2. Continued

g. Black female population

Age interval	Proportion dying	Of 100,000 born alive			Stationary population		Average remaining lifetime
Period of life between two exact ages stated in years x to $x + n$	Proportion of persons alive at beginning of age interval dying during interval $_nq_x$	Number living at beginning of age interval l_x	Number dying during age interval $_nd_x$		In the age interval $_nL_x$	In this and all subsequent age intervals T_x	Average number of years of life remaining at beginning of age interval e_x
0–1	0.01949	100,000	1,949		98,313	7,228,626	72.3
1–5	0.00329	98,051	323		391,420	7,130,313	72.7
5–10	0.00168	97,728	164		488,183	6,738,893	69.0
10–15	0.00138	97,564	135		487,518	6,250,710	64.1
15–20	0.00252	97,429	246		486,591	5,763,192	59.2
20–25	0.00460	97,183	447		484,857	5,276,601	54.3
25–30	0.00663	96,736	641		482,155	4,791,744	49.5
30–35	0.00854	96,095	821		478,556	4,309,589	44.8
35–40	0.01252	95,274	1,193		473,573	3,831,033	40.2
40–45	0.02018	94,081	1,899		465,900	3,357,460	35.7
45–50	0.03091	92,182	2,849		454,109	2,891,560	31.4
50–55	0.04461	89,333	3,985		437,103	2,437,451	27.3
55–60	0.06339	85,348	5,410		413,741	2,000,348	23.4
60–65	0.08908	79,938	7,121		382,564	1,586,607	19.8
65–70	0.11972	72,817	8,718		342,880	1,204,043	16.5
70–75	0.17292	64,099	11,084		293,205	861,163	13.4
75–80	0.23229	53,015	12,315		233,979	567,958	10.7
80–85	0.33423	40,700	13,603		168,713	333,979	8.2
85 and over	1.00000	27,097	27,097		165,266	165,266	6.1

CHAPTER 7

Measures of Fertility

The process of reproduction involves three necessary steps sufficiently obvious to be generally recognized in human culture: (1) intercourse, (2) conception, and (3) gestation and parturition. In analyzing cultural influences on fertility, one may well start with the factors directly connected with these three steps. Such factors would be those through which, and only through which, cultural conditions can affect fertility. for this reason, by way of convenience, they can be called the "intermediate variables" and can be presented schematically as follows:

I. Factors affecting exposure to intercourse ("intercourse variables")
  A. Those governing the formation and dissolution of unions in the reproductive period
     1. Age of entry into sexual unions
     2. Permanent celibacy: proportion of women never entering sexual unions
     3. Amount of reproductive period spent after or between unions
        a. When unions are broken by divorce, separation, or desertion
        b. When unions are broken by death of husband
  B. Those governing the exposure to intercourse within union
     4. Voluntary abstinence
     5. Involuntary abstinence (from impotence, illness, unavoidable but temporary separations)
     6. Coital frequency (excluding periods of abstinence)
II. Factors affecting exposure to conception ("conception variables")
     7. Fecundity or infecundity, as affected by involuntary causes
     [7a. Lactational infecundity]
     8. Use or nonuse of contraception
        a. By mechanical or chemical means
        b. By other means
     9. Fecundity or infecundity, as affected by voluntary causes (sterilization, subincision, medical treatment, etc.)

III. Factors affecting gestation and successful parturition ("gestation variables")

  10. Fetal mortality from involuntary causes

  11. Fetal mortality from voluntary causes

                                                              —DAVIS AND BLAKE (1956)

[We have added lactational infecundity to Davis and Blake's listing as item 7a, after Hobcraft and Little (1984).]

7.1. INTRODUCTION

An important distinction between crude birth and death rates is that populations may vary greatly in their proportions over age 50 or 65, where mortality is concentrated, but most tend to be similar in the proportions at ages 15–44, where fertility concentrates. As an illustration, Table 7.1 displays age distributions for the United States and six other countries, supplementing the series of Table 3.1.

Comparing summary rates for the United States and Mexico, Mexico's crude death rate is substantially lower than the U.S. CDR despite the greater U.S. life expectancy, because a much smaller proportion of the Mexican population is in the older age groups. At the fertile ages, however, the proportions in the two populations are nearly the same. The similarity, which holds across nearly all countries, allows us to develop relationships between fertility measures and make comparisons across populations in a way that is not possible for mortality measures.

Another aspect of fertility that is common to world populations is the sex ratio at birth, $_{\omega}B_{0,\,m}/_{\omega}B_{0,\,f}$, where $_{\omega}B_0$ represents births to parents of one sex across all of the fertile ages and the subscripts f, m denote the infants' sex. The sex ratio averages about 102 males per 100 females in black populations and 105 males per 100 females in other ethnicities. The ratio is higher at conception, but is brought down by higher male than female fetal losses. It also declines slightly with birth order.

As far as is known, the sex ratio is not affected by nutrition during pregnancy, or by parental preferences or stopping rules. Couples wanting sons or daughters but having daughters or sons, do not improve their chances that the next child will be of the sex they want as their family sizes increase. Where the sex of their children is important to parents, at each higher birth order the population still procreating may become more concentrated toward those without sons or without daughters, but the outcomes of their higher-order pregnancies will be sons and daughters in about equal proportions.

Table 7.1. Population Characteristics for India, United States, Indonesia, Brazil, Japan, Germany, and Mexico, c. 1980.
Sources: United Nations (1989), and United Nations Demographic Yearbooks and Population Reference Bureau World Population Data Sheets (Various Years)

Country	Population	Proportion					Crude birth rate	Crude death rate	Total fert. rate	Life exp.
		0–14	15–44 Male	15–44 Female	45–64	65+				
India	675,000,000	0.39	0.23	0.22	0.13	0.03	0.035	0.015	5.3	55
USA	225,000,000	0.22	0.23	0.24	0.19	0.12	0.016	0.009	1.9	75
Indonesia	150,000,000	0.41	0.21	0.22	0.13	0.03	0.034	0.016	4.7	50
Brazil	125,000,000	0.38	0.23	0.23	0.12	0.04	0.032	0.009	4.4	60
Japan	120,000,000	0.23	0.23	0.22	0.22	0.10	0.014	0.006	1.8	75
Germany	80,000,000	0.18	0.23	0.22	0.21	0.16	0.011	0.012	1.6	75
Mexico	75,000,000	0.46	0.21	0.21	0.09	0.03	0.032	0.006	4.8	65

7.2. COMPUTATION OF AGE-SPECIFIC, GENERAL, AND TOTAL FERTILITY RATES

Age-specific fertility rates display the proportion of women at various ages who give birth during one year, usually using 1- or 5-year age intervals from 15 to 44 or 15 to 49. For women in the age interval x to $x + n$ the ASFR is:

$$\text{ASFR}_{x, \text{F}} = {}_nf_{x, \text{F}} = {}_nB_{x, \text{F}}/{}_nN_{x, \text{F}} \qquad (7.1)$$

or, more simply,

$$\text{ASFR}_x = {}_nf_x = {}_nB_x/{}_nN_{x, \text{F}}$$

where ${}_nB_{x, \text{F}}$ represents annual births to women ages x to $x + n$ and ${}_nN_{x, \text{F}}$ is the midyear female population at the same ages. (The numerator subscripts F or M, denoting the sex of the parents, are conventionally omitted when rates are calculated for females.*)

U.S. 1980 female ASFRs are shown in Table 7.2.† They range from 2% or fewer of women at ages 35+ giving birth during the year to about 6% of women 15–19 and 30–34, and 11% of women in their 20s. These are not high rates: if 11% of women give birth each year from age 20 through 29, over the 10 years of the interval they will average only 1.1 births each (10 years × 0.11 birth per year). At 15–19 and 30–34, only about 6% of women give birth each year, adding about 0.6 birth in these 10 years. By age 35,

---

* Following standard usage, we will include the subscripts F for females and M for males to designate the sex of the parents only when that is not clear from the context. Lowercase subscripts f, m will be used to differentiate the sex of the infants. As examples, the terms ${}_\omega B_{0, \text{F}}$, ${}_\omega B_{0, \text{m, F}}$, and ${}_\omega B_{0, \text{f, F}}$ will represent total, male, and female births to women at all ages $(0, \omega)$ during one calendar year. Total births to women 20.0–24.9 are represented as ${}_5B_{20, \text{F}}$, and so forth. Omitting parental subscripts, the four terms we have highlighted become ${}_\omega B_0$, ${}_\omega B_{0, \text{m}}$, ${}_\omega B_{0, \text{f}}$, and ${}_5B_{20}$.

† Besides the ASFRs shown in Table 7.2, the NCHS also publishes *central fertility rates,* which are used in cumulating cohort fertility. Central rates divide births at age x between July 1 of year t and the following June 30 by $({}_1N_{x-1, \text{F}} + 6{}_1N_{x, \text{F}} + {}_1N_{x+1, \text{F}})/8$, where the terms in the denominator are women born in the years $t - x - 1$, $t - x$, and $t - x + 1$, and are weighted in proportion to each cohort's contribution to births in the midyear-to-midyear period. [The central cohort ${}_1N_{x, \text{F}}$ is responsible for about 3/4 of births at age x in the last half of year t and 3/4 of births at age x in the first half of year $t + 1$, and therefore for 3/4 of total births at x between July 1 and June 30. The remaining 1/4 of the births are contributed equally by the next older cohort (in year t), and the next younger cohort (in year $t + 1$).] Births at age x from January 1 to December 31 of year t are less cohort specific, as half would be to the cohort born in year $t - x - 1$ and half to the cohort born in year $t - x$.

family sizes thus average about 1.7 children. Including births at ages 35–44, the completed family size is a little over 1.8 children. Family sizes were not much larger, about 2.5 children, in the late 1920s and during the early depression years, but rose to about 3.5 children at the peak of the postwar baby boom in 1960. Figure 7.1 displays U.S. ASFRs from World War I to 1985, from U.S. Vital Statistics and Heuser (1976).

The estimates of family size we have given derive from the *total fertility rate*. Formally the TFR is found by summing across the ASFRs and adjusting for the number of years of age each ASFR spans. That is,

$$\text{TFR} = n \sum_x {}_n f_x = n \sum_x {}_n B_x / {}_n N_{x, \text{F}} \qquad (7.2)$$

where $\sum_x$ is the summation of the terms in B/N over all of the fertile ages. (A related measure is the *cumulative fertility rate*, which sums fertility to their current ages for women under 45 or 50. The rate is historical rather than cross-sectional.)

In the example of Table 7.2, the TFR is found by summing the ASFRs and multiplying by 5 (in the last column of the table). The multiplier is used because each ASFR is for a 5-year age interval: if we had used 30 single year intervals ($n = 1$ year) instead of 6 five-year intervals ($n = 5$ years), the TFR would be the sum of the 30 single year rates.

At most ages, 5-year age intervals substitute well for single year ages (Fig. 2.1), but because of interest in teen fertility, ages 15–19 are commonly

Table 7.2. Illustration of the Computation of Age-Specific and Total Fertility Rates for U.S. Females, 1980. *Source:* National Center for Health Statistics (1984–1985)

Ages	Female population	Births[a]	ASFR $_5 f_x$	Children added in interval $5 \, _5 f_x$
15–19	10,412,715	562,330	0.054	0.270
20–24	10,655,473	1,226,200	0.115	0.575
25–29	9,815,812	1,108,291	0.113	0.565
30–34	8,884,124	550,354	0.062	0.310
35–39	7,103,793	140,793	0.020	0.100
40–44	5,961,198	24,290	0.004	0.020
Total	52,833,115	3,612,258	0.068	1.840

Approximate mean age at birth = $(17.5 \times 0.270 + 22.5 \times 0.575 + \cdots + 42.5 \times 0.020)/1.840$
    = 26.0

[a] Births at ages 10–14 are included with births at 15–19, and births at 45–49 are included with births at 40–44.

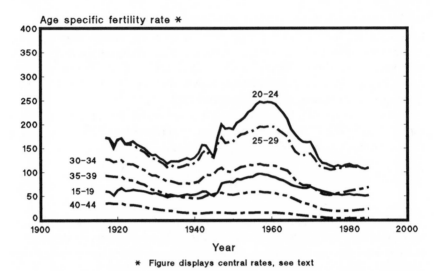

Figure 7.1. U.S. female age-specific fertility rates, 1917–1985. *Sources:* Heuser (1976), U.S. Vital Statistics (NCHS, various years).

separated into subintervals 15–17 and 18–19, or into single years. These categories are shown with fertility at age 14 in Table 7.3. Summing the rates, the number of children added at 14 and in the interval 15–19 becomes 0.266, close to the estimate of 0.270 in Table 7.2.

Birth rates for the 1980 U.S. male population are shown in Table 7.4. Although they are for the same population and year as the female rates of Table 7.2, the male rates differ in several respects. Fathers are older than

Table 7.3. U.S. 1980 Age-Specific Fertility at Ages 14–19.
Source: National Center for Health Statistics (1984–1985)

Ages	Female population	Births	ASFR $_n f_x$
14	1,850,066	10,169	0.005
15	1,990,172	28,178	0.014
16	2,045,750	63,198	0.031
17	2,063,734	106,846	0.052
18	2,098,487	153,333	0.073
19	2,214,572	200,606	0.091
15–17	6,099,656	198,222	0.032
18–19	4,313,059	353,939	0.082
15–19	10,412,715	552,161	0.053

Table 7.4. U.S. 1980 Male Age-Specific and Total Fertility Rates

Ages	Male population	Life table population $_5L_{x, M}$	Births[a, b]	ASFR $_5f_x$	Children added in interval $5 \, _5f_x$
15–19	10,755,409	488,224	202,000	0.019	0.095
20–24	10,663,231	483,870	982,000	0.092	0.460
25–29	9,705,107	478,990	1,194,000	0.123	0.615
30–34	8,676,796	474,430	790,000	0.091	0.455
35–39	6,861,509	469,323	294,000	0.043	0.215
40–44	5,708,210	462,351	98,000	0.017	0.085
45–49	5,388,249	451,697	33,000	0.006	0.030
50–54	5,620,670	435,061	19,000	0.003	0.015
Total	63,278,180		3,612,258	0.057	1.970

Approximate mean age at birth = (17.5 × 0.095 + 22.5 × 0.460 + · · · + 52.5 × 0.015)/
1.970 = 29.3

[a] Births are estimated from the 1980 census population and NCHS 1980 male age-specific fertility rates. We have rounded the numbers at individual ages since about 12% of birth certificates omit father's age.
[b] Births at ages 55+ are included with births at 50–54.

mothers by about 3 years, their fertility continues to much older ages, and their completed family sizes are larger.

To understand the difference in family sizes, the reader needs to know that in the United States in 1980 women outnumbered men at all ages over 25, and outnumbered men 3 years older than themselves, the mean age difference between parents, at all ages over 20. In computing fertility rates, births are thus averaged across smaller numbers of males than females at almost all ages, a pattern that has held for most of the 20th century (Myers, 1941). Other factors may also contribute, including errors in the 1980 census, the possible misallocation of fathers' ages that were unreported, and distortions in male and female fertility rates that result from changing marriage and birth patterns.

Besides the ASFRs and TFR, Tables 7.2 and 7.4 also show the *general fertility rate:*

$$\text{GFR}_F = {}_\omega B_0/{}_{30}N_{15, \, F} = \sum_x {}_nN_{x, \, F}({}_nB_{x, \, F}/{}_nN_{x, \, F})/{}_{30}N_{15, \, F}$$

$$\text{GFR}_M = {}_\omega B_0/{}_{40}N_{15, \, M} = \sum_x {}_nN_{x, \, M}({}_nB_{x, \, M}/{}_nN_{x, \, M})/{}_{40}N_{15, \, M}$$

(7.3)

For females, the GFR is the ASFR for the complete interval 15–44, which also makes it the average of the 1- or 5-year ASFRs weighted by the number of women in each age interval. It is therefore intermediate to the ASFRs in value: in Table 7.2, the GFR = 0.068, compared to the range of 0.004 to 0.115 in the ASFRs.

Since the GFR is an ASFR (GFR = $_{30}f_{15}$), for the female population we can estimate the total fertility rate from the GFR as

$$\text{TFR} = n \sum_x {_n}f_x \simeq 30 \text{ GFR} \qquad (7.4)$$

For the data of Table 7.2 the TFR becomes 30 (3,612,258/52,833,115) = 2.05, a figure not as accurate as our earlier estimate but of the right order of magnitude. For males the comparable figure is 40 (3,612,258/63,278,180) = 2.28.

7.3. RELATIONS BETWEEN THE GFR, TFR, AND CBR

Because the proportion of women 15–44 is similar in most world populations, at about $\frac{1}{4}$ or $\frac{1}{5}$ of total population, the general fertility rate (annual births)/(midyear female population 15–44) will typically be about four or five times the crude birth rate (annual births)/(total population). That is,

$$\text{GFR} = \text{CBR}/(_{30}N_{15,\ F}/_{\omega}N_0) \simeq 4\tfrac{1}{2} \times \text{CBR} \qquad (7.5)$$

From the relationship of the GFR to the TFR we also have for the female population:

$$\text{TFR} \simeq 30 \text{ GFR} \simeq 30 \times 4\tfrac{1}{2} \times \text{CBR} \qquad (7.6)$$

Using these expressions, the approximate GFR for the United States is $4\tfrac{1}{2}$ × 0.016 = 0.072, and the approximate TFR is 135 × 0.016 = 2.16 children. Both estimates are tolerably near the correct values.

7.4. MARITAL AND NONMARITAL FERTILITY

Historically, about 20% of first births to married women in the United States have occurred within the first 9 months of marriage. With abortion, later marriages, smaller proportions of women marrying, and higher divorce rates, pregnancy and marriage have gradually become less closely related. Whether or not children are born to married parents, a high proportion now spend part of their childhood in single parent homes.

The principal demographic measures relating to single parent homes are the marital and nonmarital fertility (illegitimacy) rates and ASFRs by marital status. The marital GFR is found as the annual number of births to women in unions divided by the number of women 15–44 (or 15–49) in

Table 7.5. U.S. 1980 Marital and Nonmarital Age-Specific
Fertility Rates. *Source:* National Center for Health Statistics
(1984–1985)

Ages	ASFR[a]	
	Women currently single $_5f_{x,-u}$	Women currently married $_5f_{x,u}$
15–19	0.028	0.350
20–24	0.040	0.204
25–29	0.031	0.146
30–34	0.019	0.073
35–39	0.008	0.022
40–44	0.002	0.004
GFR	0.028	0.098

[a] Births at ages 10–14 are included with births at 15–19, and births at 45–49 are included with births at 40–44.

unions at midyear, $_\omega B_{0,u}/_{30}N_{15,F,u}$. The nonmarital GFR is the complementary fertility rate $_\omega B_{0,-u}/_{30}N_{15,F,-u}$. The nonmarital fertility ratio is found as $_\omega B_{0,-u}/_\omega B_{0,u}$. Marital and nonmarital ASFRs are found by limiting numerators and denominators to specified age groups, as in ordinary ASFRs.

For 1980 the proportion of women who were ever married by age is displayed in Table 4.12 and Fig. 4.2. U.S. marital ($_nf_{x,u}$) and nonmarital ($_nf_{x,-u}$) ASFRs for 1980 are displayed in Table 7.5. At all ages, nonmarital fertility rates are low relative to marital fertility rates. The GFRs and numbers of births are more nearly equal: the ratio of the GFRs is about 0.28 : 1, and the ratio of births is about 0.23 : 1. (Overall, 666,000 or 18% of total births were to unmarried women.)

The table omits TFRs to married and unmarried women, which are essentially hypothetical quantities since marital status changes over time.* We might also estimate cumulative or total fertility rates for ever married and never married women, but historically most women who have borne children have also at some point been married.

7.5. THE GROSS AND NET REPRODUCTION RATES

The TFR is a measure of completed family sizes of women or of men surviving to the end of the reproductive age interval. To determine whether

* The marital total fertility rate (MTFR = $n \sum_x {_nf_{x,u}}/_nN_{x,u}$) is introduced as a link between total fertility and natural fertility in Bongaarts's proximate determinant analysis, discussed in Appendix 7A.1.

Table 7.6. Illustration of the Computation of the Gross and Net Reproduction Rates for U.S. Females, 1980

Ages	Female population	Life table population $_5L_{x, \mathrm{F}}$	Female births[a]	ASFR $_5f_{x, \mathrm{f}}$	Proportion surviving from birth to mother's age $_5L_{x, \mathrm{F}}/5l_{0, \mathrm{F}}$	Surviving daughters added in interval $_5{}_5f_{x, \mathrm{f}} \times (_5L_{x, \mathrm{F}}/5l_{0, \mathrm{F}})$
15–19	10,412,715	491,492	273,865	0.026301	0.98298	0.12927
20–24	10,655,473	490,045	597,516	0.056076	0.98009	0.27480
25–29	9,815,812	488,463	539,268	0.054939	0.97693	0.26836
30–34	8,884,124	486,634	268,233	0.030192	0.97327	0.14692
35–39	7,103,793	484,140	68,814	0.009687	0.96828	0.04690
40–44	5,961,198	480,283	11,946	0.002004	0.96057	0.00962
Total	52,833,115		1,759,642			0.87587

[a] Births at ages 10–14 are included with births at 15–19, and births at 45–49 are included with births at 40–44.

the population will increase, remain constant, or decrease gradually over time, the TFR needs to be adjusted to births of one sex and adjusted for survival. Table 7.6 shows the adjustments for daughters. In the table, female births replace total births and fertility rates for daughters replace rates for all children. Summing the fertility rates for daughters and multiplying by 5, since 5-year age intervals are used, we have the *gross reproduction rate,* or lifetime female births per 1000 women:

$$\text{GRR} = n \sum_x {}_nB_{x,\,f}/{}_nN_{x,\,F} = \text{TFR} \times {}_\omega B_{0,\,f}/{}_\omega B_0 \qquad (7.7)$$

For the example the GRR is $5(0.026223 + 0.056076 + \cdots + 0.002004)$ $= 0.89560$, calculated from female births by age of mother. Alternatively, multiplying the TFR by the overall proportion of births that are female we have GRR $= 1.83916 \times 1,759,642/3,612,258 = 0.89591$. The GRR is usually calculated by the second method, using the TFR and proportion of total births that are female, since the TFR is normally available and the proportion of births that are female is nearly constant across ages. (For the United States in 1980, the proportion of female births varies from 0.486 at ages 15–19 to 0.492 at 40–44, averaging 0.487 overall.)

A limitation of the GRR is that it estimates the number of daughters born per woman in the absence of mortality. To measure population replacement, mortality needs to be taken into account, which can be done by multiplying the ASFRs for daughters by the survival probabilities from birth to the mother's age at the delivery. The appropriate life table terms are the ${}_nL_x$ values, showing the number of women at ages x to $x + n$ per l_0 births, and nl_0, the number of births in n years, from which the ${}_nL_x$ survivors arise. The survival probability from birth to the interval x to $x + n$ becomes ${}_{x+(1/2)n}S_{0,\,F}$ $= {}_nL_{x,\,F}/(nl_0)$. Table 7.6 displays these values for the 1980 U.S. life table, and completes the calculation for the *net reproduction rate* or generational replacement rate:

$$\text{NRR} = R_0 = n \sum_x ({}_nB_{x,\,f}/{}_nN_{x,\,F})[{}_nL_{x,\,F}/(nl_0)]$$

$$\simeq \text{GRR} \times {}_5L_{25,\,F}/(5l_0) \qquad\qquad (7.8)$$

Since survival probabilities vary by a relatively small amount over the main reproductive ages, the NRR can be approximated using the GRR and an estimate of the survival probability to about the midpoint of the fertility distribution, usually near age $27\frac{1}{2}$. For the United States the approximate formula yields an NRR of $0.89591 \times 0.97693 = 0.87524$, as compared with 0.87587 using the full information from Table 7.6.

For U.S. males, the NRR is found as the product of the TFR and proportion of births that are male times the survival probability to the mean fertile age. For males, the mean fertile age is near 30, allowing us to use the proportion surviving at that exact age, $l_{30, M}/l_0$, in place of the female $_5L_{27.5, F}/(5l_0)$ centered at age $27\frac{1}{2}$. We have:

$$NRR_{Male} \simeq TFR_{Male} \times (_\omega B_{0, m}/_\omega B_0) \times l_{30, Male}/l_0$$

$$= 1.970 \times 0.513 \times 0.95336 = 0.963$$

Calculated by the more precise method of Table 7.6, the NRR is estimated as 0.965. The NRR difference repeats the disparity between the male and female TFRs.

For a population to exactly replace itself, the NRR must be 1.0, indicating that each woman (man) averages one surviving daughter (son). The U.S. 1980 NRRs of 0.876 for females and 0.964 for males are lower, and suggest that the population should be declining from one generation to the next. That has not yet happened, in part because below replacement fertility is recent and follows upon baby boom fertility rates that were about twice as high at their peak in 1959–1961, and in part because of continuing immigration into the United States. With little permanent immigration, lower historical fertility rates than the United States, and current fertility near U.S. levels, several European populations are now decreasing very slowly.

7.6. THE MEAN FERTILE AGE

In Tables 7.2 and 7.4 we used the distribution of ASFRs to estimate an approximate mean fertile age. We might also have included the number of males and females at each age as weights, to find the mean age of parents for births in the calendar year. For the latter we would have:

$$m_F = \sum_x (x + \tfrac{1}{2}n)(_nN_{x, F} \, _nf_{x, F})/\sum_x (_nN_{x, F} \, _nf_{x, F})$$

$$= \sum_x (x + \tfrac{1}{2}n)_nB_{x, F}/\sum_x {}_nB_{x, F}$$

$$= (17\tfrac{1}{2} \times 562,330 + 22\tfrac{1}{2} \times 1,226,200 + \cdots$$

$$+ 42\tfrac{1}{2} \times 24,290)/3,612,258$$

$$= 25.5$$

(7.9)

Using Table 7.4, the reader can confirm that the mean age of the fathers of 1980 infants was $m_M = 28.2$.

Of more interest to demographers than the actual ages of parents, which change every year, are the ages of the life table population of parents (the age distribution associated with the NRR). For the mean age in the life table population we replace the terms in $_nN_x$ in (7.9) by the life table population $_nL_x$. We have:

$$\mu_F = \sum_x (x + \tfrac{1}{2}n)(_nL_{x,\,F}\,_nf_{x,\,F}) \Big/ \sum_x (_nL_{x,\,F}\,_nf_{x,\,F})$$

$$= (17\tfrac{1}{2} \times 491{,}492 \times 0.026301 + 22\tfrac{1}{2} \times 490{,}045$$

$$\times 0.056076 + \cdots + 42\tfrac{1}{2} \times 480{,}283 \times 0.002004)/ \qquad (7.10)$$

$$(491{,}492 \times 0.026301 + 490{,}045 \times 0.056076$$

$$+ \cdots + 480{,}283 \times 0.002004) = 26.0$$

For males, $\mu_M = 29.2$. Both means are slightly older than the mean ages of parents for the calendar year, since the 1980 U.S. population was relatively young due to a long period of rising births after the mid-1930s.

7.7. CHILD–WOMAN RATIOS

The child–woman ratio is defined as:

$$\mathrm{CWR} = {}_5N_0/{}_{30}N_{15,\,F} \qquad (7.11)$$

where $_5N_0$ represents the midyear population of children of both sexes ages 0–4, and $_{30}N_{15,\,F}$ is the midyear female population ages 15 to 44. The value of the CWR as a fertility measure is that it can be estimated from a census, without the researcher having to know the number of annual births. Children 0–4 are used, rather than children age 0, because census underenumeration and age misreporting are worse at age 0 than at 0–4.

We can relate the CWR to the GFR by noting that if the number of births is relatively stable from year to year and infant mortality is low, the number of children 0–4 will be about four or five times the annual births. We can therefore relate the CWR to the general fertility rate, GFR $= {}_\omega B_0/{}_{30}N_{15,\,F}$, by the simple formula

$$\mathrm{CWR} \simeq 4\tfrac{1}{2} \times \mathrm{GFR} \qquad (7.12)$$

The approximation requires that both the CWR and GFR have the same denominator, either women 15–44 or 15–49. The United States had 16,348,000 children 0–4 in 1980 (Table 6A.1), making the CWR (16,348,000/52,833,000) = 0.309 for women 15–44, a figure close to the estimate of $4\frac{1}{2}$ times the GFR.

If we have access to a life table for the population, we can also use the CWR to estimate the NRR directly, by the approximation:

$$NRR_{Thompson} \simeq CWR/CWR_{life \ table} \qquad (7.13)$$

The approximation is known as *Thompson's Index*. It holds because the life table can be used to generate a stationary population. The ratio of the actual to the life table CWR will thus be a measure of the difference in family sizes between the actual population and one with similar mortality rates that exactly replaces itself.

The life table CWR is computed as:

$$CWR_{life \ table} = [(_\omega B_{0, \ m}/_\omega B_{0, \ f}) _5L_{0, \ M} + _5L_{0, \ F}]/_{30}L_{15, \ F} \qquad (7.14)$$

where $_{30}L_{15, \ F}$ is the life table female population at ages 15–44 (in 5-year interval life tables, the sum of the terms $_5L_{15, \ F} + _5L_{20, \ F} + \cdots + _5L_{40, \ F}$). Because the actual child–woman ratio includes both boys and girls at ages 0–4, the numerator of the life table CWR must also include both sexes, and needs to take into account the fact that more boys are born than girls. The term $_\omega B_{0, \ m}/_\omega B_{0, \ f}$ is the sex ratio at birth for the actual population, about 1.05 in 1980. The 1980 CWR for the United States was 0.309, and the life table CWR (from Table 6A.2) is (1.05 × 492,536 + 494,011)/2,921,057 = 0.346. For $NRR_{Thompson}$ we have 0.309/0.346 = 0.893, above the more precise estimate of 0.876 found earlier.

7.8. HIGH AND LOW FERTILITY LEVELS AND PARITY PROGRESSION

Fertility rates are substantially above U.S. levels in many world populations, but are not limitless. In even the highest fertility countries, women space children 2 years or more apart on average, and not all are building their families at the same time. In consequence, it is rare for ASFRs to be much above 0.350 or 0.400, levels equivalent to one birth every 1/0.350 = 2.9 years or 1/0.400 = 2.5 years.* Continuing over the 10 years 20–29, an ASFR of

---

* We have set the upper limit of the vertical scale in Fig. 7.1 at 400 to allow the reader to contrast current and historial U.S. fertility rates visually with natural fertility levels.

Table 7.7. Age-Specific and Total Fertility Rates for the
United States 1980, Mexico 1976, and U.S. Hutterites
1946–1950

Ages	ASFR		
	U.S.[a]	Mexico	Hutterites
15–19	0.054	0.104	0.012
20–24	0.115	0.276	0.231
25–29	0.113	0.268	0.383
30–34	0.062	0.227	0.391
35–39	0.020	0.166	0.345
40–44	0.004	0.074	0.208
45–49	0.000	0.017	0.042
CBR	0.016	0.038	0.046
GFR	0.068	0.174	0.227
CWR[b]	0.279	0.752	0.963
TFR	1.840	5.660	8.060
GRR	0.896	2.761	4.004
NRR	0.876	2.477	3.664
Approximate mean age at birth =	26.01	29.11	32.52

[a] Births at ages 10–14 are included with births at 15–19.
[b] Children 0–4/women 15–49.

0.350 implies 3.5 children per family: populations achieve higher birth rates
only with sustained high fertility at ages over 30 and perhaps at 15–19. Table
7.7 displays ASFRs and TFRs for the United States in 1980 and for a small
but exceptionally high fertility subpopulation, the Hutterite population of the
northern plains states about 1950.* (Restricted to the married population
only, 1950 Hutterite fertility rates were 0.498 at 25–29 and 0.443 at 30–34.)

An important component of fertility differences between populations is
the range over which usual family sizes vary. In the United States, more than
one-fourth of the female birth cohort of 1909–1910 remained childless, passing
through their peak fertile years during the depression of the 1930s. Female
birth cohorts of the 1950s and 1960s may have equal proportions ultimately
childless.

* Articles on Hutterite fertility include Eaton and Mayer (1953), Tietze (1957), Sheps (1965),
Laing (1980), and Robinson (1986). For an introduction to high fertility and natural fertility
populations, the reader should see Henry (1961, 1972), Leridon (1977), and Leridon and
Menken (1977). Bongaarts (1975) discusses social and biological limits to family size.

Table 7.8. U.S. 1980 Current and Retrospective Parity
Progression Ratios and Cumulative Fertility Rates.
Source: National Center for Health Statistics
(1984–1985)

Birth order	1980 births	Parity progression ratio Birth cohort		
		1955	1945	1935
0		0.56	0.86	0.92
1	0.74	0.55	0.82	0.89
2	0.47	0.32	0.52	0.73
3	0.38	0.26	0.43	0.62
4	0.38	0.25	0.41	0.56
5		0.25	0.43	0.56
6		0.25	0.43	0.55
Cumulative fertility rate		1.00	2.20	3.16

A simple measure of the variation in family sizes is the parity progression ratio, defined as

$$P_{i,\,i+1} = {_\omega}B_{0,\,i+1}/{_\omega}B_{0,\,i} \qquad |\,i \geq 1 \qquad (7.15)$$

where i represents birth order. The ratio may be taken either from births in a single calendar year, or retrospectively, from completed family size distributions. The calendar year measure is approximate, since the proportion of births of any given order depends in part on the age composition of the childbearing population. In a population that is increasing rapidly, calendar year estimates will be weighted toward younger parents, and may be much below retrospective estimates.

Parity progression ratios for U.S. 1980 births and retrospectively for women born in 1935, 1945, and 1955, (who were ages 45, 35, and 25, respectively, at the end of 1980) are shown in Table 7.8. The ratios for 1935 and 1945 birth cohorts represent nearly completed family sizes, as fertility after age 35 is low. The 1955 cohort has completed only about half of its childbearing.

Examining the table, the reader might note that the progression ratios for calendar 1980 births are close to the ratios for the 1945 birth cohort, and may approximate current fertility patterns except for the omission of the first birth probability. The relationship is inexact, in part because the age distribution of mothers, which influences birth order, varies from year to year;

and in part because ages at childbearing and completed family sizes may change across cohorts, as is evident for the 1935 and 1945 cohorts in the example.

Across cohorts, the decline in average family sizes from 3 children to 2 appears as a sharp drop in parity progression after the second birth, from 0.73 to 0.52. Only about half of women in the 1945 cohort with a second birth progressed to the third, as against about three-fourths in the 1935 cohort. The proportions of all women reaching parity 3 in the two cohorts were $(0.86)(0.82)(0.52) = 0.37$ and $(0.92)(0.89)(0.73) = 0.60$, respectively.

Mean family sizes are estimated from the parity progression ratios as the sum of the proportions reaching each parity (l_i), or

$$\mu = \sum_i l_i = \sum_i \left(\prod_{k=0}^{i-1} P_{k, k+1} \right) \qquad (7.16)$$

For the 1935 cohort we have

$$\mu \simeq 0.92 + 0.92 \times 0.89 + 0.92 \times 0.89 \times 0.73 + \cdots = 3.09$$

omitting eighth- and higher-order births. The reader can confirm that for the 1945 cohort, $\mu \simeq 2.19$. The 1945 cohort estimate is closer to the completed family size in Table 7.8 than is the 1935 cohort estimate, owing to the larger proportion of high-order births in the older cohort, not included in μ.

The reader might note that parity progression ratios are formally measures of the proportion of birth intervals of each order that are *closed* by the occurrence of the next birth. The complement is the proportion of intervals that remain open at each parity. The transitions between parities, and those from marriage to successively higher parities, can be analyzed either cross-sectionally or through life tables (see Table 4.7). Efforts to analyze closed and open intervals separately have not fared as well, since each provides only partial information on transitions (Sheps *et al.* 1970; Feeney, 1983).*

U.S. parity progression ratios are discussed in their historical context in Ryder (1986). The changes are analyzed by model schedules in Pullum *et al.* (1989). A method for estimating current fertility from parity distributions, due to Brass, will be found in Brass and Coale (1968, pp. 89–104) and Hobcraft *et al.* (1982). The Brass method is used where reporting of children ever born is relatively complete but dates of birth are not well remembered.

---

* The reader should see Feeney and Ross (1984), however, for the analysis of open birth intervals in the context of stable population theory.

7.9. RATE OF POPULATION INCREASE OR DECREASE

Since the NRR represents generational replacement, it can be converted to an estimate of long-run annual population growth or decline in the absence of migration if the generation length is known. We use the exponential relationship:

$$NRR = e^{rT}$$
$$r = \ln(NRR)/T \tag{7.17}$$

where r is the annual rate of increase or decrease and T is the generation length. In most populations the generation length T can be set at about $27\frac{1}{2}$ years. (The generation length is near the mean fertile age calculated from ASFRs. For the United States in 1980 it is about 26.0.) Setting $T = 26.0$ we have: $NRR_{US} = 0.876 = e^{26\,r}$, from which $r = -0.0051$ or -0.5% per year. The 1950 Hutterite NRR is 3.66. It is slightly smaller as a proportion of the TFR than the 1980 U.S. NRR because of higher mortality levels in the earlier period. Among Hutterite births, 0.4965 were female. For Hutterites the generation length is about $32\frac{1}{2}$ years, longer than the 26 years for the whole United States. The annual growth rate will be $r = \ln(3.66)/32.5 = 0.040$.

Both these rates are *eventual* rates of growth that would come about in the absence of migration, under the assumption that fertility and mortality remain essentially constant. That is, they are *intrinsic* to the fertility and mortality distributions of each population. The actual growth rate for the United States, the crude growth rate, will be the difference between the crude birth and death rates plus the crude migration rate (annual immigrants − annual emigrants)/(midyear population). That is,

$$CGR = CBR + CMR - CDR$$

For populations with relatively constant fertility and mortality rates over many years, the intrinsic rate of increase estimated from the NRR will be similar to the rate estimated from the difference between crude birth and death rates. The United States does not fit that pattern owing to the postwar baby boom, which contributes to elevated numbers of births in the 1980s and 1990s. For most of the developing countries, the two estimates are currently similar, but will diverge over the next generation, as the size of the parenting population stabilizes.

7.10. POPULATION DOUBLING TIMES

If migration is disregarded, the intrinsic growth rate r can be used to estimate the number of years it would take a population to double or, if the

NRR is below 1, to decline to half its initial size. The doubling time is simply the number of years τ it would take for the population to increase from N persons to $2N$ persons, or from 1 person to 2 persons since N is arbitrary. It is found by setting

$$e^{r\tau} = 2$$

and has the solution

$$\tau = \ln 2 / r \simeq 0.693 / r$$

The expression is most easily remembered if growth rates are expressed as percentages: for a population growing at 1% per year the doubling time is 69.3 or about 70 years; at 2% it becomes 35 years; at 3% 23 years. If r is negative, halving times substitute for doubling times and we have

$$\tau = \ln \tfrac{1}{2} / r \simeq -0.693 / r$$

For the United States, $r = -0.5\%$, implying that in the absence of migration the population would decline by half in $-70/-0.5 = 140$ years. The reader can confirm that the doubling time for Mexico will be found from Table 7.7 as:

$$r = \ln(2.477)/29.11 = 0.031$$

$$\tau = 70/3.1 = 22\tfrac{1}{2} \text{ years}$$

For the Hutterite data of the same table, $\tau = 17\tfrac{1}{2}$ years.

Doubling and halving time estimates are long-term values for the fertility and mortality rates that determine r. They would not hold if r changed or if net in or out migration occurred, and might not be realized for a generation or more even with fixed r and no migration, since they take no account of the age structure of the population. In the United States the postwar baby boom that peaked in the decade 1955–1964 created a large peak in the age distribution that will continue to be discernable almost to the middle of the 21st century. Population decline, if it sets in, may not occur until after 2025. In parts of Europe, slow population decreases are occurring currently.

7.11. FERTILITY, CONTRACEPTION, AND ABORTION

For the reason that women using contraception are not at high risk of pregnancy, contraceptive prevalence rates are loosely correlated with the CBR.

At one extreme, in populations with two-child families the CBR is usually about 15 per 1000 population, and about 75–80% of couples under 45 are using contraception at any given time. In six-child families the CBR is about 3 times as high, at about 45 per 1000 population, with few contraceptive users. These figures are end points of the regression line:

CBR $\simeq$ 0.045 − 0.04 × proportion of currently married women

15–44 using contraception   (7.18)

Proportion using contraception $\simeq$ (0.045 − CBR)/0.04

The expression was introduced by Nortman and Hofstatter (1975) with slightly different constants. It is not precise, since the mix of contraceptives that couples use differs from country to country, and the quality of use is influenced both by the willingness to risk a birth and by the availability of abortion. During the U.S. baby boom, for example, the family size reached 3.5 children at levels of contraceptive use similar to those of the 1.8-child 1980s families. In the developing countries the relationship is influenced by reporting of irregularly used "traditional" family planning methods having limited effectiveness, and marginally by breastfeeding. (The relationship of breastfeeding to fertility is weak because family sizes may be large even in countries where breastfeeding is prolonged, as in Nepal and Bangladesh. In both countries, breastfeeding contributes powerfully to child spacing, but spacing by itself has only a modest effect on the CBR.)

For Mexico in 1980, expression (7.18) estimates current contraceptive use at (0.045 − 0.032)/0.04 = 0.325 or $32\frac{1}{2}$% of married women, a figure that is probably low. The estimate for current contraceptive use in the United States is $72\frac{1}{2}$% by the formula, and is of the right order of magnitude. The Hutterite CBR of 0.046 in Table 7.7 is outside the range of the formula, yielding a contraceptive use estimate of $-2\frac{1}{2}$%. The correct figure is close to 0.

The reader may use the approximate relationship between the TFR and CBR suggested in Section 7.3, TFR $\simeq$ 135 CBR, to find:

TFR $\simeq$ 6 − 5 × Proportion using contraception

(7.19)

Proportion using contraception $\simeq$ 1.20 − 0.20 × TFR

Besides contraception, abortion is widely used to limit family sizes. Its effects are estimated differently, since the concepts "Percent using contraception" and "Percent using abortion" are only vaguely analogous. Contraception is utilized before pregnancy and requires continuity of use, wheras abortion may occur only following a pregnancy, with uncertainty in identifying current users other than by professed *intent*, or past use of abortion. From reported abortions, we construct the measures.

Abortion ratio

$$= (\text{annual number of abortions})/(\text{annual number of live births})$$

Age-specific abortion rate $= \text{ASAR} = (\text{annual abortions to women ages}$

$$x \text{ to } x + n)/(\text{midyear female population ages } x \text{ to } x + n)$$

Total abortion rate $= \text{TAR} = n \sum_{x} \text{ASAR}_x$

These and related measures help in defining the prevalence of abortion, but do not unambiguously measure its effects on fertility.

To see the potential impact of abortion and contraception, we need to decompose the interbirth interval (Potter, 1963; Keyfitz, 1971a). If we let I_B represent the interbirth interval, p the duration of pregnancy, i the duration of postpartum infecundity, and r the duration fecund and at risk of pregnancy, we can establish the relationship

$$I_B = r + p + i \tag{7.20}$$

which states that the interval between births is comprised of time spent at risk of pregnancy, pregnant, and in postpartum infecundity. If we assume [following Bongaarts (1978)] that a mean exposure duration of $7\frac{1}{2}$ months precedes each pregnancy when contraception is not used (that is, that the monthly probability of a pregnancy occurring is $1/7\frac{1}{2} = 0.13$), that pregnancy lasts 9 months, and that the postpartum sterile period is $1\frac{1}{2}$ months in the absence of lactation, we have $I_B = 7\frac{1}{2} + 9 + 1\frac{1}{2} = 18$ months between pregnancies, not including time added by pregnancy losses, which Bongaarts fixes at about 2 months. The corresponding interval between abortions, assuming the abortions occur after 2 months of pregnancy, will be $I_A = 7\frac{1}{2} + 2 + 1\frac{1}{2}$ $= 11$ months. By this simple model, which may not be too far off the mark, women using abortions to limit their family sizes and taking no other precautions, would average one abortion each 11 months, or nearly two abortions in the course of a normal birth interval, including in I_B pregnancy losses but not contraception or lactation.

Lactational amenorrhea lengthens the postpartum sterile period by as much as a year in a few countries, resulting in average interbirth intervals of

$l_B = 7\frac{1}{2} + 9 + 1\frac{1}{2} + 12 = 30$ months. If abortion is used to limit family sizes, the number that will be needed in the course of the normal birth interval is now $30/11 = 2.7$.

With contraception, interbirth intervals become longer through lengthening of the average period of exposure to pregnancy r. If we assume that a contraceptive with the effectiveness $0 \le e \le 1.0$ is used during the exposed period, the monthly probability of conception changes from $1/r$ to $(1 - e)/r$ and the interbirth interval increases by $r/(1 - e) - r = er/(1 - e)$ months. For a mean exposure time of $r = 7\frac{1}{2}$ months in the absence of contraception, using a contraceptive with 50% effectiveness contributes $(0.5)(7\frac{1}{2})/(0.5) = 7\frac{1}{2}$ additional months to the interbirth interval. At 75% effectiveness the gain becomes $22\frac{1}{2}$ months, at 90% effectiveness it becomes $67\frac{1}{2}$ months or $5\frac{1}{2}$ years, and at 99% it becomes more than 60 years. The reader might calculate the impact of 99% effective contraception used half the time and no contraception at other times, or equivalently, of half the population using 99% effective contraception and the other half none.*

Models that quantify the effects of contraception through decomposition of observed fertility rates into natural fertility rates and the fertility damping effects of the Davis and Blake intermediate fertility variables are introduced in Appendix 7A.1. For a life table analysis of contraception (see Table 4.7) the reader may see Potter and Avery (1975) and Trussell and Menken (1980).

7.12. THE STATISTICAL ANALYSIS OF FERTILITY

Statistical testing of standardized rates and life table differences was developed for its contribution to medical studies, where differences in the effectiveness of treatment regimens can be critical to patient survival and recovery. In fertility analysis, statistical tests are less often needed. It is useful to know if fertility rates are similar or dissimilar across populations or subgroups and whether they are stable or changing, but by the nature of the data large differences can generally be assumed to be significant and small differences inconsequential. There is also no ideal age pattern or level of fertility that populations aspire to achieve, against which current levels might be assayed. Finally, in samples of any reasonable size the nonrandom component of yearly fluctuations in fertility rates typically outweighs the random component by a substantial amount.

Where they are needed, variances of ASFRs are estimated using the convention that denominators $_nN_x$ represent risk populations analogous to the

---

* For the theoretical development of effects of contraception on birth intervals the reader should see Potter (1960), Potter and Parker (1964), Leridon (1977, pp. 121–130), and Bongaarts and Potter (1983). A more formal analysis is presented in Sheps and Menken (1973, pp. 288–310).

risk population in mortality analysis $N(x)$. The ASFR is then interpretable as a binomial probability* analogous to $_nq_x$, and we have

$$\text{Var}(_nf_x) \simeq {_nf_x}(1 - {_nf_x})/_nN_x \qquad (7.21)$$

The expression is approximate, since $_nN_x$ represents survivors in the interval $(x, x + n)$ and not at the xth birthday. It is therefore not the complete risk population. When mortality is low, however, the correspondence of the two measures is close. Formally, the expression is analogous to the approximation for the CDR [(3.13)]:

$$\text{Var}(\text{CDR}) \simeq \text{CDR}(1 - \text{CDR})/_\omega N_0$$

We also disregard the distinction between single and multiple births (about 1% of confinements and 2% of births) and rare cases of repeat births in the same calendar year.

Since the TFR is summed from the ASFRs, it has the approximate variance [analogous to (3.11)]†

$$\text{Var}(\text{TFR}) = n^2 \sum_x \text{Var}(_nf_x) \qquad (7.22)$$

To test for significant differences in the pattern and level of ASFRs between populations, we use the D statistic [(3.20)]

$$D = \left[\sum_x (ad - bc)/w_x \right]^2 \Big/ \sum_x [(a + b)(c + d)(a + c)(b + d)/ \qquad (7.23)$$

$$(a + b + c + d - 1)]/w_x^2$$

usually with weights $w_x = 1$ and terms

$$\begin{matrix} a & b \\ c & d \end{matrix} = \begin{matrix} _nN_{x,\,i} - {_nB_{x,\,i}} & _nB_{x,\,i} \\ _nN_{x,\,j} - {_nB_{x,\,j}} & _nB_{x,\,j} \end{matrix}$$

* In place of the binomial (7.2), Koop (1951; Keyfitz, 1977b, pp. 351–352) suggests the hypergeometric distribution (Johnson and Kotz, 1969, pp. 143–165; Freund, 1972, pp. 77–79, 159–160; see also Chiang, 1967, for the application of the hypergeometric in mortality analysis, and Brillinger, 1986, on the Poisson). The distinction is between sampling with (binomial) and without (hypergeometric) replacement. In demographic applications the two distributions are usually close.

† Where samples may include repeat births, (7.22) will include covariance terms, for which the reader may see Little (1982).

The reader can construct variance estimates for gross and net reproduction rates by interpreting the two terms as weighted estimates of the TFR and using the rule that the variance of a weighted function is the weight squared times the variance of the function.

7.13. SUMMARY

For the most part, fertility measures are more intuitive and simpler to work with than mortality measures. There are some intractable problems, most important among them our inability to reconcile male and female fertility estimates, but their number is small. The complexities of competing risks are absent from fertility analysis except in specialized contexts, such as contraceptive termination or failure (Tietze and Lewit, 1973; Potter and Avery, 1975; Trussell and Menken, 1980) for which the formulas of Sections 5.2 and 5.4 apply.

If fertility analysis becomes confusing, it is largely because of the variety of estimators that exist. To assist the reader, we have suggested approximate relationships between many of them. Those need not be learned—they are essentially heuristic and none are highly accurate—but the underlying reasoning should be remembered.

Of the various measures, the most widely used are the TFR, essentially a standardized estimate of completed family size, and the annual growth rate or stable growth rate. All are important because of the powerful implications of family size decisions that most of us would consider unexceptional, such as the doubling of populations within a single lifetime when family sizes average only three surviving children and the doubling within 25 years when families reach six children.

The chapter has also explored the role of breastfeeding, contraception, and abortion as they impact on completed family sizes. The models introduced are elementary but convey valuable insights. They will be utilized in Appendix 7A.1, where fertility rates are related to time spent in various exposure states, and in Chapter 8, which continues the analysis of fertility and population change in the context of population projection.

Two areas we have not discussed are natural fertility, for which the reader should see Henry (1972), Leridon (1977), and the valuable review of current knowledge in Gage *et al.* (1989); and model marriage and fertility distributions, for which the reader should see Coale (1971, 1977), Coale and McNiel (1972), and Coale and Trussell (1974, 1978). Chapter 2 introduced the normal and gamma distributions as approximations to fertility distributions, but neither is of the quality of the model distributions. Besides Henry, the reader may see Gini (1924), Potter and Parker (1964), Sheps (1964), and Sheps and Menken (1973) on models of fecundability and the birth process. For insights into differences between period and cohort measures the reader should see Ryder (1964), Keyfitz (1972), and the collection of articles in Mason and Fienberg (1985). On efforts to separate period from cohort behavior see also Glenn (1976).

APPENDIX 7A.1. FERTILITY EXPOSURE ANALYSIS

Several of the fertility measures introduced in this chapter are subsets of the intermediate fertility variables enumerated by Davis and Blake (1956). Because the effects on fertility of the key variables—time spent in unions or at risk of pregnancy, temporary or permanent sterility, breastfeeding, contraceptive use, and abortion—vary substantially within and across populations, much effort has gone into developing models to estimate their relative contributions to family size.

The fundamental model of fertility determinants is Hobcraft and Little's (1984) *fertility exposure analysis,* which uses fertility histories extracted from individual level survey data to estimate the proportion of time spent in various exposure states during a fixed reference period. Expanding on earlier work by Bongaarts (1978; Bongaarts and Potter, 1983; see also Singh *et al.,* 1985) and Gaslonde (Gaslonde and Bocaz, 1970; Gaslonde, 1972; Gaslonde and Carrasco, 1982) they identify the states (Hobcraft and Little, 1984, p. 23)*:

p_1 pregnancy, leading to a live birth
p_2 pregnancy, leading to an induced abortion
p_3 pregnancy, leading to a spontaneous abortion
p_4 pregnancy, leading to a stillbirth
l lactational infecundity
i_1 nonlactational infecundity, following a live birth
i_2 infecundity, following an induced abortion
i_3 infecundity, following a spontaneous abortion
i_4 infecundity, following a stillbirth
i_5 permanent sterility

m_1 virginity
m_2 divorce

---

* Our notation follows Hobcraft and Little (1984), except that we use r (risk) in place of their f (fecund). Sans serif variables denote the durations in exposure states in months [expressions (7.20), (7A.4), (7A.6), (7A.7)] and are distinguished from the proportion of time spent in exposure states [expressions (7A.1)–(7A.3), (7A.5)].

m_3 widowhood

m_4 separation

m_5 sexual abstinence, following a birth

m_6 terminal abstinence

c_k contraception, using method k, $k = 1, \ldots, K$

r fecund (residual), at risk of conception

If analysis is restricted to the principal intermediate variables, for women at ages x to $x + n$ we have the identity (omitting the interval subscripts n)

$$f_x = P_x[1 - d_x(-m) - d_x(-u) - d_x(c) - d_x(a) - d_x(l)] \quad (7A.1)$$

In the expression, P_x represents potential fertility at ages x to $x + n$, and is estimated from the remaining terms of the expression. That is,

$$P_x = f_x/[1 - d_x(-m) - d_x(-u) - d_x(c) - d_x(a) - d_x(l)]$$

The terms in (7A.1) are $d_x(-m)$, the proportion of time at age x spent prior to union (i.e., not yet married, hence $-m$, where the minus sign is read as "not"); $d_x(-u)$, the proportion of time spent not in union or not sexually active; and $d_x(c)$, $d_x(a)$, and $d_x(l)$, the proportions of time spent contracepting, spent in pregnancies that are aborted, and spent lactationally infecund, respectively. [The term $d_x(a)$ is omitted in the discussion that follows.] We adopt the convention that residual terms are 0 for $d_x(-m) = 1$ or $d_x(-m) + d_x(-u) = 1$. The observation period will be the interval over which the ASFRs are estimated, usually 12 or 24 months excluding very recent periods.*

Where individuals fall into more than one category in a given period (e.g., both contracepting and lactationally infecund), fractional assignments to categories or hierarchical orderings are required. Hobcraft and Little suggest the hierarchies $-u > l$ and $l > c$, which assign the overlap between time spent not in unions and time lactationally infecund to time not in unions, and assign the overlap between lactational infecundity and contraception to lactational infecundity. (In life table analyses of contraceptive failure, the period of overlap has historically been assigned wholly to contraception. The actual overlap is unassignable for at least some durations after birth.)

---

* For very recent periods, women may not know or correctly report their pregnancy status, biasing estimates of their potential fertility. Current pregnancies, for example, tend not to be reported until the middle or the last trimester in surveys, and are therefore undercounted both absolutely and relative to the annual number of births. In earlier periods, recall errors may also arise. These points are addressed in Hobcraft and Little (1984) and in Pullum et al. (1987).

The terms in (7A.1) can be expanded to form conditional exposure state probabilities. We set

$$f_x = P_x\{1 - d_x(-m)\}\{[1 - d_x(-m) - d_x(-u)]/[1 - d_x(-m)]\}$$

$$\times \{[1 - d_x(-m) - d_x(-u) - d_x(c)]/[1 - d_x(-m) - d_x(-u)]\}$$

$$\times \{[1 - d_x(-m) - d_x(-u) - d_x(c) - d_x(1)]/ \qquad (7A.2)$$

$$[1 - d_x(-m) - d_x(-u) - d_x(c)]\}$$

$$= P_x\, c_{-m,\, x}\, c_{-u,\, x|-m_x}\, c_{c,\, x|-m_x-u_x}\, c_{1,\, x|-m_x-u_xc_x} \qquad (7A.3)$$

Using (7A.2), the terms c_k in (7A.3) become: c_{-m}, the proportion of time that follows the start of the first union; c_{-u}, the ratio of time currently in union to time ever in union; c_c, the ratio of time currently in union and not contracepting to time currently in union; and c_1, the ratio of time currently in union, not contracepting, and not lactationally infecund, to time currently in union and not contracepting.

Using the 1975 National Fertility Survey for the Dominican Republic, Hobcraft and Little find the proportions of time in various exposure states for women ages 25–29 at 10–21 months prior to survey:

$$d_x(-m) = 0.116$$

$$d_x(-u) = 0.101$$

$$d_x(c) = 0.200$$

$$d_x(1) = 0.067$$

Residual terms for this population include the proportions of time spent in pregnancies (0.192), spent in postpartum infecundity or natural sterility (0.047), and spent fecund and at risk of pregnancy (0.277).

For the reference period we have used, the ASFR for the cohort is not given in Hobcraft and Little. If we allow a mean pregnancy duration of 39 weeks, however, the rate can be estimated from time spent in pregnancy as $f_x \simeq (52/39)d_x(p) = (52/39)0.192 = 0.256$. For this estimate we have*

---

* For the 12 months immediately prior to survey, the coefficients are $d_x(-m) = 0.092$, $d_x(-u) = 0.152$, $d_x(c) = 0.223$, $d_x(1) = 0.057$, and $f_x = 0.233$. The reader can confirm that for these estimates,

$$P_x = 0.233/[(0.908)(0.833)(0.705)(0.893)] = 0.489$$

$$c_{-m, x} = 1 - 0.116 = 0.884$$

$$c_{-u, x|-m_x} = (1 - 0.116 - 0.101)/(1 - 0.116) = 0.886$$

$$c_{c, x|-m_x-u_x} = (1 - 0.116 - 0.101 - 0.200)/(1 - 0.116 - 0.101) = 0.745$$

$$c_{l, x|-m_x-u_xc_x} = (1 - 0.116 - 0.101 - 0.200 - 0.067)/$$

$$(1 - 0.116 - 0.101 - 0.200) = 0.885$$

$$P_x = 0.256/[(0.884)(0.886)(0.745)(0.885)] = 0.496$$

For comparison, the 1950 Hutterite marital ASFR was 0.498 at ages 25–29 (Robinson, 1986).

The two estimates imply interbirth intervals of $I_B \simeq 1/0.496 = 24.2$ months and $I_B \simeq 1/0.498 = 24.1$ months, or a little more than the hypothetical duration of 20 months (18 months plus 20 months to allow for pregnancy losses) found using expression (7.20), $I_B = r + p + i$.

The terms of (7.20) can be estimated for the Dominican Republic data from the ratios of time spent in each state. Using a mean duration of pregnancy of $p = 39$ weeks or 9.0 months, for time at risk we find $r = 39 (0.277/0.192) = 56.3$ weeks $= 13.0$ months, and for time spent in natural sterility we have $i = 39(0.047/0.192) = 9.5$ weeks $= 2.2$ months. The estimates find the time in state j as the expected time in state i times the ratio of time in j to time in i. By this convention, the breakdown of the interval is

$$I_B = r + p + i = 13.0 + 9.0 + 2.2 = 24.2 \text{ months} \simeq 1/P_x \quad (7A.4)$$

as against our hypothetical $7\frac{1}{2} + 9 + 1\frac{1}{2} = 18$ months.

The high ratio of time at risk to time in pregnancy (0.277/0.192) and the correspondingly long exposure duration for the example (13.0 months) implies a monthly probability of only $1/13 = 0.08$ of becoming pregnant for women at risk. The value is low relative to Bongaarts's $1/7\frac{1}{2}$ months $= 0.13$ for all women 15–44, which it should exceed, and suggests either that some contraceptive methods are unreported or that others of the intermediate fertility variables have been subsumed in the residual category $d_x(r)$. Hobcraft and Little find that stratifying the sample to remove women apparently sterile $[d_x(i_5) = 0.07$, counting as sterile those at risk during the previous 5 years but not giving birth] corrects much or most of the discrepancy.

The contributions of the terms in (7A.2) to total fertility are found as weighted sums of the age-specific terms, using weights proportional to fertility.

That is,

$$\text{TFR} = P\, C_{-\text{m}}\, C_{-\text{u}|-\text{m}}\, C_{\text{c}|-\text{m}\,-\text{u}}\, C_{\text{l}|-\text{m}\,-\text{u}\,\text{c}} \qquad (7\text{A}.5)$$

where

$$P = \sum_x P_x$$

$$C_{-\text{m}} = \sum_x e_x c_{\text{m},\,x} \Big/ \sum_x e_x$$

$$c_{-\text{u}|-\text{m}} = \sum_x w_x c_{\text{u},\,x|-\text{m}} \Big/ \sum_x w_x$$

$$C_{\text{c}|-\text{m}\,-\text{u}} = \sum_x n_x c_{\text{c},\,x|-\text{m}\,-\text{u}} \Big/ \sum_x n_x$$

$$C_{\text{l}|-\text{m}\,-\text{u}\,\text{c}} = \sum_x P_x c_{\text{l},\,x|-\text{m}\,-\text{u}\,\text{c}} \Big/ P$$

The weights e_x, w_x, and n_x are found as

$e_x = f_x/[1 - d_x(-\text{m})]$, the ASFR of ever married women

$w_x = f_x/[1 - d_x(-\text{m}) - d_x(-\text{u})]$, the ASFR of currently married women

$n_x = f_x/[1 - d_x(-\text{m}) - d_x(-\text{u}) - d_x(\text{c})]$, the ASFR of currently married,

noncontracepting women (i.e., natural fertility)

Using (7A.5) with stratification of the sterile sample, Hobcraft and Little find for the terms C_k and potential fertility P:

$$\text{TFR} = P\, C_{-\text{m}}\, C_{-\text{u}|-\text{m}}\, C_{\text{c}|-\text{m}\,-\text{u}}\, C_{\text{l}|-\text{m}\,-\text{u}\,\text{c}}$$

$$= 5.35 = P(0.714)(0.754)(0.729)(0.902)$$

$$P = 15.1$$

These estimates are for the 12 months prior to survey. Except for lactation, the overall effects are greater than those at ages 25–29. The contribution to C_{-m} comes largely at ages under 25, before women enter first marriage; and those to C_{-u} and C_c come later, with union disruptions and increasing contraceptive use. Lactational amenorrhea is similar in its effects across most age intervals, as mean durations of breastfeeding average 8–9 months for all but the oldest cohorts. Hobcraft and Little assign only about half of time spent in breastfeeding to lactational infecundity, because of its overlap with immediate postpartum infecundity and its incomplete effectiveness.*

Since the effect measures in (7A.3) and (7A.5) derive from individual level fertility histories, their component terms can be incorporated in linear models, most simply of the form $\hat{d}(k) = \Sigma_j\, b_j X_j$, where b_j are regression coefficients for the attributes X_j. Other variables may be substituted for exposure times $d(k)$, including terms in $c(k)$ or fertility rates. For these and other aspects of fertility exposure analysis, the reader may see Hobcraft and Little (1984) and Pullum *et al.* (1987). Additional comments on the estimation of I_B from distributions of time in various exposure states are presented in Section 8.11.

Expression (7A.5) is a reformulation of a model originally proposed by Bongaarts (1978; Bongaarts and Potter, 1983) that is fitted using aggregate in place of individual level effect measures. In the Bongaarts proximate determinants analysis, the TFR is decomposed as the product of the natural fertility rate and the indexes

$$\text{TFR} = P_B C_{-M} C_L C_C C_A = P_B \{\text{TFR}/\text{MTFR}\}\, \{20/(18.5 + 1)\}$$

(7A.6)

$$\times \{1 - 1.08\rho e\}\, \{\text{TFR}/[\text{TFR} + 0.4\ \text{TAR}(1 + \rho)]\}$$

In the expression, P_B is the Bongaarts potential fertility rate in the absence of breastfeeding, extended postpartum sexual abstinence, and others of the fertility-inhibiting variables. Bongaarts and Potter (1983, p. 87) find the approximate value $P_B \simeq 15.3$ children; as in Hobcraft and Little, its value for a given population is determined from the expression after estimating other terms.

The indexes C_K represent fertility-depressing effects, with magnitudes between 0 and 1.0, as follows:

C_{-M} indexes the proportion in unions, and is found as the TFR divided

---

* The mean duration of breastfeeding, about 8 months, is close to the duration of pregnancy, from which we might expect $d_x(1) \simeq d_x(p)$. Owing to the partial assignment of breastfeeding to lactational infecundity, the actual ratio is substantially lower, 0.067 to 0.192 at ages 25–29.

by the MTFR.* It is the only one of the Bongaarts variables essentially preserved intact in Hobcraft and Little. The index is 1.0 if all women are married.

C_L is found as the expected interbirth interval in the absence of breastfeeding, divided by the expected interbirth interval at prevailing breastfeeding patterns. The former is estimated as $7\frac{1}{2}$ months at risk of pregnancy, 9 months in pregnancy, and $1\frac{1}{2}$ months of postpartum sterility, with an allowance of 2 months for pregnancy loss. For the latter, Bongaarts and Potter count $18\frac{1}{2}$ months plus the duration of postpartum infecundity associated with lactational amenorrhea (I), estimated as $I = 1.753e^{0.1396\mu - 0.001872\mu^2}$, or about 0.6μ for typical populations, where μ is the mean duration of breastfeeding. The index is 1.0 in the absence of breastfeeding.

C_C indexes the fertility impact of contraceptive use, and varies with both the proportion of currently married couples using contraception (ρ) and the average effectiveness (e) of the methods selected.† The constant term 1.08 adjusts for the higher proportion fecund among contraceptors than among all couples. The index is 1.0 where contraception is not used.

The index for abortion, C_A, is found as the TFR divided by the TFR plus the fertility impact of the TAR. To estimate its impact, the abortion rate is adjusted for the shortness of abortion intervals relative to birth intervals, and for contraceptive prevalence, on the argument that where contraception is widespread, fewer abortions are required for a given reduction in births than where it is less prevalent. If abortion is not used, the index is 1.0.

The reader will recognize that much of the Bongaarts model is intuitive, and he or she might suspect that its terms will not differ greatly from the Hobcraft and Little estimates based on time spent in the several exposure states. The marriage effect C_{-M} is expressed in Hobcraft and Little as the product $C_{-m}C_{-u}$, and both models express lactational infecundity through estimates of time added to the birth interval by breastfeeding. There is also a close correspondence between contraceptive prevalence and use effectiveness (Bongaarts) and the proportion of time couples are protected from pregnancy by contraceptive use (Hobcraft and Little).

The index for abortion in Bongaarts is more problematic. Like contraception or lactation, the impact of abortion is to extend the interval between

---

* Because the marital ASFR at ages 15–19 includes premarital conceptions and becomes unstable as ages at marriage change, Bongaarts and Potter (1983, pp. 81–82) set $_5f_{15,u} = (0.75)_5f_{20,u}$ for all populations.

† By method, effectiveness is estimated for most developing country populations at 0.9 for the pill, 0.95 for the IUD, 1.0 for sterilization, and 0.7 for other methods, taking into account both method quality and care in method use (Bongaarts and Potter, 1983, p. 84). To find e, the average contraceptive effectiveness, these estimates are weighted by the proportions using each method.

births, by perhaps 8–9 months using (7.20). Its impact is not conditioned on the nature and quality of prior contraception, which properly belongs to C_C, or for that matter on inadequate protection through lactational amenorrhea or others of the Davis and Blake exposure variables. (It is defended by an argument that would permit abortion effects to be subsumed in either C_C or C_L.)

Omitting contraceptive prevalence from the abortion index, it becomes $C_A^* = \text{TFR}/(\text{TFR} + 0.4\,\text{TAR})$. The expression is interpretable as the ratio of the TFR to the hypothetical rate in the absence of abortion. Substituted into (7A.6) it yields

$$\text{TFR} = P_B^* C_{-M}\, C_L\, C_C\, C_A^* = P_B^* \{\text{TFR}/\text{MTFR}\} \{20/(18.5 + \text{I})\}$$
$$\times \{1 - 1.08\rho e\} \{\text{TFR}/(\text{TFR} + 0.4\,\text{TAR})\} \tag{7A.7}$$

where P_B^* is found as $\text{TFR}/(C_{-M}C_L C_{C|m}C_A^*)$. We note that with replacement of C_A by C^*_A the impact of abortion is brought more nearly into agreement with Hobcraft and Little whose measure is time spent in pregnancies that are aborted.

For the Dominican Republic, the Bongaarts (1982) estimates for contraceptive prevalence and use effectiveness are $\rho = 0.32$ and $e = 0.89$; the mean duration of breastfeeding is estimated at $\mu = 8$ months, from which $\text{I} = 4.76$ months of postpartum infecundity. Using estimates of 5.85 for the TFR and 9.74 for the MTFR, he finds using (7A.6)–(7A.7) (Hobcraft and Rodríguez, 1982; Bongaarts, 1982):

$$\text{TFR} = P_B\, C_{-M}\, C_C\, C_L$$
$$= 5.85$$
$$= P_B\{5.85/9.74\}\{1 - (1.08)(0.32)(0.89)\}\{20/(18.5 + 4.76)\}$$
$$= P_B(0.601)(0.692)(0.860)(1.000)$$
$$P_B = 16.4$$

Using Hobcraft and Little's TFR estimate of 5.35 yields $P_B = 15.0$. The effect levels in the Bongaarts model differ from those in Hobcraft and Little, but are satisfactory as approximations from limited data.

The reader should recognize the importance of the quality of available estimates of fertility rates, breastfeeding, contraceptive use, and abortion for both Hobcraft and Little and Bongaarts. Where fertility is misreported, or pushed backward or forward in time, the contributions of the intermediate variables may be seriously distorted. More common is the underreporting of contraception and abortion, leading to overestimation of time at risk of pregnancy and therefore to low estimates of potential fertility. The reader should see Hobcraft and Little (1984) for a careful discussion of these and related issues.

CHAPTER 8

Population Projection and Projection Matrices

Professor [Leonard] Euler assumes (1) at the outset there exists a married couple aged 20, (2) their descendents also always marry at the age of 20, (3) 6 children are born to each marriage. . . . Also (4) variations must never occur; therefore twins will always be born, the first pair to each marriage coming in the 22nd, the next in the 24th and the third in the 26th year. It will be assumed (5) that all children survive, marry, and remain living until reaching age 40. . . .

On these assumptions there will be only two people initially, 4 after 2 years, 6 after 4 years, 8 after 8 years. After this no changes occur until the first two children reach their 22nd year, which takes place after 24 years, when their first two children come into the world. Two years later this couple will produce 2 more, but the couple born in the 4th year will also produce 2 children; in the 28th year 6 children will arrive; in the 30th again only 4, and so forth.

Notice that although great unorderliness seems to rule in Euler's table, the number of births belongs to a progression which is called a recurrent series and which can be produced by dividing out an algebraic fraction. While these progressions initially appear irregular, if they are continued they finally change into a geometric progression; the initially perceived irregularities decrease with time until they finally almost entirely disappear.

—JOHANN PETER SÜSSMILCH (1761)

Translated by Nathan Keyfitz (Smith and Keyfitz, 1977, pp. 81–82)

8.1. INTRODUCTION

This chapter and the next focus on population estimation and projection. The distinction between these two terms is temporal: *estimation* usually implies a judgment or guess as to the size or attributes of a historic or present

population; *projection* implies a judgment or guess as to its future direction.*
We will not maintain this distinction as rigorously as we might. The term
reverse projection is given to applications of projection methodologies to the
estimation of past populations.

The simplest population projections begin with population estimates at
two or more time points, or with the population size and either birth and
death rates or the net reproduction rate. For small areas, or where knowledge
of the population is limited, the need for more elaborate formulas may not
be great.

If greater precision is needed, we require an initial population and a
series of fertility and mortality rates by age that can be used to project survivors
by age and births by parental age in future periods. (The simple projection
outlined in the opening quotation is of this kind.) Additional terms may also
be included for migration where it is a significant factor.

An example of source data for a projection without migration is provided
in Table 8.1. The table uses 15-year age intervals (n) for illustration†: in
normal applications, 5- or at most 10-year age intervals are used for greater
precision. The projection period is the same as the width of the age intervals,
in the example 1980 to 1995, then to 2010, 2025, etc. [The projection is from
the age interval $(x, x + n)$ to the interval $(x + n, x + 2n)$, or from an average
age of $x + \frac{1}{2}n$ to $x + 1\frac{1}{2}n$. In the example, in each period the population 0–
14 is projected to ages 15–29, the population 15–29 is projected to ages 30–
44, and so forth. The projection advances each cohort 15 years in age, and
therefore 15 years in time.]

It was noticed in the early 1940s (Bernardelli, 1941; Lewis, 1942; Leslie,
1945, 1948a,b) that population projections could be handled through matrix
algebra, with the population to be projected represented as a vector **N** and
the projection equations as a matrix **M** of a relatively simple form. Among
their other properties, matrices of the population type stabilize: their elements,
the survival and birth rates, settle into fixed ratios if the matrix is repeatedly
multiplied by itself (equivalent to projecting the population into the relatively
distant future), with the result that the population age distribution also stabilizes. Manipulation of the matrix also yields the growth rate of the population
at stability (the *intrinsic growth rate r*), and provides other insights into its
behavior.

---

* The term *forecast* is used in the context of economic planning for projections to the near, or
  addressable, future. A demographer's perspective on forecasting will be found in Keyfitz (1981a).
† Where data are to be regrouped into fewer and wider age intervals to simplify population projection, Keyfitz suggests that the condensed data be adjusted to replicate source data projections
  for time $t_0 + n$, where t_0 is the initial time point and n is the interval width in the regrouped
  data. The adjustment (Keyfitz, 1977b, pp. 37–40) reduces the severity of information losses
  that arise with interval widening.

8.2. ELEMENTARY PROJECTION METHODS

The simplest population projections are constructed from the population at one time point, annual crude birth and death rates, and if migration is relevant, the net migration rate. The CBR, CDR, and CMR are not direct measures of population changes from year to year—all are constructed from annual events and the midyear population rather than from events measured from midyear to midyear—but may serve as estimates of the intensity of birth, death, and migration processes. By that interpretation, for the annual population change we will have [using (1.6), rewritten to make explicit the different reference periods in the source data]:

$$_\omega N_{0, \, exp}^{(t+1)} = {}_\omega N_0^{(t)} \exp[({}_\omega B_0^{(t-1/2, \, t+1/2)}$$

$$- {}_\omega D_0^{(t-1/2, \, t+1/2)} + {}_\omega F_0^{(t-1/2, \, t+1/2)})/{}_\omega N_0^{(t)}] \tag{8.1}$$

The expression uses $_\omega F_0$ to represent annual net migration. ($_\omega F_0$ is found as $_\omega I_0 - {}_\omega E_0$, where I represents immigrants and E represents emigrants.) For the midyear 1980 U.S. population (Hollmann, 1989), the expression yields the 1981 population:

$$_\omega N_{0, \, exp}^{(1981)} = 227{,}757{,}000 \, \exp[(3{,}612{,}000 - 1{,}990{,}000 + 750{,}000)/$$

$$227{,}757{,}000] = 227{,}757{,}000 \, e^{0.01041} = 230{,}141{,}000$$

The Bureau of the Census estimate for mid-1981 is 230,138,000, or about 3000 fewer.* The difference is due partly to changes in births, deaths, and immigration from year to year, and also partly to the formula assumption of a constant migration *rate* for the midyear-to-midyear period, rather than a fixed number of migrants as envisioned in U.S. immigration laws. Neither the 1980 nor 1981 population estimates are accurate to the number of digits shown.

For longer term population projections we may extrapolate from changes between two time points, by either of the formulas:

$$_\omega N_{0, \, exp}^{(t+n)} = {}_\omega N_0^{(t)} ({}_\omega N_0^{(k+m)}/{}_\omega N_0^{(k)})^{(n/m)} \tag{8.2}$$

---

* Had we used the demographic balancing equation [(1.5)] blending annual with midyear terms, we would have found

$$_\omega N_{0, \, lin}^{(1981)} = 227{,}757{,}000 + 3{,}612{,}000 - 1{,}990{,}000 + 750{,}000 = 230{,}129{,}000$$

$$_\omega N_{0,\text{ lin}}^{(t+n)} = {}_\omega N_0^{(t)} + (n/m)({}_\omega N_0^{(k+m)} - {}_\omega N_0^{(k)}) \qquad (8.3)$$

The formulas find annual population changes exponentially as the $1/m$ power of an m-year change, or linearly as $1/m$ times an m-year difference. The annual rate is then raised to the power n or multiplied by n to find the change over n years.

The expressions simplify if the time points and durations are coterminus; that is, if $t = k + m$ and $m = n$. For example, using the 1960 and 1970 U.S. population to project to 1980 we would have:

$$_\omega N_{0,\text{ exp}}^{(1980)} = {}_\omega N_0^{(1970)}({}_\omega N_0^{(1970)}/{}_\omega N_0^{(1960)})^{(10/10)}$$

$$= 205{,}052{,}000(205{,}052{,}000/180{,}671{,}000) = 232{,}723{,}000$$

$$_\omega N_{0,\text{ lin}}^{(1980)} = {}_\omega N_0^{(1970)} + ({}_\omega N_0^{(1970)} - {}_\omega N_0^{(1960)})(10/10)$$

$$= 205{,}052{,}000 + (205{,}052{,}000 - 180{,}671{,}000) = 229{,}433{,}000$$

Both estimates are high, although the linear formula comes closer to tracing the slowdown in growth that occurred during the 1970s. For states and localities, where changes are less predictable than at the national level, the formulas are competitive with more complex expressions.

Where birth rates have been relatively constant over several decades, and where migration is negligible, net reproduction rates and the generation length can be used for long-term population projections. Given the net reproduction rate R_0 (R_0 is the generational replacement rate, or number of daughters women have who survive to their same ages; see Section 7.5), and estimating the generation length to be about $T = 27\frac{1}{2}$ years, the intrinsic rate of population increase or decrease is found from the relationship $[(7.17)]$

$$R_0 = e^{rT}$$

$$r = \ln R_0/T$$

The expression allows us to project the population in year $t + n$ as

$$_\omega N_{0,\text{ exp2}}^{(t+n)} = {}_\omega N_0^{(t)} e^{rn} \qquad (8.4)$$

Expression (8.4) would not be used for the United States, where immigration contributes substantively to population growth, or for countries where fertility rates are changing, but is applicable to some developing country populations where family sizes remain high.

A related measure is the eventual population size that would follow an abrupt change in the NRR to replacement level ($R_0 = 1$). Originally developed by Keyfitz (1971b) and simplified by Frauenthal (1975), the estimate of the eventual population size is given by

$$_\omega N_{0,\text{ stationary}} = {_\omega N_0^{(t)}} \simeq {_\omega N_0^{(0)}} R_0^{1/2} \qquad |t \gg 0 \qquad (8.5)$$

where R_0 is the NRR prior to the change. The stationary level is reached in about one lifetime, which will give dimension to the approximation $t \gg 0$. The ratio of eventual to initial births will be about $R_0^{-1/2}$, or roughly the inverse of the change in population size.

Using (8.5) and the data of Table 7.6, the U.S. population would settle to $0.876^{1/2} = 0.94$ times its present size if the NRR recovered to 1.0. That is not a terribly helpful estimate for a population with both substantial migration and substantial momentum from the higher fertility in its recent past. For Mexico the formula suggests an eventual population 1.6 times its 1980 size with an immediate shift to an NRR of 1.0. A much larger increase is expected, since the NRR continues to be higher. The ratio of births in Mexico to births in the United States has been about 1 : 1.6 for more than a decade, and may be taken as an estimate of the near-term ratio of the two population sizes.

None of the formulas of this section incorporate much information about the populations to which they are applied, and all are most often used where detailed data are limited or unreliable, or where growth patterns are difficult to anticipate. Component formulas, which project populations using life tables and age-specific fertility rates, are normally better when data are available and the researcher is able to exercise judgment about future patterns.

8.3. COMPONENT PROJECTIONS

Component population projections begin with age distributions, and estimates or projections of age-specific fertility, mortality, and migration rates. Because they lend themselves well to matrix analysis, from which important theorems have been developed, we will introduce them in that context.

To understand the layout and application of the projection matrix, we need to look first at the equations that comprise component projections.* For simplicity, we will use only the first three age groups of the female population in Table 8.1 (ages 0–14, 15–29, and 30–44), and will project females and

---

* Readers not familiar with matrix algebra may review Searle (1966), Namboodiri (1984), or Caswell (1989, pp. 280–295) for essential formulas.

Table 8.1. U.S. 1980 Population and Births, and National Center for Health Statistics 1980 Life Table Population. *Source:* National Center for Health Statistics (1984–1985)

Ages	1980 population $_nN_x$	Life table population $_nL_x/l_0$	$_nL_{x+n}/$ $_nL_x$	Births Females $_nB_{x,\,f}$	Births Males $_nB_{x,\,m}$	Age specific fertility rates Females $_nf_{x,\,f}$	Age specific fertility rates Males $_nf_{x,\,m}$
Females:							
0–14	25,073,029	14.79376	—	0	0	0.000000	0.000000
15–29	30,884,000	14.70000	0.993662	1,410,649	1,486,172	0.045676	0.048121
30–44	21,949,115	14.51057	0.987114	348,993	366,444	0.015900	0.016695
45–59	17,924,259	13.89239	0.957398	0	0	0.000000	0.000000
60–74	14,241,832	11.90186	0.856718	0	0	0.000000	0.000000
75+	6,420,409	7.68632	0.645808	0	0	0.000000	0.000000
Total	116,492,644			1,759,642	1,852,616		
Males:							
0–14	26,217,310	14.74000	—	0	0	0.000000	0.000000
15–29	31,123,747	14.51084	0.984453	1,157,616	1,221,147	0.037194	0.039235
30–44	21,246,515	14.06104	0.969002	576,765	605,014	0.027146	0.028476
45–59	16,490,782	12.96693	0.922189	25,261	26,455	0.001532	0.001604
60–74	11,426,394	9.63350	0.742928	0	0	0.000000	0.000000
75+	3,548,413	4.04702	0.42099	0	0	0.000000	0.000000
Total	110,053,161			1,759,642	1,852,616		

daughters. The projection will be generalized for older age groups and males subsequently.

We first estimate the survival rate from ages 0–14 to 15–29, and from ages 15–29 to 30–44. If a population life table is available, the ratio of successive $_nL_x$ terms (the life table population surviving in each age interval) will normally serve to estimate survival in the real population. We set:

$$(_nL_{x+n}/_nL_x)_nN_x^{(t)} = {}_nN_{x+n}^{(t+n)} \tag{8.6}$$

where $_nN_x^{(t)}$ represents the population at ages x to $x + n$ at time t and $_nN_{x+n}^{(t+n)}$ is the population n years older at time $t + n$. For the female population of Table 8.1 we have:

$$(_{15}L_{15}/_{15}L_0)_{15}N_0^{(t)} = {}_{15}N_{15}^{(t+15)}$$

$$0.993662 \times 25,073 = 24,914$$

$$(_{15}L_{30}/_{15}L_{15})_{15}N_{15}^{(t)} = {_{15}}N_{30}^{(t+15)}$$

$$0.987114 \times 30{,}884 = 30{,}486$$

Notice that by the use of the life table $_nL_x$ series we take mortality into account but not migration, since the life table displays survivors across age and time for a fixed number of births. Migration is handled by adjusting the survival terms upwards or downwards (for net population inflow or outflow), or by adding or subtracting individuals after the projection is completed. Projections by *census survival* are of the former type: in place of the life table, survival is estimated as the ratio of the census population at ages $x + n$ to $x + 2n$ at time $t + n$ to the population ages x to $x + n$ at time t, or $_nN_{x+n}^{(t+n)}/_nN_x^{(t)}$. The ratio may be less than or greater than 1.0, depending both on mortality and on the direction and magnitude of migration between the two censuses.

To find the population ages $0-n$ at time $t + n$, who are the survivors at the end of the projection period of the children born during the period, we require three types of information. We need to know: (1) the proportion of the age groups 0 to n, n to $2n$, $2n$ to $3n$, and so forth, who will survive through part or all of the projection period; (2) the age-specific birth rates they will experience; and (3) the survival probability from birth to the $0-n$ age group.

One solution for projecting births is to use the average of the age-specific birth rates for each cohort at the start and end of the period. Formally,

$$_n\mathbf{f}_{x+(1/2)n,\text{ f, linear 1}} = \tfrac{1}{2}\left[_n f_{x,\text{ f}} + (_nL_{x+n}/_nL_x) {_n}f_{x+n,\text{ f}} \right] \tag{8.7}$$

where $_n f_{x,\text{ f}}$ and $_n f_{x+n,\text{ f}}$ are the ASFRs for births of children of one sex (here, daughters) at ages x to $x + n$ and $x + n$ to $x + 2n$, respectively, and $_nL_{x+n}/_nL_x$ is the proportion of the cohort ages x to $x + n$ who will survive to ages $x + n$ to $x + 2n$. The term $_n\mathbf{f}_{x+(1/2)n,\text{ f}}$ thus averages the current fertility of the cohort ages x to $x + n$ with its future fertility at $x + n$ to $x + 2n$, after allowing for the prospect that not all members of the cohort will be alive through the complete projection period. If (8.6) is used to project cohort survival, $_n\mathbf{f}_{x+(1/2)n,\text{ f}}$ will satisfy the projection equality for births $_nB_{x+(1/2)n}$ in the projection period:

$$_nB_{x+(1/2)n} = {_n}N_x^{(t)} {_n}\mathbf{f}_{x+(1/2)n,\text{ f}} = \tfrac{1}{2}\left(_nN_x^{(t)} {_n}f_{x,\text{ f}} + {_n}N_{x+n}^{(t+n)} {_n}f_{x+n,\text{ f}} \right)$$

The sans serif f in $_n\mathbf{f}_{x+(1/2)n,\text{ f}}$ indicates that it includes a mortality component and is not the simple average of $_n f_{x,\text{ f}}$ and $_n f_{x+n,\text{ f}}$. For projections using census survival, the term $(_nL_{x+n}/_nL_x)$ is replaced by $(_nN_{x+n}^{(t+n)}/_nN_x^{(t)})$.

Substituting the female data of Table 8.1, expression (8.7) gives:

$$_{15}f_{7.5, \ f} = \tfrac{1}{2}[_{15}f_{0, \ f} + (_{15}L_{15}/_{15}L_0)_{15}f_{15, \ f}]$$

$$= \tfrac{1}{2}(0.0 + 0.99366 \times 0.045676) = 0.022693$$

$$_{15}f_{22.5, \ f} = \tfrac{1}{2}[_{15}f_{15, \ f} + (_{15}L_{30}/_{15}L_{15})_{15}f_{30, \ f}]$$

$$= \tfrac{1}{2}(0.045676 + 0.98711 \times 0.015900) = 0.030686$$

$$_{15}f_{37.5, \ f} = \tfrac{1}{2}[_{15}f_{30, \ f} + (_{15}L_{45}/_{15}L_{30})_{15}f_{45, \ f}]$$

$$= \tfrac{1}{2}(0.015900 + 0.95740 \times 0.0) = 0.007950$$

The ASFRs are 1-year rates, and summing across all of the fertile age groups will provide an estimate of family size. For the example, in which each age interval spans 15 years, the family size becomes $15 \times (0.022693 + 0.030686 + 0.007950) = 0.919935$. Using the fertility rates of Table 8.1, it is $15 \times (0.045676 + 0.01590) = 0.92364$. The latter figure is the *gross reproduction rate,* and is the number of daughters each woman would have in her lifetime in the absence of mortality. For the projection we have had to take female mortality into account, which gives a slightly smaller estimate.

Besides (8.7), we may estimate $_nf_{x+(1/2)n, \ f}$ terms by interpolating from $_nf_{x, \ f}$ to $_nf_{x+(1/2)n, \ f}$ and surviving the population $_nN_x$ to midinterval. Interpolation formulas are presented as expression (2.3) and are applied to 1980 U.S. fertility rates for 5-year age intervals in Table 2.1. Either the cubic or fifth-order formula, with the endpoint adjustments shown in the table, will produce estimates of higher quality than the essentially linear averaging that is applied in (8.7).

Survival to midinterval is most easily estimated by adjusting from the complete interval estimator $_nS_{x+(1/2)n} = \ _nL_{x+n}/_nL_x$. If survival is linear over the interval, at midinterval we will have

$$_{(1/2)n}S_{x+(1/2)n, \ \text{linear}} = \tfrac{1}{2}(1 + \ _nL_{x+n}/_nL_x) \tag{8.8}$$

Alternatively, if the survival probability is assumed to be constant in the interval we will have

$$_{(1/2)n}S_{x+(1/2)n, \ \text{exp}} = (_nL_{x+n}/_nL_x)^{1/2} \tag{8.9}$$

Using 5-year age intervals, the two expressions will be similar in magnitude for the fertile age range. We note from Chapter 4 that linear estimators are usually slightly better than exponential estimators for human survival, and recommend using (8.8) when the two survival estimates differ.

Combining cubic or fifth-order interpolation of $_nf_{x,\,f}$ with midinterval survival estimates from (8.8), the fertility terms become

$$_n\mathbf{f}_{x+(1/2)n,\,f,\,\text{linear 2}} = (1/2)_nS_{x+(1/2)n,\,\text{linear}}\,_nf_{x+(1/2)n,\,f}$$

$$= \tfrac{1}{2}(1 + {}_nL_{x+n}/{}_nL_x)_nf_{x+(1/2)n,\,f} \tag{8.10}$$

The reader can confirm that with cubic interpolation of $_nf_{x+(1/2)n,\,f}$, (8.10) yields

$$_{15}\mathbf{f}_{7.5,\,f} = (0.99683)(0.021844) = 0.021775$$

$$_{15}\mathbf{f}_{22.5,\,f} = (0.99356)(0.034637) = 0.034414$$

$$_{15}\mathbf{f}_{37.5,\,f} = (0.97870)(0.005095) = 0.004986$$

For the example we will use (8.7), since (8.10), although better for 5-year age interval data, is less satisfactory for interval widths of 15 years, which concentrate fertility into very few age groups.*

To adjust the estimates of (8.7) from annual births to children in the age interval $0-n$ (in the example, $0-14$) at the end of the period, we may use the life table ratio of persons $0-14$ to births ($_{15}L_0/l_0$). Combining this expression with the fertility estimates at each age, we will have:

$$_{15}N_0^{(t+15)} = \tfrac{1}{2}(_{15}L_0/l_0)\{_{15}N_0^{(t)}[_{15}f_{0,\,f} + (_{15}L_{15}/_{15}L_0)_{15}f_{15,\,f}]$$

$$+ {}_{15}N_{15}^{(t)}[_{15}f_{15,\,f} + (_{15}L_{30}/_{15}L_{15})_{15}f_{30,\,f}] \tag{8.11}$$

$$+ {}_{15}N_{30}^{(t)}[_{15}f_{30,\,f} + (_{15}L_{45}/_{15}L_{30})_{15}f_{45,\,f}]\}$$

To put this expression in matrix format we need to simplify our notation, which we can do by setting

$$_n\phi_{x+(1/2)n} = \tfrac{1}{2}(_nL_0/l_0)[_nf_{x,\,f} + (_nL_{x+n}/_nL_x)_nf_{x+n,\,f}]$$

$$= (_nL_0/l_0)_n\mathbf{f}_{x+(1/2)n,\,f} \tag{8.12}$$

---

* We test for estimator quality by the closeness of the intrinsic roots of the expressions to roots found from the source data. This point is discussed in Section 8.5.

using the Greek ϕ (phi) to mean "fertility." For our example, the terms are:

$$_{15}\phi_{7.5} = 14.79376 \times 0.022693 = 0.33571$$

$$_{15}\phi_{22.5} = 14.79376 \times 0.030686 = 0.45396$$

$$_{15}\phi_{37.5} = 14.79376 \times 0.007950 = 0.11761$$

Notice that multiplication by $_{15}L_0$ yields a family size estimate of 0.33571 + 0.45396 + 0.11761 = 0.90728 daughters. Because it includes a partial adjustment for mortality, the sum of the $_n\phi_{x+(1/2)n}$ terms approximates the completed family size a little better than does the gross reproduction rate.

Collecting the formulas for survival and for births, the basic projection will be equivalent to solving three equations:

$$
\begin{aligned}
_{15}\phi_{7.5}\,_{15}N_0^{(t)} \quad &+ \quad _{15}\phi_{22.5}\,_{15}N_{15}^{(t)} \quad + \, _{15}\phi_{37.5}\,_{15}N_{30}^{(t)} = \,_{15}N_0^{(t+15)} \\
(_{15}L_{15}/_{15}L_0)_{15}N_0^{(t)} + \qquad\quad 0 \qquad\quad + \qquad 0 \qquad = \,_{15}N_{15}^{(t+15)} \\
0 \qquad\quad + (_{15}L_{30}/_{15}L_{15})_{15}N_{15}^{(t)} + \qquad 0 \qquad = \,_{15}N_{30}^{(t+15)}
\end{aligned}
\tag{8.13}
$$

In matrix notation these terms become

$$
\begin{bmatrix}
_{15}\phi_{7.5} & _{15}\phi_{22.5} & _{15}\phi_{37.5} \\
_{15}L_{15}/_{15}L_0 & 0 & 0 \\
0 & _{15}L_{30}/_{15}L_{15} & 0
\end{bmatrix}
\begin{bmatrix}
_{15}N_0^{(t)} \\
_{15}N_{15}^{(t)} \\
_{15}N_{30}^{(t)}
\end{bmatrix}
=
\begin{bmatrix}
_{15}N_0^{(t+15)} \\
_{15}N_{15}^{(t+15)} \\
_{15}N_{30}^{(t+15)}
\end{bmatrix}
\tag{8.14}
$$

$$\mathbf{M} \qquad\qquad\quad \mathbf{N}^{(t)} \ = \quad \mathbf{N}^{(t+15)}$$

Comparing the equations and the matrix, it will be evident that each of the elements of $\mathbf{N}^{(t+15)}$ is the sum of the products of a row of the matrix and the column vector $\mathbf{N}^{(t)}$. The convention that rows multiply columns applies to matrices generally, and gives rise to the simple rule that the product of a $c \times d$ matrix and a $d \times e$ matrix is a $c \times e$ matrix. In the example, a 3×3 matrix multiplies a 3×1 matrix to produce a second 3×1 matrix. (The term *vector* applies to any $n \times 1$ or $1 \times n$ matrix.)

For our example, we enter the terms in ϕ in the first row of the matrix and the survival terms from Table 8.1 in the subdiagonals. We then have for the 15-year projection:

$$
\begin{bmatrix}
0.33571 & 0.45396 & 0.11761 \\
0.99366 & 0.00000 & 0.00000 \\
0.00000 & 0.98711 & 0.00000
\end{bmatrix}
\begin{bmatrix}
25,073 \\
30,884 \\
21,949
\end{bmatrix}
=
\begin{bmatrix}
25,019 \\
24,914 \\
30,486
\end{bmatrix}
$$

$$\mathbf{M} \qquad\qquad\quad \mathbf{N}^{(1980)} \ = \quad \mathbf{N}^{(1995)}$$

The reader can confirm that the 1995 population estimates are found from the matrix as:

$$0.33571 \times 25{,}073 + 0.45396 \times 30{,}884 + 0.11761 \times 21{,}949 = 25{,}019$$

$$0.99366 \times 25{,}073 + 0.00000 \times 30{,}884 + 0.00000 \times 21{,}949 = 24{,}914$$

$$0.00000 \times 25{,}073 + 0.98711 \times 30{,}884 + 0.00000 \times 21{,}949 = 30{,}486$$

8.4. LONGER TERM PROJECTIONS AND POPULATION STABILITY

Part of the power of the matrix lies in its ability to simplify long-range projections. To find the population at time $t + 30$ by expression (8.13) we have to first solve for $\mathbf{N}^{(t+15)}$ and then repeat the multiplication substituting $\mathbf{N}^{(t+15)}$ for $\mathbf{N}^{(t)}$ on the left-hand side of the equations. Using the projection matrix $\mathbf{M}$ and the population vectors $\mathbf{N}^{(t)}$ and $\mathbf{N}^{(t+15)}$, the multiplication simplifies to

$$\mathbf{N}^{(t+30)} = \mathbf{M}\mathbf{N}^{(t+15)} = \mathbf{M}(\mathbf{M}\mathbf{N}^{(t)}) = \mathbf{M}^2\mathbf{N}^{(t)}$$

Projection to any future time point reduces to the problem of raising $\mathbf{M}$ to the appropriate power. This is usually left to the computer, but follows the rule that the ijth element of $\mathbf{M}^2$ is the product–sum of row i and column j of $\mathbf{M}$. For our example, element 11 (row 1 column 1) of $\mathbf{M}^2$ will be $_{15}\phi_{7.5} \times {}_{15}\phi_{7.5} + {}_{15}\phi_{22.5} \times ({}_{15}L_{15}/{}_{15}L_0) + {}_{15}\phi_{37.5} \times 0.0 = 0.33571 \times 0.33571 + 0.45396 \times 0.99366 + 0.11761 \times 0.0 = 0.56378$, element 12 (row 1 column 2) will be $_{15}\phi_{7.5} \times {}_{15}\phi_{22.5} + {}_{15}\phi_{22.5} \times 0.0 + {}_{15}\phi_{37.5} \times ({}_{15}L_{30}/{}_{15}L_{15}) = 0.33571 \times 0.45396 + 0.45396 \times 0.0 + 0.11761 \times 0.98711 = 0.26849$, and so forth. The reader can confirm the correctness of the matrix terms by substituting terms in $_nN_x^{(t+15)}$ for terms in $_nN_x^{(t)}$ in (8.13), and then substituting for $_nN_x^{(t+15)}$ the expressions in $_nN_x^{(t)}$ that produce them. The substitutions generate expressions for $_nN_x^{(t+30)}$ as functions of $_nN_x^{(t)}$ whose coefficients are those of $\mathbf{M}^2$.

Raised to very high powers, the elements of the projection matrix stabilize, in the sense that the ijth element of $\mathbf{M}^{k+1}$ will equal a constant (the 15-year intrinsic growth rate $\lambda = e^{15r}$) times the ijth element of $\mathbf{M}^k$. The elements of **M** also settle into fixed ratios with respect to each other, and the population converges to the stable form*

$$_nN_x = \lambda^{-x/n}(_nL_x/_nL_0)_nN_0 \qquad (8.15)$$

[Note: matrices in which fertility is nonzero only at a single age, or where all of the fertile age groups share a common factor, converge *cyclically*, with births fluctuating from period to period in a fixed pattern. (An example would be a population in which fertility was confined to the second and fourth age groups, which have 2 as a factor. The population would oscillate between two stable distributions.) Oscillations do not occur in human populations, but are sometimes generated in projections when very few age intervals are used.]

For our example, we begin with the initial projection matrix:

$$\mathbf{M} = \begin{bmatrix} 0.33571 & 0.45396 & 0.11761 \\ 0.99366 & 0.00000 & 0.00000 \\ 0.00000 & 0.98711 & 0.00000 \end{bmatrix}$$

After squaring the matrix **M** 5 times (which raises it to the 32nd power, equivalent to a projection 480 years into the future) we have

$$\mathbf{M}^{32} = \begin{bmatrix} 0.08710 & 0.05328 & 0.01086 \\ 0.09174 & 0.05611 & 0.01144 \\ 0.09599 & 0.05871 & 0.01197 \end{bmatrix}$$

and again multiplying by **M** gives

$$\mathbf{M}^{33} = \begin{bmatrix} 0.08218 & 0.05026 & 0.01024 \\ 0.08655 & 0.05294 & 0.01079 \\ 0.09056 & 0.05539 & 0.01129 \end{bmatrix}$$

Dividing any element of $\mathbf{M}^{33}$ by the corresponding element of $\mathbf{M}^{32}$ will produce an estimate of the population growth rate (the matrix *eigenvalue* λ) during the projection period. For example, using element 11, $\lambda = 0.08218/$

---

* The reader may construct the projection matrix for Euler's example in the opening quotation. Euler was the first to recognize that populations stabilize if their fertility and mortality rates remain fixed. A loose proof was given by Alfred Lotka in the 1920s (Lotka, 1939), and a rigorous proof by W. Feller in 1939, both using calculus. The matrix proofs date to Perron (1907a,b) and Frobenius (1908, 1909, 1912, 1917). On the rate of convergence to stability see Coale (1968), who finds that even very sharp initial perturbations in births are largely damped within about one lifetime.

0.08710 = 0.9435; using element 13, $\lambda = 0.01024/0.01086 = 0.9429$; and using element 32, $\lambda = 0.05539/0.05871 = 0.9435$. Had we displayed more significant digits, all three estimates would have given $\lambda = 0.94344$. The intrinsic growth rate r becomes $r = \ln\lambda/15 = -0.00388 \simeq -0.004$, using $\lambda = e^{15r}$. At 1980 fertility and mortality rates, the U.S. population would eventually decline.

Expression (8.15) allows us to estimate the stable age distribution as a function of the size of one of the age groups (in the expression the youngest age group has been used). To test this, we multiply $\mathbf{M}^{32}\mathbf{N}^{(1980)}$ and find

$$_{15}N_0^{(2460)} = 4{,}068{,}000$$

$$_{15}N_{15}^{(2460)} = 4{,}284{,}000$$

$$_{15}N_{30}^{(2460)} = 4{,}483{,}000$$

Setting $_{15}N_0^{(2460)}$ to 4,068,000 and using (8.15), the numbers in the next two age groups would be:

$$_{15}N_{15}^{(2460)} = 4{,}285{,}000$$

$$_{15}N_{30}^{(2460)} = 4{,}483{,}000$$

The two sets of estimates yield virtually identical results, confirming that the age distribution has stabilized. (Notice also that the ratio of the row entries in each column of $\mathbf{M}^{32}$ or $\mathbf{M}^{33}$ is the same as the ratio of the age groups. For example, in $\mathbf{M}^{32}$ element 21/element 11 $= 0.09174/0.08710 \simeq 1.053$ $= {}_{15}N_{15}^{(2460)}/{}_{15}N_0^{(2460)}$, and element 32/element 22 = 0.05871/0.05611 ≃ 1.046 $= {}_{15}N_{30}^{(2460)}/{}_{15}N_{15}^{(2460)}$. The age distribution necessarily stabilizes in the same ratio as the rows of the projection matrix from which it is derived, becoming independent of the initial age structure except as to the population size.)

What happens to the matrix when women above age 45 are included? Survival ratios for 1980 are $_{15}L_{45}/_{15}L_{30} = 0.95740$, $_{15}L_{60}/_{15}L_{45} = 0.85672$, and $_{15}L_{75}/_{15}L_{60} = 0.64581$, and adding these into the projection matrix gives:

$$\mathbf{M} = \begin{bmatrix} 0.33571 & 0.45396 & 0.11761 & 0.0 & 0.0 & 0.0 \\ 0.99366 & 0.0 & 0.0 & 0.0 & 0.0 & 0.0 \\ 0.0 & 0.98711 & 0.0 & 0.0 & 0.0 & 0.0 \\ 0.0 & 0.0 & 0.95740 & 0.0 & 0.0 & 0.0 \\ 0.0 & 0.0 & 0.0 & 0.85672 & 0.0 & 0.0 \\ 0.0 & 0.0 & 0.0 & 0.0 & 0.64581 & 0.0 \end{bmatrix}$$

$$\mathbf{M}^{32} = \begin{bmatrix} 0.08710 & 0.05328 & 0.01086 & 0.0 & 0.0 & 0.0 \\ 0.09174 & 0.05611 & 0.01144 & 0.0 & 0.0 & 0.0 \\ 0.09599 & 0.05871 & 0.01197 & 0.0 & 0.0 & 0.0 \\ 0.09741 & 0.05958 & 0.01214 & 0.0 & 0.0 & 0.0 \\ 0.08846 & 0.05410 & 0.01103 & 0.0 & 0.0 & 0.0 \\ 0.06055 & 0.03703 & 0.00755 & 0.0 & 0.0 & 0.0 \end{bmatrix}$$

The zeros in the last three columns of $\mathbf{M}^{32}$ mean that women over age 45 in 1980 will make no long-term contribution to population change. All of their children had already been born at the outset of the projection period. For the same reason, the first three rows and columns are those of the earlier 3×3 matrix. All that has been added by enlarging the matrix is an additional series of stable ratios corresponding to the upper part of the age distribution. These could have been found from (8.15) with less work, after raising the 3×3 matrix to a high power to derive λ.

The model we have introduced is *Markovian,* in that the population distribution at $t + n$ is dependent on the distribution at t and the transition matrix $\mathbf{M}$, and is independent of earlier states. Models can also be constructed with memory, but in demography their applications remain limited.

8.5. DIRECT ESTIMATION OF λ

The closeness of the matrix projection to stability at various time points can be checked by estimating λ directly from the initial fertility and survival rates. To do so we again need to make use of (8.15).

We begin by noting that at stability, for $_{15}N_0$ persons at age 0–14 there will be $\lambda^{-1}(_{15}L_{15}/_{15}L_0)_{15}N_0$ persons at ages 15–29 and $\lambda^{-2}(_{15}L_{30}/_{15}L_0)_{15}N_0$ persons ages 30–44. At the fertility rates $_{15}\phi_{7.5}$, $_{15}\phi_{22.5}$, $_{15}\phi_{37.5}$ the population 0–14 at time $t + 15$ will be

$$_{15}N_0^{(t+15)} = {}_{15}\phi_{7.5}\, {}_{15}N_0^{(t)} + \lambda^{-1}(_{15}L_{15}/_{15}L_0)_{15}\phi_{22.5}\, {}_{15}N_0^{(t)}$$

$$+ \lambda^{-2}(_{15}L_{30}/_{15}L_0)_{15}\phi_{37.5}\, {}_{15}N_0^{(t)}$$

$$= {}_{15}N_0^{(t)}[_{15}\phi_{7.5} + \lambda^{-1}(_{15}L_{15}/_{15}L_0)_{15}\phi_{22.5} \qquad (8.16)$$

$$+ \lambda^{-2}(_{15}L_{30}/_{15}L_0)_{15}\phi_{37.5}]$$

Since the population is stable, however,

$$_{15}N_0^{(t+15)} = \lambda_{15}N_0^{(t)}$$

Substituting this expression in (8.16) and canceling the terms in $_{15}N_0^{(t)}$ on both sides gives

$$\lambda = {}_{15}\phi_{7.5} + \lambda^{-1}(_{15}L_{15}/_{15}L_0)_{15}\phi_{22.5} + \lambda^{-2}(_{15}L_{30}/_{15}L_0)_{15}\phi_{37.5} \quad (8.17)$$

Multiplying both sides of this expression by λ^2 and rearranging terms, we have

$$\lambda^3 - {}_{15}\phi_{7.5}\lambda^2 - (_{15}L_{15}/_{15}L_0)_{15}\phi_{22.5}\lambda - (_{15}L_{30}/_{15}L_0)_{15}\phi_{37.5} = 0$$
$$(8.18)$$
$$\lambda^3 - 0.33571\lambda^2 - 0.45396\lambda - 0.11761 = 0$$

Expression (8.18) is the *characteristic equation* of the renewal function, in that it defines the relationship between fertility, mortality, and the rate of population growth at stability. For the three age interval example the expression is a cubic polynomial, with roots (found by computer or programmable calculator):

$$\lambda_1 = 0.94656, \qquad r_1 = (\ln\lambda_1)/15 = -0.00366$$

$$\lambda_2 = -0.30543 + 0.17459i, \qquad r_2 = -0.06951 + 0.17459i$$

$$\lambda_3 = -0.30543 - 0.17459i, \qquad r_3 = -0.06951 - 0.17459i$$

The first root is the intrinsic growth rate and is close to the matrix estimate 0.94344. The other roots (which could have been estimated from the projection matrix M) are complex conjugates and track the fluctuations in births before they ultimately stabilize. They have a periodicity of $2\pi/0.17459 = 36.0$ years, or about a generation. [Higher order polynomials have additional roots, but these have shorter periodicities and are less easily interpretable. The terms $i = (-1)^{1/2}$ cancel in the actual projection.]

As a test of the quality of the projection matrix, we may compare the roots found as expression (8.18) with the roots of the maternity function for the source fertility distribution (Table 8.1).

$$_n\phi_x = (_nL_0/l_0)_nf_{x,\,f}$$
$$(8.19)$$
$$\lambda = \lambda^{1/2}{}_{15}\phi_0 + \lambda^{-1/2}(_{15}L_{15}/_{15}L_0)_{15}\phi_{15} + \lambda^{-1.5}(_{15}L_{30}/_{15}L_0)_{15}\phi_{30}$$

Expression (8.19) differs from (8.18) by the absence of half interval survival adjustments, either $_{(1/2)n}S_{x+(1/2)n}$ [from (8.8)] or $_nL_{x+n}/_nL_x$ [(8.9)], which are not needed when terms in $_n f_{x,\,f}$ are substituted for terms in $_n f_{x+(1/2)n,\,f}$; and by the earlier time indexes on λ corresponding to the younger ages to which the fertility terms $_n f_{x,\,f}$ apply. The fractional powers on λ are handled by substituting $\kappa = \lambda^{1/2}$ in (8.19). With the substitution, and after rearranging terms and multiplying through by κ^5, we will have

$$\kappa^2 - {}_{15}\phi_0 \kappa - ({}_{15}L_{15}/{}_{15}L_0){}_{15}\phi_{15}\kappa^{-1} - ({}_{15}L_{30}/{}_{15}L_0){}_{15}\phi_{30}\kappa^{-3} = 0$$

$$\kappa^5 - {}_{15}\phi_0 \kappa^4 - ({}_{15}L_{15}/{}_{15}L_0){}_{15}\phi_{15}\kappa^2 - ({}_{15}L_{30}/{}_{15}L_0){}_{15}\phi_{30} = 0 \qquad (8.20)$$

$$\kappa^5 - 0 - 0.67144\kappa^2 - 0.23072 = 0.$$

The largest root of the expression is found to be $\kappa_1 = 0.97119$, and therefore for λ_1 we have $\lambda_1 = \kappa_1^2 = 0.94322$. Had we fitted (8.17) using the interpolated fertility estimates of (8.10) in place of (8.7), we would have:

$$\lambda^3 - 0.32213\lambda^2 - 0.50911\lambda - 0.07376 = 0$$

$$\lambda_1 = 0.94412$$

The estimate error using (8.10) is about four times as large as that of (8.7).

8.6. THE GENERATION LENGTH

The characteristic equation (8.17) estimates the growth rate of the population at stability. To find the generation length, we also need the net reproduction rate (NRR or R_0), representing the number of daughters women have who will survive to their same ages, or generational replacement rate. The NRR is found by summing the lifetime fertility for one woman just born [(7.8)]:

$$\mathrm{NRR} = R_0 = \sum_x \left({}_n L_x \, {}_n f_{x,\,f} \right) \Big/ l_0 \qquad (8.21)$$

The expression uses $_n L_x / l_0$ to estimate the number of years lived in the interval, and therefore the number of years during which the fertility rate is $_n f_{x,\,f}$. For our example,

$R_0 = ({}_{15}L_0\, {}_{15}f_0,\, {}_f + {}_{15}L_{15}\, {}_{15}f_{15},\, {}_f + {}_{15}L_{30}\, {}_{15}f_{30},\, {}_f)/l_0$

$= 14.79376 \times 0.0 + 14.70000 \times 0.045676$

$+\ 14.51057 \times 0.015900 = 0.90215$

[The reader may note that the net reproduction rate R_0 is a little less than the sum of the fertility terms ${}_n\phi_{x+(1/2)n}$ that make up the first row of the projection matrix (in the example, 0.90728). The matrix projection survives infants into the age interval $0-n$, a younger age than the age of their mothers at the birth.]

Under stability, the annual population growth rate r and net reproduction rate R_0 are related through the generation length T as $R_0 = e^{rT}$. Taking logs of both sides and substituting the R_0 and r estimates into the expression, we find: $T = \ln(R_0)/r = \ln(0.90215)/-0.00390 = 26.4$ years. The estimate is younger than the 35.9 years found from the roots of (8.17). The latter figure is the time between peaks in annual births before the age distribution stabilizes: it would be closer to the generation length if more age intervals were used in the projection.*

8.7. THE STABLE POPULATION EQUIVALENT

A question that arises in projections is the closeness of the initial population age distribution to its *stable population equivalent,* a stable population with the same long-term growth pattern and same eventual size as the initial population. To find the stable equivalent, we project from the stable population back to the present. The female population in 2475 (the 33rd period) is nearly stable, with ${}_{15}N_0^{(2475)} = 3.838$ million, ${}_{15}N_{15}^{(2475)} = 4.042$ million, and ${}_{15}N_{30}^{(2475)} = 4.229$ million. For $\lambda = 0.94344$, after 33 periods we have $\lambda^{33} = 0.15519$, representing the ratio of the stable population at time 33 to the

---

* In continuous analysis, the generation length is the approximate midpoint (Keyfitz, 1977b, pp. 141–147) between the mean age at fertility in the stationary population (μ) and the mean age at fertility in the stable population (A_r). For our example the estimate is

$$\mu = \sum_x (x + \tfrac{1}{2}n)({}_nL_x\, {}_nf_x)/\sum_x ({}_nL_x\, {}_nf_x) = 26.00$$

$$A_r = \sum_x (x + \tfrac{1}{2}n)(\lambda^{-x/n}\, {}_nL_x\, {}_nf_x)/\sum_x (\lambda^{-x/n}\, {}_nL_x\, {}_nf_x) = 26.50$$

$$T \simeq (\mu + A_r)/2 = 26.25$$

initial stable population. Dividing $_nN_x^{(1980+nk)}/\lambda^k = {_nN_x^*}^{(1980)}$, we find $_{15}N_0^{*\,(1980)} = 24.7$ million, $_{15}N_{15}^{*\,(1980)} = 26.0$ million, $_{15}N_{30}^{*\,(1980)} = 27.3$ million. The stable equivalent population thus numbers 78.0 million at ages 0–45, as compared with 77.9 million in the actual population. The age ratios of the stable equivalent population to the actual population are 0.99, 0.84, and 1.24, respectively. These numbers can be interpreted to mean that the youngest age group was in nearly a stable pattern at the outset of the projection period, but that the 15–29 age group is substantially larger and the 30–44 group is substantially smaller than it would be expected to be at 1980 fertility and mortality rates.

8.8. PROJECTIONS WITH BOTH SEXES

A complete population projection includes both sexes and all age groups. For males and females beyond the reproductive ages, (8.6) is used to project from one period to the next. To include male births we can construct a projection model similar to that for females, by substituting the male population and survival terms in Table 8.1 for the equivalent female terms and substituting fathers' fertility rates for sons in place of mothers' fertility rates for daughters. In practice that is not often done. Separate male and female projections usually yield different estimates of the stable growth rate λ, because ages at marriage and age differences between husbands and wives change from year to year, and in each year a different set of couples contributes to births.

Consistent estimates for males can be produced most easily by using the female fertility distributions to project sons as well as daughters, since the difference in the number of boys and girls born in any given year is small: in the United States about 105 boys are born per 100 girls.

Using the female fertility distribution for sons $_nf_{x,\,m,\,F}$ and indexing other terms as pertaining to males (M) or females (F), the male population 0–14 would be estimated by

$$_{15}N_{0,\,M}^{(t+15)} = \tfrac{1}{2}(_{15}L_{0,\,M}/l_0)$$

$$\times \{_{15}N_{0,\,F}^{(t)}[_{15}f_{0,\,m,\,F} + (_{15}L_{15,\,F}/_{15}L_{0,\,F})_{15}f_{15,\,m,\,F}]$$

$$+ {_{15}N_{15,\,F}^{(t)}}[_{15}f_{15,\,m,\,F} + (_{15}L_{30,\,F}/_{15}L_{15,\,F})_{15}f_{30,\,m,\,F}] \tag{8.22}$$

$$+ {_{15}N_{30,\,F}^{(t)}}[_{15}f_{30,\,m,\,F} + (_{15}L_{45,\,F}/_{15}L_{30,\,F})_{15}f_{45,\,m,\,F}]\}$$

Continuing with our earlier example, for 1980 male and female populations (Table 8.1) expression (8.22) yields the male population:

$$_{15}N_{0,\,m}^{(1995)} = \tfrac{1}{2}(14.74000)[25,073(0.0 + 0.99366 \times 0.048121)$$

$$+\ 30,884(0.048121 + 0.98711 \times 0.016695)$$

$$+\ 21,949(0.016695 + 0.95740 \times 0.0)] = 26,241$$

Using (8.11) with the substitution of the male terms of Table 8.1 for the female terms, we would have:

$$_{15}N_{0,\,m}^{(1995)} = \tfrac{1}{2}(14.74000)[26,217(0 + 0.98445 \times 0.039235)$$

$$+\ 31,124(0.039235 + 0.96900 \times 0.028476)$$

$$+\ 21,246(0.028476 + 0.92219 \times 0.001604)$$

$$+\ 16,491(0.001604 + 0.74293 \times 0.0)] = 27,678$$

The two estimates differ by about 5%, which is substantial. It is explained in part by the fact that at the ages of highest fertility (roughly, 22–26 for women and 25–29 for men in 1980) women outnumbered men by roughly 7% and were caught in a marriage squeeze. For most of the 1990s, men will outnumber women at these ages and the pattern should reverse. Both effects are outcomes of the baby boom that peaked about 1960.

The complete projection matrix for both sexes using births of sons and daughters to mothers is shown below. The reader might rewrite the projection equations in algebraic form to confirm that the model satisfies (8.6), (8.11), and (8.22).

0.336	0.454	0.118	0.0	0.0	0.0	0.0	0.0	0.0	0.0	0.0	0.0	25,073		25,019
0.994	0.0	0.0	0.0	0.0	0.0	0.0	0.0	0.0	0.0	0.0	0.0	30,884		24,914
0.0	0.987	0.0	0.0	0.0	0.0	0.0	0.0	0.0	0.0	0.0	0.0	21,949		30,486
0.0	0.0	0.957	0.0	0.0	0.0	0.0	0.0	0.0	0.0	0.0	0.0	17,924		21,014
0.0	0.0	0.0	0.857	0.0	0.0	0.0	0.0	0.0	0.0	0.0	0.0	14,242		15,356
0.0	0.0	0.0	0.0	0.646	0.0	0.0	0.0	0.0	0.0	0.0	0.0	6,420	=	9,197
0.352	0.475	0.123	0.0	0.0	0.0	0.0	0.0	0.0	0.0	0.0	0.0	26,217		26,367
0.0	0.0	0.0	0.0	0.0	0.0	0.984	0.0	0.0	0.0	0.0	0.0	31,124		25,809
0.0	0.0	0.0	0.0	0.0	0.0	0.0	0.969	0.0	0.0	0.0	0.0	21,247		30,159
0.0	0.0	0.0	0.0	0.0	0.0	0.0	0.0	0.922	0.0	0.0	0.0	16,491		19,594
0.0	0.0	0.0	0.0	0.0	0.0	0.0	0.0	0.0	0.743	0.0	0.0	11,426		12,252
0.0	0.0	0.0	0.0	0.0	0.0	0.0	0.0	0.0	0.0	0.420	0.0	3,548		4,800

$$\mathbf{M} \qquad \mathbf{N}^{(1980)} = \mathbf{N}^{(1995)}$$

The projection matrix for the two-sex model is simpler than it may appear. It is comprised of four smaller matrices arranged as discrete blocks. The left half of the matrix projects the surviving female population (the coefficients of rows 2–6) and children 0–14 (daughters in row 1, sons in row 7) for the next period. The right half of the matrix projects surviving males (rows 8–12). Since the female population does not contribute to surviving males at ages 15+, the lower left quadrant of the matrix is 0 except for the female contribution to male births. Similarly, the upper right quadrant, which would project female births and survivors through the male population, is 0. If births were attributed to males, or part to each sex, rows 1 and 7 would include additional nonzero terms.

The matrix can be partitioned into its component blocks by rewriting it to be:

$$\mathbf{M} = \begin{bmatrix} \mathbf{M}_{11} & \mathbf{M}_{12} \\ \mathbf{M}_{21} & \mathbf{M}_{22} \end{bmatrix} \tag{8.23}$$

The submatrices are $\mathbf{M}_{11}$, projecting female survival and births, $\mathbf{M}_{22}$ projecting male survival, $\mathbf{M}_{21}$ projecting male births to females, and $\mathbf{M}_{12}$, projecting female births to males (here, none).

Each of the submatrices is of dimension 6×6. Like the original matrix, they can be further subdivided. We might, for example, break each submatrix into urban and rural population components or labor force components, as in the multistate life table example in Section 5.3. A matrix projection for that example will be introduced in Section 9.3.

8.9. BACKWARD AND INVERSE PROJECTION

Besides the forward projections of populations we have outlined, projections can also be used to reconstruct past populations. Like forward projection, projections into the past require an initial population and fertility and mortality information, except that fertility and mortality are now used to reconstruct the population that has died.

Unfortunately, just as an infinite range of current populations can be constructed that project to the same stable distribution, an infinite range of past populations can be constructed that project to the current distribution. Errors propagate, producing implausibly large or small numbers and negative numbers that contribute to the confusion of possible origin states.

The ease with which implausible results are generated is illustrated by the example of Section 8.3. After projecting the U.S. female population from 1980 to 1995 using (8.14): $\mathbf{MN}^{(1980)} = \mathbf{N}^{(1995)}$, we may invert $\mathbf{M}$ to reconstruct the 1980 population as $\mathbf{M}^{-1}\mathbf{N}^{(1995)} = \mathbf{N}^{(1980)}$. The inverse projection becomes

$$\begin{bmatrix} 0.00000 & 1.00638 & 0.00000 \\ 0.00000 & 0.00000 & 1.01306 \\ 8.50268 & -2.87265 & -3.91028 \end{bmatrix} \begin{bmatrix} 25,019 \\ 24,914 \\ 30,486 \end{bmatrix} = \begin{bmatrix} 25,073 \\ 30,884 \\ 21,951 \end{bmatrix}$$

$$\mathbf{M}^{-1} \qquad\qquad \mathbf{N}^{(1995)} \quad = \quad \mathbf{N}^{(1980)}$$

The reader may sense that the inverse is less than ideal: the population 30–44 is back projected from surviving offspring 0–44 who are only partly theirs, with negative weights on the contributions of two of the three age intervals. Projected back three more periods, to 1935, the model yields the curious result $_{15}N_{30}^{(1935)} = -115,000 \times 10^3$. The problem is not simply that we have reconstructed the past with wrong fertility and mortality rates, although that has contributed: the negative terms in the matrix are a trap that can eventually be sprung by the propagation of simple rounding errors.

In practice, the projection problem is more complex than we have made it, as projection matrices that extend beyond the fertile age span (see the example of Section 8.4) will have only zeros in their final column and cannot be inverted: in essence, if the final age interval does not contribute to survivorship at any younger ages it cannot be reconstructed after it is extinct.

Backward projection is made more tractable by the use of *generalized inverses,* which invert survival probabilities (compare $\mathbf{M}_{12}^{-1}$ with $\mathbf{M}_{21}$ in the source matrix, and $\mathbf{M}_{23}^{-1}$ with $\mathbf{M}_{32}$) at ages below the final age and reconstruct the final interval (here, $\mathbf{M}_{33}^{-1}$) from the stable population as $_{\omega-f}N_f^{(\text{stable})}/{}_nN_{f-n}^{(\text{stable})}$, or from the principal intrinsic roots $\lambda_i \,|\, i = 1, 2, 3, \ldots$, and source population terms at the older ages (Greville and Keyfitz, 1974). The use of several roots allows some of the instability of the source distribution to be preserved in backward projection, but also introduces negative terms into the matrix and limits the duration for which the projections can be constructed before anomalous population estimates arise.

We can do better in reconstructing historical populations where estimates of births and deaths are available, since the inverse projection must satisfy the demographic balancing equation [(1.5)], written for back projection as

$$_\omega N_0^{(t-1)} = {}_\omega N_0^{(t)} - {}_\omega B_0^{(t-1,\, t)} + {}_\omega D_0^{(t-1,\, t)} \qquad (8.24)$$

For simplicity we omit net migration. Use of the balancing equation requires that both fertility and mortality be estimated, since the extinct terminal population is found as the residual when births and mortality at all younger ages are substituted into (8.24). The reader may consult Wrigley and Schofield (1982) and Lee (1974a, 1985) for adjustments to the basic projection equations that allow for some uncertainty in (8.24), and for techniques that extend backward projection to the distant past, where uncertainty is greatly magnified.

Conditions under which reconstructed past populations may fail to converge to present distributions are discussed in Wachter (1986).

8.10. CHOICE OF ASSUMPTIONS

The population projections outlined here are *component projections,* and were first suggested by Edmund Cannan in 1895. Although they are markedly better in concept than projections without age, their history has not been one of resounding success. In the United States, P. K. Whelpton produced population projections in the mid-1930s that closely matched the actual 1940 U.S. population, but his series and most others produced over the next 30 years needed substantial adjustment as early as the next census. In the 1930s it was not foreseen that the small family sizes of the late 1920s and the depression years would be succeeded by moderately larger and then dramatically larger family sizes in the first two decades after the outbreak of World War II in Europe. Later, in 1960 and 1961 the rapid retrenchment that began in 1962 was not foreseen. Nor, in the years after the War, were the implications for population growth of the assault on infectious diseases in the developing countries widely anticipated.*

The critical problem in projections has consistently been fertility. Mortality, except as it affects infants and children, can be under- or overstated by fairly substantial amounts without greatly distorting projections, since its impact is largely at the oldest ages where numbers of people are typically small and remaining lifetimes are not long. By contrast, the difference between family sizes of two, three, or four surviving children is a difference between an essentially constant population, one doubling about each 70 years, and one doubling about each 35 years. With hindsight, we know that family sizes can move upward or downward across this range, and downward across an even wider range, in as little as 15 years. These are not necessarily the temporal limits of fertility shifts, but are more than enough to make even well-reasoned projections become curiosities in the lifetimes of their creators.†

---

* A compact summary of population projections for the United States will be found in Petersen and Petersen (1986, pp. 715–718).

† It has not helped to model fertility on economic behavior or historical time series (Ahlburg, 1983; Butz and Ward, 1977), or to presuppose cyclic behavior, at least for the United States, although theory does not completely preclude the latter (Easterlin, 1961, 1973; Smith, 1981a,b; Frauenthal and Swick, 1983; Wachter and Lee, 1989). Nor have models in which populations increase toward asymptotic limits fared well (Verhulst, 1838, 1845, 1847; Pearl and Reed, 1920) despite the essential plausibility of assuming that growth cannot remain rapid indefinitely. Experience continues to reduce demographic confidence that future U.S. fertility can be modeled with any precision. A valuable perspective on the U.S. convergence to small family sizes is Westoff (1978). The reader should also see Lee (1980) and Udry (1983) on decision processes and family size.

For the United States, additional complications are introduced by immigration, only part of which is documented in migration statistics and decennial censuses. To the extent that the balance of immigrants and emigrants can be estimated, they can be accommodated in projections by adjustment of survival probabilities or by the addition or subtraction of the estimated migrant population at the end of each projection period. These methods are reviewed in Chapter 9.

8.11. OTHER PROJECTION MODELS

The methods used for population projection generalize to other models. Consider the problem of estimating the mean length of the birth interval from information on its components, pregnancy, postpartum sterility, and exposure prior to the start of the next pregnancy. The three states can be interpreted as a transition vector, with women "aging" from pregnancy to postpartum infecundity to exposure and a subsequent pregnancy. If the time unit is months, then the proportion completing pregnancy and moving into postpartum sterility each month will be 1/9 of those who are pregnant. Likewise, if the mean infecund period is 17 months, then 1/17 of women will leave infecundity and become exposed to the risk of another pregnancy each month. We will set the probability of pregnancy at 0.2 per month among women at risk, or 20%. With these conventions we have the projection equations:

$$
\begin{aligned}
8/9 \, p^{(t)} \qquad\qquad\quad + 1/5 \, r^{(t)} &= p^{(t+1)} \\
1/9 \, p^{(t)} + 16/17 \, i^{(t)} \qquad\qquad &= i^{(t+1)} \\
1/17 \, i^{(t)} + 4/5 \, r^{(t)} &= r^{(t+1)}
\end{aligned}
\tag{8.25}
$$

where the proportions who leave each state and those who remain in it sum to 1.0 (we have used the codes p = proportion of time spent in pregnancy, i = proportion of time in postpartum infecundity, r = proportion of time at risk). In matrix form the model becomes

$$
\underbrace{\begin{bmatrix} 8/9 & 0 & 1/5 \\ 1/9 & 16/17 & 0 \\ 0 & 1/17 & 4/5 \end{bmatrix}}_{\mathbf{M}} \underbrace{\begin{bmatrix} p^{(t)} \\ i^{(t)} \\ r^{(t)} \end{bmatrix}}_{\mathbf{K}^{(t)}} = \underbrace{\begin{bmatrix} p^{(t+1)} \\ i^{(t+1)} \\ r^{(t+1)} \end{bmatrix}}_{\mathbf{K}^{(t+1)}}
\tag{8.26}
$$

As before, raising the matrix to the 32nd power we find

$$\mathbf{M}^{32} = \begin{bmatrix} 0.2891 & 0.2908 & 0.2909 \\ 0.5493 & 0.5476 & 0.5492 \\ 0.1615 & 0.1616 & 0.1599 \end{bmatrix}$$

The entries have not quite stabilized at this point. Ultimately the column entries will settle to $p = 9/31 = 0.2903$ pregnant, $i = 17/31 = 0.5484$ in postpartum amenorrhea, and $r = 5/31 = 0.1613$ exposed to risk. Births, not shown, number $1/9$ of pregnancies $= 0.03226$ per month at stability. They might have been included separately from pregnancy or postpartum sterility by revising (8.26) to become a 4×4 matrix with entries

$$\underbrace{\begin{bmatrix} 8/9 & 0 & 0 & 1/5 \\ 1/9 & 0 & 0 & 0 \\ 1/9 & 0 & 16/17 & 0 \\ 0 & 0 & 1/17 & 4/5 \end{bmatrix}}_{\mathbf{M}} \underbrace{\begin{bmatrix} p^{(t)} \\ b^{(t)} \\ i^{(t)} \\ r^{(t)} \end{bmatrix}}_{\mathbf{K}^{(t)}} = \underbrace{\begin{bmatrix} p^{(t+1)} \\ b^{(t+1)} \\ i^{(t+1)} \\ r^{(t+1)} \end{bmatrix}}_{\mathbf{K}^{(t+1)}} \tag{8.27}$$

The matrix could also be written

$$\underbrace{\begin{bmatrix} 8/9 & 0 & 0 & 1/5 \\ 1/9 & 0 & 0 & 0 \\ 0 & 1 & 16/17 & 0 \\ 0 & 0 & 1/17 & 4/5 \end{bmatrix}}_{\mathbf{M}} \underbrace{\begin{bmatrix} p^{(t)} \\ b^{(t)} \\ i^{(t)} \\ r^{(t)} \end{bmatrix}}_{\mathbf{K}^{(t)}} = \underbrace{\begin{bmatrix} p^{(t+1)} \\ b^{(t+1)} \\ i^{(t+1)} \\ r^{(t+1)} \end{bmatrix}}_{\mathbf{K}^{(t+1)}} \tag{8.28}$$

In either matrix form, the birth function b does not change the model result at stability, since births are simply $1/9$ of pregnancies.

In Appendix 7A.1 the proportion of time women spend in various exposure states was used to estimate the interbirth interval and durations of postpartum infecundity and exposure to pregnancy risks in the absence of contraception and lactation. The durations can also be found from the projection matrix, by treating the proportions of time in different states as stable outcomes. Using Hobcraft and Little (1984) estimates for the Dominican Republic, for the proportion of time in various states we have $p^{(t)} = p^{(t+1)} = d_x(p) = 0.192$, $r^{(t)} = r^{(t+1)} = d_x(r) = 0.277$, and merging contraception, lactation, and sterility into the infecund category, $i^{(t)} = i^{(t+1)} = d_x(c, l, i) = 0.314$. We seek the expected duration of infecundity i, the probabilities $1/i$ that persons leave and $(i - 1)/i$ that they remain in the infecund subset, the duration of risk r, and the probabilities $1/r$ that persons become pregnant and $(r - 1)/r$ that they remain at risk. These terms will be solutions to the projection model

$$
\begin{bmatrix}
8/9 & 0 & 1/r \\
1/9 & (i-1)/i & 0 \\
0 & 1/i & (r-1)/r
\end{bmatrix}
\begin{bmatrix}
0.192 \\
0.314 \\
0.277
\end{bmatrix}
=
\begin{bmatrix}
0.192 \\
0.314 \\
0.277
\end{bmatrix}
\qquad (8.29)
$$

$$
\mathbf{M} \qquad\qquad \mathbf{K}^{(t)} \;=\; \mathbf{K}^{(t+1)}
$$

where the duration of pregnancy is taken to be 9 months as before. The algebra of the projection matrix is

$$
(8/9)(0.192) + \quad 0 \quad + \quad (1/r)(0.277) \quad = 0.192
$$
$$
(1/9)(0.192) + [(i-1)/i](0.314) + \quad 0 \quad = 0.314 \qquad (8.30)
$$
$$
0 \quad + \quad (1/i)(0.314) \quad + [(r-1)/r](0.277) = 0.277
$$

The reader can solve (8.30) to confirm that $r = 13.0$ months and $i = 14.7$ months. The projection matrix is therefore

$$
\mathbf{M} =
\begin{bmatrix}
8/9 & 0.0 & 1/13.0 \\
1/9 & 13.7/14.7 & 0.0 \\
0.0 & 1/14.7 & 12.0/13.0
\end{bmatrix}
\qquad (8.31)
$$

And for the interbirth interval we will have,

$$
I_B = r + p + i = 13.0 + 9.0 + 14.7 = 36.7 \text{ months}
$$

The sterile period includes the proportions of time spent in contraception, lactation, and natural sterility, $d_x(c) = 0.200$, $d_x(l) = 0.067$, and $d_x(i) = 0.047$, respectively. Using these estimates, the total sterile period can be disaggregated into $(0.200/0.314)14.7 = 9.4$ months spent contracepting, $(0.067/0.314)14.7 = 3.1$ months lactating, and $(0.047/0.314)14.7 = 2.2$ months in natural sterility. For persons not contracepting or breastfeeding the interbirth duration is thus

$$
I_B = r + p + i = 13.0 + 9.0 + 2.2
$$

$$
= 24.2 \text{ months, in agreement with } (7A.4).
$$

8.12. SUMMARY

Population projection has been a perennial headache for demographers. We are expected to be good at it, and the essential methodologies are difficult to fault, but our insight cannot be said to be outstanding. Nor is that of economists in their efforts to link population and economic projections. The failures are not necessarily critical: if we err by a few percent in projecting the U.S. population over a decade or two, the target figure will be reached near the anticipated date, and projections to the more distant future require few immediate actions. Even projections of the retirement age population 25 or 30 years hence are of marginal current interest: if the past is any guide, the amounts invested in the social security fund by the working population will have little bearing on the amounts the survivors among them eventually draw. I make these points because even demographers tend not to realize the enormous impunity with which long-term projection can actually be approached. It is important that assumptions be competent, but not necessary that the future conform to them.

For demographers the more interesting aspects of projections are the insights on current population characteristics that derive from stable population theory. Using stable theory it is possible to construct the age distributions toward which populations are converging and to abstract from the current fertility and mortality distributions to the numbers and rates of birth and death that would eventually occur. The estimates are not always hypothetical. In the developing world, where information is often limited, many populations are close enough to their stable forms to allow the substitution of stable estimates for missing or suspect data. [A review of these and other techniques for developing country data will be found in Leslie and Gage (1989).]

We have not qualified these uses by introducing variance estimates for population projections. For those the reader is referred to Sykes (1969), Schweder (1971), and Lee (1974b). The essential finding of these works is that the statistical precision of projections is high, even with serially correlated error terms (Lee, 1974b). Where projections become seriously out of line with actual population changes, the cause is invariably that the researcher's assumptions about future fertility, mortality, and migration were not borne out.

The projection matrix itself is a remarkably versatile tool. Besides population projection, we have used it to model interbirth intervals (Section 8.11) and time in the different exposure states in fertility exposure analysis (Appendix 7A.1). Among other problems that require the solution of a series of simultaneous equations are data interpolation methods, outlined in Chapter 2 and Appendix 2A.1. The use of matrices in conventional population projections is due largely to Leslie (1945, 1948a, 1948b). Besides Leslie's work, the reader should see Sykes (1969), Parlett (1970), and Hanson (1989) on projection matrices, and Lee (1975) on spectral decomposition of the matrix.

The chapter has touched briefly on historical demography in the context of backward population projections. The field of historical demography is far larger, drawing both on general history and on local registries that have sometimes allowed individual families to be traced through several generations. The classic works in family reconstitution are Henry (1956), Fleury and Henry (1956), and Gautier and Henry (1958). English introductions to historical demography will be found in Hollingsworth (1969) and Willigan and Lynch (1982). The interested reader should also see the collected papers in Glass and Eversley (1965), Wrigley (1966), Wrigley and Schofield (1981), Cook and Borah (1971, 1974), and Dyke and Morrill (1980).

CHAPTER 9

Migration in Population Analysis

> 5. *The next Observation we shall offer, is, The time wherein the City hath been* Re-peopled *after a great* Plague; *which we affirm to be by the second year. For in 1627, the* Christnings *(which are our Standard in this Case) were 8408, which in 1624 next preceding the* Plague *year 1625 (that had swept away above 54000) were but 8299, and the* Christnings *of 1626 (which were but 6701) mounted in one year to the said 8408.*
>
> 6. *Now the Cause hereof, for as much as it cannot be a supply for Procreations;* Ergo, *it must be by new Affluxes to* London *out of the Countrey.*
>
> 7. *We might fortifie this Assertion by shewing, that before the* Plague-year, *1603, the* Christnings *were about 6000, which were in that very year reduced to 4789, but crept up the next year 1604, to 5458, recovering their former ordinary proportion in 1605 of 6504, about which proportion it stood till the year 1610.*
>
> 8. *I say, it followeth, that, let the* Mortality *be what it will, the City repairs its loss of Inhabitants within two years, which Observation lessens the Objection made against the value of houses in* London, *as if they were liable to great prejudice through the loss of Inhabitants by the* Plague.
>
> —JOHN GRAUNT (1662)

9.1. INTRODUCTION

Migration contributes with fertility and mortality to the demographic balancing equation [expression (1.5)]

$$_{\omega}N_0^{(t+n)} = {_{\omega}}N_0^{(t)} + {_{\omega}}B_0^{(t,\ t+n)} - {_{\omega}}D_0^{(t,\ t+n)} + {_{\omega}}I_0^{(t,\ t+n)} - {_{\omega}}E_0^{(t,\ t+n)} \quad (9.1)$$

where $_{\omega}N_0$ represents total population, $_{\omega}B_0$ represents births, $_{\omega}D_0$ represents deaths, and $_{\omega}I_0$ and $_{\omega}E_0$ are in-migration and out-migration, respectively. [The difference $_{\omega}I_0 - {_{\omega}}E_0$ is net in-migration, introduced as $_{\omega}F_0$ in (8.1).] The interval width $(0, \omega)$ is taken to represent the whole of life. The superscripts designate that the population size is estimated at t and $t + n$; and that births, deaths, and migrants are estimated for the interval $(t, t + n)$.

Besides (9.1), which is exact, population changes can be approximated linearly, by substituting the midinterval population $_\omega N_0^{(t+0.5n)}$ for $_\omega N_0^{(t)}$ to estimate $_\omega N_0^{(t+1.5n)}$ where annual changes in other terms of (9.1) are small. We may also use (2.1) to find $_\omega N_0^{(t+1.5n)} \simeq 2_\omega N_0^{(t+0.5n)} - _\omega N_0^{(t-0.5n)}$, if the balance of annual changes in births, deaths, and migrants is approximately constant from year to year. Changes can also be modeled geometrically, by interpreting annual crude birth, death, and migration rates as measures of the average intensity of changes during the year. If the rates are constant over time, we will have [(1.6)]

$$_\omega N_{0,\,exp}^{(t+1.5n)} = {}_\omega N_0^{(t+0.5n)} \exp[({}_\omega B_0^{(t,\,t+n)} - {}_\omega D_0^{(t,\,t+n)}$$

$$+ {}_\omega F_0^{(t,\,t+n)})/{}_\omega N_0^{(t+0.5n)}] \tag{9.2}$$

$$= {}_\omega N_0^{(t+0.5n)} e^{CGR_n}$$

where CGR_n is the n-year crude growth rate.

None of these expressions will typically estimate population changes with precision, since the crude rates and population estimates are offset in time, and since the underlying population composition is ignored, but the estimates they give will not err greatly if the projection interval n is short.

Applications of (9.1) and (9.2) were introduced in simple population projections in Section 8.2. The role of migration in population change was also considered in the context of multistate life tables in Section 5.3, where age- and residence-specific transition probabilities were estimated. In this chapter we attempt to bring migration analysis into sharper focus. Section 9.2 reviews definition and measurement, which are less straightforward than in fertility and mortality analysis. In Section 9.3 we introduce projection matrices with migration, essentially similar in form to the two-sex projection matrix of Section 8.8. Section 9.4 considers the adjustment of migration projections for compositional stability. As in two-sex population projections, certain ratios—males to females, parents to children—would be expected to hold for regional and subregional migration projections. In Section 9.5 formulas are introduced for controlled projections, in which local area estimates are adjusted to sum to independently generated estimates at the state or national level. Finally, in Section 9.6 we consider problems that arise in small-area population estimates and projections, where adjustments for survival and migration require particular care.

9.2. DEFINITION AND MEASUREMENT

Fertility and mortality are unambiguous events, but migration is not. People may move across national boundaries or across a street, and may remain relatively permanently at a given location or leave again almost immediately. Or they may commute between several locations, any of which they may define as their usual place of residence. The conventions used to identify migrants and nonmigrants will be relevant to all of the measures of migration we introduce.

Methodologically, where the immediate purpose of migration estimates is not population projection, the estimates can be generated from life tables showing the proportion of individuals resident in location i at time t who leave in the interval $(t, t + 1)$. For migration, the conventional mortality probability $_nq_x = {}_nD_x/N(x)$ is revised to

$$_nq_x = {}_nE_x^{(t, t+1)}/N(x)^{(t)} \qquad |_nE_x^{(t, t+1)} \in N(x)^{(t)} \qquad (9.3)$$

for out-migrants in $(t, t + 1)$ from the resident population at t, $N(x)^{(t)}$. The restriction $_nE_x \in N(x)$ indicates that the numerator is a subset of the denominator, and may not be a complete count of migrants in the interval. The life table might also be constructed retrospectively, to show the proportion of those residing in i at time $t + 1$ who resided elsewhere at t,

$$_nq_x = {}_nI_x^{(t, t+1)}/N(x)^{(t+1)} \qquad |_nI_x^{(t, t+1)} \in N(x)^{(t+1)} \qquad (9.4)$$

In this formulation, $_nI_x$ represents the survivors at $t + 1$ of in-migrants in $(t, t + 1)$.

For life table estimates using total migrants and census or midperiod populations, we require formulas analogous to the central population $_np_x$ estimators, expressions (4.9) and (4.10). Using (4.9), the life table emigration probability becomes

$$_nq_{x,\text{ linear}} = {}_nE_x^{(t, t+1)}/N(x)^{(t)}$$

$$= median\ of\{0, 1, {}_nE_x^{(t, t+1)}/({}_nN_x^{(t+1/2)}/n \qquad (9.5)$$

$$+ \tfrac{1}{2}{}_nD_x^{(t, t+1)} - \tfrac{1}{2}{}_nI_x^{(t, t+1)} + \tfrac{1}{2}{}_nE_x^{(t, t+1)})\}$$

where $_nI_x$ and $_nE_x$ need not belong to $_nN_x^{(t+1/2)}$ but may not count the same individuals, or individuals included in $_nD_x$. The limiting values apply where mortality or migration distributions are not uniform during the year, and lead to $_nq_x$ estimates outside the range $(0, 1)$.

Mortality may be taken into account in (9.3) and (9.5) by revising the numerators to $_nD_x + {}_nE_x$ and using multiple decrement or cause-eliminated life tables to estimate $_nq_{x,\text{ migration}}$, possibly with further disaggregation by initial migrant destination, using $_nE_{x,\ i \to j}$. We might also disaggregate immigrants by last prior residence, but would not normally be interested in formulations of (9.4) with mortality, as the events $_nI_x$ and $_nD_x$ are not competing decrements.

The life table presents an incomplete picture of migration behavior, since only a single departure or arrival for individual j would be recorded in $_nE_x$ or $_nI_x$. In reality, at least some individuals are likely to enter and leave i numerous times during $(t, t + 1)$, and a life table for first departure or arrival will not be the same as a life table based on actual location at t and at $t + 1$.

A different approach is taken in multistate life tables and population projections, where interest is in the proportion of individuals in location i at time t who are in location j at $t + n$. The timing of the first departure and durations at intermediate destinations are not of concern.

An elementary model of this type was introduced in Section 5.3 for rural-to-urban migration and for transitions between labor force activity and inactivity. The transition probabilities generalize as $[(5.11)]$:

$$_nt_{x+(1/2)n, \; i \to j}^{(t, \; t+n)} = \begin{cases} 0 & |_n\nu_{x+n, \; j}^{(t+n)} \leq {}_n\nu_{x, \; j}^{(t)} \\ (_n\nu_{x+n, \; j}^{(t+n)} - {}_n\nu_{x, \; j}^{(t)})/(1 - {}_n\nu_{x, \; j}^{(t)}) & \\ |_n\nu_{x+n, \; j}^{(t+n)} > {}_n\nu_{x, \; j}^{(t)} & \end{cases}$$

$$_nt_{x+(1/2)n, \; j \to i}^{(t, \; t+n)} = \begin{cases} 0 & |_n\nu_{x+n, \; j}^{(t+n)} \geq {}_n\nu_{x, \; j}^{(t)} \\ (_n\nu_{x, \; j}^{(t)} - {}_n\nu_{x+n, \; j}^{(t+n)})/(_n\nu_{x, \; j}^{(t)}) & \\ |_n\nu_{x+n, \; j}^{(t+n)} < {}_n\nu_{x, \; j}^{(t)} & \end{cases} \tag{9.6}$$

$$_nt_{x+(1/2)n, \; i \to i} = 1 - {}_nt_{x+(1/2)n, \; i \to j}$$

$$_nt_{x+(1/2)n, \; j \to j} = 1 - {}_nt_{x+(1/2)n, \; j \to i}$$

where $_n\nu_{x, \; j}^{(t)} = {}_nN_{x, \; j}^{(t)}/{}_nN_x^{(t)}$ is the proportion of the population in j at ages x to $x + n$ and time t, and $_n\nu_{x+n, \; j}^{(t+n)}$ is the proportion in j at ages $x + n$ to $x + 2n$ and time $t + n$. The changes in the proportions in i and j across age and time establish the transition probabilities for the model, which will be net flows $_nF_x$.

If the source data include individual migration histories, the transition probabilities can be improved to

$$_nt_{x+(1/2)n, \; i \to j}^{(t, \; t+n)} = {}_nN_{x+n, \; (i \to)j}^{(t+n)}/{}_nN_{x, \; i}^{(t)} \tag{9.7}$$

where the subscript $(i \to)j$ on $_nN_{x+n}^{(t+n)}$ identifies persons in j at time $t + n$ who were in i at time t. Using (9.7), migrant flows both to and from j can be estimated.

In more complex models the transition matrix may be made non-Markovian: that is, the probability of migration from i to j in the interval $(t, t + n)$ may depend on the individual's previous migration history, or on his or her duration at i.

A variety of identification problems may add to the complexity of migration analysis. For every transition model the specific migration probabilities will depend on the geographic boundaries of i and j, and on the conventions used to distinguish between moves qualifying and not qualifying as migrations.* For many purposes, conventional measures of location (census tracts, county or state lines, national borders) serve well, although some will vary by user (e.g., U.S. regions) or over time (postal and telephone area codes).

Problems also arise where individuals may claim more than one residence, either because they relocate seasonally or for reasons associated with university attendance, state or federal taxes, voting, and so forth. U.S. census counts for counties with major universities, for example, may show substantially fewer young adults than are usually resident, since students may be missed by the census, or may be enumerated either at the university, at their parents' homes, or at other residences. The problem of identification is compounded where multiple data sources with differing levels of completeness are used.

In many settings the difficulties of quantifying migration are mitigated by the relative stability of patterns over time. In the United States, the states that drew the largest numbers of migrants during the 1980s, California, Florida, and Texas, also did so in earlier decades. Growth rates in all three states, shown in Fig. 9.1, have been relatively constant for more than a century, despite sharp compositional shifts between fertility (1940–1965) and migration (1965–1990) as driving forces in population change. In most states the next decades should see some slowing of population changes, as fertility continues to be low and the baby boom generation is passing out of the ages of highest migration.†

---

* The reader should see Kephart (1988) for a valuable perspective on the influence of level of aggregation on migration patterns.

† Migration peaks occur near birth and at ages 20–34, and in some populations again at the retirement or postretirement ages. Rogers et al. (1978; see also Rogers and Castro, 1982, 1984; Rogers, 1988) have suggested the model

$$M(x) = a_1 \exp[-\alpha_1 x] + a_2 \exp\{-\alpha_2(x - \mu_2) - \exp[-\lambda_2(x - \mu_2)]\}$$

$$+ a_3 \exp\{-\alpha_3(x - \mu_3) - \exp[-\lambda_3(x - \mu_3)]\} + c$$

where x represents age, μ_2 and μ_3 are the two migration peaks after infancy, and c is a constant representing the lowest rate of migration observed. The remaining constant terms determine the height and spread of each peak.

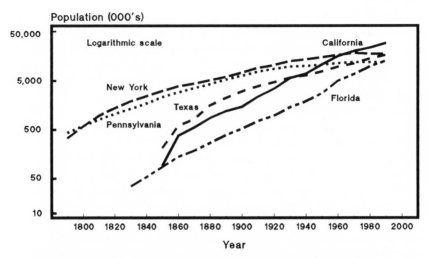

Figure 9.1. Selected state populations, 1790–1990. *Source:* U.S. Dept. of Commerce (1975, Series A-195, pp. 24–37; 1990, T. 26, p. 20).

9.3. THE MULTISTATE PROJECTION MATRIX

Projection of populations with migration may follow the simple models of Sections 8.2 and 9.1, or may follow cohort component methods in a manner analogous to the two-sex projection of Section 8.8. For the one-sex model with two regions we partition **M** into the submatrices [(8.23)]

$$\mathbf{M} = \begin{bmatrix} \mathbf{M}_{11} & \mathbf{M}_{12} \\ \mathbf{M}_{21} & \mathbf{M}_{22} \end{bmatrix}$$

where $\mathbf{M}_{11}$ and $\mathbf{M}_{22}$ comprise transition probabilities within regions 1 and 2, and $\mathbf{M}_{12}$ and $\mathbf{M}_{21}$ are transfer probabilities between the regions. [The reader should recall from (8.23) that in the matrix formulation $\mathbf{M}_{12}$ represents transition probabilities to region 1 from region 2, and $\mathbf{M}_{21}$ represents transitions to 2 from 1.]

Recalling our earlier example of rural-to-urban migration in Mexico (Section 5.3*), we utilized submatrices of dimension 6 × 6 to project populations in 15-year age intervals. The submatrices can be expanded and further

---

* The reader should review Section 5.3 for the details of the example, which is based on Tabah (1968). For a projection with two-way migration between California and the rest of the United States, see Rogers (1968, p. 14).

subdivided. We might, for example, break each submatrix into labor force and non-labor force components, raising M_{ij} to dimension 12×12 and M to dimension 24×24. For the two-sex model with rural-to-urban migration, M_{ij} is also of dimension 12×12.

The data of Tables 5.8 and 5.9 allow us to reproduce only quadrant M_{22} of the 1960-to-1975 transition matrix for Mexico. For that quadrant, the terms of the projection matrix and the projected population will be

$$
\begin{bmatrix}
0.0 & 0.0 & 0.0 & 0.0 & 0.0 & 0.0 & 0.0 & 0.0 & 0.00 & 0.0 & 0.0 & 0.0 \\
0.953 & 0.0 & 0.0 & 0.0 & 0.0 & 0.0 & 0.212 & 0.0 & 0.0 & 0.0 & 0.0 & 0.0 \\
0.0 & 0.925 & 0.0 & 0.0 & 0.0 & 0.0 & 0.0 & 0.203 & 0.0 & 0.0 & 0.0 & 0.0 \\
0.0 & 0.0 & 0.833 & 0.0 & 0.0 & 0.0 & 0.0 & 0.0 & 0.158 & 0.0 & 0.0 & 0.0 \\
0.0 & 0.0 & 0.0 & 0.604 & 0.0 & 0.0 & 0.0 & 0.0 & 0.0 & 0.094 & 0.0 & 0.0 \\
0.0 & 0.0 & 0.0 & 0.0 & 0.317 & 0.0 & 0.0 & 0.0 & 0.0 & 0.0 & 0.0 & 0.0 \\
0.0 & 0.0 & 0.0 & 0.0 & 0.0 & 0.0 & 0.703 & 0.0 & 0.0 & 0.0 & 0.0 & 0.0 \\
0.0 & 0.0 & 0.0 & 0.0 & 0.0 & 0.0 & 0.0 & 0.681 & 0.0 & 0.0 & 0.0 & 0.0 \\
0.0 & 0.0 & 0.0 & 0.0 & 0.0 & 0.0 & 0.0 & 0.0 & 0.629 & 0.0 & 0.0 & 0.0 \\
0.0 & 0.0 & 0.0 & 0.0 & 0.0 & 0.0 & 0.0 & 0.0 & 0.0 & 0.494 & 0.0 & 0.0 \\
0.0 & 0.0 & 0.0 & 0.0 & 0.0 & 0.0 & 0.0 & 0.0 & 0.0 & 0.0 & 0.284 & 0.0
\end{bmatrix}
\begin{bmatrix}
4089 \\ 2208 \\ 1358 \\ 787 \\ 341 \\ 96 \\ 4286 \\ 2251 \\ 1310 \\ 761 \\ 374 \\ 105
\end{bmatrix}
=
\begin{bmatrix}
— \\ 4805 \\ 2499 \\ 1338 \\ 547 \\ 108 \\ — \\ 3013 \\ 1533 \\ 824 \\ 376 \\ 106
\end{bmatrix}
$$

$$M_{22} \qquad\qquad N_M^{(1960)} \;=\; N_M^{(1975)}$$

$$(9.8)$$

The projection omits the 1975 female population, projected using quadrant M_{11}, and the 1975 male population ages 0–14, which is contributed by the urban and rural female populations (quadrant M_{21}). Quadrant M_{12}, representing male contributions to the 1975 female population, would be 0.

For the projection, 1960 population estimates, $N_M^{(1960)}$, are taken from Table 5.8. The elements of M_{22} are found from Table 5.9. For the urban and rural nonmigrant populations, survival from ages $(x, x + n)$ to ages $(x + n, x + 2n)$ is found using (8.6) and the $_nL_x$ terms of the table. That is, for $_nS_{x+(1/2)n}$ we use $_nL_{x+n}/_nL_x$. As examples, we have

$$_{15}S_{7.5,\,u \to u} = {}_{15}L_{15,\,u}/{}_{15}L_{0,\,u} = 139{,}987/146{,}865 = 0.953$$

$$_{15}S_{52.5,\,r \to r} = {}_{15}L_{60,\,r}/{}_{15}L_{45,\,r} = 19{,}110/38{,}662 = 0.494$$

Note that the $_nL_x$ terms in Table 5.9 are $r \to r$ and $u \to u$ migration–survival probabilities, displaying the life table populations who both survive and remain in each area (hence, the large discrepancy between the urban and rural survival terms.)

If two censuses were available, for the urban and rural nonmigrant populations we might also have used *census survival* estimates (Section 8.3). For rural nonmigrants, we would have

$$_nS_{x+(1/2)n,\ r\to r} = [_nN^{(t+k)}_{x+k,\ r}/_nN^{(t)}_{x,\ r}]^{n/k} \tag{9.9}$$

where the power n/k adjusts the survival estimate from the k-year interval between censuses to the n-year interval between age groups. If the census at $t + k$ also disaggregated the urban population by place of residence at t, (9.9) would also estimate $_nS_{x+(1/2)n,\ r\to u}$ and $_nS_{x+(1/2)n,\ u\to u}$.

Table 5.9 is not used for the rural-to-urban migrant population, since as we have constructed the table the $_nL_x$ series for migrants includes both new migrants and the survivors of migrants at earlier ages. For the projection matrix we require only transfer and survival probabilities at the time of migration. The probabilities can be computed from the source of information in Tables 5.5 and 5.6, using the geometric approximation

$$_{15}S_{x+7.5,\ r\to u,\ exp} = (_{15}S_{x,\ r\to u}\ _{15}S_{x+15,\ r\to u})^{1/2} \tag{9.10}$$

where the terms in $_nS_{x,\ r\to u}$ are estimated as

$$_nS_{x,\ r\to u} = _np_{x,\ r\to u}\ _nt_{x,\ r\to u} = (_np_{x,\ r}\ _np_{x,\ u})^{1/2}\ _nt_{x,\ r\to u} \tag{9.11}$$

Using Tables 5.5 and 5.6, the transition probability for the age group 30–44 will be

$$_{15}S_{37.5,\ r\to u} = [(0.9007 \times 0.8408)^{1/2}$$

$$\times (0.2137)(0.7584 \times 0.7125)^{1/2}(0.1835)]^{1/2} = 0.1584$$

The reader can confirm the matrix estimates at other ages. Note, however, that for ages 60–74, (9.10) and (9.11) yield $_{15}S_{67.5,\ r\to u} = [(0.4000 \times 0.4101)^{1/2}(0.1619)(0.0000 \times 0.0000)^{1/2}(0.0279)]^{1/2} = 0.0$ a result that is inconsistent with the source data of Table 5A.1. For the final ages we might have substituted the linear approximation

$$_{15}S_{x+7.5,\ r\to u,\ lin} = \tfrac{1}{2}(_{15}S_{x,\ r\to u} + _{15}S_{x+15,\ r\to u}) \tag{9.12}$$

which yields the transition estimate

$$_{15}S_{67.5,\ r\to u,\ lin} = \tfrac{1}{2}[(0.4000 \times 0.4101)^{1/2}(0.1619)$$

$$+ (0.0000 \times 0.0000)^{1/2}(0.0279)] = 0.0328$$

This estimate could also have been found from Tables 5.7b and 5.7c, which show $(9 + 46 + 69)$ transfers between ages 60 and 74 among $(131 + 1765)$ survivors at age 60, and no transfers in the interval 75+. Averaging these proportions; we have $\frac{1}{2}[(9 + 46 + 69)/(131 + 1765) + 0] = 0.0327$.

From (9.8) the increase in the male population at ages 15 and above is projected to be 58% from 1960 to 1975, disaggregated as a 94% increase in the urban population and 22% increase in the rural population. The changes represent a shift from 50% to 61% urban over the 15 years of the projection.

The actual population change and urban shift over the period were greater. The 1975 male population ages 15+ was about 7% above the projection, due in part to increasing life expectancies over the period and in part to higher current estimates of the 1960 population base than were used in (9.8). The proportion urban was 63%. Table 9.1 displays the two sets of estimates, showing differences by both residence and age.

To complete the projection matrix will require the three other 12×12 submatrices, M_{11}, M_{12}, and M_{21}. The complete matrix will be dimension 24×24, becoming 48×48 if labor force status is also distinguished. As the complexity of the matrix increases, the user will need to carefully review its internal consistency (Section 9.4) to assure that age, sex, and activity ratios remain plausible across the various categories.

The complete multistate matrix M would be expected to stabilize over time. Where the population is incremented only through fertility, a sufficient condition for stability is that in those of the component submatrices with fertility terms, the nonzero terms may not be concentrated entirely at ages that can be indexed as integer multiples of a common base, leaving gaps at some intermediate ages.* Human fertility normally satisfies that condition, as it extends over several adjacent age intervals even at interval widths of 15 years. Discussions of stability in multistate models will be found in Rogers (1968, 1975), Espenshade *et al.* (1982), Sivamurthy (1982), Mitra (1983), and Cerone (1987). For this example, the stable population is almost wholly urban, since rural-to-urban migration flows absorb most of the rural population increase, and are not offset (in these data) by any urban-to-rural flows.

9.4. IMPOSED CONSTRAINTS

Like population projections with separate birth functions for male and female infants, migration projections need to preserve certain ratios between ages and sexes. Apart from new settlement areas and temporary migrations,

---

* As an example, indexing the interval $(0, n)$ as 1, the age intervals $(3n, 4n)$ and $(5n, 6n)$ become 4 and 6, with the common base 2. If fertility concentrated solely at those two ages, populations would stabilize only cyclically. Except in very small (3×3) matrices, human fertility probabilities will be nonzero across several contiguous intervals, assuring eventual stabilization of the matrix.

Table 9.1. Projected and Estimated Male Populations for Mexico, 1975. *Source:* United Nations (1976, Table 7, pp. 146–147)

| Ages | 1960 population (000s) | | | Proportional change to 1975[a] | | | | | |
| | Urban est. | Rural est. | Total est. | Urban | | Rural | | Total | |
				Proj.	Est.	Proj.	Est.	Proj.	Est.
0–14	4089	4286	8,375	+0.18	+0.28	−0.30	−0.34	−0.07	−0.03
15–29	2208	2251	4,459	+0.13	+0.25	−0.32	−0.28	−0.10	−0.02
30–44	1358	1310	2,668	−0.01	+0.06	−0.37	−0.35	−0.19	−0.14
45–59	787	761	1,548	−0.30	−0.19	−0.51	−0.39	−0.40	−0.29
60–74	341	374	715	−0.75	−0.60	−0.78	−0.70	−0.77	−0.65
75+	96	105	201						
Total	8879	9087	17,966	9297	10,250	5852	5913	15,149	16.163

$^a {}_n N_x^{(t+15)}/{}_n N_x^{(t)} - 1.$

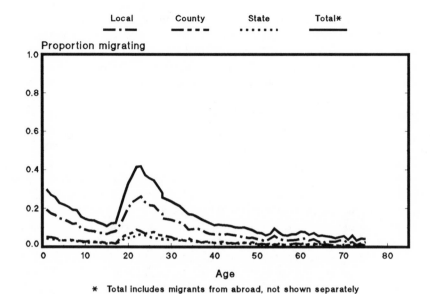

Figure 9.2. U.S. migration rates, March 1980–March 1981. *Source:* Hansen and Boertlein (1983, T. 6, p. 16).

sex ratios tend to vary relatively little among populations apart from the influences of differential mortality. Age ratios are more variable, since migration peaks both at relatively young working ages, roughly 20–34, where marriages and job changes are expected (the peak is also reflected in the migration patterns of their young children), and to some extent at the retirement ages, where climate strongly influences residential preferences. These patterns are brought out in Fig. 9.2, which displays proportions migrating during a 1-year period following the 1980 census.* In more detailed projections, linguistic, religious, and ethnic concentration or dispersal can also be factored into migration models. Distinctions can also be made between potential migrant and nonmigrant subsets (movers and stayers) within area populations.

The variety of patterns that occur will sometimes defeat conventional component projections, since it is unlikely that aggregate transition probabilities will be in a stable balance among relevant groups at any particular time. As in the disparity between male and female marriage and fertility

---

* The reader may compare Fig. 9.2 with Table 5A.1, which displays 5-year rural-to-urban migration probabilities for Mexico c. 1960. The Mexico data show a much more uniform pattern across ages, as older workers are less vested in the local economy than is usual in wealthier areas.

patterns noted in Chapter 7, migration patterns may be in continuous adjustment. As a result, the medium or longer term consequences for population projections of utilizing a fixed set of annual or quinquennial migration estimates may be untenable, or at least unpersuasive.

Where an initial projection requires adjustment, the corrections can be imposed on the transition probabilities, or by reformulating the projection model to generate selected subpopulations as functions of others. The approach is an extension of the procedures by which infants are projected as functions of the adult population at the reproductive ages. Projection of older children as functions of the adult population is similar to projection of infants, since it requires only that the parental cohorts be reverse survived to the time of the children's births, and that the children then be survived forward for the number of years required to bring them to their ages at the end of the projection period. For the multistate projections the children would be assigned the migration probabilities of their parents, at least to ages 10–14.

We illustrate the procedure using the projection model in Section 8.3 to project the female population 15–29 in location j at time $t + 15$ as a function of the female population ages 15–29, 30–44, and 45–59 in location i at time t. We have, from (8.11),

$$_{15}N_{15,\,(i\to)j}^{(t+15)} = \tfrac{1}{2}\left(_{15}L_{15}/l_0\right)\{\,_{15}N_{15,\,i}^{(t)}\,_{15}t_{22.5,\,i\to j}[\left(_{15}L_0/_{15}L_{15}\right)_{15}f_0 + {}_{15}f_{15}]$$

$$+\ _{15}N_{30,\,i}^{(t)}\,_{15}t_{37.5,\,i\to j}[\left(_{15}L_{15}/_{15}L_{30}\right)_{15}f_{15} + {}_{15}f_{30}] \qquad (9.13)$$

$$+\ _{15}N_{45,\,i}^{(t)}\,_{15}t_{52.5,\,i\to j}[\left(_{15}L_{30}/_{15}L_{45}\right)_{15}f_{30} + {}_{15}f_{45}]\}$$

The expression substitutes $\left(_{15}L_{x-15}/{}_{15}L_x\right)_{15}N_x^{(t)} = {}_{15}N_{x-15}^{(t-15)}$ for $_{15}N_x^{(t)}$ in (8.11) to back-age the parenting cohorts to $t - 15$ to generate the interval births $_\omega B_0^{(t-15,\,t)}$, and substitutes $_{15}L_{15}/l_0$ for $_{15}L_0/l_0$ to survive the birth cohort to ages 15–29 at $t + 15$. The subscript $(i\to)j$ on $_{15}N_{15}^{(t+15)}$ identifies the population as the survivors in j of migrants from i. [The terms in $_{15}L_x/{}_{15}L_{x+15}$ partially cancel against the terms in $_{15}L_{x+15}/{}_{15}L_x$ in (8.11), accounting for the slightly different appearance of the two expressions.] Using the data of Section 8.3, the reader can confirm that for a single region $i = j$ expressions (8.11) and (9.13) are equivalent.

In the multistate model the migration probabilities for the cohort ages 15–29, $_{15}t_{22.5,\,i\to j}$, would be those of the parents only if families largely remained intact at those ages and at the parental ages used in the projection.

(At ages 5–9 and 10–14 in 5-year interval projections,* parental migration probabilities would be expected to apply. For the 15-year age intervals of the example, different probabilities are more likely.)

Including migrants to j from other regions, the complete projection by (9.13) would find $_{15}N^{(t+15)}_{15,\,j} = \sum_i {}_{15}N^{(t+15)}_{15,\,(i\to)j}$ persons ages 15–29 in j at $t + 15$. Besides the differences between this estimate for region j and the conventional projection $_{15}N^{(t)}_{15,\,j} = \sum_i {}_{15}N^{(t)}_{0,\,i}\,{}_{15}l_{7.5,\,i\to j}\,({}_{15}L_{15,\,(i\to)j}/{}_{15}L_{0,\,i})$, there may be differences in the total populations $_{15}N^{(t+15)}_{15}$ found by the two methods, since (9.13) assigns the parenting cohorts the fertility, survival, and migration probabilities of their places of residence during $(t, t + 15)$ and not during $(t - 15, t)$, when the children were born. If there is substantial disagreement between the two $_{15}N^{(t+15)}_{15}$ estimates, and therefore in the survival ratios $_{15}N^{(t+15)}_{15}/{}_{15}N^{(t)}_0$ found by the two methods, the user may want to expand the projection matrix to allow migrating and nonmigrating populations to be projected separately.

After childhood and at the retirement ages, where fertility does not enter, unintended discrepancies in age and sex composition can be resolved more simply than at young ages. The projections may be constructed initially for one sex, and at their completion the researcher can use independently estimated sex ratios by age to impute numbers for the omitted sex. Formally, to introduce males into a one-sex projection for the female population, for region j we would set

$$_nN^{(t)}_{x,\,\mathrm{M},\,j} = \sum_i {}_nN^{(t)}_{x,\,\mathrm{F},\,(i\to)j}(_\omega B_{0,\,\mathrm{M}}/_\omega B_{0,\,\mathrm{F}})(_nL_{x,\,\mathrm{M}}/_nL_{x,\,\mathrm{F}}) \qquad (9.14)$$

where the terms in $_\omega B_0$ estimate the sex ratio at birth and terms in $_nL_x$ provide the ratio of males to females surviving at ages x to $x + n$. The expression can be simplified by presetting the terms in parentheses, using observed ratios or model tables. Where these terms differ by region or over time, the popula-

---

* The reader can show that for the 5-year projections we would have

$$_5N^{(t+n)}_{5,\,i\to j} = \tfrac{1}{2}(_5L_5/l_0)\{_5N^{(t)}_{15,\,i}\,_5l_{17.5,\,i\to j}[(_5L_{10}/_5L_{15})_5f_{10} + {}_5f_{15}]$$

$$+ {}_5N^{(t)}_{20,\,i}\,_5l_{22.5,\,i\to j}[(_5L_{15}/_5L_{20})_5f_{15} + {}_5f_{20}] + \cdots$$

$$+ {}_5N^{(t)}_{45,\,i}\,_5l_{47.5,\,i\to j}[(_5L_{40}/_5L_{45})_5f_{40} + {}_nf_{45}]\}$$

$$_5N^{(t+n)}_{10,\,i\to j} = \tfrac{1}{2}(_5L_{10}/l_0)\{_5N^{(t)}_{20,\,i}(_5L_{10}/_5L_{20})_5l_{22.5,\,i\to j}[_5f_{10} + (_5L_{15}/_5L_{10})_5f_{15}]$$

$$+ {}_5N^{(t)}_{25,\,i}(_5L_{15}/_5L_{25})_5l_{27.5,\,i\to j}[_5f_{15} + (_5L_{20}/_5L_{15})_5f_{20}] + \cdots$$

$$+ {}_5N^{(t)}_{50,\,i}(_5L_{40}/_5L_{50})_5l_{52.5,\,i\to j}[_5f_{40} + (_5L_{45}/_5L_{40})_5f_{45}]\}$$

tion figures may be aggregated and the various ratios $[_nN_{x,\text{M}}^{(t)} : _nN_{x,\text{F}}^{(t)}]$, $[_nN_{x,\text{M}}^{(t)} : _nN_{x+n,\text{M}}^{(t)}]$, $[_nN_{x,\text{F}}^{(t)} : _nN_{x+n,\text{F}}^{(t)}]$, $[(_nN_{x,\text{M}}^{(t)}/_nN_{x+n,\text{M}}^{(t)}) : (_nN_{x,\text{F}}^{(t)}/_nN_{x+n,\text{F}}^{(t)})]$ checked to assure that the population distributions by age are plausible. If the distribution eventually stabilizes, the stable populations that are generated for each projection matrix may also indicate whether the model probabilities are reasonable or unreasonable.

9.5. CONTROLLED PROJECTIONS

In the United States, mortality and fertility rates differ by ethnicity, but not greatly by state. One- or five-year population projections for the separate ethnic groups at the national level should therefore agree closely with projections generated at the state level and aggregated. They do not. At the state level, migration usually contributes nonnegligibly to projections, at rates that are not reconcilable with those in the competing projections of other states.

Constructing state population estimates by disaggregating from national population figures would assure consistency. With Bureau of the Census access to internal revenue and social security address files and annual vital statistics reports, and with state reports of school enrollments (see Section 9.6) it is also possible to estimate migration patterns with some confidence. Not with complete confidence: vital statistics and administrative records locate part but not all of the U.S. population.*

To reconcile state or regional level projections (and local projections from the state level figures) where the sum of the state series is reasonably close to a national projection, the series may be *controlled* (rescaled) to the national figure. For the separate age, sex, and ethnic groups at the state level we set

$$_nN_{x,\,j}^{*} = \,_nN_{x,\,j}\left(_nN_x \Big/ \sum_j \,_nN_{x,\,j}\right) \tag{9.15}$$

where $_nN_x$ is the national population estimate and j indexes combinations of the subset categories apart from age. The asterisk identifies the controlled state or local estimate.

---

* In Texas, where net migration in the 1970s and 1980s fluctuated sharply with oil revenues, the last 1980 population projections prior to the 1980 census were low by about 1 million persons, or 7%, relative to the census enumeration. The last 1990 projections before the 1990 census were high by about the same amount. In both cases the Bureau of the Census was aware of the problem, but could not resolve it prior to the census. The numbers will be found in U.S. Statistical Abstracts for the relevant years.

If the initial quality of particular state or local estimates is high enough that further correcting is not warranted, (9.15) can be adjusted by subtracting the satisfactory estimates from $_nN_x$ and from $\Sigma_j \, _nN_{x,\, j}$, limiting the correction to the remaining areas. (The same procedure would also be followed for institutional and other fixed populations in local area projections; see Section 9.6.)

Besides subpopulations not needing adjustment, there may be some requiring more correction than others. Particularly when the discrepancy between $_nN_x$ and $\Sigma_j \, _nN_{x,\, j}$ is substantial, the researcher should examine the uncorrected state or local projections for possible suspect figures, and review the model assumptions from which they were derived.

9.6. SMALL-AREA ESTIMATION AND PROJECTION

Small-area populations introduce complexities in projection and estimation that are rarely found in larger units. The projections may need to distinguish a variety of special populations, such as residents of nursing homes, the military, university students, and prisoners, *to the extent that they are drawn from outside the projection area*. These *placed* populations can usually be regarded as fixed, and therefore need not be projected as a component of the area population (Davis, 1988). Denoting these individuals as $_\omega N_{0,\, p}$ and the residual population as $_\omega N_{0,\, -p}$, the balancing equation (9.1) for small areas becomes

$$
\begin{aligned}
_\omega N_0^{(t+n)} &= {_\omega N_{0,\, p}} + {_\omega N_{0,\, -p}^{(t+n)}} \\[2mm]
&= {_\omega N_{0,\, p}} + {_\omega N_{0,\, -p}^{(t)}} + {_\omega B_0^{(t,\, t+n)}} \\[2mm]
&\quad - {_\omega D_0^{(t,\, t+n)}} + {_\omega I_0^{(t,\, t+n)}} - {_\omega E_0^{(t,\, t+n)}}
\end{aligned}
\tag{9.16}
$$

Unfortunately, when its terms must be approximated, (9.16) is only sometimes better than simpler linear or geometric projection [(8.2), (8.3), and (9.2)]. The problems in using it derive from the instability of birth, death, and migration counts when numbers of events are small. Disaggregated by age, in some intervals small populations may experience no events, and even a single event may imply an event rate that is unsustainable.

In component projections, model birth, survival, and migration rates can substitute for small-area rates, but may yield population estimates at some ages that revert to their initial values after rounding off fractions. In consequence, few or no changes except the gradual aging of the population may be projected. The assignment of random number operators to the birth and transition probabilities may improve the realism of the projection, but can introduce other anomalies, as small children remaining whose parents have migrated.* Inspection of the completed projections may suggest other incongruities.

To a greater extent than larger regions, small-area populations are also subject to unpredictable changes as employers enter or leave. If the areas are relatively near large urban centers, these changes may be more a function of events in the central area than of local conditions. When that is the case, future area changes may be more appropriately estimated linearly than exponentially, with the central area taken as the projection base.

Finally, the separation of placed or otherwise fixed populations $_\omega N_{0,\,p}$ may not be straightforward. Census or institutional estimates for these populations may be incomplete, or may not separate individuals by local or nonlocal prior residence. For projections, only those who are not local need to be counted in $_\omega N_{0,\,p}$. Their number can sometimes be estimated from differences between the area and the regional or state age distributions: nonlocal university students would appear as an excess in the population ages 18–22, military populations will be slightly older and predominantly male, and prison populations slightly older again. The populations of nursing homes will be largely female and largely over 70.

The problems of population estimation and projection for local areas may be partly mitigated by other available indicator data. These include vital statistics for local area births $_\omega B_0$ and deaths $_\omega D_0$ since the last census, available in the United States from state records; and school enrollment data for children by county of residence, compiled as part of the Federal–State Cooperative Program for Population Estimates (FSCPE).

The Bureau of the Census also has access to federal income tax records for estimating individual and family migration, and uses these *administrative records* together with births and deaths to estimate intercensal county and state population changes, by expression (9.1).

In place of tax records, which are not released for public use, state and local populations are widely estimated from changes in housing units or electrical hookups, possibly differentiated by type of building (Smith, 1986). Using *housing units* the population estimate for area j at time $t + n$ would be

$$_\omega N_{0,\,j}^{(t+n)} = {}_\omega N_{0,\,j,\,p} + {}_\omega N_{0,\,j,\,-p}^{(t)}(K_j^{(t+n)}/K_j^{(t)}) \qquad (9.17)$$

where $K_j^{(t)}$ is the housing stock at the time of the census (year t), $K_j^{(t+n)}$ is

---

* Given the event probability $_n q_x$, the event is determined to occur to individual j if a random number r drawn from the uniform distribution satisfies $0.0 \leq r \leq {}_n q_x < 1.0$. Where the event is migration, transfers of partners and children may be assigned in proportion to transfers of adults of one sex.

an estimate of housing stock at $t + n$, and $_\omega N^{(t)}_{0, j, -\text{p}}/K^{(t)}_j$ is the census ratio of population to housing.

Births and deaths, and automobile registrations, selected taxes, electrical or telephone hookups, or school enrollments can also be translated into total population estimates by *ratio correlation* regression, which regresses the change in the ratio of the local area population $_\omega N_{0, j}$ to the regional or state population $_\omega N_0$ as a function of earlier changes in the ratios of the selected attributes K_i. The estimating model has the form

$$
(_\omega N^{(t)}_{0, j, -\text{p}}/_\omega N^{(t)}_0)/(_\omega N^{(t-m)}_{0, j, -\text{p}}/_\omega N^{(t-m)}_0)
$$
$$
= \sum_i [b_i(K^{(t)}_{i, j}/K^{(t)}_i)/(K^{(t-m)}_{i, j}/K^{(t-m)}_i)] + e
\tag{9.18}
$$

where e is a stochastic error term with mean and variance $(0, \sigma^2)$, and the fitting is to two time points (we have used $t - m$ and t) at which all of the terms in (9.18) are known. The expression omits any populations $_\omega N_{0, j, \text{p}}$ whose numbers are expected to remain fixed for area j; adjustment is not usually needed at the aggregate level. After finding the regression coefficients b_i, the local population in year $t + n$ is estimated from (9.17) and (9.18) as

$$
_\omega N^{(t+n)}_{0, j} = {}_\omega N_{0, j, \text{p}} + (_\omega N^{(t)}_{0, j, -\text{p}} \, _\omega N^{(t+n)}_0/_\omega N^{(t)}_0)
$$
$$
\times \left[\sum_i b_i(K^{(t+n)}_{i, j}/K^{(t+n)}_i) \middle/ (K^{(t)}_{i, j}/K^{(t)}_i) \right]
\tag{9.19}
$$

Expressions (9.18) and (9.19) are generalizations of simpler projections that extrapolate from the ratios of local to larger area populations, disregarding the components K. Given $(_\omega N^{(t-m)}_{0j, -\text{p}}/_\omega N^{(t-m)}_0)$ and $(_\omega N^{(t)}_{0, j, -\text{p}}/_\omega N^{(t)}_0)$, the population of j is estimated at $t + n$ using (2.1) or (2.2). We have

$$
_\omega N^{(t+n)}_{0, j, \text{lin}} = {}_\omega N_{0, j, \text{p}} + {}_\omega N^{(t+n)}_0[(n + m)(_\omega N^{(t)}_{0, j, -\text{p}}/_\omega N^{(t)}_0)
$$
$$
- n(_\omega N^{(t-m)}_{0, j, -\text{p}}/_\omega N^{(t-m)}_0)]/m
\tag{9.20}
$$

$$
_\omega N^{(t+n)}_{0, j, \text{exp}} = {}_\omega N_{0, j, \text{p}} + {}_\omega N^{(t+n)}_0
$$
$$
\times (_\omega N^{(t)}_{0, j, -\text{p}}/_\omega N^{(t)}_0)^{1+n/m}/(_\omega N^{(t-m)}_{0, j, -\text{p}}/_\omega N^{(t-m)}_0)^{n/m}
\tag{9.21}
$$

However populations are estimated or projected, if a series is complete to the state level, or complete for other administrative areas for which independent estimates exist, the local series may need to be controlled by age and sex to agree with the aggregate total. For the adjustment the number in each age and sex category is multiplied by the ratio of the independent estimate to the projected sum, again separating placed subpopulations whose numbers are essentially fixed. For ages x to $x + n$, we will have,

$$_nN^{*\;(t+n)}_{x,\;j} = {}_nN_{x,\;j,\;p} + {}_nN^{(t+n)}_{x,\;j,\;-p}\left({}_nN^{(t+n)}_x - \sum_i {}_nN_{x,\;i,\;p}\right)\bigg/ \sum_i {}_nN^{(t+n)}_{x,\;i,\;-p} \quad (9.22)$$

After completing area estimates or projections, the user may survive the initial population from t to $t + n$ using the life table survival probabilities at each age [(4.18) and (8.6)], $_nS_{x+(1/2)n} = {}_nL_{x+n}/{}_nL_x$. The difference between the population found from (9.17), (9.19), or (9.20) and the population projected using the life table will represent the contribution of migration to the change from t to $t + n$.

For details on these and other techniques for estimation and projection, the reader should see Pittenger (1976), Byerly (1987), National Research Council (1980), Lee and Goldsmith (1982), Galdi (1985), Felton (1986), and Smith (1986, 1987). For the reasons we have outlined, having to do with the instability of small-area measures, none of the estimating formulas is wholly satisfactory. The researcher may need to reject one or another formula for particular areas where estimated population totals or age distributions are implausible.

9.7. SUMMARY

The formal analysis of migration has taken two directions in the United States. In one direction, analysis focuses toward the practical problems that arise in attempting to estimate and project populations; in the other, the flexibility of matrix analysis is applied to multistate population projections where population sizes are assumed large enough to provide robust estimates of survival and transition probabilities. In the former category are works by Pittenger (1976), Lee and Goldsmith (1982), and the other contributions cited immediately above. The latter category includes works by Rogers (1968, 1975, 1984), Rees and Wilson (1977), Land and Rogers (1982), and Schoen (1988).

Two problems complicate migration analysis. The first is one of definition. Whereas births and deaths are unambiguous events, individuals may change residences frequently, moving over short or long distances at each change. Some of the moves will not be of interest to the researcher, but any conventions he or she uses to exclude them may not be adopted by other investigators. Hence, the same study sample may yield multiple estimates of migration rates.

The other problem in migration analysis, shared by two-sex population projections, is associated with the difficulty of reconciling differences among subgroup transition probabilities, and with the stochastic and nonstochastic variability that arises where population sizes are small.

A variety of methods can be used to circumvent the most troublesome problems. In Bureau of the Census estimates, they are addressed by finding local area and county populations using more than one formula, and averaging the results. The procedure does not assure correct estimates, but limits the number of areas for which errors are extreme. Projection to stability is also useful for identifying unsupportable outcomes, as imbalances by age and sex outside the limits that are commonly observed.

References

Aalen, O. O. A linear regression model for the analysis of life times. *Statistics in Medicine,* 1989, *8,* 907–925.

Ahlburg, D. Good times, bad times: A study of the future path of U.S. fertility. *Social Biology,* 1983, *30,* 17–23.

Alterman, H. *Counting People: The Census in History.* New York: Harcourt, Brace & World, 1969.

Althauser, R. P., and Wigler, M. Standardization and component analysis. *Sociological Methods and Research,* 1972, *1,* 97–135.

Anderson, J. E., Rodrigues, W., and Thome, A. M. T. Breastfeeding and use of the health care system in Bahia State, Brazil: Three multivariate analyses. *Studies in Family Planning,* 1984, *15,* 127–135.

Ansell, C. *On the Rate of Mortality . . . .* London: National Life Assurance Society, 1874.

Arthur, W. B., and Stoto, M. A. An analysis of indirect mortality estimation. *Population Studies,* 1983, *37,* 301–314.

Barclay, G. W. *Techniques of Population Analysis.* New York: Wiley, 1958.

Barrett, J. C. Transformations for model life tables. *Genus,* 1976, *32,* 1–10.

Batten, R. W. *Mortality Table Construction.* Englewood Cliffs, N.J.: Prentice–Hall, 1978.

Beard, R. E., Pentikäinen, T., and Pesonen, E. *Risk Theory: The Stochastic Basis of Insurance* (3rd Ed.). London: Chapman & Hall, 1984 (1969).

Beekman, J. A. *Two Stochastic Processes.* Stockholm: Almqvist & Wiksell, 1974.

Beers, H. S. Modified-interpolation formulas that minimize fourth differences. *Record of the American Institute of Actuaries,* 1945, *24,* 14–20.

Behar, C. L. Malthus and the development of demographic analysis. *Population Studies,* 1987, *41,* 269–281.

Benitez, R., and Cabrera, G. *Proyecciones de la Población de Mexico 1960–1980.* Mexico City: Banco de Mexico, 1966. [Cited in Tabah (1968).]

Benjamin, B. *Health and Vital Statistics.* London: Allen & Unwin, 1968.

Bennett, N. G., and Garson, L. K. The centenarian question and old-age mortality in the Soviet Union, 1959–1970. *Demography,* 1983, *20,* 587–606.

Berkson, J. Application of the logistic function to bio-assay. *Journal of the American Statistical Association,* 1944, *39,* 357–365.

Berkson, J. Why I prefer logits to probits. *Biometrics,* 1951, *7,* 327–339.

Berkson, J., and Gage, R. P. Calculation of survival rates for cancer. *Proceedings of the Staff Meetings of the Mayo Clinic,* 1950, *25,* 270–286.

Bernardelli, H. Population waves. *Journal of the Burma Research Society,* 1941, *31 (Part 1),* 1–18. [Parts of this article are reprinted in Smith and Keyfitz (1977, pp. 215–219).]

Bernoulli, D. Essai d'une nouvelle analyse de la mortalité causée par la petite Vérole . . . . *Histoire de L'Académie Royale des Sciences* (Paris), 1766, *Année 1760*, 1–45. [An English translation will be found in Bradley (1971). See also Birnbaum (1979).]

Birnbaum, Z. W. On the mathematics of competing risks. *Vital and Health Statistics*, 1979, *Series 2, No. 77.*

Böhmer, P. E. Theorie der unabhängigen Wahrscheinlichkeiten Rapports. *Mémoires et Procès-verbaux de Septième Congrès International d'Actuaries (Amsterdam)*, 1912, *2*, 327–343. [Cited in Namboodiri and Suchindran (1987).]

Bongaarts, J. Why high birth rates are so low. *Population and Development Review*, 1975, *1*, 289–296.

Bongaarts, J. A framework for analyzing the proximate determinants of fertility. *Population and Development Review*, 1978, *4*, 105–132.

Bongaarts, J. The fertility-inhibiting effects of the intermediate fertility variables. *Studies in Family Planning*, 1982, *13*, 179–189.

Bongaarts, J., and Potter, R. G., Jr. *Fertility, Biology and Behavior: An Analysis of the Proximate Determinants.* New York: Academic Press, 1983.

Bradley, L. *Smallpox Inoculation: An Eighteenth Century Mathematical Controversy.* Nottingham: Adult Education Dept., University of Nottingham, 1971.

Brass, W. A critique of methods for estimating population growth in countries with limited data. *Bulletin de l'Institut International de Statistique*, 1971, *44*, 397–412.

Brass, W. *Methods for Estimating Fertility and Mortality from Limited and Defective Data.* Chapel Hill: Laboratories for Population Statistics, Carolina Population Center, University of North Carolina, 1975. [On the robustness of Brass mortality estimates see Arthur and Stoto (1983).]

Brass, W., and Coale, A. J. Methods of analysis and estimation. In W. Brass, A. J. Coale, P. Demeny, D. F. Heisel, F. Lorimer, A. Romaniuk, and E. van de Walle (Eds.), *The Demography of Tropical Africa.* Princeton, N.J.: Princeton University Press, 1968, pp. 88–142.

Breslow, N. E., and Day, N. E. Indirect standardization and multiplicative models for rates, with reference to the age adjustment of cancer incidence and relative frequency data. *Journal of Chronic Diseases*, 1975, *28*, 289–303.

Breslow, N. E., and Day, N. E. *Statistical Methods in Cancer Research II: The Design and Analysis of Cohort Studies.* Lyon: International Agency for Research on Cancer, 1987.

Brillinger, D. R. The natural variability of vital rates and associated statistics. *Biometrics*, 1986, *42*, 693–712. [See also the Discussion, pp. 712–734.]

Butz, W. P., and Ward, M. P. The emergence of countercyclical U.S. fertility. The Rand Corporation, 1977.

Byerly, E. State population and household estimates, with age, sex, and components of change: 1981 to 1986. *Current Population Reports*, 1987, *Series P-25, No. 1010.*

Cannan, E. The probability of a cessation of the growth of population in England and Wales during the next century. *Economic Journal*, 1895, *5*, 505–515.

Carrier, N. H., and Farrag, A. M. The reduction of errors in census populations for statistically underdeveloped countries. *Population Studies*, 1959, *12*, 240–285.

Carrier, N. H., and Hobcraft, J. *Demographic Estimation for Developing Societies: A Manual of Techniques for the Detection and Reduction of Errors in Demographic Data.* London: Population Investigation Committee, London School of Economics, 1971.

Caswell, H. *Matrix Population Models.* Sunderland, Mass.: Sinauer Associates, 1989.

Centers for Disease Control. Premature mortality in the United States: Public health issues in the use of years of potential life lost. *Morbidity and Mortality Weekly Report*, 1986, *35 (Suppl. 2S).*

Cerone, P. On stable population theory with immigration. *Demography*, 1987, *24*, 431–438.

Chiang, C. L. A stochastic study of the life table II: Sample variance of the observed expectation of life and other biometric functions. *Human Biology,* 1960, *32,* 221–238.

Chiang, C. L. Standard error of the age-adjusted death rate. *Vital Statistics—Special Reports,* 1961, *47 (9).*

Chiang, C. L. Variance and covariance of life table functions estimated from a sample of deaths. *Vital and Health Statistics,* 1967, Series 2, No. 20.

Chiang, C. L. *Introduction to Stochastic Processes in Biostatistics.* New York: Wiley, 1968.

Chiang, C. L. *The Life Table and Its Applications.* Malabar, Fla.: Krieger, 1984.

Cho, L. J., and Retherford, R. D. Comparative analysis of recent fertility trends in East Asia. *Proceedings of the 17th General Conference of the IUSSP,* 1973, *2,* 163–181.

Choldin, H. M. Statistics and politics: The "Hispanic issue" in the 1980 census. *Demography,* 1986, *23,* 403–418.

Clogg, C. C., and Eliason, S. R. A flexible procedure for adjusting rates and proportions, including statistical methods for group comparisons. *American Sociological Review,* 1988, *53,* 267–283.

Coale, A. J. Convergence of a human population to a stable form. *Journal of the American Statistical Association,* 1968, *63,* 395–435.

Coale, A. J. Age patterns of marriage. *Population Studies,* 1971, *25,* 193–214.

Coale, A. J. The development of new models of nuptiality and fertility. *Population,* 1977, *32 (Special Number, September),* 131–154.

Coale, A. J., and Guo, G. Revised regional model life tables at very low levels of mortality. *Population Index,* 1989, *55,* 613–643.

Coale, A. J., and Kisker, E. E. Mortality crossovers: Reality or bad data? *Population Studies,* 1986, *40,* 389–401.

Coale, A. J., and Kisker, E. E. Defects in data on old-age mortality in the United States: New procedures for calculating mortality schedules and life tables at the highest ages. *Asian and Pacific Population Forum,* 1990, *4 (1),* 1–31.

Coale, A. J., and McNiel, D. R. The distribution by age of the frequency of first marriage in a female cohort. *Journal of the American Statistical Association,* 1972, *67,* 743–749.

Coale, A. J., and Trussell, T. J. Model fertility schedules: Variations in the age structure of child-bearing in human populations. *Population Index,* 1974, *40,* 185–258; 1975, *41,* 572 (erratum note).

Coale, A. J., and Trussell, T. J. Finding the two parameters that specify a model schedule of marital fertility rates. *Population Index,* 1978, *44,* 203–213.

Coale, A. J., Demeny, P., and Vaughan, B. *Regional Model Life Tables and Stable Populations* (2nd Ed.). New York: Academic Press, 1983. [See also the revised tables for very low mortality populations in Coale and Guo (1989).]

Cook, S. F., and Borah, W. *Essays in Population History: Mexico and the Caribbean.* Two volumes. Berkeley: University of California Press, 1971, 1974.

Cox, D. R. Regression models and life tables. *Journal of the Royal Statistical Society, Series B,* 1972, *34,* 187–220.

Cox, D. R., and Oakes, D. *Analysis of Survival Data.* London: Chapman & Hall, 1984.

Davis, K., and Blake, J. Social structure and fertility: An analytic framework. *Economic Development and Cultural Change,* 1956, *4,* 211–235.

Davis, S. T. Methodology for experimental county population estimates for the 1980's. *Current Population Reports.* 1988, Series P-23, No. 158.

DeGruttola, V., and Lagakos, S. W. Analysis of doubly censored survival data, with application to AIDS. *Biometrics,* 1989, *45,* 1–11.

Diamond, I. D., McDonald, J. W., and Shah, I. H. Proportional hazards models for current status data: Application to the study of differentials in age at weaning in Pakistan. *Demography,* 1986, *23,* 607–620.

Drolette, M. E. The effect of incomplete follow-up. *Biometrics,* 1975, *31,* 135–144.

Duggar, B. C., and Lewis, W. F. Comparability of diagnostic data coded by the 8th and 9th revisions of the International Classification of Diseases. *Vital and Health Statistics,* 1987, *Series 2, No. 104.*

Dupâquier, J., and Grebenik, E. (Eds.). *Malthus Past and Present.* London: Academic Press, 1983.

Durbin, J., and Watson, G. S. Testing for serial correlation in least squares regression I. *Biometrika,* 1950, *37,* 409–428.

Durbin, J., and Watson, G. S. Testing for serial correlation in least squares regression II. *Biometrika,* 1951, *38,* 159–178.

Durbin, J., and Watson, G. S. Testing for serial correlation in least squares regression III. *Biometrika,* 1971, *58,* 1–19.

Dyke, B., and Morrill, W. T. (Eds.). *Genealogical Demography.* New York: Academic Press, 1980.

Easterlin, R. A. The American baby boom in historical perspective. *American Economic Review,* 1961, *51,* 896–911.

Easterlin, R. A. Relative economic status and the American fertility swing. In E. B. Sheldon (Ed.), *Family Economic Behavior.* Philadelphia: Lippincott, 1973, pp. 170–233.

Eaton, J. W., and Mayer, A. J. The social biology of very high fertility among the Hutterites. *Human Biology,* 1953, *25,* 206–264.

Elandt-Johnson, R. C. Various estimators of conditional probabilities of death in follow-up studies: Summary of results. *Journal of Chronic Diseases,* 1977, *30,* 247–256.

Elandt-Johnson, R. C., and Johnson, N. L. *Survival Models and Data Analysis.* New York: Wiley, 1980.

Elveback, L. Estimation of survivorship in chronic disease: The 'actuarial' method. *Journal of the American Statistical Association,* 1958, *53,* 420–440.

Ericksen, E. P., Kadane, J. B., and Tukey, J. W. Adjusting the 1980 census of population and housing. *Journal of the American Statistical Association,* 1989, *84,* 927–944.

Espenshade, T. J., Bouvier, L. R., and Arthur, W. B. Immigration and the stable population model. *Demography,* 1982, *19,* 125–133.

Farr, W. *English Life Table.* London: Longman, 1864.

Farr, W. *20th Annual Report of the Registrar General of England and Wales.* London: H. M. Stationary Office, 1857. [Parts of this report are reprinted in New York Academy of Medicine (1975). The opening quotation in Chapter 3 is from pp. 128–130 of the New York Academy of Medicine reprint.]

Feeney, G. Population dynamics based on birth intervals and parity progression. *Population Studies,* 1983, *37,* 75–89.

Feeney, G., and Ross, J. A. Analyzing open birth interval distributions. *Population Studies,* 1984, *38,* 473–478.

Feller, W. Die Grundlagen der Volterraschen Theorie des Kampfes ums Dasein in Wahrschein-lichkeitstheoretischer Behandlung. *Acta Biotheoretica,* 1939, *5,* 11–40.

Felton, G. R. Evaluation of population estimation procedures for counties 1980. *Current Population Reports,* 1986, *Series P-25, No. 984.*

Ferry, B., and Smith, D. P. Breastfeeding differentials. *World Fertility Survey Cross-National Summaries, No. 23.* Voorburg, The Netherlands: International Statistical Institute, 1983.

Fleiss, J. L. *Statistical Methods for Rates and Proportions.* New York: Wiley, 1981.

Fleury, M., and Henry, L. *Des Registres Paroissiaux à l'Histoire de la Population: Manuel de Dépouillement et d'Exploitation de l'État Civil Ancien.* Paris: Presses Universitaires de France, 1956.

Frauenthal, J. Birth trajectory under changing fertility conditions. *Demography,* 1975, *12,* 447–454.

Frauenthal, J., and Swick, K. Limit cycle oscillations of the human population. *Demography,* 1983, *20,* 285–298.

Freedman, D. A., and Navidi, W. C. Regression models for adjusting the 1980 census. *Statistical Science,* 1986, *1,* 1–39. [Cited in Ericksen *et al.* (1989).]

Freeman, D. H., Jr. *Applied Categorical Data Analysis.* New York: Dekker, 1987.

Freund, J. E. *Mathematical Statistics* (2nd Ed.). Englewood Cliffs, N.J.: Prentice–Hall, 1972.

Fries, J. F. Aging, natural death, and the compression of morbidity. *New England Journal of Medicine,* 1980, *303,* 130–135.

Fries, J. F., and Crapo, L. M. *Vitality and Aging: Implications of the Rectangular Curve.* San Francisco: Freeman, 1981.

Frobenius, G. F. Über Matrizen aus positiven Elementen. *Sitzungsberichte der Königlich Preussischen Akademie der Wissenschaften zu Berlin,* 1908, 471–477. [Cited in Rogers (1968).]

Frobenius, G. F. Über Matrizen aus positiven Elementen (II). *Sitzungsberichte der Königlich Preussischen Akademie der Wissenschaften zu Berlin,* 1909, 514–518. [Cited in Rogers (1968).]

Frobenius, G. F. Über Matrizen aus nicht negativen Elementen. *Sitzungsberichte der Königlich Preussischen Akademie der Wissenschaften zu Berlin,* 1912, 456–477. [Cited in Rogers (1968).]

Frobenius, G. F. Über zerlegbare Determinanten. *Sitzungsberichte der Königlich Preussischen Akademie der Wissenschaften zu Berlin,* 1917, 274–277. [Cited in Rogers (1968).]

Gage, T. B., McCullough, J. M., Weitz, C. A., Dutt, J. S., and Abelson, A. Demographic studies and human population biology. In M. A. Little and J. D. Haas (Eds.), *Human Population Biology.* New York: Oxford University Press, 1989, pp. 45–65.

Gail, M. A review and critique of some models used in competing risk analysis. *Biometrics,* 1975, *31,* 209–222.

Galdi, D. Evaluation of 1980 subcounty population estimates. *Current Population Reports,* 1985, *Series P-25, No. 963.*

Gaslonde, S. Programa de estudios comparativos sobre aborto inducido y uso de anticonceptivos en America Latina. *Centro Latino Americano de Demografia (CELADE),* 1972, *Series A, No. 118.* [Cited in Hobcraft and Little (1984).]

Gaslonde, S., and Bocaz, A. Método para medir variaciones en el nivel de fecundidad. *Centro Latino Americano de Demografia (CELADE),* 1970, *Series A, No. 107.* [Cited in Hobcraft and Little (1984).]

Gaslonde, S., and Carrasco, E. The impact of some intermediate variables on fertility: Evidence from the Venezuela National Fertility Survey 1977. *World Fertility Survey Occasional Papers, No. 23.* Liège: International Statistical Institute, 1982.

Gautier, É., and Henry, L. *La Population de Crulai, Paroisse Normande.* Paris: Presses Universitaires de France, 1958.

George, S. L., and Desu, M. M. Planning the size and duration of a trial studying the time to some critical event. *Journal of Chronic Diseases,* 1973, *17,* 15–24.

Gini, C. Premières recherches sur la fécundabilité de la femme. *Proceedings of the International Mathematics Congress,* pp. 889–892. Toronto, 1924. [An English translation will be found in Smith and Keyfitz (1977, pp. 367–371).]

Glass, D. V., and Eversley, D. E. C. (Eds.). *Population in History.* London: Arnold, 1965.

Glenn, N. D. Cohort analysts' futile quest: Statistical attempts to separate age, period and cohort effects. *American Sociological Review,* 1976, *41,* 900–903.

Glick, P. C. Marriage, divorce, and remarriage by year of birth: June 1971. *Current Population Reports,* 1972, *Series P-20, No. 239.*

Glick, P. C., and Norton, A. J. Number, timing, and duration of marriages and divorces in the United States: June 1975. *Current Population Reports,* 1976, *Series P-20, No. 297.*

Goldman, N., and Lord, G. A new look at entropy and the life table. *Demography,* 1986, *23,* 275–282.

Goldman, N., Pebley, A. R., and Lord, G. Calculation of life tables from survey data: A technical note. *Demography,* 1984, *21,* 647–653.

Gompertz, B. On the nature of the function expressive of the law of mortality. *Philosophical Transactions,* 1825, *27,* 513–585. [Parts of this article are reprinted in Smith and Keyfitz (1977, pp. 279–282).]

Graunt, J. *Natural and political observations mentioned in a following index, and made upon the Bills of Mortality.* London, 1662. Republished with an introduction by B. Benjamin in *Journal of the Institute of Actuaries,* 1964, *90,* 1–64. [Parts of this book are reprinted in Smith and Keyfitz (1977, pp. 11–20).]

Greenwood, M. A report on the natural duration of cancer. *Reports on Public Health and Medical Subjects, No. 33.* London: His Majesty's Stationery Office, 1926.

Greenwood, M. *Medical Statistics from Graunt to Farr.* New York: Arno Press, 1977 (orig. ed. 1948).

Greville, T. N. E. Short methods of constructing abridged life tables. *Record of the American Institute of Actuaries,* 1943, *32,* 29–42.

Greville, T. N. E. The general theory of osculatory interpolation. *Transactions of the Actuarial Society of America,* 1944, *45, Pt. II,* 202–265.

Greville, T. N. E. United States abridged life tables 1945. *Vital Statistics Special Reports,* 1947, *23 (11),* 243–249.

Greville, T. N. E. Mortality tables analyzed by cause of death. *Record of the American Institute of Actuaries,* 1948, *37,* 283–294.

Greville, T. N. E., and Keyfitz, N. Backward population projection by a generalized inverse. *Theoretical Population Biology,* 1974, *6,* 135–142.

Hajnal, J. Aspects of recent trends in marriage in England and Wales. *Population Studies,* 1947, *1,* 72–92.

Halley, E. An estimate of the degrees of the mortality of mankind. *Philosophical Transactions,* 1693, *17,* 596–610.

Halli, S. S., and Rao, K. V. *Advanced Techniques in Population Analysis.* New York: Plenum Press, 1992.

Hansen, K. A., and Boertlein, C. G. Geographical mobility: March 1980 to March 1981. *Current Population Reports,* 1983, *Series P-20, No. 377.*

Hanson, P. E. Leslie matrix models. *Mathematical Population Studies,* 1989, *1,* 37–67.

Henry, L. *Anciennes Familles Genevoises: Étude Démographique, XVIᵉ–XXᵉ Siècle.* Paris: Presses Universitaires de France, 1956.

Henry, L. *On the Measurement of Human Fertility: Selected Writings.* M. C. Sheps and E. Lapierre-Adamcyk (Eds.). New York: Elsevier, 1972.

Heuser, R. L. *Fertility Tables for Birth Cohorts by Color.* Rockville, Md.: U.S. Dept. of Health, Education and Welfare, National Center for Health Statistics, 1976.

Hobcraft, J., and Little, R. J. A. Fertility exposure analysis: A new method for assessing the contribution of proximate determinants to fertility differentials. *Population Studies,* 1984, *38,* 21–45, 191 (erratum note).

Hobcraft, J., and Rodríguez, G. The analysis of repeat fertility surveys: Examples from Dominican Republic. *World Fertility Survey Scientific Reports, No. 29.* Voorburg, The Netherlands: International Statistical Institute, 1982.

Hobcraft, J., Goldman, N., and Chidambaram, V. C. Advances in the P/F ratio method for the analysis of birth histories. *Population Studies,* 1982, *36,* 291–316.

Hoem, J. M. The construction of increment–decrement life tables: A comment on articles by R. Schoen and V. Nelson. *Demography,* 1975, *12,* 661.

Hollingsworth, T. H. *Historical Demography.* Ithaca, N.Y.: Cornell University Press, 1969.

Hollmann, F. W. United States population estimates, by age, sex, race, and Hispanic origin: 1980 to 1988. *Current Population Reports,* 1989, *Series P-25, No. 1045.*

Horiuchi, S., and Coale, A. J. A simple equation for estimating the expectation of life at old ages. *Population Studies,* 1982, *36,* 317–326.

Horiuchi, S., and Preston, S. Age-specific growth rates: The legacy of past population dynamics. *Demography,* 1988, *25,* 429–441.

Hosmer, D. W., and Lemeshow, S. *Applied Logistic Regression.* New York: Wiley, 1989.

Householder, A. S. *The Numerical Treatment of a Single Nonlinear Equation.* New York: McGraw–Hill, 1970.

Hsieh, J. A probabilistic approach to the construction of competing-risk life tables. *Biometric Journal,* 1989, *3,* 339–357.

Huebner, S. S., and Black, K., Jr. *Life Insurance* (10th Ed.). Englewood Cliffs, N.J.: Prentice–Hall, 1982 (orig. ed. 1915).

Jaffe, A. J. *U.S. Bureau of the Census: Handbook of Statistical Methods for Demographers* (3rd printing). Washington, D.C.: U.S. Government Printing Office, 1960 (orig. ed. 1951).

Jain, A. K., and Sivin, I. Life-table analysis of IUDs: Problems and recommendations. *Studies in Family Planning,* 1977, *8,* 25–47.

Johnson, N. L., and Kotz, S. *Discrete Distributions.* New York: Wiley, 1969.

Jordan, C. W., Jr. *Society of Actuaries Textbook on Life Contingencies* (2nd Ed.). Chicago: Society of Actuaries, 1975 (orig. ed. 1967).

Judge, G. W., Griffiths, W. E., Hill, R. C., and Lee, T.-C. *The Theory and Practice of Econometrics.* New York: Wiley, 1980.

Kaplan, E. L., and Meier, P. Nonparametric estimation from incomplete observations. *Journal of the American Statistical Association,* 1958, *53,* 457–481.

Kephart, G. Heterogeneity and the implied dynamics of regional growth rates: Was the nonmetropolitan turnaround an artifact of aggregation? *Demography,* 1988, *25,* 99–113.

Keyfitz, N. Sampling variance of standardized mortality rates. *Human Biology,* 1966, *38,* 309–317.

Keyfitz, N. How birth control affects births. *Social Biology,* 1971a, *18,* 109–121.

Keyfitz, N. On the momentum of population growth. *Demography,* 1971b, *8,* 71–80.

Keyfitz, N. On future population. *Journal of the American Statistical Association,* 1972, *67,* 351–352.

Keyfitz, N. Cause of death in future mortality. In International Union for the Scientific Study of Population, *International Population Conference, Mexico,* Vol. 1. Liège: IUSSP, 1977a, pp. 483–503.

Keyfitz, N. *Introduction to the Mathematics of Population* (2nd Ed.). Reading, Mass.: Addison–Wesley, 1977b (orig. ed. 1968).

Keyfitz, N. The limits of population forecasting. *Population and Development Review,* 1981a, *7,* 589–603.

Keyfitz, N. Statistics, law, and census reporting. *Society,* 1981b, *18,* 5–12.

Keyfitz, N. *Applied Mathematical Demography* (2nd Ed.). New York: Wiley, 1985 (orig. ed. 1977).

Keyfitz, N., and Flieger, W. *World Population: An Analysis of Vital Data.* Chicago: University of Chicago Press, 1968.

Keyfitz, N., and Flieger, W. *Population: Facts and Methods of Demography.* San Francisco: Freeman, 1971.

Keyfitz, N., and Frauenthal, J. An improved life table method. *Biometrics,* 1975, *31,* 889–899.

Keyfitz, N., and Littman, G. S. Mortality in a heterogeneous population. *Population Studies,* 1979, *33,* 333–343.

Kim, Y. J., and Strobino, D. M. Decomposition of the difference between two rates with hierarchical factors. *Demography,* 1984, *21,* 361–372.

Kitagawa, E. Components of a difference between two rates. *Journal of the American Statistical Association,* 1955, *50,* 1168–1194.

Kitagawa, E. Standardized comparisons in population research. *Demography,* 1964, *1,* 296–315.

Klebba, A. J., and Dolman, A. B. Comparability of mortality statistics for the seventh and eighth revisions of the International Classification of Diseases. *Vital and Health Statistics,* 1975, *Series 2, No. 66.*

Klebba, A. J., and Scott, J. H. Estimates of selected comparability ratios based on dual coding of 1976 death certificates by the eighth and ninth revisions of the International Classification of Diseases. *Monthly Vital Statistics Reports,* 1980, *28 (11), Supplement.*

Koop, J. C. Notes on the estimation of gross and net reproduction rates by methods of statistical sampling. *Biometrics,* 1951, *7,* 155–166.

Krishnamoorthy, S. Classical approach to increment–decrement life tables: An application to the study of the marital status of United States females, 1970. *Mathematical Biosciences,* 1979, *44,* 139–154.

Lachin, J. M. Introduction to sample size determination and power analysis for clinical trials. *Controlled Clinical Trials,* 1981, *2,* 93–113.

Lagakos, S. W. Inference in survival analysis: Nonparametric tests to compare survival distributions. In V. Miké and K. E. Stanley (Eds.), *Statistics in Medical Research.* New York: Wiley, 1982, pp. 340–364.

Laguerre, E. N. Sur une méthode pour obtenir par approximation les racines d'une équation algébraique qui a toutes ses racines réelles. *Nouvelles Annales de Mathématiques, 2e Serie,* 1880, *19,* 161–171, 193–202.

Laing, L. M. Declining fertility in a religious isolate: The Hutterite population of Alberta, Canada, 1951–1971. *Human Biology,* 1980, *52,* 288–310.

Land, K. C., and Hough, G. C., Jr. New methods for tables of school life, with applications to U.S. data from recent school years. *Journal of the American Statistical Association,* 1989, *84,* 63–75.

Land, K. C., and Rogers, A. (Eds.). *Multidimensional Mathematical Demography.* New York: Academic Press, 1982.

Land, K. C., and Schoen, R. Statistical methods for Markov-generated increment–decrement life tables with polynomial gross flow functions. Pp. 265–346 in Land and Rogers (1982).

Land, K. C., Hough, G. C., Jr., and McMillen, M. M. Voting status life tables for the United States, 1968–1980. *Demography,* 1986, *23,* 381–402.

Lawless, J. F. *Statistical Models and Methods for Lifetime Data.* New York: Wiley, 1982.

Lee, E. S., and Goldsmith, H. F. (Eds.). *Population Estimates: Methods for Small Area Analysis.* Beverly Hills: Sage, 1982.

Lee, R. D. Estimating series of vital rates and age structures from baptisms and burials: A new technique. *Population Studies,* 1974a, *28,* 495–512.

Lee, R. D. Forecasting births in post-transition populations: Stochastic renewal with serially correlated fertility. *Journal of the American Statistical Association,* 1974b, *69,* 607–617.

Lee, R. D. Natural fertility, population cycles and the spectral analysis of births and marriages. *Journal of the American Statistical Association,* 1975, *70,* 295–304.

Lee, R. D. Aiming at a moving target: Period fertility and changing reproductive intentions. *Population Studies,* 1980, *34,* 205–226.

Lee, R. D. Inverse projection and back projection: A critical appraisal, and comparative results for England, 1539 to 1871. *Population Studies,* 1985, *39,* 233–248.

Leridon, H. *Human Fertility: The Basic Components.* Chicago: University of Chicago Press, 1977.

Leridon, H., and Menken, J. A. (Eds.). *Natural Fertility.* Liège: Ordina, 1977.

Leslie, P. H. On the use of matrices in certain population mathematics. *Biometrika,* 1945, *33,* 183–212. [Parts of this article are reprinted in Smith and Keyfitz (1977, pp. 227–238).]

Leslie, P. H. On the distribution in time of the births in successive generations. *Journal of the Royal Statistical Society A,* 1948a, *111,* 44–53.

Leslie, P. H. Some further notes on the use of matrices in population mathematics. *Biometrika,* 1948b, *35,* 213–245.

Leslie, P. W., and Gage, T. B. Demography and human population biology: Problems and progress. In M. A. Little and J. D. Haas (Eds.), *Human Population Biology.* New York: Oxford University Press, 1989, pp. 15–44.

Lesthaeghe, R., and Page, H. J. The post-partum non-susceptible period: Development and application of model schedules. *Population Studies,* 1980, *34,* 143–169.

Lewis, E. G. On the generation and growth of a population. *Sankhya,* 1942, *6,* 93–96. [Reprinted in Smith and Keyfitz (1977, pp. 221–225).]

Lexis, W. *Einleitung in die Theorie der Bevölkerungs-Statistik.* Strasbourg: Trubner, 1875. [An English translation of pp. 5–7, introducing the Lexis diagram, will be found in Smith and Keyfitz (1977, pp. 39–41).]

Liao, T. F. A flexible approach for the decomposition of rate differences. *Demography,* 1989, *26,* 717–726.

Littell, A. Estimation of the T-year survival rate from follow-up studies over a limited period of time. *Human Biology,* 1952, *24,* 87–116.

Little, R. J. A. Sampling errors of fertility rates from the WFS. *World Fertility Survey Technical Bulletins No. 10.* Voorburg, The Netherlands: International Statistical Institute, 1982.

Little, R. J. A., and Pullum, T. W. The general linear model and direct standardization: A comparison. *Sociological Methods and Research,* 1979, *7,* 475–501.

Lotka, A. *Théorie Analytique des Associations Biologiques.* Paris: Hermann, 1939.

Malthus, T. R. *An Essay on the Principle of Population* and *A Summary View of the Principle of Population.* Edited by A. Flew. Harmondsworth, Middlesex: Penguin Books, 1970 (orig. ed. 1798, 1830).

Manton, K. G., and Myers, G. C. Recent trends in multiple-cause mortality, 1968 to 1982: Age and cohort components. *Population Research and Policy Review,* 1987, *6,* 161–176.

Manton, K. G., and Stallard, E. *Recent Trends in Mortality Analysis.* New York: Academic Press, 1984.

Manton, K. G., and Stallard, E. *Chronic Disease Modelling.* London: Griffin, 1988.

Manton, K. G., Tolley, H. D., and Poss, S. S. Life table techniques for multiple-cause mortality. *Demography,* 1976, *13,* 541–564.

Mason, W. M., and Fienberg, S. E. *Cohort Analysis in Social Research.* Berlin: Springer-Verlag, 1985.

Massalee, A. Z. *The Population of Liberia.* C.I.C.R.E.D./United Nations, 1974.

McNiel, D. R., Trussell, T. J., and Turner, J. C. Spline interpolation of demographic data. *Demography,* 1977, *14,* 245–252.

McNown, R., and Rogers, A. Forecasting mortality: A parameterized time series approach. *Demography,* 1989, *26,* 645–660.

Menken, J. A., Trussell, T. J., Stempel, D., and Babakol, O. Proportional hazards life table models: An illustrative analysis of sociodemographic influences on marriage dissolution in the United States. *Demography,* 1981, *18,* 181–200.

Miller, L. Estimates of the population of the United States, by age, race and sex: 1980 to 1982. *Current Population Reports,* 1983, *Series P-25, No. 929.*

Miller, L. Estimates of the population of the United States by age, sex, and race: 1980 to 1983. *Current Population Reports,* 1984, *Series P-25, No. 949.*

Milne, J. *A Treatise on the Valuation of Annuities and Assurances on Lives and Survivors.* London, 1815. [Excerpted in Smith and Keyfitz (1977, pp. 27–34).]

Mitra, S. Generalizations of immigration and the stable population model. *Demography,* 1983, *20,* 111–115.

Mitra, S., and Romaniuk, A. Pearsonian type I curve and its fertility projection potentials. *Demography,* 1973, *10,* 351–365.

Mode, C. J., Avery, R. C., Littman, G. S., and Potter, R. G., Jr. Methodological issues underlying multiple decrement life table analysis. *Demography,* 1977, *14,* 87–96.

Mosley, W. H., Werner, L. W., and Becker, S. The dynamics of birth spacing and marital fertility in Kenya. *World Fertility Survey Scientific Report No. 30.* London: World Fertility Survey, 1982.

Myers, R. J. Errors and bias in reporting of ages in census data. *Transactions of the Actuarial Society of America,* 1940, *41,* 395–415.

Myers, R. J. The validity and significance of male net reproduction rates. *Journal of the American Statistical Association,* 1941, *36,* 275–282.

Namboodiri, K. *Matrix Algebra: An Introduction.* Beverly Hills: Sage, 1984.

Namboodiri, K., and Suchindran, C. M. *Life Table Techniques and Their Applications.* New York: Academic Press, 1987. [See also the review by Smith (1989).]

National Center for Health Statistics. *Vital Statistics of the United States, 1980.* Three volumes. Washington, D.C.: U.S. Government Printing Office, 1984–1985.

National Center for Health Statistics. *U.S. Decennial Life Tables for 1979–81, Vol. 1, No. 1: United States Life Tables.* Hyattsville, Md.: Public Health Service, U.S. Dept. of Health and Human Services, 1985.

National Center for Health Statistics. *U.S. Decennial Life Tables for 1979–81, Vol. 1, No. 3: Methodology of the National and State Life Tables.* Hyattsville, Md.: Public Health Service, U.S. Dept. of Health and Human Services, 1987.

National Research Council. Panel on small-area estimates of population and income. *Estimating Population and Income of Small Areas.* Washington, D.C.: National Academy Press, 1980.

New York Academy of Medicine. *Vital Statistics: A Memorial Volume of Selections from the Reports and Writings of William Farr.* Metuchen, N.J.: Scarecrow Press, 1975 (orig. ed. 1885).

Newell, C. *Methods and Models in Demography.* New York: Guilford Press, 1988.

Nortman, D., and Hofstatter, E. *Population and Family Planning Programs, A Factbook* (7th ed.). New York: The Population Council, 1975.

Nour, E.-S., and Suchindran, C. M. The construction of multi-state life tables: Comments on the article by Willekens et al. *Population Studies,* 1984, *38,* 325–328.

Page, H. J. Patterns underlying fertility schedules: A decomposition by both age and marriage duration. *Population Studies,* 1977, *31,* 85–106.

Parlett, B. Ergodic properties of populations I: The one sex model. *Theoretical Population Biology,* 1970, *1,* 191–207.

Pearl, R. Factors in human fertility and their statistical evaluation. *The Lancet,* 1933, *225,* 607–611.

Pearl, R., and Reed, L. J. The rate of growth of the population of the United States since 1790 and its mathematical representation. *Proceedings of the National Academy of Science,* 1920, *6,* 275–288.

Perron, O. Grundlagen für eine Theorie des Jakobischen Kettenbruchalgorithmus. *Mathematische Annalen,* 1907a, *64,* 1–76. [Cited in Rogers (1968).]

Perron, O. Zur Theorie der Matrizen. *Mathematische Annalen,* 1907b, *64,* 248–263. [Cited in Rogers (1968).]

Petersen, W., and Petersen, R. *Dictionary of Demography.* Two volumes. New York: Greenwood Press, 1986.

Pittenger, D. B. *Projecting State and Local Populations.* Cambridge, Mass.: Ballinger, 1976.

Pollard, A. H., Yusuf, F., and Pollard, G. N. *Demographic Techniques.* Elmsford, N.Y.: Pergamon Press, 1981 (orig. ed. 1974).

Pollard, J. H. *Mathematical Models for the Growth of Human Populations.* London: Cambridge University Press, 1973.

Pollard, J. H. Bias in graduated life table functions. *Demography,* 1979, *16,* 131–135.

Pollard, J. H. The expectation of life and its relationship to mortality. *Journal of the Institute of Actuaries,* 1982, *109,* 225–240.

Pollard, J. H. On the decomposition of changes in the expectation of life and differentials in life expectancy. *Demography,* 1988, *25,* 265–276.

Population Reference Bureau. *World Population Data Sheet.* Washington, D.C.: Population Reference Bureau, Inc., various years.

Potter, R. G., Jr. Length of observation period as affecting the contraceptive failure rate. *Milbank Memorial Fund Quarterly,* 1960, *38,* 140–152.

Potter, R. G., Jr. Birth intervals: Structure and change. *Population Studies,* 1963, *17,* 155–166.

Potter, R. G., Jr., and Avery, R. C. Use-effectiveness of contraception. In C. Chandrasekaran and A. I. Hermalin (Eds.), *Measuring the Effect of Family Planning Programs on Fertility.* Dolhain, Belgium: Ordina Editions, 1975. [For the actuarial formulas in this article the reader may substitute expressions (4.2) and (5.16).]

Potter, R. G., Jr., and Parker, M. P. Predicting the time required to conceive. *Population Studies,* 1964, *18,* 99–116.

Prentice, R. L., Kalbfleisch, J. D., Peterson, A. V., Jr., Flournoy, N., Farewell, V. T., and Breslow, N. E. The analysis of failure times in the presence of competing risks. *Biometrics,* 1978, *34,* 541–554.

Pressat, R. *Demographic Analysis.* Chicago: Aldine–Atherton, 1972.

Preston, S. H., and Bennett, N. G. A census-based method for estimating adult mortality. *Population Studies,* 1983, *37,* 91–104.

Preston, S. H., Keyfitz, N., and Schoen, R. *Causes of Death: Life Tables for National Populations.* New York: Seminar Press, 1972.

Pullum, T. W., Casterline, J. B., and Shah, I. H. Adapting fertility exposure analysis to the study of fertility change. *Population Studies,* 1987, *41,* 381–399.

Pullum, T. W., Tedrow, L. M., and Herting, J. R. Measuring change and continuity in parity distributions. *Demography,* 1989, *26,* 485–498.

Reed, L. J., and Merrell, M. A short method for constructing an abridged life table. *American Journal of Hygiene,* 1939, *30,* 33–62.

Rees, P. H., and Wilson, A. G. *Spatial Population Analysis.* London: Arnold, 1977.

Rives, N. W., Jr., and Serow, W. J. *Introduction to Applied Demography: Data Sources and Estimation Techniques.* Beverly Hills: Sage, 1984.

Robinson, W. C. Another look at the Hutterites and natural fertility. *Social Biology,* 1986, *33,* 65–76.

Rogers, A. *Matrix Analysis of Interregional Population Growth and Distribution*. Berkeley: University of California Press, 1968.

Rogers, A. *Introduction to Multiregional Mathematical Demography*. New York: Wiley, 1975.

Rogers, A. (Ed.). *Migration, Urbanization, and Spatial Population Dynamics*. Boulder: Westview Press, 1984.

Rogers, A. Age patterns of elderly migration: An international comparison. *Demography*, 1988, *25*, 355–370.

Rogers, A., and Castro, L. J. Model schedules in multistate demographic analysis: The case of migration. Pp. 113–154 in Land and Rogers (1982).

Rogers, A., and Castro, L. J. Model migration schedules. Pp. 41–91 in Rogers (1984).

Rogers, A., Raquillet, R., and Castro, L. J. Model migration schedules and their applications. *Environment and Planning A*, 1978, *10*, 475–502.

Rosenwaike, I. A new evaluation of United States census data on the extreme aged. *Demography*, 1979, *16*, 279–288.

Rosenwaike, I. A note on new estimates of the mortality of the extreme aged. *Demography*, 1981, *18*, 257–266.

Rosenwaike, I., and Logue, B. Accuracy of death certificate ages for the extreme aged. *Demography*, 1983, *20*, 569–585.

Ryder, N. B. The process of demographic translation. *Demography*, 1964, *1*, 74–82.

Ryder, N. B. Observations on the history of cohort fertility in the United States. *Population and Development Review*, 1986, *4*, 617–643.

Schoen, R. The geometric mean of the age-specific death rates as a summary index of mortality. *Demography*, 1970, *7*, 317–324.

Schoen, R. Constructing increment–decrement life tables. *Demography*, 1975, *12*, 313–324, 571 (erratum note).

Schoen, R. Calculating life tables by estimating Chiang's a from observed rates. *Demography*, 1978, *15*, 625–635.

Schoen, R. *Modeling Multigroup Populations*. New York: Plenum Press, 1988.

Schoen, R., and Nelson, V. E. Marriage, divorce, and mortality: A life table analysis. *Demography*, 1974, *11*, 267–290.

Schweder, T. The precision of population projections studied by multiple prediction methods. *Demography*, 1971, *8*, 441–450.

Searle, S. R. *Matrix Algebra for the Biological Sciences*. New York: Wiley, 1966.

Sheps, M. C. On the time required for conception. *Population Studies*, 1964, *18*, 85–97.

Sheps, M. C. An analysis of reproductive patterns in an American isolate. *Population Studies*, 1965, *19*, 65–80.

Sheps, M. C., and Menken, J. A. *Mathematical Models of Conception and Birth*. Chicago: University of Chicago Press, 1973.

Sheps, M. C., Menken, J. A., Ridley, J. C., and Lingner, J. W. Truncation effect in birth interval data. *Journal of the American Statistical Association*, 1970, *65*, 678–693.

Shryock, H. S., and Siegel, J. S. (Eds.). *The Methods and Materials of Demography*. Two volumes. Washington, D.C.: U.S. Dept. of Commerce, Bureau of the Census, 1971.

Singh, S., Casterline, J. B., and Cleland, J. G. The proximate determinants of fertility: Subnational variations. *Population Studies*, 1985, *39*, 113–135. [In the appendix to this article (p. 133), the Index of marriage CM should be written as $C_m = F/F_M = \Sigma f(a)/\Sigma [f(a)/m(a)] = \Sigma f(a)/\Sigma g(a)$, where $f(a)$ is the age-specific fertility at age a, $m(a)$ is the age-specific proportion of time spent in marriage or informal unions at age a, and $g(a)$ is the marital age-specific fertility rate at a. The summations are across the fertile age range.]

Sivamurthy, M. *Growth and Structure of Human Population in the Presence of Migration*. New York: Academic Press, 1982.

Slater, C., and Smith, D. P. Ischemic heart disease: Footprints through the data. *American Journal of Clinical Nutrition*, 1985, *42*, 329–341.

Slud, E., and Hoesman, C. Moderate- and large-deviation probabilities in actuarial risk theory. *Advances in Applied Probability*, 1989, *21*, 725–741.

Smith, D. P. The problem of persistence in economic–demographic cycles. *Theoretical Population Biology*, 1981a, *19*, 125–146.

Smith, D. P. A reconsideration of Easterlin Cycles. *Population Studies*, 1981b, *35*, 247–264.

Smith, D. P. Durbin–Watson statistics for model life tables. *Asian and Pacific Census Forum*, 1983, *9 (4)*, 7–9. [Sample weights for weighted least squares are given incorrectly in this source. The formula should be, for $l_0 = 1$: $w_{lx} = l_x^2 (1 - l_x)^2 / \text{Var}(l_x) = (1 - l_x)^2 / \sum_{a=0}^{x-n} [_n q_a^2 / (_n D_a \, _n p_a)]$. In samples with approximately equal numbers in each interval, the user may substitute the approximate weights $w_{lx} = l_x (1 - l_x)$. I am indebted to Michael Stoto for this correction.—DS]

Smith, D. P. Robustness of $_5 q_x$ estimators under non-stationarity. *Demography*, 1984, *21*, 613–622.

Smith, D. P. Formulas for cause deleted life tables. *Statistics in Medicine*, 1985a, *4*, 155–162.

Smith, D. P. Regression analysis of "current status" life tables on duration of breastfeeding in Sri Lanka. *Social Biology*, 1985b, *32*, 90–101.

Smith, D. P. Review of Namboodiri and Suchindran, *Life Table Techniques and Their Applications*. *Contemporary Sociology*, 1989, *18*, 81–83.

Smith, D. P., and Keyfitz, N. (Eds.). *Mathematical Demography: Selected Papers*. Berlin: Springer-Verlag, 1977.

Smith, S. K. A review and evaluation of the housing unit method of population estimation. *Journal of the American Statistical Association*, 1986, *81*, 287–296.

Smith, S. K. Tests of forecast accuracy and bias for county population projections. *Journal of the American Statistical Association*, 1987, *82*, 991–1003.

Spencer, G. Projections of the population of the United States, by age, sex and race: 1983 to 2080. *Current Population Reports*, 1984, *Series P-25, No. 952*.

Sprague, T. B. Explanation ov a new formula for interpolation. *Journal of the Institute of Actuaries*, 1881, *22*, 270–285.

Süssmilch, J. P. *Die göttliche Ordnung* (2nd ed.). Berlin, 1761.

Sykes, Z. M. Some stochastic versions of the matrix model for population dynamics. *Journal of the American Statistical Association*, 1969, *64*, 111–130.

Tabah, L. Représentations matricielles de perspectives de population active. *Population*, 1968, *23*, 437–476. [An English translation of part of this article will be found in Smith and Keyfitz (1977, pp. 239–254).]

Teachman, J. D. The relationship between Schoen's ∇ and a log-linear measure. *Demography*, 1977, *14*, 239–241.

Tietze, C. Reproductive span and rate of reproduction among Hutterite women. *Fertility and Sterility*, 1957, *8*, 89–97. [Reprinted in Tietze and Lincoln (1987, pp. 328–332).]

Tietze, C., and Lewit, S. Recommended procedures for the statistical evaluation of intrauterine contraception. *Studies in Family Planning*, 1973, *4*, 35–42. [Reprinted in Tietze and Lincoln (1987, pp. 77–87). For the actuarial formulas in Tietze the reader may substitute expressions (4.2) and (5.16).]

Tietze, S. L., and Lincoln, R. (Eds.). *Fertility Regulation and Public Health: Selected Papers of Christopher Tietze*. Berlin: Springer-Verlag, 1987.

Trussell, T. J. A re-estimation of the multiplying factors for the Brass technique for determining childhood survivorship rates. *Population Studies*, 1975, *29*, 97–108.

Trussell, T. J., and Hammerslough, C. A hazards-model analysis of the covariates of infant and child mortality in Sri Lanka. *Demography*, 1983, *20*, 1–26.

Trussell, T. J., and Menken, J. A. *Life Table Analysis of Contraceptive Use-Effectiveness.* Seminar on the Use of Surveys for the Analysis of Family Planning Programs, Bogota, Colombia, October 28–31. Liège, Belgium: International Union for the Scientific Study of Population, 1980. [This article presents an excellent introduction to multiple decrement life tables for contraceptive use. For illustration the authors use the actuarial estimator, our expression (4.6). In place of their cause-eliminated estimators, their expressions (7)–(9), the reader is advised to use Greville's estimator, our expression (5.16), which is generally of higher quality. Trussell and Menken's methodological discussion will also be found in Vaughan *et al.* (1980, pp. 49–57) and in Trussell and Menken (1982).]

Trussell, T. J., and Menken, J. A. Life table analysis of contraceptive failure. In A. I. Hermalin and B. Entwistle (Eds.), *The Role of Surveys in the Analysis of Family Planning Programs.* Liège: Ordina, 1982, pp. 537–571.

Trussell, T. J., and Richards, T. Correcting for unmeasured heterogeneity in hazard models using the Heckman–Singer procedure. Pp. 242–276 in Tuma (1985).

Trussell, T. J., and Rodríguez, G. Heterogeneity in demographic research. In J. Adams, D. A. Lam, A. I. Hermalin, and P. E. Smouse (Eds.), *Convergent Issues in Genetics and Demography.* New York: Oxford University Press, 1990, pp. 111–133.

Trussell, T. J., Martin, L. G., Feldman, R., Palmore, J. A., Concepcion, M., and Datin Noor Laily Bt. Dato' Abu Bakar. Determinants of birth-interval length in the Philippines, Malaysia and Indonesia: A hazard-model. *Demography,* 1985, *22,* 145–168.

Tuma, N. B. (Ed.). *Sociological Methodology, 1985.* San Francisco: Jossey–Bass, 1985.

Udry, J. R. Do couples make fertility plans one birth at a time? *Demography,* 1983, *20,* 117–128.

United Nations. Department of International Economic and Social Affairs. *United Nations Demographic Yearbook.* New York: United Nations, various years.

United Nations. Department of International Economic and Social Affairs. *Manual X: Indirect Techniques for Demographic Estimation.* New York: United Nations, 1983.

United Nations. Department of International Economic and Social Affairs. *MortPak—The United Nations Software Package for Mortality Measurement. Batch-oriented Software for the Mainframe Computer.* New York: United Nations, 1988a.

United Nations. Department of International Economic and Social Affairs. *MortPak-Lite—The United Nations Software Package for Mortality Measurement. Interactive Software for the IBM-PC and Compatibles.* New York: United Nations, 1988b.

United Nations. Department of International Economic and Social Affairs. *Global Estimates and Projections of Population by Sex and Age: The 1988 Revision.* New York: United Nations, 1989.

United States. Department of Commerce. Bureau of the Census. *Historical Statistics of the U.S., Colonial Times to 1970. Bicentennial Edition.* Two volumes. Washington, D.C., 1975.

United States. Department of Commerce. Bureau of the Census. Population and per capita money income estimates for local areas: Detailed methodology and evaluation. *Current Population Reports,* 1980, *Series P-25, No. 699.*

United States. Department of Commerce. Bureau of the Census. *Statistical Abstract of the United States, 1990.* Washington, D.C., 1990.

Vaughan, B., Trussell, T. J., Menken, J. A., and Jones, E. F. Contraceptive efficacy among married women aged 15–44 years: United States. *Vital and Health Statistics,* 1980, *Series 23, No. 5.*

Vaupel, J. W. How change in age-specific mortality affects life expectancy. *Population Studies,* 1986, *40,* 147–157.

Vaupel, J. W., and Yashin, A. I. The deviant dynamics of death in heterogeneous populations. Pp. 179–211 in Tuma (1985).

Vaupel, J. W., Manton, K. G., and Stallard, E. The impact of heterogeneity in individual frailty on the dynamics of mortality. *Demography*, 1979, *16*, 439–454.

Verhulst, P.-F. Notice sur la loi que la population suit dans son accroissement. *Correspondance Mathématique et Physique Publiée par A. Quételet*, 1838, *10*, 113–121. [An English translation will be found in Smith and Keyfitz (1977, pp. 333–337).]

Verhulst, P.-F. Recherches mathématiques sur la loi d'accroissement de la population. *Nouveaux Mémoires de l'Académie Royale des Sciences et Belles Lettres (Brussels)*, 1845, *18*, 3–41; 1847, *20*, 4–32.

Wachter, K. W. Ergodicity and inverse projection. *Population Studies*, 1986, *40*, 275–287.

Wachter, K. W., and Lee, R. D. U.S. births and limit cycle models. *Demography*, 1989, *26*, 99–115.

Westoff, C. C. Some speculations on the future of marriage and fertility. *Family Planning Perspectives*, 1978, *10*, 79–83.

Whelpton, P. K. An empirical method for calculating future population. *Journal of the American Statistical Association*, 1936, *31*, 457–473.

Wicksell, S. D. Nuptiality, fertility, and reproductivity. *Skandinavisk Aktuarietidskrift*, 1931, 149–157. [Part of this article is reprinted in Smith and Keyfitz (1977, pp. 315–322).]

Willekens, F. J., Shah, I. H., Shah, J. M., and Ramachandran, P. Multi-state analysis of marital status life tables: Theory and applications. *Population Studies*, 1982, *36*, 129–144. [See also the comment by Nour and Suchindran (1984).]

Willigan, J. D., and Lynch, K. A. *Sources and Methods of Historical Demography*. New York: Academic Press, 1982.

Wilson, E. B. The standard deviation of sampling for life expectancy. *Journal of the American Statistical Association*, 1938, *33*, 705–708.

Wood, J. C. (Ed.) *Thomas Robert Malthus: Critical Assessments*. Four volumes. London: Croom Helm, 1986.

Wrigley, E. A. (Ed.). *An Introduction to English Historical Demography*. New York: Basic Books, 1966.

Wrigley, E. A., and Schofield, R. S. *The Population History of England, 1541–1871*. Cambridge, Mass.: Harvard University Press, 1982.

Wrigley, J. M., and Nam, C. B. Underlying versus multiple causes of death: Effects on interpreting cancer mortality differentials by age, sex, and race. *Population Research and Policy Review*, 1987, *6*, 149–160.

Wu, M., Fisher, M., and DeMets, D. Sample sizes for long-term medical trials with time-dependent dropout and event rates. *Controlled Clinical Trials*, 1980, *1*, 109–121.

Wunsch, G. J., and Termote, M. G. *Introduction to Demographic Analysis*. New York: Plenum Press, 1978.

Xie, Y. An alternative purging method: Controlling the composition-dependent interaction in an analysis of rates. *Demography*, 1989, *26*, 711–716.

Author Index

Bibliographic citations are indicated by italics.

Subject Index

Figures and tables are indicated by italics.

DATE DUE

HIGHSMITH 45-220